PARADIGMS OF JUSTICE

This book explores the relation between redistribution and recognition, two key paradigms in the contemporary discourse on justice. Combining insights from the traditions of critical social theory and analytical political philosophy, the volume offers a multifaceted exploration of this incredibly inspiring conceptual couple from a plurality of perspectives. The chapters engage with concepts such as universal basic income, property-owning democracy, poverty, equality, self-respect, pluralism, care, and work, all of which have an impact on individuals' recognition as well as on distributive policies.

An important contribution to the field of political and social philosophy, the volume will be useful to scholars and researchers of politics, law, human rights, economics, social justice, as well as policymakers.

Denise Celentano is Postdoctoral Fellow in Ethics and Economics at the Centre for Research on Ethics at the University of Montreal, Canada. She was previously a Berggruen Postdoctoral Fellow in Philosophy at New York University, US. Her research explores problems of social justice and equality, with a focus on work as an issue of justice.

Luigi Caranti is Professor of Political Philosophy at the Università di Catania, Italy. He has worked as a researcher in various institutions including the School of International and Public Affairs at Columbia University, US, the Australian National University, and the Philipps-Universität – Marburg, Germany. His studies mainly concern the philosophy of Kant and he has contributed extensively to the theoretical, practical, aesthetic, and political dimensions of Kant's thought. Currently, his research focuses on the philosophical theory of human rights.

PARADIGMS OF JUSTICE

Redistribution, Recognition, and Beyond

Edited by Denise Celentano
and Luigi Caranti

Routledge
Taylor & Francis Group
LONDON AND NEW YORK

First published 2021
by Routledge
2 Park Square, Milton Park, Abingdon, Oxon OX14 4RN

and by Routledge
605 Third Avenue, New York, NY 10017

Routledge is an imprint of the Taylor & Francis Group, an informa business

British Library Cataloguing-in-Publication Data
A catalogue record for this book is available from the British Library

Library of Congress Cataloging-in-Publication Data
Names: Celentano, Denise, editor. | Caranti, Luigi, editor.
Title: Paradigms of justice: redistribution, recognition, and beyond / edited by Denise Celentano and Luigi Caranti.
Identifiers: LCCN 2020021689 (print) | LCCN 2020021690 (ebook)
Subjects: LCSH: Distributive justice. | Social justice. | Critical theory.
Classification: LCC HB523 .P374 2021 (print) | LCC HB523 (ebook) | DDC 339.2 — dc23
LC record available at https://lccn.loc.gov/2020021689
LC ebook record available at https://lccn.loc.gov/2020021690

ISBN: 978-1-138-59427-2 (hbk)
ISBN: 978-1-003-09993-2 (ebk)

Typeset in Sabon
by Apex CoVantage, LLC

CONTENTS

CONTRIBUTORS

Nunzio Alì is a postdoctoral researcher at the Department of Political Science at the University of Catania, Italy. A former postdoctoral researcher at the Department of Political Science at the University of São Paulo, Brazil (2018–2020). He holds a PhD in Philosophy from Universidade Federal de Santa Catarina (2018). His research interests include theories of justice, economic inequality, and human rights.

Sarah Bufkin is Examination Fellow at All Souls College, Oxford, UK, where she is a DPhil candidate in Political Theory. She is also Stipendiary Lecturer in Politics at Queen's College, Oxford. Her research focuses on the ethics of racialized subject formation in the contemporary United States, with a particular focus on the problems of visibility and voice.

Jurgen De Wispelaere is Policy Fellow at the Institute for Policy Research (IPR), University of Bath, and Visiting Researcher at the Department of Business and Management, Stockholm School of Economics in Riga (SSE Riga), Latvia. He has published on basic income in leading journals and edited volumes. He is the co-author (with Evelyn Forget) of *Basic Income Experiments: Theory, Practice, and Politics* (2021) and co-editor of *Basic Income: An Anthology of Contemporary Research* (2013) and *The Ethics of Stakeholding* (2003).

Jean-Philippe Deranty is Professor of Philosophy at Macquarie University, Sydney, Australia. He is the author of *Beyond Communication. A Critical Study of Axel Honneth's Social Philosophy* (2009) and the editor of numerous collections in contemporary critical theory, including the debate between Axel Honneth and Jacques Rancière, *Recognition or Disagreement* (edited with Katia Genel, 2016). His most recent publications include the co-authored volume, *The Return of Work in Critical Theory* (2018).

Caroline Guibet Lafaye is permanent research fellow at the National Center for Scientific Research (CNRS), France. Her research in ethics is devoted to identifying right solutions in a context of strong pluralism about ethical and medical dilemmas, as well as moral and religious conflicts in civil society. She is also interested in issues raised by egalitarianism, liberalism, and distributive justice. She wrote several papers on these topics and two books: *La justice comme composante de la vie bonne* [Justice as a Component of the Good Life] (2006), *Justice sociale et éthique individuelle* [Social Justice and Individual Ethics] (2006), and *Le juste et l'inacceptable. Les sentiments d'injustice contemporains et leurs raisons* (2012).

Naïma Hamrouni is Canada Research Chair in Feminist Ethics and Professor of Political Philosophy and Applied Ethics at the Université du Québec à Trois-Rivières, Quebec. Her current work aims at offering an understanding of the diverse forms of epistemic oppression and relational inequalities experienced in given institutional contexts by minorities. Her research has been published in several books, such as *In Yet a Different Voice* (2000), *Vulnerability, Autonomy, and Applied Ethics* (2016), *Le care, éthique féministe actuelle* (2015), and in different journals, such as *World Political Science* (2017), *Philosophiques* (2017), *Politiques et Sociétés* (2016), and *Recherches féministes* (2015).

Gavin Kerr is an independent researcher currently based near Bonn in Germany. His research interests lie in the areas of politics, philosophy, and economics, particularly in relation to the ideas of predistribution, property-owning democracy, and market freedom. He is the author of *The Property-Owning Democracy: Freedom and Capitalism in the Twenty-First Century* (2017). His current research focuses on the importance of land in economic theory and practice and on the relevance of land economics to the issue of environmental sustainability.

Arto Laitinen is Professor of Social Philosophy at Tampere University, Finland. He is an editor of the *Journal of Social Ontology*. His publications include *Strong Evaluation without Moral Sources: On Charles Taylor's Philosophical Anthropology and Ethics* (2008), *Hegel on Action* (co-edited with C. Sandis, 2010), *Recognition and Social Ontology* (co-edited with H. Ikäheimo, 2011), *Solidarity: Theory and Practice* (co-edited with A.B. Pessi, 2014), and *Dimensions of Personhood* (co-edited with H. Ikäheimo, 2007).

Christian Lazzeri is Professor of Philosophy at the University of Paris Nanterre, France. His areas of interest and specialty are political and social philosophy, theories of recognition, deliberation and conflict, and power. Among his publications are *La reconnaissance aujourd'hui* (with Alain Caillé, 2009) and *Reconnaissance, identité et intégration sociale* (with Soraya Nour, 2011).

Kathleen Lynch is Professor Emerita of Equality Studies at University College Dublin (UCD), and a Professor in the School of Education. She played a leading role in establishing the UCD Equality Studies Centre (1990) and the UCD School of Social Justice (2004/2005). Her recent co-authored books include *New Managerialism in Education: Commercialisation, Carelessness and Gender* (2012, 2015) and *Affective Equality: Love, Care and Injustice* (2009). Her forthcoming book, *Care and Capitalism* (2021), will be published by Polity Press, Cambridge.

Renante Pilapil is Professor at the Ateneo de Davao University (Philippines), specializing in political philosophy and ethics. He finished his PhD in Philosophy from KU Leuven (Belgium) and went to Columbia University (US) for his postdoctoral studies under the supervision of Frederick Neuhousser and Axel Honneth. His works have appeared in various international journals including *Ethical Perspectives*, *Res Publica*, *Thesis Eleven*, among others. Currently, he also serves as the editor-in-chief of *Tambara*, the academic journal of the Ateneo de Davao University.

Alessandro Pinzani is Professor of Ethics and Political Philosophy at the Department of Philosophy of the Federal University of Santa Catarina, Florianópolis, Brazil. His publications include *Jurgen Habermas* (2007), *An den Wurzeln moderner Demokratie* (2009), and *Money, Autonomy, and Citizenship* (with W. Leão Rego, 2018).

INTRODUCTION

In both academic and public debates, redistribution and recognition are key categories shaping the vocabularies of justice of our time. Usually labelled as 'paradigms' or 'pictures' of justice (Young 1990; Fraser and Honneth 2003; Forst 2014), theories and perspectives within each tend to share some background assumptions about what problems justice should address, and how to do so. Normative discourses about goods, resources, income, wealth, and opportunities are usually referred to as relating to the distributive paradigm, whereas concerns about identity, social status, and esteem are traced back to the paradigm of recognition. Broadly conceived, they point to the economic and the social sphere respectively. Not only do they provide different accounts of what justice is and how it ought to be conceptualized, they are also rooted in distinct philosophical traditions and display different styles of thought. Yet, the legitimacy itself of these distinctions is a subject of contention, for competing monisms tend to advocate the superiority of one perspective over the other. Some argue that the material side of justice has some sort of preeminence, other dimensions being somewhat derived from it, and, as such, seen as normatively secondary. Others argue that behind individuals' economic demands lies a more fundamental expectation of recognition, which should be the primary focus of justice. Attempts to consider these paradigms jointly have been proposed, as well as suggestions on possible ways to overcome their limits.

After almost two decades from the publication of the well-known debate between Axel Honneth and Nancy Fraser (2003), the question of whether redistribution and recognition are complementary, mutually exclusive, insufficient, or essentially inadequate accounts of justice is still open.[1] Despite the popularity of these concepts, the relation between them is yet to be fully explored, both from a practical and a theoretical perspective: How does the economic discourse intertwine with recognition dynamics? What are the recognition implications of individuals' access to goods? What could recognition teach us about the most desirable or morally preferable ways to distribute them? How can the relation between the redistributive and the recognition-based models of justice help us understand the interconnections between economic structures and social relations, in both descriptive and normative terms? How does this relation suggest that justice is concerned with problems that go beyond redistribution and recognition? Indeed, there might be reasons specifically related to recognition for which certain distributive measures ought to be preferred over others; likewise, the extent to which recognition can be abstracted from access to resources and opportunities remains under-explored.

To be sure, the recent philosophical debate has expressed similar concerns by focusing on the concept of relational equality with regard to distributive justice (Scheffler 2015; Schemmel 2011). Though the notion of relational equality is broader than that of recognition, and essentially different: even if both emphasize the normative relevance of the quality of social relations, recognition's scope is narrower, and is not primarily or necessarily concerned with equality (see Chapters 4 and 5 in this volume).

The book offers a multifaceted exploration of this peculiar, and still incredibly inspiring conceptual couple, from a number of different perspectives. The richness and variety of insights about justice and the social world enabled by the joint consideration of these paradigms suggest that their fertility can hardly be overestimated. Each chapter hosted in this volume shows in its own way and from a different angle how fruitful it is to think about distributive justice through the lens of recognition, and vice versa. It is also shown, on the other hand, that there are problems and phenomena that systematically escape their grasp – that other concepts, other grids are needed. For instance, some authors complete them with additional categories or reframe them to capture underrepresented domains of justice, such as work or the affective domain of life.

The volume is divided into four parts. In Part I 'The "recognition side" of distributive justice', the reader will find a number of attempts to read distributive models and concepts through the lens of recognition. Universal basic income (Chapter 1), property-owning democracy and predistribution (Chapter 2) but also specific policies like the *Bolsa Familia* – a conditional cash transfer to the poor realized in Brazil (Chapter 3) – are examined in their recognition implications. Part II 'Dimensions of equality' narrows the focus on the value of equality understood in various ways. A joint consideration of redistribution and recognition prompts a substantive, rather than formal consideration of equality, seen either as 'real equality' (Chapter 4), or as an enabling concept of peer contribution to social cooperation (Chapter 5), or in its relation to the affective domain of life (Chapter 6). Part III 'Rethinking grammars of oppression and inclusion' provides a multifaceted account of oppression and inclusion in their relation to distributive justice and recognition. It explores the insufficiency of the distributive paradigm when it comes to the exclusion of women and racialized people from institutional political life (Chapter 7), and the difficulties raised by recognition with regard to racial inequalities (Chapter 9). But it also provides a defence of distributive justice from criticisms, highlighting its advantages with regard to its capacity to accommodate reasonable pluralism (Chapter 8). Finally, Part IV 'Moral economies of respect and esteem', focuses on broader economic concepts like the capitalist market (Chapter 10), as well the notions of social esteem (Chapter 11), self-esteem and self-respect (Chapter 12), by reclaiming a redistributive grid in the analysis through the concepts of work, exchanges, and outcomes.

Let us outline the content of the chapters in further detail. In 'Basic income in the recognition order: respect, care, and esteem' (Chapter 1), Jurgen De Wispelaere and Arto Laitinen aim to complement freedom-based justifications of basic income with a recognition-theoretical perspective unfolded through the concepts of respect, care, and social esteem. While arguing that respect and care for well-being can ground basic income from a recognition perspective, they also engage with the challenge of clarifying the tension between social esteem and basic income. A tension particularly hard to tackle, given that social esteem has to do with the sphere of social relations, being positional and differential, while basic income pertains to the sphere of goods, being universal and egalitarian.

In 'Freedom, recognition, and the property-owning democracy: towards a predistributive model of justice' (Chapter 2), Gavin Kerr addresses another distributive model, property-owning democracy. In particular, he explores whether property-owning democracy can be plausibly understood in terms of recognition via the concept of social freedom. Kerr observes that despite their very different methodologies, Axel Honneth's and John Rawls' ideas of freedom present relevant similarities if property-owning democracy departs somewhat from the original sense developed by James Meade, and if its 'predistributive' aspects are understood as progressive.

In 'Redistribution, misrecognition, domination: a look at Brazilian society' (Chapter 3), Alessandro Pinzani examines a particular case of welfare provision for the poor. As a policy of conditional cash transfer realized in Brazil, the case of the *Bolsa Familia* raises a series of normative questions about distributive justice, recognition, and political participation that prove relevant to our understanding of individual autonomy. Moving beyond a narrow reading of the significance of distributive public policies, Pinzani assesses the impact of *Bolsa Familia* on individuals' subjectivity by resorting to the notions of epistemic oppression, hegemony, and systemic domination.

In 'Redistribution and recognition from the point of view of real equality: Anderson and Honneth through the lens of Babeuf' (Chapter 4), Jean-Philippe Deranty assesses the republican and socialist theories of 'real equality' offered by two critics of the distributive paradigm, Elizabeth Anderson and Axel Honneth. By using Babeuf's egalitarianism as a critical reference point, Deranty discusses the challenges that this early theorist of full equality raises to both Anderson's and Honneth's view, and explores the overlaps and differences of their conceptions of real equality as well as their implications for redistribution.

In 'Work justice beyond redistribution and recognition' (Chapter 5), Denise Celentano argues that work raises specific concerns of justice and explores whether and how distributive and recognition perspectives provide resources to address them. To this purpose, she assesses the normative relevance of property-owning democracy and of universal basic income for labour justice, and critically discusses four concepts of work identified in the recognition paradigm. Drawing on a synthesis of the concepts of social equality and participatory parity, she argues for a more structural and egalitarian understanding of status inequalities in the division of labour than that offered by the recognition paradigm. The norm of 'contributive parity' aims at reframing the critical-normative approach to work, demanding that individuals be enabled to contribute to social cooperation as peers.

In 'Affective equality and social justice' (Chapter 6), Kathleen Lynch argues that existing accounts of redistribution and recognition do not adequately account for the 'affective domain of life'. According to Lynch, love, care, and solidarity cannot be reduced to other spheres of justice – they constitute a discrete, irreducible field of social practices and normative concerns. She proposes a structural, rather than individualist reading of them, represented as 'sites of political import' that generate specific injustices. In this view, mere access to love, care, and solidarity is not sufficient: it is actually experiencing them that matters.

In 'Vulnerable political life: distributive justice, critical theory, and critical care ethics' (Chapter 7), Naïma Hamrouni contributes to defining the contours of a critical care ethics in contrast to distributive models of justice, liberal feminist approaches, and critical theory. She highlights the systematically excluding logic of the 'organizational and labour culture of political life', which denies our 'ordinary vulnerability' even at an epistemic level, and the inability of distributive justice to grasp the logic of exclusion of women and racialized people from the institutional practice of politics.

In 'Redistribution, recognition, and pluralism: a Rawlsian criticism of Fraser' (Chapter 8), Luigi Caranti and Nunzio Alì critically address Nancy Fraser's model of justice. They focus in particular on the difficulties raised by her notion of social institutions and contest the assumption that injustices of misrecognition are not adequately captured by the Rawlsian paradigm, at least if broadly and charitably interpreted. They argue that some of the injustices that Fraser attributes to the recognition paradigm can be grasped by the distributive approach, while other injustices denounced by Fraser are better conceptualized in terms of moral wrongs, if one wants to end up with a theory of justice compatible with reasonable pluralism.

In 'The politics of white misrecognition and practices of racial inequality' (Chapter 9), Sarah Bufkin explores the relation between maldistribution and misrecognition with regard to the reproduction of racial inequalities.

Drawing on the seminal work of Frantz Fanon, James Baldwin, and Raoul Peck, Bufkin highlights the controversial aspects of recognition when it comes to racial justice, given that White imaginaries shape normative standards of recognition – a point that neither Honneth's nor Fraser's accounts seem to capture adequately.

In 'A moral economy? Honneth, recognition, and the capitalist market', Renante Pilapil (Chapter 10) critically examines the reading of the capitalist market recently proposed by Axel Honneth. Pilapil is sceptical of Honneth's optimistic account of the market in terms of solidarity and recognition, and expresses doubts about his methodology as well, warning about the risks of his moral interpretation of economic practices. He argues that complementing Honneth's 'experiential' approach with a 'structural' one enables to better capture the normative dimensions involved in the market.

In 'Social esteem between recognition and redistribution' (Chapter 11), Christian Lazzeri explores the different meanings of the concept of esteem in relation to redistribution, focusing on cooperation and exchanges under capitalism. Both Honneth's and Fraser's accounts of the moral economy of esteem are discussed. Lazzeri's conclusion is that the way these authors describe the relation between economic structures and categories of recognition raises theoretical and practical problems that suggest to rethink their models.

In 'Recognition vs redistribution: the case of self-respect' (Chapter 12), Caroline Guibet Lafaye argues that self-respect should be reframed from the perspective of fundamental social 'achievements', rather than being merely conceptualized in the language of opportunities. She argues that the point of justice is not as much what people have, but what they can actually achieve with what they have. For this reason, rather than being seen from the perspective of primary goods, self-respect should be considered as a 'primary outcome'.

Each contribution in this volume explores in its own way the intermeshing between economic structures, social, cultural, and political dynamics, and how each originally reflects on the moral economies that operate behind social phenomena, while warning against the risks implicit in a merely economic reading of the same phenomena. Overall, the book shows that redistribution and recognition provide valuable resources to think about justice and that their joint consideration increases our chances to capture aspects that one-dimensional accounts tend to overlook. However, the book also suggests that further grids are necessary to grasp relevant and crucial dimensions of life escaped by both approaches.

Note

1 The subsequent literature, for example, integrates the very important political paradigm (Fraser 2008).

References

Forst, Rainer. 2014. *Justification and Critique*. Trans. by C. Cronin. Cambridge: Polity Press.

Fraser, Nancy. 2008. *Scales of Justice: Reimagining Political Space in a Globalizing World*. Cambridge: Polity Press.

Fraser, Nancy, and Axel Honneth. 2003. *Redistribution or Recognition? A Political-Philosophical Exchange*. New York: Verso.

Scheffler, Samuel. 2015. 'The Practice of Equality'. In Fourie, C., Fabien Schuppert, and Ivo Wallimann-Helmer (eds.) *Social Equality: On What It Means to Be Equals*. Oxford: Oxford University Press, pp. 21–44.

Schemmel, Christian. 2012. 'Distributive and Relational Equality'. *Politics, Philosophy & Economics*, 11(2): 123–148.

Young, Iris M. 1990. *Justice and the Politics of Difference*. Princeton: Princeton University Press.

Part I

THE 'RECOGNITION SIDE' OF DISTRIBUTIVE JUSTICE

1

BASIC INCOME IN THE RECOGNITION ORDER

Respect, care, and esteem

Jurgen De Wispelaere and Arto Laitinen

1 Introduction

Justifications of the proposal to grant each individual member in the polity an unconditional cash grant – an unconditional basic income – draw support from both principled and pragmatic arguments (Barry 1996; Van der Veen 1997). The leading principled justification proposes that basic income is a precondition for individuals having the freedom to live their lives in accordance with their own values and plans. This freedom-based argument comes in many forms, including a liberal-egalitarian (Maskivker 2011; Birnbaum 2012), republican (Pettit 2007; Casassas and DeWispelaere 2016), and even a libertarian variant (Tomasi 2012; Zwoliski 2012). It is most importantly associated with the real-libertarian justification advocated by Philippe Van Parijs (1995) or, more recently, the status freedom proposed by Karl Widerquist (2013).[1]

Freedom-based arguments typically adopt an individualist stance in which social agents – including groups in either aggregate or corporatist form – feature in one of two instrumental guises. On the one hand, social agents are modelled as part of an agent's preferences or life plans: for instance, I prefer to live my life with a partner rather than on my own and expect social policy to support this free choice. On the other hand, social agents are often modelled as constraints or impediments on my free choices: for instance, I would like to engage in a more creative manner with my job, but my boss imposes a strictly controlled regime on all her employees, reducing my freedom at work. In both these cases, social agency remains decidedly instrumental and 'thin', failing to capture the variety of ways in which human agents interact with each other at different levels and consequently are embedded in social networks that are constituted by virtue of social interaction. In short, the freedom-based approach is missing a social ontology.

In this chapter we propose to examine the justification of basic income from a recognition-theoretical perspective as a complement to the freedom-based justification. Rather than seeing freedom and recognition as competing approaches, we suggest that both share important features and can be fruitfully combined to achieve a more plausible account of the role a basic income could play in an individual's life. Basic income advocates and recognition theorists have by and large ignored each other.[2] This is odd to the extent that basic income debates already contain important recognition-theoretical components. For instance, basic income advocates have made a strong case for the importance of granting each individual an unconditional basic income as a condition for securing equal dignity, regarding basic income as one of the social determinants of self-respect (McKinnon 2003; Maskivker 2011). This respect-recognizing case for basic income largely turns on the fact that its universal application mirrors and promotes the equal standing of each member of society, while the lack of conditions avoids the reliance on undignified and intrusive social monitoring by state agents (Van Parijs and Vanderborght 2017). Similarly, the critical link between basic income and promoting care for others – a second key feature of what Axel Honneth (2003a, 2003b) refers to as the 'recognition order' of a society – is widely acknowledged and debated, especially in the feminist basic income literature (Zelleke 2011). While dignity and care offer recognition theorists a way into the basic income debate, the relation between both and their role within a broader theory of recognition remains under-theorized.

In what follows we first characterize three modes of recognition: respect, care, and social esteem. We argue that a strong recognition-theoretical argument for basic income emerges from combining considerations of universal respect and care (or concern) for well-being. We then turn towards what is arguably the most challenging mode of recognition for defenders of basic income: social esteem. Esteem is a critical feature of Honneth's recognition order but at the same time appears in constant tension with the basic income ideal. We examine this tension by focusing on the particular nature of esteem as a relational and positional good. Conceptually distinguishing different forms of social esteem, we offer several ways in which a universal basic income can be made compatible with a recognition order that gives pride of place to differential esteem.

2 Three kinds of recognition: respect, care, and esteem

From a recognition-theoretical perspective there are three main forms of the recognition order of a society: respect for equal dignity, concern or care for others, and social esteem (Honneth 1995, 2003b; Ikäheimo 2002; Laitinen 2002, 2010). This section briefly sets out each of these forms or modes to stage the scene for examining their relation with basic income in subsequent sections.

First, *respect* is responsive to the equal dignity of human persons. Every person is assumed to have an equal positive standing; divisions into first- and second-class forms of personhood are inimical to the equal dignity principle. Equal respect is a universalistic form of recognition that abstracts from the numerous differences between individuals and is often expressed in the form of basic rights that apply equally to all members in the relevant social order. Hegel's (1807) famous master-slave dialectic is a prime example of a failure of mutual recognition, since both masters and slaves suffer from lack of recognition as equals. The special relational good of being positioned as a 'social equal' must be distinguished from the positional desire to be a 'social better'. Fukuyama (1992) refers to these fundamentally oppositional desires as *isothymia* (the desire to be recognized as an equal) and *megalothymia* (the desire to be recognized as better than others). This distinction between egalitarian isothymia and competitive megalothymia will be relevant for the recognition-theoretical defence of basic income.[3]

Second, *care or concern* for the well-being and suffering of others, especially those who are regarded as needy and vulnerable, is a key mode of recognition. But care or concern comes in two distinctive forms. In its most familiar form, care is highly selective and partial and attached to a specific person – such as a family member, for instance. This form of care or 'love' is *singular*. But care can nevertheless also be *universal* when it responds not to a specific person or relationship but instead to the many predicaments that are common to members of humanity. This type of care – or concern – is often triggered by disasters such as war, flooding, or hunger in even the remotest parts of the world. In its universalistic modality, care often takes on a sufficientarian stance reflecting the norm that every person ought to live a minimally decent life compatible with basic human dignity. In the next section, we argue that the universalistic mode of care for others makes for a forceful case for basic income when joined with equal respect.

A third form of recognition, *social esteem*, is distinct from both universal and singular modes of recognition. Esteem is fundamentally responsive to the relevant differences of individuals, including their merits, efforts, contributions, achievements, and talents. Esteem is *particular* in that it is sensitive to *what kind of a person* is being estimated. It focuses on the general properties that esteemed persons should hold, independent of which specific person effectively ends up holding them. Genuine esteem is different from singular care because it does not respond to specific relationships, ignoring friendship, kinship, or co-nationality. Social esteem also eschews the universality and equality attached to each person and instead focuses on the differential ranking of persons based on their abilities and achievements. Where respect and dignity recognize equal standing, social esteem recognizes difference and allocates positive and negative esteem in accordance to the differential ranking established by different esteem criteria (Taylor 1992; Laitinen 2002; Ikäheimo and Laitinen 2007).

3 Respect, care, and basic income

From a recognition-theoretical perspective, respect and care offer obvious ways to consider how basic income would fit into a recognition order. As mentioned previously, basic income advocates have made a strong case for the importance of granting each an individual unconditional basic income as a condition for securing first of all dignity and respect, including viewing basic income as a social determinant of self-respect (e.g., McKinnon 2003; Pinzani 2010; Van Parijs and Vanderborght 2017). The respect-recognizing case for basic income turns on the fact that its universal application mirrors and promotes the equal standing of each member of society (Pateman 2003; Morales 2019). Furthermore, the lack of conditions avoids the reliance on undignified and intrusive social monitoring by state agents, which has reached endemic forms in conditional welfare support (Handler and Babcock 2006). A basic income regime fulfils Philip Pettit's so-called eyeball test: with a regular basic income each individual has the robust capacity to 'look others in the eye without reason for the fear or deference that a power of interference might inspire; they can walk tall and assume the public status, objective and subjective, of being equal in this regard with the best' (Pettit 2012: 84; see also Pettit 2007). Mulligan (2013: 159) sees as the main connection between basic income and recognition the granting of 'the necessary material security to enable basic relations of reciprocal recognition'.[4]

Another straightforward defence of basic income considers the relationship between the recipients of basic income and the recognizer as one of concern or care for its most vulnerable or marginalized citizens. As outlined in the previous section, care in the recognition order has both a universalistic and particularistic character. Care is universal where we – typically the state, but in democratic states ultimately its citizens – collectively embrace our responsibility towards the vulnerable (Goodin 1985). But care is also simultaneously particularistic because care relations typically take the form of a carer (or care institution) caring for a particular person in need. The universal and the particular dimension are closely linked in the recognition order by virtue of the fact that both the carer and the person in need of care are owed recognition of their particular needs. In many societies those in need of care are increasingly left to their own devices but also those who are taking up care roles are often insufficiently supported (Alstott 2005). Enter basic income, which discharges our collective responsibility of concern and care by offering necessary support for those in need – without stigmatizing those in need by requiring they engage in 'shameful revelation' (Wolff 2006) – but also, crucially, for those who undertake care roles in society (Zelleke 2011).

Respect and care each offer a route for recognition-theorists to embrace basic income, but importantly the recognition order must balance both to avoid the danger of paternalism on the one hand, and the danger of insensitivity to actual welfare on the other. A key feature of the recognition-based justification of basic income is that it simultaneously promotes the respect and care dimensions of the recognition order and, in doing so, reinforces the structural connection between respect and care. Historically, as social support systems evolved from forms of voluntary charity and philanthropy to legally recognized social rights, the concern for well-being has matched the concern for autonomy and dignity (Waldron 1988). Policies that focus primarily on the concern or care for the needs and welfare of vulnerable citizens, risk imposing paternalistic measures that promote welfare at the cost of autonomy and dignity. By contrast, policies that preserve dignity may do so at the cost of paying insufficient attention to their welfare: this is the case when formal rights do not offer 'real' access to or opportunities for welfare (Van Parijs 1995). Honneth (2003b: 149) made this point when he argued that

> [t]he normative argument which made social-welfare guarantees in a certain sense "rationally" unavoidable is essentially the hardly disputable assertion that members of society can only make actual use of their legally guaranteed autonomy if they are assured a minimum of economic resources, irrespective of income.

The key insight of the basic income discussion is that the secure provision of an income floor is a precondition for *both* respect (or dignity) and the well-being of each member in a society. Moreover, providing income security in an unconditional and universal manner assures that society *simultaneously* expresses respect and care. In other words, basic income mutually reinforces the recognition of care and respect *horizontally* – the interpersonal recognition of equal standing across society – as well as *vertically* – the hierarchical interaction between state apparatus and citizens. This interlocking of considerations of respect, care, and the institution of a basic income is a central insight for recognition theorists and offers a solid basis upon which to build a recognition-theoretical justification for basic income. In the remainder of this chapter we address the challenges posed by the third form of recognition for basic income.

4 Basic income in the economy of esteem: two challenges

If respect and care offer a good recognition-theoretical case for basic income, what about the third form of recognition – social esteem? At first blush, social esteem seems to throw a big spanner into the recognition-theoretical justification of basic income. As outlined in section 2, social esteem by its nature eschews universality and equality attached to each person and instead focuses on the differential ranking of persons who are compared on the basis of their abilities and achievements. Where respect and egalitarian concern recognize equal standing, social esteem explicitly recognizes difference. Without difference, no esteem – after all, it is precisely what makes us different that allows for the ranking of social esteem. This distinguishes esteem from dignity and respect.[5] Furthermore, esteem cannot be granted merely because someone has a clear *need* for social esteem: esteem granted as a mere response to perceived need for esteem fails to be genuine esteem.

Instead, genuine esteem appropriately responds to *achievement*, which also sets it apart from care or concern.

Basic income is attractive from the perspective of recognizing care and respect in large part because of a shared focus on equality and universalism. But these features, hardwired into the basic income policy design, are chafing when viewed through the lens of social esteem. Recognizing social esteem is all about appreciating differential achievement (or its proxy, effort), and it would appear basic income has little or nothing to contribute in this regard. This would suggest social esteem and basic income are at best mutually disinterested in one another.[6] But this may be too optimistic a scenario, for there is a good case to be made that basic income is not neutral but rather inimical to social esteem. The provision of an income guarantee that is deliberately designed to ignore contingent circumstances such as effort, talent, or achievement can be said to crowd out esteem itself. On the one hand, basic income crowds out esteem by replacing support mechanisms conditional on certain achievements, which would be a potential basis for conferring esteem. On the other hand, basic income, deliberately eschewing achievement or effort as an eligibility condition, also sends a clear message that appears to downplay their social and moral relevance – this is the stated aim of many of those advocating basic income (e.g., Van Parijs and Vanderborght 2017). Recognition theorists might therefore worry basic income causes a form of expressive harm by depreciating social esteem as a valid mode of recognition.

The recognition literature offers a second challenge to basic income, more specifically tied to the social value attributed to employment and being employed in the recognition order. Axel Honneth, for instance, has argued that cooperation in the division of labour is a positive feature of a society intent on recognizing esteem: in a nutshell, through employment every worker enjoys social esteem associated with the social appreciation of their contributive effort and achievement. In this, Honneth (2003a, 2003b) follows Hegel, Durkheim, and Meade in linking social division of labour to social solidarity – everyone should occupy a social position that allows them to contribute to the common good. The occupational honour conferred to those in a profession is linked to a general recognition that all job-holders have in common. Honneth (1998: 775) sees this as relevant for democracy as well: following Dewey, he maintains that a just division of labour is a prerequisite of democracy, which is best seen as a reflective form of governing the society built on such division of labour (cf. Mulligan 2013: 158–159).

To be sure, a strict focus on labour market positions carries with it the risk of a particular form of *mis*recognition, already pointed out by Honneth (2003a, 2003b). The emphasis given to paid compared to unpaid labour is both ungrounded and objectionably gendered. Women doing 'invisible' household work should receive equal recognition for their critical social contribution. Honneth writes:

> the extent to which something counts as "achievement", as a cooperative contribution, is defined against a value standard whose normative reference point is the economic activity of the independent, middle-class, male bourgeois. What is distinguished as "work", with a specific, quantifiable use for society, hence amounts to the result of a group-specific determination of value – to which whole sectors of other activities, themselves equally necessary for reproduction (e.g. household work) fall victim.
>
> (Honneth 2003b: 141)

For Honneth, then, social esteem should not be strictly linked to employment, but to social cooperation more broadly. Both paid *and* unpaid work should count as valid contributions to the common good and merit to be esteemed accordingly.

This view is endorsed by other recognition theorists as well. If only paid work is esteemed, 'a large proportion of the population is denied the opportunity to achieve equal esteem for similar activities because of the prioritization of paid work over other forms of work' (Mulligan 2013: 165). Recognizing unpaid work without distortion would also relieve the psychological distress related to periods of unemployment, and remove the stigma related to being a 'jobseeker' (Mulligan 2013: 166). It could also foster gender equality in circumstances where the less recognized unpaid forms of work are predominantly carried out by female workers. Timo Jütten adopts a similar view:

> In the modern capitalist recognition order people gain social esteem through their work and, therefore, depend on it for their self-worth. This explains why forced unemployment, precarious employment, and low paid work are experienced as threats to human dignity: they suggest to those who experience them that they are of little social usefulness and value to society. Therefore, my interim conclusion was that in order to protect the dignity of their members, modern societies must strive to achieve full employment, protect employment security, and decent pay, and broaden the range of estimable activities in which citizens can engage in outside of the workplace or instead of paid labour.
>
> (Jütten 2017: 277)[7]

Now, recognizing societal useful unpaid work points to a direction where *almost* everyone is seen as a contributor. The closest corresponding policy proposal is not basic income, however, but *participation income* as outlined and defended by the economist Tony Atkinson (1996, 2015). Participation income broadens conditional support by abolishing means-testing and introducing a social participation requirement that includes care work, volunteering, engaging in education, or training in addition to actual labour market participation. While many basic income advocates perceive it as a close cousin of, or even a feasible pathway towards, the implementation of a fully unconditional basic income (e.g., Van Parijs and Vanderborght 2017), others insist the persistence of conditions retains a division between those eligible to income support and those not (De Wispelaere and Stirton 2007, 2018).

From the perspective of recognizing social esteem this seems to be as far as we should go: participation income but not basic income could offer a viable and sufficiently broad-based approach to the recognition of social esteem.[8] In short, the tension between basic income and social esteem remains firmly in place even where we broaden social participation beyond employment. Put together, the two challenges outlined in this section strongly suggest that recognition theorists are right to remain wary about embracing basic income: even where care and respect offer good reasons for supporting basic income, social esteem introduces a major kink in the cable. And because social esteem remains a valid and irreducible mode of recognition, this represents a serious concern for the recognition-theoretical justification of basic income. In the remainder of this chapter we examine whether we can find a way to make basic income more palatable for recognition theorists by rendering it compatible with the economy of esteem.

5 Unpacking social esteem

Social esteem is a 'container concept' that captures a number of different realities that need to be unpacked. Acknowledging the multifaceted nature of social esteem offers room for bridging the apparent chasm between basic income and social esteem.

In the first place, consider how the debates about the role of employment that feature as the central battleground for social esteem in contemporary society are entirely focused on *contributions to the common good* (Honneth 1995; Ikäheimo and Laitinen 2010; Jütten 2017). The central idea is that the advanced division of labour allows people to contribute in their specific way to the societal good and be recognized for their contribution. But production-related social esteem is but one of the many ways in which contemporary society allocates esteem. A complex society is made up of many cultures that often comprise distinct local subcultures, featuring norms and rules on the basis of which people can be differentially esteemed and obtain differential honour, status, or rank. Not all such 'pockets of esteem' (Laitinen 2015) need adopt a quasi-productivist mode of recognition; many will allocate esteem in ways that are not easily fitted into a discourse of 'contributing to the common good'. In short, social esteem can be based on contributions to society but also associated with non-contributive agency; basic income might not be in tension with the latter but in fact promote the use of non-productivist esteem indicators for seeking social distinction.

Second, we have characterized social esteem as a particularist mode of recognition. But could esteem have a universalistic dimension as well? There exist basic forms of social esteem that are arguably egalitarian and can be met with a one-size-fits-all logic (Laitinen 2002, 2015). Consider, for instance, the universal demand not to suffer the negative esteem of stigmatization. Stigmatization falls foul of the principle that each individual is entitled to a basic level of dignity and respect: it produces *disrespect*. But the constant vilification of the poor, the unemployed, or immigrants, both in popular discourse and in social policy and state regulation, also engenders a problematic form of *negative esteem*. Stigmatization as a failure of equal respect is a failure to be difference-blind; stigmatization as a failure of deserved esteem, by contrast, is a failure to respond appropriately to differences associated with the stigmatized person (or group) and thus misrecognize the desert basis of their achievements.

Further, and more positively, each person is arguably owed a basic level of positive esteem as a 'useful member of a society' (Laitinen 2015, cf. Honneth 2003b). Merely by occupying a role in the social space, by being a 'citizen' or a 'peer', one is entitled to the basic, default esteem that comes with that role – independently of individual variation in how well one performs in that role. This type of basic esteem need not be positional or competitive: one need not view others' success as diminishing one's own success, but such esteem can be co-realizable. In cases of collective action, everyone's success can even be tied together: Tuomela's (2007) 'collectivity condition' holds in that a member of a collective succeeds only if others experience success as well. The social esteem at stake here is *non-competitive* but nonetheless *relational*: the value of the mutual esteem between different contributors may reside in the kind of relationship between them – which could be grounded in the value of solidarity, for instance. In what follows, we discuss how basic income relates to such relational, non-positional goods of esteem.

This brings us to a third question: how is social esteem related to the positional desire to fare better than others, to win in competitions for positional goods? Rutger Claassen (2008) has argued that a good such as money can be desired both positionally and non-positionally. It matters to have more money than your neighbour, but it also matters to have a certain amount of money to allow you to satisfy your basic needs independent of how much money others have. By contrast, many would insist that social esteem (or honour) is an intrinsically positional good: esteem matters only as part of a ranked system in which some are more esteemed than others. But this view is incomplete in several ways.

We need to distinguish between *deserved* and *undeserved* esteem: the desire to always get more and more esteem (whether deserved or not) must be distinguished from the desire to get as much esteem (recognition, status) as one deserves – no less but also no more. The classic source for this is the *Nicomachean Ethics*, where Aristotle argues for the primary desire to be good and only secondarily to be honoured because of it. Adequate regard implies a person wants to be recognized in accordance to the normative significance of their features: misrecognition can happen both when a person's positive contributions are not recognized *and* when she receives esteem for something she is not responsible for. Social esteem is also intimately related to *self-esteem*: esteem is a social precondition for self-esteem.[9] But in contrast to esteem itself, self-esteem is not intrinsically relational or positional. One's desire for self-esteem is essentially independent of the levels of self-esteem in others. A key condition for self-esteem is that the social esteem on which it relies must be authentic and sincerely deserved. In other words, the desire for deserved self-esteem feeds back into the desire for deserved social esteem. The search for *adequate* recognition effectively dampens or tempers excessive competition for the positional good of esteem.

In addition, the relational goods of esteem come in positional competitive variants but also in egalitarian variants. What Francis Fukuyama (1992) calls *megalothymia* is the desire to do better than others – a desire for positional goods whose value decreases proportionally to the extent that more people have it. By contrast, what Fukuyama refers to as *isothymia* is the desire to be an equal to others.[10] It would appear then that esteem may be more similar to money than initially thought. Both money and esteem can be desired positionally – one wants more of each good compared to others (megalothymia) – or relationally but non-positionally – one has a strong desire to have as much as others have (isothymia). On the latter, non-positional approach, one desires to be regarded as better than others only if one *is* better than others and desires to be regarded as equal to others only if one *is* equal to others. The main problem with kinds of esteem that are insensitive to judgements of desert is that these do not provide appropriate feedback on the features that drive self-esteem. A tyrant may be praised by the subjects as a great poet and a great athlete, but if entirely motivated by fear or a desire to please these expressions fail to communicate the message that the tyrant is being regarded as a great poet and a great athlete. In the final section we revisit the link between basic income and social esteem, keeping in mind the more complex picture of social esteem briefly outlined here.

6 Esteem-proofing basic income

If basic income and social esteem are in tension, as the argument in section 4 leads us to believe, basic income proponents have three argumentative strategies at their disposal. The first is to downplay or even deny the relevance of social esteem altogether, but this is simply an implausible strategy given the established role of esteem in recognition theory. The second would be to argue that while esteem is problematic, the positive linkage with respect and care balances out concerns to reach an all-things-considered positive justification. We believe this strategy, too, underestimates the critical role of esteem in the recognition order. A third strategy, which we explore in this final section, is to employ the more complex picture of social esteem outlined in section 5 to argue that the concerns themselves may be less pronounced than initially thought.

To begin with, the references to the role of dignity in relation to both respect and care invokes the absence of stigma, which represents an unacceptable form of negative esteem as well. To rehearse a point made earlier, unlike food banks or highly conditional state benefits, basic income expressly eschews stigmatization at the level of discourse as well as policy design. It is worth noting, therefore, that a universal and unconditional basic income is not only compatible with, but also likely reinforces, the universal desire for an absence of unjustified negative esteem.

Next, admittedly universal one-size-fits-all policies are ill-equipped to offer appropriate feedback on individual contributions – and therefore cannot satisfy the *desire for self-esteem* – nor be responsive to status differentials – and thus fail to satisfy the *desire for positional esteem*. This means they are seriously limited as a means of communicating social esteem. In a recent paper Nick Smith has stated this point forcefully:

> If UBI [universal basic income] is to be made an expression of esteem in the performance of a role, either one or both of the following qualifications would need to be made. Either the esteem conferred would need to be qualified so that it no longer had conditions, or the UBI would need to be qualified so that it was no longer unconditional. The problem with first strategy, however, is that it inevitably abstracts from the content of the role, making it such that anyone can occupy it and occupy it equally well. Esteem thus morphs into the respect all owe each other qua persons and loses its distinctiveness both as a form of recognition and as a criterion of social freedom. The problem with the second strategy is that it inevitably takes the radicality out of the UBI idea and makes it indistinguishable from various conditional incomes. UBI thus morphs into the citizen's wage, or a carer's allowance or a householder's income, depending on the primary social role that the basic income is meant to enable and esteem.
>
> (Smith 2019: 17)

Smith has a valid point: basic income is incapable of conferring esteem because a universal and unconditional entitlement axiomatically negates any link with achievement. But a plausible and justifiable recognition order requires more than merely ensuring positive and negative esteem is apportioned appropriately in line with relevant achievements. A core element of an egalitarian recognition order requires that the distribution of *opportunities to contribute* is also given due attention, for the apportioning of esteem itself is indirectly affected by the prevailing opportunity structure.[11] Bringing opportunities to contribute in line with, for instance, a more egalitarian outlook is perfectly compatible with discharging social esteem according to differential contribution. Or to put it differently, the apportioning of appropriate reward (or opprobrium) following socially beneficial (or harmful) contributions is at best orthogonal to the prior allocation of the very opportunities to engage in such contributory activity. There are good reasons to think that differential social esteem is more justified when access to the sources of social esteem themselves is rendered more equally available.[12]

Enter basic income, which through its universal and unconditional character is said to secure an 'opportunity floor' for all citizens (Van Parijs and Vanderborght 2017). Whatever the prevailing recognition order has established as esteem-worthy contributions, basic income aims to improve opportunities to contribute especially for those who are currently situated at the vulnerable or marginalized end of the social spectrum. This way, we argue, basic income plays a key role in securing what we might call the 'preconditions for social esteem', which in turn means the positional and competitive economy of esteem will be tamed by background measures such as basic income in order to avoid clashing with the need for securing dignity in all three dimensions: care, respect, and esteem itself. Failing to provide a decent floor for opportunities to contribute directly affects citizens' well-being (care or concern) but equally may threaten their rights status (respect). With respect to esteem, too, we believe a recognition order that combines social recognition with the equal or perhaps maximin allocation of opportunities for securing esteem is preferable over its alternative.[13]

Finally, we note that Axel Honneth's (2003b) and Timo Jütten's (2017) argument concerning the good society esteem-wise is in an important sense egalitarian or universal[14]: *everyone* ought to have the positive esteem that follows from contributing to society. Honneth stresses the division of labour and the social esteem that comes *equally* to everyone in a role qua contributor, even though the roles themselves vary extensively in character, effort, productivity, and so on. On this view, all contributions to the common good represent a threshold value and this is why Honneth thinks all employed people deserve the basic social esteem that comes with holding down a job. But recall that Honneth is equally keen to stress that the unpaid labour of care workers should be included in this recognition order; social contribution cannot just be restricted to participation in the formal labour market.

Basic income may go some way towards 'radicalizing' the basis of social esteem and thus altering the recognition order itself. The move to expand social participation to include care, household, and voluntary work in the sphere of valuable contributions can be followed by another shift where any rigid divide between a 'working life' and other valuable forms of social existence fades. At this point, social esteem need not be based on contributions but instead could be based on other valuable particularities that allow individuals to seek the relevant distinction to satisfy a desire for esteem.

In relation to this shift, Timo Jütten comments on the Rawlsian ideal of an equal distribution of the social basis of respect:

> While an equal distribution of social esteem is utopian, due to the fact that people differ in their abilities and inclinations, and therefore cannot or do not contribute equally to socially shared goals, in a well-ordered society there is a threshold of social esteem that is sufficient for a dignified life which even the least advantaged can meet, so that nobody falls below this threshold and must live an undignified life.
>
> (Jütten 2017: 276)

What would be the basis of social esteem, if not paid or unpaid work? Here the basic income debate expounds a strong Millian tendency to value 'experiments in living' both for their own sake but also in terms of their social value (Van Parijs and Vanderborght 2017). The starting point is that policies that are grounded in and insist on institutionalizing lists of socially valuable activities inescapably fail to capture the full range of human experience and existence, or the myriad ways in which human ingenuity itself reimagines and revitalizes an ever-changing social world. The strength of a basic income provided to all on an unconditional basis is that it adopts a radical bottom-up vision by which individuals themselves – typically in some collaborative form – produce activities that prove to be valuable for some others in some form. These activities may not be appreciated by the dominant institutions or even the majority of 'users', but that does not mean they do not represent a genuine social value and deserve to be recognized as such. Those engaging in such activities in turn ought to be given the appropriate esteem for their particular achievement. The potential of basic income, in other words, is to vastly expand the pockets of esteem (Laitinen 2015) and to allow for social esteem to emerge in a kind of Hayekian spontaneous order instead of in the form of a highly regulated, but inevitably restraining, top-down engineered social order.

7 Conclusion

In this chapter we have explored the justification of basic income from the perspective of recognition theory. We first suggested that the easy road into a recognition-theoretical justification of basic income is through its connections with, respectively, dignity or respect and care or concern for other people's well-being. The basic income literature offers plenty of vantage points from which to argue that instituting a universal and unconditional cash grant would recognize respect and care. In addition, however, we argued that basic income is of particular interest to recognition theorists because of its ability to mutually reinforce the respect and care forms of recognition.

Recognition theorists seem to leave firm ground when we start thinking about basic income from the perspective of the third mode of recognition – social esteem. Because esteem is intricately connected with differential achievement, it appears to be at constant loggerheads with a policy that is characterized by universalism and unconditionality. This chapter both describes the challenges basic income justification faces with regard to esteem and offers several arguments for how basic income advocates could mitigate these challenges. We conclude that a better understanding of the multifaceted and complex nature of social esteem offers a number of avenues for thinking basic income could operate within, and even support, a recognition order that gives appropriate space for the human desire to seek esteem, status, and rank.

Acknowledgements

Earlier versions of this chapter were presented at the 2018 BIEN Congress (24–26 August, Tampere) and the 2018 Power Conference (27–29 August, Tampere). We would like to thank the audiences at both events for constructive criticism that by and large leaves our self-esteem in place. Arto Laitinen would like to acknowledge the support from the Faculty of Social Sciences, Tampere University, and the research project Robotics and the Future of Welfare Services (Academy of Finland, Strategic Research Council). Jurgen De Wispelaere is grateful to the Independent Social Research Foundation (ISRF) for funding a political economy research fellowship and to Tampere University for funding a guest professorship during which this chapter was drafted. Our special thanks go to Roosa Eriksson for research assistance.

Notes

1 A second principled justification grounds basic income in democracy and individuals' foundational right to participation in the decision-making process of the polity (Pateman 2003, 2004; Goodhart 2007; for a recent review, see Morales 2019).

2 Notable exceptions include Mulligan (2013), Laitinen (2015), Schmidt am Busch (2011), and Smith (2019).

3 There is room for debate whether equality of persons is merely an accidental outcome, a consequent of the principle that all persons ought to be regarded appropriately, and it just happens to be so that the basic dignity of all persons is equal. The view of Harry Frankfurt (1987), for instance, is that equality as such does not matter. What matters is that everyone is treated *adequately*. A rival view is that the equality realized in equal relationships between persons is intrinsically valuable: it is a relational, comparative value. In this essay, we accept both normative premises: persons ought to be treated adequately in light of their basic dignity, and equality in social relations is valuable in itself. Our focus is on complementing these considerations of respect and dignity by other considerations.

4 The link between social rights and social citizenship goes back to T.H. Marshall's classic account (see King and Waldron 1988, for an illuminating discussion). Basic income pushes the argument by insisting on the *unconditional* provision of social rights as a condition of social citizenship.
5 See Brennan and Pettit (2000) for 'the economy of esteem'. The relation between dignity and rank is complicated (Waldron 2007).
6 In this case, we might consider adopting basic income while leaving people to search elsewhere to satisfy their need for social esteem, effectively creating 'pockets of esteem' (see Laitinen 2015).
7 However, Jütten (2017) adds that the comparative and positional nature of social esteem may come with a dark side similar to the first challenge outlined previously.
8 Note, however, that the extent to which a participation income advances the case of gender equality remains disputed (Zelleke 2018).
9 Relatedly, see the Rawlsian idea of the social bases of self-respect as a universally desired (and desirable) primary good (Rawls 2003).
10 Note that Fukuyama (1992) fails to notice that both of these desires can again come in desert-sensitive and desert-insensitive variants; combining both dimensions allows for a more realistic multidimensional conception of social esteem.
11 For a discussion of opportunities to contribute in the context of people with disabilities, see De Wispelaere and Casassas (2014).
12 This is at least a partial response to another concern raised by Smith (2019: 17), namely that basic income offers mere possibilities whereas esteem requires actualization or performance. Our response would be that even if we grant the performance condition, the allocation of opportunities to perform esteem-worthy activities should not be dismissed out of hand.
13 Two important qualifications are worth pointing out at this stage. First, in this section we envisage the opportunity to contribute as an internal shift within an existing recognition order. This is to be distinguished from the more expansive shift in changing the recognition order itself. Second, the reference to 'contribution' varies with the particularities of the recognition order. We deliberately leave open what counts as contribution, partially discussed in section 3.
14 It also resembles Nancy Fraser's (2003a, 2003b) argument for participatory parity.

References

Alstott, A.L. 2005. *No Exit: What Parents Owe Their Children and What Society Owes Parents*. New York, NY: Oxford University Press.

Aristotle. 2004. *Nicomachean Ethics*. Cambridge: Cambridge University Press.

Atkinson, A.B. 1996. 'The Case for a Participation Income', *The Political Quarterly*, 67(1): 67–70.

Atkinson, A.B. 2015. *Inequality: What Can Be Done?* Cambridge, MA: Harvard University Press.

Barry, B. 1996. 'Real Freedom and Basic Income', *Journal of Political Philosophy*, 4(3): 242–276.

Birnbaum, S. 2012. *Basic Income Reconsidered: Social Justice, Liberalism, and the Demands of Equality*. New York: Palgrave.

Brennan, G. and P. Pettit. 2000. 'The Hidden Economy of Esteem', *Economics and Philosophy*, 16(1): 77–98.

Casassas, D. and J. De Wispelaere. 2016. 'Republicanism and the Political Economy of Democracy', *European Journal of Social Theory*, 19(2): 283–300.

Claassen, R. 2008. 'The Status Struggle. A Recognition-based Interpretation of the Positional Economy', *Philosophy & Social Criticism*, 34(9): 1021–1049.

De Wispelaere, J. and D. Casassas. 2014. 'A Life of One's Own: Republican Freedom and Disability', *Disability & Society*, 29(3): 402–416.

De Wispelaere, J. and L. Stirton. 2007. 'The Public Administration Case Against Participation Income', *Social Service Review*, 81(3): 523–549.

De Wispelaere, J. and L. Stirton. 2018. 'The Case Against Participation Income – Political, Not (Merely) Administrative', *The Political Quarterly*, 89(2): 262–267.

Frankfurt, H. 1987. 'Equality as a Moral Ideal', *Ethics*, 98(1): 21–43.

Fraser, N. 2003a. 'Distorted Beyond All Recognition: A Rejoinder to Axel Honneth', in *Redistribution or Recognition? A Political-Philosophical Exchange*, pp. 198–236. New York: Verso.

Fraser, N. 2003b. 'Social Justice in the Age of Identity Politics: Redistribution, Recognition, and Participation', in *Redistribution or Recognition? A Political-Philosophical Exchange*, pp. 7–109. New York: Verso.

Fukuyama, F. 1992. *The End of History and the Last Man*. New York: Free Press.

Goodhart, M. 2007. '"None So Poor That He Is Compelled to Sell Himself": Democracy, Subsistence, and Basic Income', in S. Hertel and L. Minkler (eds), *Economic Rights: Conceptual, Measurement, and Policy Issues*, pp. 94–114. Cambridge: Cambridge University Press.

Goodin, R.E. 1985. 'Vulnerabilities and Responsibilities: An Ethical Defense of the Welfare State', *American Political Science Review*, 79(3): 775–787.

Handler, J. and A. Babcock. 2006. 'The Failure of Workfare: Another Reason for a Basic Income Guarantee', *Basic Income Studies*, 1(1): 1–22.

Hegel, G.W.F. 1807/1977. *The Phenomenology of Spirit*. Oxford: Oxford University Press.

Honneth, A. 1995. *The Struggle for Recognition: The Moral Grammar of Social Conflicts*. Cambridge: Polity.

Honneth, A. 1998. 'Democracy as Reflexive Cooperation: John Dewey and the Theory of Democracy Today', *Political Theory*, 26(6): 763–783.

Honneth, A. 2003a. 'The Point of Recognition: A Rejoinder to the Rejoinder', in *Redistribution or Recognition? A Political-Philosophical Exchange*, pp. 237–267. New York: Verso.

Honneth, A. 2003b. 'Redistribution as Recognition: A Response to Nancy Fraser', in *Redistribution or Recognition? A Political-Philosophical Exchange*, pp. 110–197. New York: Verso.

Ikäheimo, H. 2002. 'On the Genus and Species of Recognition', *Inquiry*, 45(4): 447–462.

Ikäheimo, H. and A. Laitinen. 2007. 'Analyzing Recognition: Identification, Acknowledgement and Recognitive Attitudes Towards Persons', in B. van den Brink and D. Owen (eds), *Recognition and Power*, pp. 33–56. New York: Cambridge University Press.

Ikäheimo, H and A. Laitinen. 2010. 'Esteem for Contributions to the Common Good: The Role of Personifying Attitudes and Instrumental Value', in M. Seymour (ed.), *The Plural States of Recognition*, pp. 98–121. London: Palgrave MacMillan.

Jütten, T. 2017. 'Dignity, Esteem, and Social Contribution: A Recognition-Theoretical View', *The Journal of Political Philosophy*, 25(3): 259–280.

King, D. and J. Waldron. 1988. 'Citizenship, Social Citizenship and the Defence of Welfare Provision', *British Journal of Political Science*, 18(4): 415–43.

Laitinen, A. 2002. 'Interpersonal Recognition: A Response to Value or a Precondition of Personhood?', *Inquiry*, 45(4): 463–478.

Laitinen, A. 2010. 'On the Scope of Recognition: The Role of Adequate Regard and Mutuality', in Schmidt am Busch and Zurn (eds), *The Philosophy of Recognition*, pp. 319–342. Lanham: Lexington.

Laitinen, A. 2015 'Recognition, Solidarity, and the Politics of Esteem: The Case of Basic Income', in *Recognition and Freedom: Axel Honneth's Political Thought*, pp. 57–78. Leiden: Brill.

Maskivker, J. 2011. *Self-Realization and Justice: A Defense of Freedom from Employment*. New York: Routledge.

McKinnon, C. 2003. 'Basic Income, Self-Respect and Reciprocity', *Journal of Applied Philosophy*, 20(2): 143–158.

Morales, L. 2019. 'The Democratic Case for a Basic Income', *Law, Ethics and Philosophy*, 6: 120–137.

Mulligan, R. 2013. 'Universal Basic Income and Recognition Theory – A Tangible Step towards an Ideal', *Basic Income Studies*, 8(2): 153–172.

Pateman, C. 2003. 'Freedom and Democratization: Why Basic Income Is to Be Preferred to Basic Capital', in K. Dowding, J. De Wispelaere and S. White (eds), *The Ethics of Stakeholding*, pp. 130–148. Basingstoke: Palgrave.

Pateman, C. 2004. 'Democratizing Citizenship: Some Advantages of a Basic Income', *Politics and Society*, 32(1): 89–105.

Pettit, P. 2007. 'A Republican Right to Basic Income?', *Basic Income Studies*, 2(2): 1–8.

Pettit, P. 2012. *On the People's Terms: A Republican Theory and Model of Democracy*. Cambridge: Cambridge University Press.

Pinzani, A. 2010. 'Minimal Income as Basic Condition for Autonomy', *Veritas – Revista de Filosofia da Pucrs*, 55(1): 9–20.

Rawls, J. 2003. *Justice as Fairness: A Re-Statement*. Cambridge, MA: Harvard University Press.

Schmidt am Busch, H.-C. 2011. "*Anerkennung*" *als Prinzip der kritischen Theorie*. Berlin, Boston: de Gruyter.

Smith, N.H. 2019. 'Basic Income, Social Freedom and the Fabric of Justice', *Critical Review of International Social and Political Philosophy*. Online First doi:10.1080/13698230.2019.1585152.

Taylor, C. 1992. 'The Politics of Recognition', in A. Gutmann (ed.), *Multiculturalism: Examining the Politics of Recognition*, pp. 25–73. Princeton: Princeton University Press.

Tomasi, J. 2012. *Free Market Fairness*. Princeton: Princeton University Press.

Tuomela, R. 2007. *The Philosophy of Sociality: The Shared Point of View*. Oxford: Oxford University Press.

van der Veen, R. 1997. 'Real Freedom and Basic Income: Comment on Brian Barry', *Journal of Political Philosophy*, 5(3): 274–286.

Van Parijs, P. 1995. *Real Freedom for All: What (if Anything) can Justify Capitalism?* Oxford: Clarendon Press.

Van Parijs, P. and Y. Vanderborght. 2017. *Basic Income: A Radical Proposal for a Free Society and a Sane Economy*. Cambridge, MA: Harvard University Press.

Waldron, J. 1988. 'When Justice Replaces Affection: The Need for Rights', *Harvard Journal of Law & Public Policy*, 11: 625.

Waldron, J. 2007. 'Dignity and Rank', *European Journal of Sociology*, 48(2): 201–237.
Widerquist, K. 2013. *Independence, Propertylessness, and Basic Income: A Theory of Freedom as the Power to Say No*. New York: Palgrave Macmillan.
Wolff, J. 2006. 'Fairness, Respect, and the Egalitarian Ethos', *Philosophy and Public Affairs*, 27(2): 97–122.
Zelleke, A. 2011. 'Feminist Political Theory and the Argument for an Unconditional Basic Income', *Policy and Politics*, 39(1): 27–42.
Zelleke, A. 2018. 'Work, Leisure, and Care: A Gender Perspective on the Participation Income', *The Political Quarterly*, 89(2): 273–279.
Zwolinski, M. 2012. 'Classical Liberalism and the Basic Income', *Basic Income Studies*, 6(2): 1–14.

2

FREEDOM, RECOGNITION, AND THE PROPERTY-OWNING DEMOCRACY

Towards a predistributive model of justice

Gavin Kerr

1 Introduction

In his *Lectures on the History of Moral Philosophy* (2008), John Rawls identified two distinct traditions of liberal political thought – the liberalisms of freedom and of happiness – with which each major conception of justice could in his view be associated. Justice as fairness, his own conception, he associated firmly with the liberalism of freedom. And as he made clear in his later work, he regarded the property-owning democracy (POD) as one of the two forms of socio-economic organization under which the principles associated with this conception of justice would be fully realizable (the other being a form of liberal socialism). Rawls' rejection of the institutions of welfare state capitalism (WSC) and his endorsement of those of the POD – which initially seemed puzzling to some commentators – can perhaps best be explained as a corollary of his association of WSC with the liberalism of happiness, and more specifically with the tradition of classical utilitarianism. The arguments presented by Rawls in favour of the POD and against WSC are very much grounded in the criticisms of the utilitarian tradition which he developed in work beginning in the 1950s, and in the modernization of the tradition of social contract theory which he presented in *A Theory of Justice*.

Since the publication of the latter work in 1971, the focus of political and social theoretical enquiry has shifted away from what some regard as an excessively narrow concern with questions relating to distributive justice, and towards a broader set of issues relating to the 'politics of recognition', including multiculturalism, multi-nationalism, the politics of race and of gender, identity politics, and the accommodation of difference (Zurn 2005). The question I would like to address in this chapter is whether Rawls' critique of WSC and his endorsement of the POD can plausibly be interpreted and understood in terms of the politics of recognition. I argue that Rawls' view might plausibly be connected with the idea of recognition via the conception of social freedom developed by Axel Honneth. However, this is only the case, so I argue, if the idea of the POD is conceived very differently from the way in which it was conceived by James Meade, the thinker who did most to develop the idea, and if the 'predistributive' mechanisms of the POD are as effectively progressive as their proponents have suggested.

2 Property-owning democracy vs welfare state capitalism

The term 'property-owning democracy' was first used in the 1920s by Scottish Conservative politician Noel Skelton, who sought to provide a set of policy options which would offer working class voters an alternative to the collectivism offered by the socialists and communists. Skelton suggested a number of ways in which the benefits of private property might be extended to a much larger proportion of the population, including the encouragement of profit-sharing and co-partnership in industrial production, the expansion of agricultural small-holdings, and the introduction of cooperative principles into larger agricultural enterprises (Jackson 2012). However, like the earlier 'distributionists', Skelton did not envisage a significant role for state action in the achievement of this objective (Jackson 2012: 39).

In stark contrast to Skelton's pragmatic conception of the POD, the conception developed by revisionists in the British Labour Party in the 1950s, most notably economist James Meade, emphasized an active role for the state in generating a much more progressive and egalitarian diffusion of privately owned capital (Jackson 2012). Meade called for the aggressive taxation of transfers of wealth between generations, and for the public financing of state investment funds which would acquire significant stakes in private industry (1993: 54). Both of these measures would generate funds for a 'social dividend', which could then be distributed in the form of a universal basic income and a substantial investment in education and training in order to reduce inequality in the distribution of human capital.

Meade's proposals amounted, as Alan Thomas has recently suggested, to 'a macro-level restructuring of the balance between income from labour and income from the holding of capital' (Thomas 2017: 155). While this restructuring of the relation between capital and labour required an active role for the state, particularly in breaking up large estates and broadening the distribution of privately owned capital, an important effect of this kind of state action would be to modify the underlying *ex ante* distribution of capital (both human and non-human) and in this way to reduce the need for the redistribution of *ex post* labour income (Jackson 2005). In other words, the government of a POD would put more emphasis on the pre-emptive dispersal of income from capital – income 'not related to the pay which [individuals] receive from their work' – and less emphasis on providing redress through the welfare system for inequalities that arise from large accumulations of capital passed from one generation to the next (Meade 1993: 7).

Meade's ideas were enormously attractive to Rawls, who thought that the full realization of his conception of political justice would require the basic structure of society to 'disperse the ownership of wealth and capital' and thus 'prevent a small part of society from controlling the economy and indirectly political life itself' (1999: xiv–xv). The distinctive feature of the POD as envisaged by both Meade and Rawls was a focus on the 'predistributive' mechanism of the diffusion of privately owned productive resources (including both human and non-human capital) rather than the redistribution of the incomes generated against a background of highly inequitable 'predistributions' of productive resources. The key distinction between predistribution and redistribution plays an important part in the detailed analysis and defence of the POD model recently presented by Alan Thomas (2017). On Thomas's account, the diffusion of capital through the ongoing taxation of wealth is a *pre*distributive rather than a *re*distributive mechanism because it ensures that the bargaining positions from which agents enter the labour market are strong enough to eliminate (or at least significantly reduce) the need for the subsequent redistribution of income derived from the marketing of labour (Thomas 2017).

By providing all citizens with access to capital *as of right*, and in this way securing what Rawls referred to as 'background justice' in the distribution of productive assets, predistribution strengthens the bargaining position of labour in respect of capital, indirectly affecting the distribution of labour income by enhancing the bargaining power of those who would previously have had to rely solely on their income from labour (Thomas 2017). In this way, Thomas argues, the diffusion of capital through the taxation and distribution of large accumulations of wealth empowers less advantaged citizens by removing their dependence on *both* the welfare services and benefits funded by redistributive income taxation *and* the wages offered by employers. The citizens of a society that takes the form of a POD do not simply receive welfare 'benefits' at difficult times in their lives when the income which they can obtain from marketing their labour is insufficient to support a minimally decent standard of living. As Rawls put it, the intention in setting up the institutions of a POD

> is not simply to assist those who lose out through accident or misfortune (although that must be done), but rather to put all citizens in a position to manage their own affairs on a footing of a suitable degree of social and economic equality. The least advantaged are not, if all goes well, the unfortunate and unlucky – objects of our charity and compassion, much less our pity – but those to whom reciprocity is owed as a matter of political justice among those who are free and equal citizens like everyone else.
>
> (Rawls 2001: 139)

The citizens of such a society enjoy access to permanent streams of income which derive from the ownership of capital in various forms – including universal equity ownership, the incentivization of small savers via the tax system, and social ownership in the form of sovereign wealth funds – as well as publicly funded high quality education and training for all, and access to temporary 'demogrants' which enable them to invest in productive enterprise, or in other projects connected with their determinate conceptions of the good (Thomas 2017: 211–212; Williamson 2012). This is how the institutions of the POD are intended to generate 'a macro-level restructuring of the relation between labour and capital' (Thomas 2017: 211). In these socio-economic conditions, in which there would be no propertyless class wholly dependent on income from labour, and no 'underclass' of citizens wholly dependent on income from welfare benefits funded by taxing other people's labour income, both the least advantaged members of society and the 'squeezed middle' would find themselves in a position to enjoy the independence and autonomy conferred by the ownership of property, avoiding the domination which might otherwise be exercised by employers, bankers, bureaucrats, and so on (Thomas 2017). In this sense, Thomas suggests, a POD may be regarded as a non-capitalistic private property-based society.

But while Meade and Rawls both envisaged the institutions of the POD as being fundamentally predistributive (though neither actually used the term 'predistribution'), one major difference between the otherwise broadly similar conceptions of the POD was their contrasting views of the way in which the POD relates to other institutional models, in particular welfare state capitalism and liberal socialism. While Meade saw the institutions of the POD as but one element of a just socio-economic system which also incorporated welfare state and socialist institutions, for Rawls the POD was one of two socio-economic systems whose institutions are *sufficient* for the full realization of justice as fairness because they are *explicitly intended to satisfy* the principles of justice. WSC, by contrast, was the socio-economic system whose institutions are intended to satisfy a version of the principle of utility[1] (Freeman 2013: 17; Thomas 2017: 187). In other words, Rawls envisaged both WSC and the POD as abstract models associated with the traditions of classical utilitarianism and social contractarianism respectively (Freeman 2013).

Because the institutions of WSC are better suited to the realization of the principle of utility than to the realization of Rawls' much more demanding 'difference principle',[2] these institutions are limited to the 'sufficientarian' aim of the provision of 'safety-net' protections against accident and misfortune, in the form of a 'floor' below which no citizen should be allowed to fall (Rawls 1999: xv; Rawls 2001: 137–138; Thomas 2017: 190). Capitalist welfare-state societies would therefore be characterized by large and inheritable inequalities in the distribution of wealth, as well as significant inequalities in the initial distribution of property and skill endowments. The 'social minimum' specified in such a society would be secured through a redistribution of the income generated from inequitable initial distributions of endowments of human and non-human capital and would fall far short of the social minimum secured in a society that took the form of a POD (Rawls 1999: xv; Rawls 2001: 139). Moreover, although the underlying utilitarian rationale for the institutions of WSC might demand the partial realization of some aspects of Rawls' principles of justice, the socio-economic inequalities resulting from the institutionalization of the principle of utility rather than the difference principle would make these goals – particularly that of providing special protection to the political liberties[3] – much more difficult to achieve (Thomas 2017: 186–187).

On Rawls' account, then, WSC and POD are both committed, to varying degrees, to free-market institutions and a substantial degree of private ownership, but differ in (1) the central aims and values that are embodied and promoted in their institutions, (2) the extent of the social and economic inequalities that each form of organization permits, and (3) the means by which these inequalities are to be restricted. These differences arise from the absence in WSC of a principle of 'deep' reciprocity – the idea that 'social institutions are not to take advantage of contingencies of native endowment, or of initial social position, or of good or bad luck over the course of a life, except in ways that benefit everyone, including the least favored' (Rawls 2001: 124). Rawls regarded the absence in WSC of the principle of reciprocity as a function of its underlying utilitarian rationale and its place within the tradition of the liberalism of happiness rather than the liberalism of freedom (Freeman 2013).

In contrast, the importance of the principle of reciprocity to the idea of the POD derives from the underlying contractarian rationale for this form of socio-economic organization and reflects its place within the tradition of the liberalism of freedom. But what *form* of freedom is protected by the institutions of the POD? In the next section I argue that despite their contrasting methodological approaches, the concept of freedom which is implicit in Rawls' theory of justice is similar in many respects to the idea of freedom expressed explicitly in the work of Axel Honneth.

3 The idea of social freedom

A leading thinker in the tradition of critical theory, Honneth has been at the forefront of the movement, which has been growing since the 1990s, to place the concept of recognition at the centre of political and social theory. In his most recent work, Honneth (2014; 2017) focuses his attention on the idea of freedom as the central value of Western modernity, and the normative criterion in terms of which social institutions and practices can be evaluated as just or unjust. Deploying his Hegel-inspired methodological approach of 'normative reconstruction', Honneth identifies the institutions, practices, and social developments through which freedom has been realized in modern liberal societies, as well as the pathological 'misdevelopments' which have hindered its realization. One of Honneth's most important (and controversial) contentions is that, along with the family and democratic politics, the market economy is also one of the spheres within which freedom is embodied and realized (2014: 196). However, the form of freedom whose actualization Honneth discerns in the institutions and practices of modernity is not a 'negative' form of freedom that consists in the absence of external limits to the pursuit of one's unreflected interests, of the sort commonly associated with the thought of Thomas Hobbes and with the libertarian political philosophy of Robert Nozick. The idea that this form of freedom might constitute the core value of Western modernity is rejected by Honneth on the basis that it is too narrow to incorporate a comprehensive vision of the fundamental interests of citizens, failing to account for the importance of autonomy in both the political and the personal spheres (2014: 54–55). Nor, however, does Honneth identify a more positive or 'reflexive' conception of freedom that emphasizes the importance of personal and political autonomy as the value whose actualization is sufficient for the realization of social justice. While the freedom of reflexive autonomy does indeed represent a significant improvement on negative freedom, it fails to account for the fact that the social conditions that enable citizens to become autonomous agents are *constituent components of freedom*, rather than external to it (Honneth 2014: 79).

Although negative and reflexive freedom are both necessary *preconditions* for the realization of freedom, their institutionalization provides only *opportunities* for freedom by creating the legal and moral spaces that allow citizens to question and temporarily withdraw from the social world. The actual *realization* of freedom occurs through the performance of and participation in the social roles and practices that exist within the three spheres of personal relationships, democratic politics, and the market economy (Honneth 2014: 48–50). Moreover, freedom can be fully realized only when those performing and participating in social roles and practices recognize that the (reflexively determined) interests and well-being of each are complemented by and inseparable from the interests and well-being of all (Honneth 2014: 48–49). In other words, freedom can be fully realized only when the individual freedom of reflexive autonomy has expanded into an intersubjective form of freedom, through the mutual recognition by each subject of the fact that the realization of the desires and aims of each is conditional on, and partly constituted by, the realization of the desires and aims of the other (Honneth 2014: 44–45, 86).

The form of freedom with which Honneth is concerned – which he refers to as 'social freedom' – is thus firmly grounded in the idea of recognition: each individual's freedom is constituted through processes of mutual recognition which manifest themselves in the three spheres of ethical life, so that each is recognized as a condition of the other's freedom. The idea that freedom thus conceived is realized in the spheres of personal relationships and democratic politics is more plausible and less controversial than the idea that it is also realized in the sphere of the market economy. However, Honneth's claim here is that the promise of social freedom is *implicit* in the market economy: it is only when markets are embedded within deliberative discursive mechanisms and legal regulation that they become forms of cooperation which benefit all members of society (2014: 184–188). Since such moral and ethical foundations are *intrinsic* aspects of a legitimate market economy, the neoliberal policies implemented since the late 1970s are to be regarded as serious misdevelopments, or 'deviations from the norms underlying the market system', which have radically undermined the pursuit of social justice (Honneth 2014: 196, 252). Moreover, Honneth does not identify the market economy with capitalism and considers it obvious 'that a completed "socialization" of the market could only be possible under post-capitalist conditions' (2015: 224).

We can now return to the question posed at the end of the previous section. It is clear that the institutions of the POD do not protect a merely negative form of freedom of the kind associated with the thought of Hobbes and the ideology of economic neoliberalism. While many of the kinds of rights and liberties typically associated with the idea of negative liberty – the freedoms of expression, association, religious belief, and so on – are indeed secured by Rawls' first principle of justice, many of the *economic* rights and liberties which are also typically associated with this form of freedom, such as the right to private property in the means of production, are not. It is the exclusion of the latter from the first principle of justice that prevents this principle from restricting the operation of the second principle, which regulates the distribution of social and economic advantages.

The exclusion of formal rights of private ownership from the first principle of justice derived ultimately from the way in which Rawls specified the foundational conceptions of social cooperation and free and equal citizenship from which he constructed his theory of justice. Rawls conceived of social cooperation not simply as efficiently coordinated behaviour, but rather as cooperation between persons who hold a conception of their own good and who engage in cooperation in order to advance this conception in accordance with terms of cooperation and publicly recognized rules and procedures which each participant can reasonably be expected to accept as fair and appropriate (2001: 6). From this 'central organizing idea' of society as a fair system of cooperation Rawls then derived the idea of free and equal persons, arguing that persons capable of engaging in social cooperation over a complete life must be regarded as having two 'moral powers': the capacity for a sense of justice and the capacity for a conception of the good (2001: 18–19).

Since the principles of justice secure citizens' fundamental interests in the development and exercise of the capacity for a conception of the good – which is the capacity to form, pursue, and if necessary revise a conception of the good – the form of freedom that these principles protect might plausibly be identified as a version of Honneth's conception of individual freedom as reflexive autonomy. The citizens of a Rawlsian well-ordered society are free in the sense that they are capable of revising and changing their conceptions of the good so that these conceptions are not fixed but form and develop as they mature, and may change more or less radically over the course of life (Rawls 2001: 20–21). However, as we have seen, the moral capacities of the citizens of a well-ordered society also include the capacity for a sense of justice, which is the capacity to understand, to apply, and to act from (and not merely in accordance with) the principles of justice that specify the fair terms of social cooperation (Rawls 2001: 18–19). Guided and motivated by their sense of justice, the citizens of such a society are free in the sense that all are regarded as 'self-authenticating sources of valid claims', which is to say that all are regarded as being entitled to make claims on basic social and economic institutions so as to advance their conceptions of the good (provided that these conceptions fall within the range permitted by the public conception of justice) (Rawls 2001: 23).

There is a sense, then, in which the form of freedom secured by justice as fairness may plausibly be said to constitute a version of Honneth's conception of social freedom. The citizens of a Rawlsian well-ordered society are motivated by their sense of justice to act in accordance with fair terms of social cooperation and regard these terms *as* fair only when the distribution of 'primary social goods' (including the social and material resources covered by the second principle of justice) is such that all citizens are assured the all-purpose means with which to develop and exercise their two moral powers. If we accept a Rawlsian rather than a Meadean interpretation of the POD – that is, if we specify the institutions of the POD not merely as one element of a just social system but rather as sufficient for the full realization of justice as fairness, embodying the values expressed by the idea of society as a fair scheme of cooperation among citizens conceived as free and equal persons – then we may plausibly evaluate this form of socio-economic organization as just in the sense specified by Honneth. We can thus define the POD as a socio-economic system whose institutions are designed to satisfy all of the demands of political and social justice, including those that arise in all of the spheres – culture, gender, race, sexuality, and so on – highlighted by recognition and critical theorists during the past several decades.[4]

Consider, for example, the impact of the institutionalization of a POD on gender justice, particularly in the context of caregivers and their dependents. Ingrid Robeyns has argued, as part of a critique of the POD from the perspective of caregivers and their dependents, that 'gender justice and a proper acknowledgement of care' demand the implementation of a set of measures which would be financially very costly, consisting in 'a mix of labour market regulations, social security provisions, and public services (such as nurseries and care institutions for the elderly and the disabled) which are funded, and controlled or provided, by the government' (2012: 175). It follows from this, Robeyns argues, that the institutions of the POD as envisaged by Rawls will need to be supplemented with a range of social policies and institutions which are not intrinsic to the idea of the POD if significant progress towards gender justice and justice for the recipients of care is to be achieved.

It is important to emphasize, however, that the POD – on its Rawlsian interpretation as the socio-economic system whose institutions are designed to satisfy all of the demands of political and social justice – must incorporate, not only the capital-dispersing mechanisms emphasized by Rawls but all of the institutions which are necessary for the realization of political and social justice. A Rawlsian predistributionist property-owning democrat would therefore argue in response to Robeyns that the sorts of policies and institutions which she highlights are not in fact extrinsic to the idea of the POD. Such institutions are essential to the full realization of justice as fairness and are therefore essential features of a POD, even if their importance was not adequately recognized by Rawls himself.[5]

There is, however, a limit to the extent to which the predistributionist property-owning democrat can rely on this sort of argumentative strategy. One cannot simply argue that the POD is by definition whichever set of institutions one considers most likely to satisfy the demands of justice as fairness. While the POD is unlike WSC in its commitment to the progressive predistribution of privately owned capital and productive resources, it is similar to WSC in its incorporation of free-market institutions and the private ownership of a substantial proportion of capital and productive resources, as well as a range of redistributive or regulatory mechanisms (such as those highlighted by Robeyns). The institution of private property is central to the notion of the POD. What this means is that unlike a liberal socialist society, a POD *cannot* incorporate workplace democracy and the public control of capital investment as mandatory requirements. Thus, even if we define the POD along Rawlsian rather than Meadean lines, we must still choose between the POD (which does *not* incorporate mandatory workplace democracy and public control of capital investment) and liberal socialism (which *does* incorporate these features).

The question which must now be addressed, then, is whether there are reasons to suppose that these features of liberal socialism might be essential features of a society in which all of the demands of political justice are fully satisfied and in which social freedom is fully realized. If the answer to this question is affirmative, then the claim that a POD would be a fully just society must be rejected.

4 Property-owning democracy vs liberal socialism

Although Honneth has indicated in his most recent work that the 'socialisation of the market' that is essential to the realization of social freedom is possible only 'under post-capitalist conditions' (2015: 224), he has not provided a detailed account of the form that these conditions might take, suggesting that a renewed version of socialism 'would have to leave it up to experimentation whether the market, civil society or the democratic constitutional state represents the most appropriate steering principle when it comes to realizing social freedom in the economic sphere' (2017: 58–59). I shall therefore address the question posed at the end of the previous section by considering a range of arguments presented by Joshua Cohen (1989) in favour of a form of democratic socialism that incorporates the two features that in my view distinguish liberal socialism (LS) from POD.

I consider first the requirement that all productive enterprises are to be owned and managed by the workers in these enterprises. In such enterprises

> all and only the workers on the firm have voting rights concerning the operations of the firm – including what to produce, how much to produce, what the distribution of earnings among members should be, and whether to expand the scale of operations.
>
> (Cohen 1989: 40)

The form of socialism outlined by Cohen is in this respect similar to the model of 'Economic Democracy' proposed by David Schweikart (2012) in explicit contrast to the POD model. Under Economic Democracy, large firms that constitute the 'commanding heights' of the economy are publicly owned, but legally controlled by those who work for the firm, rather than by the state (Schweikart 2012: 210).

In Cohen's view, the institution of workplace democracy is an essential feature of any properly functioning deliberative democracy because it helps to foster the conditions within which all citizens can learn to exercise their deliberative capacities (1989: 46). This view, Cohen argues, is strengthened by what he refers to as the 'psychological support' and 'parallel case' arguments.[6] The former states that capitalist property relations are ill-suited to a democratic society because such relations 'vest final authority in the owners of capital', thereby limiting 'the extent of intra-firm democracy . . . fostering passivity and a narrower basis of political judgment' (1989: 29). Capitalist property relations therefore fail to contribute to the formation of an active character and to the development of a sense of the common good, and thus fail to generate a fully democratic state.[7] The latter holds that the private ownership of capital should be abolished, or at least heavily restricted, because it interferes with the democratic governance of enterprises, which itself is justified for the same kinds of reasons that justify the democratic governance of a liberal society. Thus, workers should have the right to determine the rules that regulate workplace cooperation through their own deliberation, given that they have the capacity to assess these rules, and that a productive enterprise, like the state, constitutes a form of cooperation for common benefit (Cohen 1989: 27).

If Cohen is right then the commitment to a Honnethian conception of social freedom which is implicit in the idea of social cooperation upon which justice as fairness is grounded would seem to support a liberal socialist institutional model that requires the legal enforcement of workplace democracy. The implication of the 'psychological support' and 'parallel case' arguments would seem to be that the effective protection of citizens' fundamental interests in the development and exercise of their capacities for rationality and reasonableness would be possible only in a socialist society in which productive enterprises are organized along democratic lines. And since the development and exercise of these moral capacities is an essential aspect of the social freedom of intersubjective reflexive autonomy, this form of freedom would appear to be realizable in a LS society, but not in a POD.

However, there are of course ways in which one might object to Cohen's argument. First, one might point out that in a modern liberal society mandatory workplace democracy is not an essential condition for a viable and inclusive democratic process, since it is likely that there will be contexts other than that of the workplace within which the deliberative capacities might be exercised and an active character and sense of the common good developed. One way of responding to this objection would be to argue that although there are indeed other contexts within which these capacities and character traits might be exercised and developed, the workplace is nevertheless by far the most important such context, since it is the place in which many people spend most of their time and energy, not necessarily because they choose to do so but often because they are compelled by economic circumstances. On this view, workplace democracy would enable citizens to develop and exercise their deliberative capacities much more fully and effectively than would be possible if they worked predominantly in non-democratic hierarchically structured workplaces (O'Neill 2008: 35–36).

But might there be costs attached to the legal enforcement of workplace democracy which outweigh such benefits? One possible cost concerns the constraints which would be imposed on the freedom of citizens who believe they have good reason to set up or become involved with an enterprise in which decisions concerning the amount of capital to be invested and the direction in which this investment is to be channelled are *not* necessarily made by all those who work for the enterprise in question. One might believe, for example, that a commitment to certain kinds of moral values (environmental sustainability, social responsibility, the values connected with a particular set of religious beliefs, and so on) might be achievable only within the context of an enterprise organized hierarchically rather than democratically. The opportunity to form such an enterprise might therefore plausibly be thought to protect fundamental interests connected with the pursuit of a conception of the good.[8] While much more would need to be said before drawing any firm conclusions, it is certainly not clear that a society in which workplace democracy is legally mandated would be a society within which social freedom is most fully realizable.

Second, one might argue in relation to the 'parallel case' argument that although productive enterprises do indeed comprise forms of cooperation for mutual advantage, a productive enterprise is nevertheless a very different kind of association from that of a civil association, and the deliberative ideal of justification does not carry over from one form of association to the other in the way that Cohen suggests (Taylor 2014: 453). An enterprise is a different kind of cooperative association from a civil association firstly because it is a *purposive* association that incorporates aims and objectives in addition to the common purpose of the citizens of a democratic state, and secondly because it is a form of association from which members can exit while remaining free to pursue their conceptions of the good.[9] For these reasons, it does not follow from the idea that the *state* ought to be governed democratically that *productive enterprises* ought also to be governed democratically.

Perhaps a more appropriate approach would be to focus on the effective protection of the substantive opportunity of workers to exit from existing productive enterprises in order to form new enterprises that are more compatible with their moral values and commitments, such as that of workplace democracy. This might mean not only that formal rights to freedom of occupation must be protected but also that substantive rights to access to the property and capital needed to exit from an existing productive enterprise in order to form an alternative one must be secured (Taylor 2014: 453–454; Thomas 2017: 219). Such a substantive right of exit would need to take account of numerous practical considerations, such as high exit costs faced by workers (including the costs associated with locating a new job and making the transition to it, and the costs faced by workers whose contribution to a specific firm depends upon an investment in developing firm-specific human capital in order to increase productivity in that specific firm (Hsieh 2008: 89)), as well as the costs attached to forming a new enterprise (including those resulting from significant barriers to entry). But if the arguments connecting workplace democracy with the capacity for a conception of the good are at least partially sound, then the realization of social freedom would require that a substantive right of exit be secured, however challenging this right would be to implement. And since a POD is by definition a society whose institutions facilitate the full realization of social freedom, the institutions necessary to secure a substantive right of exit must be an essential feature of a POD.

I shall now consider the second core feature of a liberal socialist society, the requirement that productive resources be publicly rather than privately controlled. According to what Cohen refers to as the 'structural constraints argument', the requirement for public control of the investment of productive resources stems from the fact that private control 'limits the democratic character of the state by subordinating the decisions and actions of the democratic state to the investment decisions of capitalists' (1989: 28). Private control of the investment of productive resources generates a situation in which political decisions 'are structurally constrained because the fate of parties and governments depends on the health of the economy, the health of the economy on investment decisions by capitalists, and investment decisions by capitalists on their expectations of profits' (Cohen 1989: 28). Public control of the investment of capital and productive resources therefore removes the significant and unjustifiable constraints on the collective choices of citizens imposed by private control of the investment of these resources.

The problem with this line of argument is that even if we accept the idea that public control of capital investment is a requirement of an ideal deliberative process and an essential condition for the protection of the political liberties, we might at the same time think that the possibility for citizens to exercise a certain amount of private control of capital investment is an essential condition for the protection of *some other* significant personal liberty, and therefore a necessary feature of a society in which social freedom is fully realizable. We can highlight the plausibility of this thought by taking a closer look at the specific scenario described by Cohen as an example of the structural constraints problem. In the scenario described by Cohen 'citizens in a capitalist democracy want simultaneously to increase the rate of growth and to redistribute income', when 'doing so requires both stimulating investment and increasing the progressivity of the tax system' (1989: 28). Private control of investment would be an obstacle to this collective decision because capitalists can be expected to feel disinclined to invest their capital when they expect that more of their gains will be taxed away. Since this obstacle may reasonably be expected to result in long-term material losses for the whole society, the citizens of this capitalist democracy will choose not to introduce the scheme after all, despite their desire to do so.

Public control of investment is therefore required by Cohen's deliberative democratic ideal because it facilitates the implementation of the collective democratic decision to increase the rate of growth and redistribute the income that this growth generates. In Cohen's socialist society, public decisions about 'the share of national income to be devoted to investment and the desired pattern of that investment' would be implemented 'by fixing the terms on which capital is rented to firms' (Cohen 1989: 40). The aim of this form of public control would be to remove the limit on deliberation imposed by private control 'by making the conditions of economic life part of the subject matter of political debate' (Cohen 1989: 41–42). The socialization of control over the investment of productive resources is also a distinguishing feature of the model of Economic Democracy defended by David Schweikart (2012). In the liberal socialist society as envisaged by Schweikart, publicly owned financial capital would be loaned out to businesses by public banks whose officers would 'rank loan applications according to the projected profitability of the investment request, its job creating potential, *and whatever additional considerations the community wishes to impose*' (Schweikart 2012: 212, emphasis added).

Thus, under the models of liberal socialism defended by both Cohen and Schweikart, if a democratic decision is made to increase the rate of economic growth and share the proceeds of this growth fairly, and if in order to achieve this objective access to productive resources is limited to enterprises that are intended and designed to generate significant financial profits (which may take the form of dividend payments to worker-owners), then only these kinds of enterprises will have access to productive resources. The implementation of such a policy would presumably serve the interests of citizens who affirm conceptions of the good that incorporate values and beliefs that are compatible with the objective of increasing the rate of growth (which would presumably be the majority of citizens if the policy in question is the result of a fair democratic process). The same could be said of any other condition that is attached to access to productive resources in order to realize some democratically endorsed cultural, religious, or other goal or objective.

But in a modern liberal society characterized by reasonable pluralism and the affirmation of a wide variety of reasonable conceptions of the good it is likely that a minority of citizens, perhaps even a substantial minority, will affirm conceptions of the good that incorporate values and commitments which are *not* compatible with the democratically endorsed objective of increasing the rate of economic growth, or realizing some other perfectionist cultural or religious values. In these cases, citizens who affirm the conception of the good in question will seek to pursue aims and objectives that may not be compatible with the goal of maximizing financial profits, or with the broader goal of increasing the rate of economic growth. Even when the pursuit of any particular perfectionist objective (whether economic, cultural, religious, or some other) is approved democratically, there will in any modern pluralistic liberal society always be a substantial minority of citizens for whom the pursuit of this objective is undesirable. In such societies the enforced pursuit of such objectives is contrary to the fundamental interest in the exercise of the capacity for a conception of the good and is therefore incompatible with the realization of social freedom.

This inevitable incongruence between the various conceptions of the good held by the citizens of modern liberal societies highlights a significant degree of tension between the two features of the form of LS under consideration (democratic worker control of enterprises and public control of investment) and casts doubt on the coherence of the model. Consider the case described by Schweikart of a democratically organized enterprise the workers in which decide not to give top priority to maximizing income, but rather to reorganize work 'so as to make it more satisfying, more skill enhancing, more in accord with "the Aristotelian Principle"',[10] and choose 'to sacrifice a bit of "efficiency", and hence income to do so' (2012: 18). This is the kind of scenario that in Schweikart's view is compatible with the incentive structure of a democratically organized enterprise, but incompatible with that of a capitalist enterprise or an enterprise that exists within the institutional context of a POD. It is also a scenario that is consistent with Cohen's characterization of worker-managed firms as outlined previously.

The problem for the liberal socialist is that in a society in which productive resources are publicly owned and production and investment publicly controlled, the conditions attached by the public authorities and investment agencies to access to capital and productive resources will be likely to prevent workers in democratically organized firms from exercising any real control over the operations of the enterprise, particularly those operations with which Cohen and Schweikart are primarily concerned. If high interest rates or a high level of taxation (or any other conditions) are attached to access to productive resources in order to realize some democratically endorsed objective, then the capacity of workers in democratically organized firms to determine, for example, what and how much is produced, or to determine any other aspects of the operation of the firm, might be greatly restricted. If capital and other productive resources are publicly owned and their utilization subject to public control, there is then an obvious and serious limitation placed on the autonomy of those engaged in the productive utilization of these resources. This problem would seem to be unavoidable in a society in which 'the conditions of economic life' are made 'part of the subject matter of political debate'.

The socialization of ownership and control of productive resources does much more than secure equal participation in the democratic process: such an institution also provides the majority of citizens with the power to compel unwilling minorities to pursue particular perfectionist aims and objectives. To be sure, (roughly) equal participation in the democratic process is one of the fundamental interests of the citizens of a liberal society, who exercise their capacities for reasonableness and a sense of justice by expressing, through participation in the democratic process, their considered judgements about the demands of justice and the institutions and policies needed to satisfy these demands. However, any tension which might exist between citizens' fundamental interests in exercising their capacities for rationality (by pursuing a conception of the good) and their capacities for reasonableness (by participating in the democratic process) is not appropriately resolved by socializing the ownership and control of productive resources.

If democratic politics are indeed constrained by the structural power of privately owned productive resources, this is not something that can justifiably be remedied by abolishing the private ownership and control of these resources. The fundamental interest in democratic political participation must always be balanced against the fundamental interest in pursuing a conception of the good, and the institution of private property is essential to the effective protection of this fundamental interest. These competing interests would be balanced by POD institutions designed, as Rawls put it, to 'disperse the ownership of wealth and capital, and thus to prevent a small part of society from controlling the economy, and indirectly, political life itself' (1999: xiv–xv; 2001: 137–140). Additional constitutional safeguards might then be put in place in order to insulate the political process from any concentrations of economic and social power that remain (Rawls 1996: 328).

This of course does not mean that there can be no public control exercised over the investment of capital in a just liberal society. But what it does mean is that there must be a significant role for the exercise of private control over the investment of capital in such a society, even if a substantial proportion of productive resources are publicly controlled. This triple strategy – of constitutional safeguards, plus measures designed to ensure the broad dispersal of privately owned property, plus a substantial degree of public control of capital investment – would surely represent a more effective balancing of the relevant competing fundamental interests than the socialization of control over the investment of all (or most) capital and productive resources. If a liberal socialist society entails the latter approach, then the ideal of social freedom would appear to be more fully realizable in a POD (which *can* incorporate a substantial degree of *public* control of capital) than in a liberal socialist society (which *cannot* incorporate a substantial degree of *private* control of capital).

5 Conclusion

Rawls theorized the POD as an abstract model of socio-economic organization whose institutions were explicitly intended to facilitate the realization of the principles of justice as fairness. These principles he regarded as the most appropriate terms of social cooperation between citizens conceived as free and equal – that is, as moral persons who have fundamental interests in developing and exercising their capacities for reasonableness and rationality. Viewed from this perspective, a POD may be regarded as the most complete institutional expression of the values of freedom and equality, at least if the criticisms of liberal socialism put forward in the previous section are broadly accepted. And the form of freedom which these institutions express is neither the 'negative' liberty associated with the tradition of classical liberalism, nor a simple form of individual autonomy or self-realization but rather a form of social freedom – the mutual recognition by each subject of the fact that the realization of the desires and aims of each is conditional on, and partly constituted by, the realization of the desires and aims of the other.

There is, however, an obvious sense in which Rawls' usages of the terms 'property-owning democracy' and 'welfare state capitalism' were unfortunate and unhelpful. Rawls' excessively negative evaluation of the redistributive institutions of welfare state capitalism – which clearly need not give rise to the extreme socio-economic inequalities suggested by Rawls – is as problematic as his excessively positive evaluation of the predistributive institutions of the POD, which are surely insufficient by themselves to secure the full realization of justice as fairness. It might perhaps make more sense to follow Meade in calling for a combination of welfare-state, property-owning democracy, and liberal socialist institutions than to follow Rawls in expanding the definition of the POD to incorporate all of the institutions of a just liberal society. On this view, it is only by combining both redistributive *and* predistributive institutions, together with the exercise of democratic public control over a substantial amount of productive resources, that a liberal society can plausibly be expected to become a truly free society.

Notes

1 More specifically, Rawls associated WSC with what he called the principle of 'restricted utility', which incorporates Rawls' first principle of justice, but replaces his 'difference principle' with a principle demanding that the distribution of income and wealth maximize average utility, constrained by a guaranteed minimum income (2001: 120–130).
2 The difference principle requires that inequalities in the distribution of social and economic advantages improve the positions of the least advantaged members of society.
3 As required by Rawls' first principle of justice (Rawls 2001: 149).
4 Another way in which the idea of the POD might be connected with that of recognition is via the idea of freedom as non-domination developed most notably by Philip Pettit (1997). The conception of the POD elaborated and defended by Thomas (2017) explicitly incorporates a commitment to the protection of this form of freedom. As a number of scholars have recently suggested, the idea of freedom as non-domination, properly developed and understood, complements and embodies the moral concept of recognition in the political sphere (Schuppert 2013; Snyder 2017). If, as Thomas has claimed, the institutions of the POD may be expected to generate the social conditions within which non-domination is 'structurally impossible', then these institutions may also be said to be grounded in the idea of recognition (2017: 144).
5 Thomas expresses a similar point in the following way: 'In a society that implements the correct principle of reciprocity markets will be restructured so as to make them fair: we can reasonably predict, to take an important example, that care work currently disproportionately done by women will not be categorized as an unpaid leisure activity in such a restructured market' (2017: 198–199).
6 On the 'psychological support' argument see Hsieh 2008; and O'Neill 2008. On the 'parallel case' argument see also Dahl 1985: Ch. 4; Walze 1983: 291–303; and Young 1979: 30–46).
7 A version of the psychological support argument is suggested by Rawls, when he poses the question whether in a well-ordered society worker-managed firms should be subsidized on the grounds that they may be 'more likely to encourage the democratic political virtues needed for a constitutional regime to endure' (2001: 178).
8 See Kerr (2017, Ch. 5) for a more detailed argument to this effect.
9 This is precisely why Rawls was reluctant to identify a well-ordered society as either a community or an association: in his view any sort of political society is a 'complete and closed social system', which has 'no final ends and aims in the

way that persons or associations do' (1996: 42, n44). Citizens cooperate in a well-ordered society in order 'to assure one another political justice', while people cooperate as members of an association in order 'to realize ends falling under their different comprehensive conceptions of the good' and 'to achieve whatever it is that moved them to join the association, which will vary from one association to another' (1996: 42, n44).

10 Rawls' "Aristotelian Principle" states that 'other things equal, human beings enjoy the exercise of their realized capacities (their innate and trained abilities) and their enjoyment increases the more the capacity is realized, or the greater its complexity' (Rawls 1999: 374).

References

Cohen J. 1989. "The Economic Basis of Deliberative Democracy". *Social Philosophy and Policy*, Vol. 6, No. 2, 25–50.

Dahl R. 1985. *A Preface to Economic Democracy*. Berkeley: University of California Press.

Freeman S. 2013. "Property-Owning Democracy and the Difference Principle". *Analyse & Kritik*, Vol. 35, No. 1, 9–36.

Honneth A. 2014. *Freedom's Right: The Social Foundations of Democratic Life*. Joseph Ganahl (tr.). New York: Columbia University Press.

Honneth A. 2015. "Rejoinder". *Critical Horizons*, 16(2): 204–226.

Honneth A. 2017. *The Idea of Socialism*. Cambridge: Polity Press.

Hsieh N. 2008. "Survey Article: Justice in Production". *The Journal of Political Philosophy*, Vol. 16, No. 1, 72–100.

Jackson B. 2005. "Revisionism Reconsidered: Property-Owning Democracy and Egalitarian Strategy in Post-War Britain". *Twentieth Century British History*, Vol. 16, No. 4, 416–440.

Jackson B. 2012. "Property-Owning Democracy: A Short History". In: Martin O'Neill and Thad Williamson (eds.) *Property-Owning Democracy: Rawls and Beyond*. Oxford: Wiley Blackwell.

Kerr G. 2017. *The Property-Owning Democracy: Freedom and Capitalism in the Twenty-First Century*. New York and Oxford: Routledge.

Meade J. 1993 (1964). *Liberty, Equality and Efficiency*. Basingstoke, UK: Macmillan.

O'Neill M. 2008. "Three Rawlsian Routes Towards Economic Democracy". *Revue de Philosophie Economique*, Vol. 8, 29–55.

Pettit P. 1997. *Republicanism: A Theory of Freedom and Government*. Oxford: Oxford University Press.

Rawls J. 1996. *Political Liberalism*. New York: Columbia University Press.

Rawls J. 1999. *A Theory of Justice (Revised Edition)*. Cambridge, MA: Harvard University Press.

Rawls J. 2001. *Justice as Fairness: A Restatement*. Cambridge, MA: Harvard University Press.

Rawls J. 2008. *Lectures on the History of Political Philosophy*. Cambridge, MA: Harvard University Press.

Robeyns I. 2012. "Care, Gender, and Property-Owning Democracy". In: Martin O'Neill and Thad Williamson (eds.), *Property-Owning Democracy: Rawls and Beyond*. Oxford: Wiley Blackwell, 163–179.

Schuppert F. 2013. "Discursive Control, Non-Domination and Hegelian Recognition Theory: Marrying Pettit's Account(s) of Freedom with a Pippinian/Brandomian Reading of Hegelian Agency". *Philosophy and Social Criticism*, Vol. 39, No. 9, 893–905.

Schweikart D. 2012. "Property-Owning Democracy or Economic Democracy?". In: Martin O'Neill and Thad Williamson (eds.), *Property-Owning Democracy: Rawls and Beyond*. Oxford: Wiley Blackwell, 201–222.

Snyder M. 2017. "Recognition and Redistribution: Finding Common Ground between Two Conceptions of Freedom". *Theory in Action*, Vol. 10, No. 3, 16–37.

Taylor R. 2014. "Illiberal Socialism". *Social Theory and Practice*, Vol. 40, No. 3, 433–460.

Thomas A. 2017. *Republic of Equals: Predistribution and Property-Owning Democracy*. New York: Oxford University Press.

Walzer M. 1983. *Spheres of Justice*. New York: Basic Books.

Williamson T. 2012. "Realizing Property-Owning Democracy: A 20-Year Strategy to Create an Egalitarian Distribution of Assets in the United States". In: Martin O'Neill and Thad Williamson (eds.), *Property-Owning Democracy: Rawls and Beyond*. Oxford: Wiley Blackwell, 225–248.

Young I. M. 1979. "Self-determination as a Principle of Justice". *The Philosophical Forum*, Vol. 11, 30–46.

Zurn C. 2005. "Recognition, Redistribution, and Democracy: Dilemmas of Honneth's Critical Social Theory". *European Journal of Philosophy*, Vol. 13, No. 1, 89–126.

3

REDISTRIBUTION, MISRECOGNITION, DOMINATION

A look at Brazilian society

Alessandro Pinzani

As a result of her debate with Axel Honneth (Fraser and Honneth 2003), Nancy Fraser has claimed that theories of social justice should take three dimensions into account: redistribution, recognition, and representation or political participation. The present chapter discusses this claim by referring to a field study on the *Bolsa Familia* (henceforth, PBF), a conditional cash transfer (CCT) programme implemented by the Brazilian federal government for the last 15years. The research (Leão Rego and Pinzani 2018) focused on the way the programme affected the subjectivity of the participants. In particular, it showed that a regular income might deeply affect the way in which participants in such programmes perceive themselves and are perceived by others. The present chapter shall question the impact of the PBF on the social and political awareness of its recipients and analyze the finding that the programme had very little impact on the way the Brazilian poor relate to political life.

The first part of the chapter focuses on the impact of the PBF on the personal autonomy of its beneficiaries. This needs an explanation, since neither Honneth nor Fraser discusses this concept. Both authors do, though, have as the ultimate goal of their respective theories the development of an individual capable of acting freely. However, this is not in the sense of the liberal concept of freedom as mere absence of coercion, that is, as the formal capacity to choose between options. They think rather of individual freedom in the more substantial sense of a social freedom that can be exerted only within a context of social relations with others. This is a main aspect of Honneth's thought, not only in his *Freedom's Right* (Honneth 2014), where social freedom is openly discussed, but already in *The Struggle for Recognition* (Honneth 1996), where different forms of misrecognition are all seen as violations of personality. The corresponding lacks of self-confidence, self-respect, and self-esteem, then, result in severe hindrances of the individual's ability to act autonomously. This is also a main aspect of Fraser's thought, in which the tripod of redistribution, recognition, and representation can be seen as concerning the material and political conditions under which individuals can lead autonomous lives in the previously stated strong sense of social freedom. From this point of view, both thinkers carry out a form of social criticism that can be considered to represent an ethical critique[1]; that is, a critique that aims at showing that the present societal structures and the power relations within society are imposing a form of 'bad' life on its members. It is worth noting here that although Fraser holds that her approach is strictly deontological, this does not preclude it from having an ethical aspect, in my view. Her critique concerns a life which provokes a suffering that, although experienced individually, is in fact social both in the sense that it affects mostly social groups (e.g., the poor, women, ethnic, and sexual minorities) and that its causes lie in the very way society is organized as a whole. In the second part of the essay, I shall discuss the obstacles that the women we interviewed have to face on their way to higher levels of personal autonomy and to more active political participation. I shall refer to the notions of epistemic oppression, hegemony, and systemic domination.

Before starting our discussion, I would like to advance some remarks on methodological questions. One could observe that mixing empirical facts and normative arguments is either bad sociology or bad philosophy. I am aware of the difficulties connected with this enterprise, but I share Adorno's view that it is impossible to draw a sharp distinction between these two disciplines, since it is not possible to distinguish completely between facts and theory (Adorno 2008: 23ff. and 2011: 18). Or, as Peter Winch says (2008: 3) 'any worthwhile study of society must be philosophical in character and any worthwhile philosophy must be concerned with the nature of human society'. By adopting this view, I am not claiming that normative arguments need to be founded on or justified by empirical facts, nor that empirical facts serve to prove such arguments to be 'true' or valid. Rather, I hold that they help us to elaborate normative arguments that are closer to reality since they take into account from the very beginning the way in which reality is socially shaped. This is true, for example, of the concept of personal autonomy and of the normative premises and consequences that go together with the meaning it commonly assumes in moral and political theories.

1 Money and personal autonomy

In the following, I shall discuss first whether the PBF as a CCT programme can be seen as a policy that, by redistributing money, results also in a form of recognition (1.1) and whether it also creates better conditions for political participation (1.2).

1.1 Redistribution and recognition: the case of the PBF

In view of the Fraser/Honneth debate, one could ask whether social programmes that directly transfer money to their recipients under certain conditions (CCT-programmes) are to be considered exclusively as aiming at redistribution, or whether they have at least an implicit effect with regard to recognition. In this section, we shall consider a specific case, namely that of the Brazilian *Bolsa Família* Programme. For our goals we do not need to enter into the details of the programme itself. It suffices to say that it grants a basic allowance (at present R$ 140 per month; for comparison's sake, the official minimum salary is presently [March 2019] R$ 998) to families whose per capita income falls below a poverty line of R$ 140 per month (or a severe poverty line of R$ 70) as defined by the federal government. There are also variable allowances for school-age children and teenagers up to a maximum of five persons. If, for example, the family has seven children, it will receive an allowance for only five (up to a maximum of approximately R$ 300), although *all* of them have to fulfil the conditions for receiving the grant, namely: 1) all school-age children must regularly attend school, and 2) all children in the family must be regularly vaccinated. It is evidently, to use Fraser's vocabulary (Fraser and Honneth 2003: 72ff.), an affirmative, not a transformative remedy: as such it acknowledges and satisfies claims of recognition and/or of redistribution, while at the same time leaving untouched the social structures that provoke these claims in the first place (transformative remedies, on the contrary, aim at modifying the deeper social causes of injustice). Its main goal was and is to help people to come out of severe poverty, not to eradicate poverty itself. (The governments led by the Workers' Party introduced more than 50 special programmes to fight poverty, but the right-wing governments under Michel Temer and Jair Bolsonaro have cancelled most of them.) Under president Rousseff the programme affected 55 million Brazilians, but both the Temer and the Bolsonaro administrations have excluded from it an increasing number of families.

In order to ascertain the effects that the PBF has on the subjectivity of its recipients, we performed a field study over five years (2006 to 2011), interviewing more than 150 women. We chose women because the allowance is distributed through a debit card, whose titular is in almost every case the female member of the family considered to be the head of the household: a single woman living alone or, in the case of families with children, a mother, a grandmother, an aunt, an older sister, etc. We opted for the methodology of the open interview, since question-forms or interviews with fixed questions would not allow us to reach deeper levels of the respondents' subjectivity. Furthermore, we noticed that we had to adapt the formulation of our questions to the different interlocutors, some of whose linguistic codes varied quite significantly.

Our starting point was Georg Simmel's *Philosophy of Money* (Simmel 2004).[2] The German thinker claims that money has a liberating dimension as it makes its owners more respectable and respected in a world dominated by monetary relations. Money allows people to make decisions about their lives and has a levelling effect, since the person who uses it to buy a good or a service can be rich or poor, noble or plebeian, male or female. Furthermore, it liberates individuals from the personal bonds of economic dependency on their family or other individuals (Simmel 2004: 299ff.). Simmel defines independence not as a total lack of dependence on anyone else in order to reach one's goals (this is impossible, since we always have to rely on others' cooperation), but as the ability to *buy* the assistance of others, instead of depending on their friendly inclinations, on their benevolence or even on their charity (as Adam Smith had already remarked in a different context: Smith 1976: 26). It was quite common that the women we interviewed described their situation after starting to receive the PBF by using the expression '*sentir-se mais à vontade*', or, 'feeling more at ease' in comparison to the period in which they had no regular income. A woman from Pasmadinho (MG) affirmed that 'there is more freedom in money, because with money you can buy what you want' – a sentence Simmel would doubtless have agreed with. Starting from his thesis, we aimed to test the hypothesis that the experience of receiving a regular basic income for the first time in their lives represented a radical change in the women's sense of personal autonomy. But what is meant here by autonomy?

Autonomy is a multi-layered concept. There are several levels of autonomy and on each level one can be autonomous to different degrees. (In this the concept radically differs from the liberal concept of freedom as absence of coercion.) On a first level, being autonomous means to be able to choose a specific strategy for action. This implies being able to formulate goals and having beliefs about these goals through which we are more likely to achieve them. Therefore, we are more likely to understand, at least to a certain extent, which consequences may result from our actions. This level comes close to what is traditionally called agency (Schlosser 2015). At a higher level, autonomy indicates the capacity to take responsibility for our actions. This is connected to further conditions, such as being conscious of oneself as an agent or taking a reflexive stance towards one's agency and being able to formulate reasons in a shared language and to justify our actions to ourselves and/or others. On a yet higher level people are considered to be autonomous when they are able to act according to a personal life plan and to consider themselves and others as capable of establishing mutual relations of moral and legal obligation. This third kind of autonomy fully deserves the name of personal autonomy and can be developed at several degrees. A person becomes more autonomous (1) to the extent that she can plan her life on a longer term because of an availability of the material conditions for this and to the extent that she begins to determine her life plan not by simply accepting the models offered by her environment, both the narrow one (family, friends, restricted community) and the wider one (her culture, her religious creed etc.), but by reflecting upon such models and possibly by distancing herself from them. (For instance, a woman coming from a very chauvinistic and patriarchal family who decides to live alone, even at the price of moving to another city or to a faraway place.) Furthermore, a person becomes more autonomous (2) the more she establishes her rights and duties (for herself and for others) based on a personal examination (and possible rejection) of the principles and values learnt from her family or church or community. (For instance, a brother of the aforementioned woman who comes to consider his sister's life model as morally legitimate and who starts to attribute to women – in general – rights that the other family members still denied based on their chauvinistic views.) This kind of autonomy should not be understood in a merely atomistic sense; it has rather an intersubjective dimension, particularly with regards to the second aspect of mutual recognition as moral and legal subjects. In this sense, it comes close to Honneth's concept of social freedom. The women we interviewed tended to see themselves as embedded in a wider net of moral relationships, particularly of duties connected to their roles as mothers, wives, daughters, etc. While the acceptance of these roles might be a consequence of an oppressive education, these persons consider the ability to perform their corresponding duties as a central facet of their individual freedom.[3] Their familiar roles do not simply represent the precondition to develop their individual freedom, they are essential to the factual realization of this freedom. From *their* point of view, being a good mother, for instance, is a way of exerting personal autonomy. They do not see the grant as their personal money but as a means to improving their families' quality of life.

Autonomy (even agency, i.e., the basic level of autonomy) has a strong social dimension: the actor's social position and biography shape the way she develops her capacity to act autonomously. External factors such as family, community, education (or lack thereof), public policies of all kinds, social hierarchies (which can be rigid or allow for some social mobility) affect people in a way that shapes their ability to grasp their world, their social reality, the meanings and consequences of their actions, etc. Internal factors (e.g., intelligence) are also so deeply affected by social external factors that in many cases they can become irrelevant: a malnourished child will have problems properly developing her intellectual faculties and this depends on her external circumstances, not on her genes. Therefore, no one is completely responsible for one's own level of autonomy, and this alone should lead us to mistrust any normative position that holds individuals *fully* responsible for their choices. Bad choices can be (and often are) the result of bad social circumstances. This is not tantamount to embracing social determinism; my claim is rather that we must abandon the belief that individuals have always had or may reach at some point in their life a fully-fledged form of autonomy. As we shall see, however, it is precisely this idea that is at the core of the epistemic bias that leads so many people (including the poor themselves) to develop a wrong picture of the situation of those living in poverty.

All the women we interviewed claimed that the PBF had a tremendous impact on their capacity to plan their lives in the short and medium term, as the following examples should show. During one interview, a woman from Maragogi (AL) brought up the idea that the PBF has afforded her more freedom: 'When I get it, I've got my own money. I go out and I buy things. I don't like to keep asking him [her husband], not a bit'. Another woman from Demerval Lobão (PI) asserted emphatically: 'My card is the only thing that has brought me credit in my life. Before this I didn't have anything. It's not much, though, because I'd like to have a better life'. She was not referring only to the financial credit the shop-owners of the town accorded to her now that she was known to receive a regular monthly income; she meant it also in the moral sense of being considered a reliable person, and she told us how differently people looked at her in shops and on the street. Further, one woman from Piri Piri (PI) claimed that through the PBF she felt acknowledged as a person for the first time in her life. Finally, one from Inhapi (AL) affirmed that before receiving the grant, she felt like a wild animal that starts the day searching for food for its children, but the PBF made her feel human at last.

The circumstance that they were receiving a monthly monetary income allowed them to introduce significant material changes in their families' lives. All the women claimed that the grant allowed them to minimally plan monthly expenses for paying bills and buying food, clothing, and stationery for their children.[4] One woman from Povoado da Cruz (AL) was particularly proud of being able to save enough money on the grant to finally buy mattresses for her family, so that they could for the first time sleep on a proper bed. Another from the semi-rural periphery of São Luís (MA) was using the grant to pay for the transport for her grandson to attend an art school in the capital, since he was particularly talented at drawing and wanted to pursue a career as an artist.

One could therefore claim that through the PBF these women got the chance to reach some form of minimal autonomy (ranging from an increase in their choices as consumers to the capacity to plan their own and their families' lives on a longer term than they were used to). This is not tantamount to claiming that the programmes always had this side effect. Unfortunately, there is no automatism that leads from receiving a minimal monetary income to developing personal autonomy. The programme however opened up some space for this process. It cracked open the rigid corset that imprisons poor people because of their lack of resources. It remains an affirmative remedy and does not affect the underlying structures that cause poverty.[5] However, the words of the woman who claimed that through the PBF she was first recognized as a person point to a central issue of our discussion, since they suggest that redistribution can directly translate into recognition. In her case, she meant that her difficulty in meeting her and her family's basic needs had been finally acknowledged by the federal government, which therefore had decided to help her. This leads us to our second question: what is the effect of the PBF on the political attitudes of its beneficiaries?

1.2 From redistribution to political participation?

As we have seen (1.1), social policies like the PBF have a dimension that goes beyond the mere (re)distribution of goods and services (in this case: money), since they have a profound impact on the recipients' subjectivity and autonomy. Receiving a regular monetary income might deeply affect the way in which beneficiaries conceive of themselves. In this sense, the PBF should not only be seen as a policy of redistribution but also as a possible instrument for tackling issues of misrecognition. But what about the third dimension mentioned by Fraser: representation? Does the PBF also have a political dimension? Does it impact the way in which its recipients see themselves as citizens? Does it foster their eagerness, willingness, or capacity to participate in the political process of decision-making? Does it allow for increased participation or does it lead to a greater representation of their interests both on the institutional level and in the public sphere?

Most women attributed the responsibility for the changes in their life to President Lula. They explained Lula's decision to implement the PBF through the fact that he himself had been poor and had suffered from hunger. We could ascertain among the women we interviewed a strong identification with him precisely because of this circumstance. They considered Lula to be one of them, who had managed to gain the power necessary to help the poor out of solidarity with their plight. In a sense, they were right, for the social policies created by the Lula administration aimed precisely at eradicating misery in the short term and poverty in the long. Lula himself referred to his own experience as a poor child whose mother (his father left the family very early) frequently struggled not only to make ends meet but even to guarantee regular meals. He often highlighted that he had experienced hunger as a child and that 'only those who have suffered hunger know what it means to wake up hungry in the night: the fight against hunger became an obsession in my life' (quoted in Damous 2018). Despite this personalization of the PBF (more generally, of the social policies introduced under the Lula administration), many women claimed that they felt that the Brazilian *government* was taking their suffering seriously for the first time.

Interestingly, though, almost no women referred to the grant as the object of a right. They did not use the language of rights, and when they did, they often referred to the grant as a right and as a favour from the government at the same time. A woman from Maragogi (AL) observed: 'I think it's a right. It's a right, of course, because we depend on a right from the government. It's not a favour because we pay taxes'. Two other women, also from Maragogi, had a different opinion: 'It's a big favour, because it's a help to those who don't have anything, right?' said one, while the other stated: 'I've got two opinions. Sometimes, I think that it's a favour and sometimes I think it's their duty'. A woman from Demerval Lobão (PI) thought that the PBF was 'a kindness from him [Lula] to the people, because many people needed it', and that 'the people deserve it because they went there and voted and put him [Lula] into office'. The grammar of right and the grammar of personal ties and favours intertwine in such testimonies.

When asked about their attitude towards voting (which in Brazil is mandatory), they often confessed that they do not like it, mostly because they perceived it as useless, since no real change happens in their life. For this reason, they claimed only to cast their ballot with real conviction for the presidential election; their experiences after Lula's victory in 2002 made clear how this vote could change things for them. Their coldness and distance towards elections and politics in general are the result of decades (if not centuries) of neglect by all kinds of governments: local, regional, and federal. They often claimed that politicians seem to remember their existence only during electoral campaigns, but forget them altogether once they get into power. Therefore, they singled out Lula for not having forgotten his promise to help the poor once elected. In this sense they were right: the PBF is a governmental programme, not a state policy, and the right-wing governments under Temer and Bolsonaro have started to reduce it steadily. Their enthusiasm for Lula (for whom – they claimed – they would vote over and over again) is an expression of their positive experience with his personal care for the poor rather than a political stance with regard to the programme of the Workers' Party. They still remain divided and unarticulated as a social group. Differently from other groups struggling for recognition (e.g., Afro-Brazilians, LGBT+ movements) or for redistribution (e.g., unions) they do not coalesce in order to advance specific demands. They remain objects of policies but are not yet subjects of politics (Pinzani 2012).

More generally, the women we interviewed never established a connection between their situation of deprivation and the unequal distribution of resources that characterizes Brazilian society. They do not see themselves as victims of social injustice, and, when asked about the existence of the rich and the poor, they tend to give answers that rationalize or naturalize inequality. Among the answers they gave were that the rich work harder than the poor (although the women actually spend the whole day working hard in the fields or in menial jobs); that there have always been rich and poor (like there have always been blondes and brunettes); or even that God is showing people His benevolence by showering them with riches (this is connected to the so-called theology of prosperity, which is preached in most of the evangelical churches they frequent). Therefore, they generally do not see any reason to engage in politics to change society or to defend their interests.

Our findings appear to confirm Fraser's claim that redistributive policies can be connected to some form of social recognition, although in the case of the PBF these policies are not connected to social struggles or to normative demands explicitly advanced by their beneficiaries. The PBF opens a path for developing increasingly wider forms of personal autonomy; however, one has to acknowledge that there is no automatism that leads from attaining (through CCT programmes) the material conditions for autonomy to its concrete development. Powerful hindrances impede this process taking place in every case and proceeding linearly and continuously. Furthermore, this seems not to apply to political autonomy, that is, to the capacity to act as active, reflexive political subjects. In the second part of this essay, I shall present a possible explanation for this phenomenon, while at the same time discuss the obstacles that hinder or make difficult an ampler development of personal autonomy in the wider sense.

2 Hermeneutic injustice, hegemony, and systemic domination

We have seen that social policies (in our case the PBF) can have positive effects in starting processes through which individuals may increasingly develop higher levels of autonomy. At the same time, however, we have had to acknowledge that, more often than not, this autonomy scarcely rises above the level of a basic capacity to act in relative independence from others or from the material restraints of the individual's immediate environment. Participants can start planning their life with more ease in the short and middle term, but, since the allowance is still minimal, apart from some exceptions (e.g., the grandmother paying for the bus for her grandson to go to art school) this new ability does not go beyond their capacity to organize their spending in the more or less immediate future. This represents an important change in the way they face life's challenges and see themselves as more autonomous subjects, but their options for material improvement remain limited to what the allowance can buy for them. While this might of course curb or sober our expectations with regard to the positive effects of social programmes on their recipients, it allows for a deeper analysis of poverty in general. As we observed previously, the mere redistribution of goods or services is not enough to eradicate poverty because it has dimensions that go beyond the simple lack of material resources by an individual or a family. It is rather the way society is structured that causes their situation (including their lack of resources). This might sound trivial, but many theories of social justice insist on focusing on the situation of individuals or households and offer therefore individual solutions (e.g., empowerment, education, etc.) that can be considered to be affirmative rather than transformative remedies. Poverty is not an individual problem, but has social roots that remain unchanged not only because of its structural causes or of specific economic interests but also because of a negative attitude towards the poor from the rest of society – like in the case of Brazil, which cannot be defined as a poor country that lacks the resources to eradicate poverty. This latter aspect is often overlooked by theories that see poverty just as an objective condition of material need. This view neglects two relevant aspects: first, the fact that poverty deeply affects the self-perception of the poor; that is, it has a non-material dimension that goes beyond the ones usually described in the literature (Townsend 1987); second, the fact that the poor may suffer forms of prejudice and discrimination from the majority of society (cf. Cortina 2017). In the following I shall discuss these two aspects. As we shall see, both are interconnected, insofar as the prejudice suffered by the poor influences their perception of themselves and of their situation, effectively hindering their personal and political autonomy. Nevertheless, I shall treat these aspects separately for presentation's sake. I shall focus on Brazil because in my view social criticism can only be parochial and have as its object either a specific society (like the Brazilian one) or at most a specific aspect shared by different societies. I shall first try to understand how the poor see themselves (2.1) and why they do not tend to organize in order to advance demands of recognition, representation, or even redistribution (2.2).

2.1 *The poor's self-perception*

The social investigation of poverty faces a major problem: it is forced to take as its source of knowledge the depositions of individuals whose epistemic reliability it tends to question or even to deny. The poor do not give evidence on their situation from the objective standpoint of an impartial observer. They refer to their subjective experience, that is, to the way they experience their poverty. In doing so, however, more often than not they adopt a language that is not their own and that reflects rather those assumed by the socially dominant view on poverty, as in the case of the women we interviewed. We were puzzled by the discrepancy between their accounts of their plights, in which they gave voice to their suffering, on the one side, and on the other the way they tended to explain their situation, usually blaming themselves. In order to understand this phenomenon, which has been described also by Christopher Zurn by means of the concept of second-order disorders (Zurn 2011), I would like to recur first to Miranda Fricker's concept of epistemic oppression (Fricker 1999) and, second, I shall refer briefly to Gramsci's concept of hegemony.

In a first attempt at roughly defining epistemic oppression, Fricker references the fact that 'the powerful have some sort of unfair advantage' over the powerless 'in "structuring" our understandings of the social world' (Fricker 1999: 191). In doing so she mobilizes vague, generic categories (the powerful, the powerless) that need some clearer definition.[6] Individuals have a plural, intersectional identity and can belong to different social groups. They might face their social world in different ways according to which aspect of their identity is more affected by a specific experience (their ethnicity, their gender, their sexual orientation, their social status, etc.). On the other hand, notwithstanding the intersectional character of the personal identity developed by the members of society, one can identify specific social experiences that are shared by those who belong to a specific group, for example, the racial discrimination suffered by black people independently from their gender or social position. This is not tantamount to claiming that they share the *same* social experience. As Fricker points out with reference to the feminine standpoint, 'it need only depend on the idea that some of women's social experiences have *similarities* in virtue of their subjects being women' (1999: 201). This allows us to define the standpoint of a specific social group without falling into the opposite mistakes of either assuming an essentialist concept of it (as if there might exist something like a feminine nature opposed to the masculine) or denying the possibility of identifying a common experience shared by the members of the group (as if every social experience were essentially individual in its character and could not possibly lead to any kind of generalization). Against this view, Fricker claims that it is possible to circumscribe social experiences (e.g., experiences of discrimination or silencing) that are similarly lived by members of a social group. This allows us to identify the specific standpoint of that group despite the individual differences among its members. It should be possible therefore to talk of the social experience of the poor notwithstanding the fact that poor individuals differ from each other in many respects. From this point of view, it is possible then to speak of the standpoint of the poor as opposed to the standpoint of economically and socially privileged groups of a specific society, so that the categories of 'powerful' and 'powerless' become less vague.[7]

It is now possible to claim that the standpoint of the poor is marginalized in the sense that the poor's social experiences are not deemed relevant in order to understand how a specific society is structured. It is rather the standpoint of more privileged groups that is considered to represent an objective or even a 'true' interpretation of the social world. These groups need not be represented by the highest echelon of the social ladder, by the wealthiest strata of society. More often than not all groups that gain advantages from present social arrangements (from the economic elite to the lower-middle class) tend to share a number of beliefs, values, and social practices that can be seen as forming a specific standpoint through which they see and experience their social world. In taking this standpoint, they marginalize and disqualify alternative standpoints; that is, they negate the relevance of the social experience of those who suffer under present social arrangements. This hermeneutic discrimination can affect the poor for no other reason than their being poor and can be therefore called hermeneutic injustice. Hermeneutic injustice becomes epistemic injustice when, by silencing the social experiences of specific social groups, it hinders our ability to gain knowledge of society. This is, for instance, the case when poverty is reduced to a lack of material resources and explained by the poor's alleged lack of initiative, education, or intelligence. This prejudiced view prevents us from having a more realistic view of society. When a group 'suffers epistemic injustice in a systematic way, then it will be appropriate to talk of epistemic oppression', as Fricker remarks (1999: 208), and it is undeniable that the poor suffer such oppression. Actually, one could even talk of epistemic domination, since they often lack the capacity to articulate an alternative epistemic standpoint. To epistemic domination corresponds of course an 'epistemic advantage' (Fricker 1999: 208) for the 'powerful'. Their standpoint is considered to offer the only legitimate view of society, so that their narrative becomes the only acceptable one and ends up being accepted also by the 'powerless', even though it might go against their personal experience. This happens mostly when the privileged standpoint is incessantly repeated in the political arena by dominant parties and by governing politicians as well as in the public sphere by mass media that uncritically accepts it. This happens, for instance, in Brazil with *Rede Globo* and the other commercial broadcasting and publishing corporations that dominate the market in the absence of an effective public broadcast corporation.[8] This is not tantamount to claiming that the Brazilian media wilfully spread an ideological view that blames the poor, although this may well be the case up to a certain point. I would rather assume that we face here an epistemic bias.

Social groups may have an epistemic bias that leads them not to see social injustice in their society. This is not a form of cynicism or an ideological attempt to conceal the real power relation, but a certain inability to grasp how their society is actually structured and how its institutions reproduce social injustice. When middle class Brazilians blame the poor for their own poverty and see the poor's laziness, lack of intelligence, or sheer irresponsibility as its main causes, they are not necessarily being cynical. They are simply judging the poor's situation by using the same parameters they use to judge their own lives, that is, individual responsibility and individual merit. Of course, they are wrong in applying these parameters to themselves in the first place, for, as we have seen, individual autonomy is actually the result of external social factors on which individuals have hardly any influence, particularly when it comes to the conditions under which they are born (which social class, which social group, which family, etc.) and have been educated. Further, they are also wrong because they think it is legitimate to judge someone's social position or economic condition simply by looking at their individual choices and actions without taking into account the social context in which those choices and courses of action were pursued. They do not seem to consider the role of family, social groups, education, etc. in which those individuals *happen* to live (not by choice, *nota bene*).

On the other side, this epistemic bias regarding how to evaluate one's life, has for the middleclass the positive effect of justifying in their eyes their own privileged position, which they do not attribute to the social conditions under which they have come to the world, but exclusively to their individual merit. It is then easy to see how this epistemic bias crystallizes in a view of social reality that justifies the status quo they profit from. It is at this point that this specific standpoint (the privileged standpoint) is presented to society as a whole as the only valid one and becomes hegemonic.

As it is well known, hegemony is an ambiguous concept. Gramsci uses it in different contexts and with reference to different phenomena (Gramsci 1992 and 1996).[9] For our purpose, it suffices to say that, generally speaking, the concept refers to the way a social group conquers and exerts power – be it social, political, economic, or intellectual. One of its main mechanisms is to formulate a specific view of society and of social relations that is presented as the only objective and true one, although it represents a partial point of view in which, basically, the interests of the hegemonic class or classes are presented as the general interests of society as a whole (Gramsci 1996: 179ff.). In order to impose this standpoint on all other classes, different instruments are mobilized; academic discourse, school curricula, and mass media, however, play an eminent role in its spreading (Gramsci 1992: 152ff. and 1996: 199ff.).[10] In the case of Brazil, the dominant narrative has remained basically unaltered through all the regime changes: from colony to independent state, from monarchy to republic. It claims that society is naturally hierarchically structured and that those on the bottom (i.e., slaves and, after abolition, which happened very late, in 1888, former slaves) occupy their position because of their ethnical, intellectual, and moral inferiority. The narrative has been repeated for centuries in schools and academia, newspaper columns and church pulpits, by politicians, preachers, and pundits.[11] This goes some way to explaining how racism became so ingrained in the dominant view of social reality that most members of the dominant classes (the elite and the so-called middle class)[12] claim that Brazilian society is not racist.[13] The naturalization of racial, economic and social inequality (not to mention the strong gender inequality that characterizes South American societies) is the result of the hegemonic view according to which social positions are the result of 'how things are'. In recent years, this narrative has been partly substituted by a more neoliberal one, according to which social positions are the result of individual merit. The latter view is only tepidly defended by the elite, since their privileges are based mainly on inheritance and since most of its members are rentiers rather than entrepreneurs. However, it is strongly present in the public discourse, from media to academia, and it has also been internalized by the poor, as we have seen.

There are of course differences in the way the hegemonic standpoint is de facto accepted and internalized by the subordinate groups. There might be forms of resistance that manifest themselves in different ways. These can take the form of what James C. Scott (1990) has called 'hidden transcripts'; that is, they can result in a discourse that disallows the official one, but too often remains circumscribed to small circles: to local communities, to friends and family, sometimes to the individual herself. Or they can surface through attempts to expressly voice alternative standpoints via independent media, social networks, or forms of cultural expressions that have escaped the mainstream mechanism of producing culture, information, and entertainment (in Brazil this might be the case with favela funk music). As important as they obviously are, these forms of resistance do not however subvert the epistemic privilege of the standpoint of the powerful and its dominance over the standpoint of the powerless. The latter therefore tend to remain under the spell of the interpretation of their own situation offered by those who created it in the first place.

The result of the hegemonic view within Brazilian society is that poor people tend to believe that they have no possibility of modifying their situation because they lack the resources that are necessary to attain this goal. They consider themselves to be too uneducated, too dumb, too weak, too incapacitated to find a way out of the mess of their lives (cf. Lavinas 2014 and Marins 2017). They face, in Honneth's (1996) use of the terms, both a lack of self-esteem and lack of self-respect. They do not believe that they are able to meet their own needs (not to mention the needs of their family), to develop their own talents (if they believe they have any at all), to pursue some long-term life plan (presuming that they manage to see their own lives in a long-term prospective). In this sense, they have no self-esteem because they internalize a dominant discourse that individualizes the responsibility of poverty and attributes its causes to some personal fault of the poor, not to structural problems. The lack of self-esteem makes them furthermore endure different forms of humiliation imposed on them by officials (social workers, teachers, school directors, police officers, etc.) or by persons who exert some power on them (shop owners, bank clerks, doctors, etc.). This leads to a lack of self-respect, with its cause in the refusal of their social and legal equality, which is not acknowledged by those agents who occupy a socially higher position and claim for themselves not only a privileged epistemic standpoint but also a superior moral status (cf. Cortina 2017).

Loss of self-esteem and loss of self-respect are therefore caused by forms of misrecognition, the causes of which are social, even when they depend apparently on the individual behaviour of some authorities or power holders. It is mostly individuals who deny them their rights, but this happens because society condones such a denial, so that its perpetrators have nothing to fear. Quite on the contrary, within society their attitude is justified for being grounded on the alleged moral inferiority of the poor: they are lazy, stupid, sneaky, and deserve therefore to be treated badly. Conversely, these individuals think that their superior position of power entitles them to act as they do towards the poor. Their personal attitude rests on a social culture that justifies both discrimination against the poor and the very social structure that provokes and maintains poverty. When they despise, discriminate against, and humiliate the poor they act in a sense as representatives of society. The resulting loss of self-esteem and self-respect on the poor's part is therefore provoked by the dominance of the epistemic standpoint of the powerful, that is, by the way in which it explains poverty and identifies its causes in the alleged personal faults of the poor.

2.2 From objects of policies to subjects of politics?

The discrepancy between the subjective experience of suffering and the hegemonic, 'objective' explanation of their situation deeply affects the subjectivity of the women we interviewed. The adoption of the hegemonic standpoint when it comes to evaluating their situation does not represent merely a hindrance to a correct understanding of the causes of their suffering; it forms further a powerful obstacle for the development of their personal autonomy, since it implies the previously mentioned lack of self-respect and self-esteem. Not only are they victims of misrecognition, but it is as if they were misrecognizing themselves. The cause of this phenomenon is epistemic domination, whose role should once more be highlighted and put into the wider context of the social causes of poverty.

The women we interviewed suffer under multiple forms of domination. It is not epistemic domination itself that causes poverty, although it might represent a powerful hindrance in the fight against poverty. The roots of the latter go deeply into the structure of a specific society and very often have a historical character. Among the immediate structural causes for poverty are, for example, the unequal distribution of material resources and the lack of public policies aiming to reduce this inequality. Their effects, however, are magnified by their temporal persistence. In Brazil, this goes back to colonial times and is mostly connected with slavery and the way it was abolished. (After their emancipation, the slaves were abandoned by the government and practically treated as non-citizens.) Three hundred years of slavery had and still have a momentous impact on the subjectivity both of the enslaved and of their masters, as well as on the social views of their descendants. What some call 'the Brazilian social apartheid' (Michel-Muniz 2018)[14] maintains itself not only through the use of police brutality or through the violent imposition of discriminating rules. The fact that institutions and social practices promoting discrimination or even class segregation have prospered for centuries and are still extremely powerful cannot be simply explained with reference to material differences in power. As Gramsci (1992 and 1996) and later Arendt (1970) convincingly argued, power cannot be based only on the brute use of force. If it wants to remain stable, it needs to convince those who are submitted to it of its necessity. It is here that hegemonic and epistemic domination comes into play, helping to rationalize, reinforce, and maintain structural domination. Their interplay (which is always to be considered in its historical dimension) provokes what I would like to call systemic domination precisely in order to highlight its temporal and dynamic character as opposed to the rather static idea of a 'structural' domination.

Systemic domination asks for transformative remedies. In the case of poverty, this would mean firstly a thorough redistribution of material resources, not only in monetary terms but also and primarily in terms of public investments in education (including civic and vocational education), health care, infrastructures, and, possibly, through the creation of public companies that offer job opportunities when private initiative fails to do so. Such public activity, however, is simply unthinkable if the dominant standpoint on poverty blames the poor for their condition, as happens in Brazil. In cases like the Brazilian one, then, it is necessary first to criticize and deconstruct the dominant discourse on poverty and its causes. This is tantamount to demanding that redistributive policies go together with policies aiming at eliminating social misrecognition and its negative effects on the poor. Introducing legal norms against discrimination (as advocated by Cortina 2017) can be a first step; even more effective could be the introduction in school curricula of the study of poverty and its causes as a mandatory subject. The question of political representation remains untouched by such policies, though. As we have seen, the women we interviewed limit their political participation to casting a ballot every four years. They do not organize, and when they try to do so, e.g., on the local level, their voices remain unheard. They are deeply disaffected with politics and mistrust politicians with the exception of Lula and similar figures they can identify with. It is not easy to imagine what kind of state policies could change this state of things. One could wager on the positive effects of redistributive policies and of the critique of the dominant standpoint on poverty, in the hope that, by removing the most powerful material and immaterial hindrances to the development of personal autonomy, the poor would manage to develop also a desire for greater political participation; but also in this case, there would be no automatism leading to the expected results. Such scenarios however cannot be discussed here.

Acknowledgements

I would like to thank Kim Butson for revising the text. This work was supported by the CNPq under Grant 306784/2014–9 and was finished during a stay at the Czech Academy of Sciences.

Notes

1 On the threefold kinds of social criticism (functional, moral, and ethical, respectively) see Jaeggi (2016). On the ethical character of Honneth's *Sozialphilosophie* see Jaeggi and Celikates (2017).

2 In the following paragraphs I recall material exposed in Leão Rego and Pinzani (2016 and 2018).

3 The objection that the PBF ties the women to the roles imposed on them by society does not take into account the fact that the women see their individual lives as embedded in a complex network of social relations (parenthood, wider family ties, neighbourhood, religious communities, etc.) and that they perceive their actions as always taking place within the context of this network. They are not able to imagine a different context of life for themselves (this 'narrow-mindedness' is not peculiar to them, however, and is widely shared among social

classes). One might wish that they managed one day to attain this capacity, but one would be wrong to consider them as merely passive victims of social relations they do not accept. When this is the case, they are sometimes able to react and to reject the demands of their social environment on their lives: they might decide to use a contraceptive pill or even to ask a doctor to perform an ovariectomy on them; they might leave their parents' house; they might renounce their church; they can warn their daughter against the traditional view according to which they are supposed to marry and have children at an early age (all these strategies were actually adopted by some of the women we talked to). Of course, these revolts find insuperable limits in the women's capacity to maintain themselves (and their children) after leaving their husbands or parents but also in the previously mentioned incapacity of thinking of an alternative life. I shall come back to this point in the second part of this essay.

4 One can recognize in these kinds of expenses what Viviana Zelizer (1989: 353) has called the poor's morality of household spending.

5 One major obstacle to developing a higher level of autonomy is doubtless represented by the insufficiency of the material resources distributed through the PBF. Most women complained that the grant was 'just a help', its value being too low to allow for significant changes in their *material* conditions. On the other hand, they also acknowledged that it gave them certain security with regard to the short-term future. (They knew they could rely on that money every month.) In other words, at the same time they lamented the insufficient character of the grant, they highlighted its relevance for creating some space for them to act with certain autonomy, without being fully subject to material necessity and without depending on the benevolence of others. In this sense, the PBF contributes to giving to its participants the material basis on which they can develop some sense of self-esteem (in Honneth's terms).

6 This vagueness echoes the way in which Howard Becker in his famous essay "Whose Side are We On?" (1967) distinguishes between subordinate and superordinate parties.

7 The same of course can be said of Becker's categories of subordinate and superordinate parties.

8 On the dominant view on poverty and the poor in Brazil see Lavinas (2014) and Marins (2017).

9 According to him 'hegemony' can be 'cultural', 'intellectual', 'moral', 'social', 'political', or 'economic'; the corresponding adjective 'hegemonic' is applied to such heterogeneous things such as 'nation', 'position', 'point of view', 'apparat', 'action', 'system', etc. (Cospito 2016: 59).

10 One can observe this with the so-called neoliberal revolution that allegedly took place in the 1980s. As a matter of fact, the ground for this momentous shift in the social view that was dominant in Western capitalist countries was prepared through decades of patient, incessant intellectual efforts by academics, journalists, politicians, and pundits, whose history have been already told by many authors (e.g., Bourdieu and Boltanski 1976; Foucault 2008; Mirowski and Plehwe 2009; Stedman Jones 2012). This shift happened often through apparently neutral governmental decisions, like when the French government stopped building social housing and started offering citizens low interest credit that it had dealt with private banks (Bourdieu 2005). In doing so, what was seen as a social right of citizens (the right to a decent housing) became a matter of individual responsibility (citizens were allowed using the borrowed money to build a house or a mansion, if they wanted, although this might involve their impossibility to payback their debt).

11 With regard to preachers, I would like to refer to the so-called theology of prosperity, which is widespread within Pentecostal Evangelical churches and claims that God wants us to become rich and despises those who do not make the corresponding effort.

12 What Brazilians call middle class represent actually a small parcel of society and would be considered middle-high class elsewhere. It is composed by free professionals and high rank public servants (judges, university professors, bureaucrats, etc.) and comprehend the fiscal classes A and B, although class A (formed by those, whose income is more than ten times the legal minimum wage) includes also the billionaires and the economic elite (this gives to people earning slightly more than 10.000 reais the illusion that they belong to the elite, whose monthly income measures in the hundreds of thousands or millions).

13 When the Lula government introduced affirmative action policies for public universities, it was common to hear from pundits and common people that it was such policies that created racism. Probably many made this claim in good faith. This peculiar blindness towards racial issues found an ideological justification in Giberto Freyre's concept of 'racial democracy' (Freyre 1964, first published in Brazil in 1933).

14 Class segregation is omnipresent in everyday life: in shopping habits (the wealthy go to well-protected, socially segregated shopping malls, while the poor go to *comércio* neighbourhoods in dilapidated inner cities); even in buildings, with their insupportable distinction between social and service lifts, highlighting the social apartheid that divides not only the rich from the poor, but members of higher classes from simple workers (the cleaning lady, the delivery boy, or the electrician are not worthy of sharing the same lift with the residents). Even before the law, inequality reigns. Not only informally, due to the fact that rich people can hire lawyers, while poor people have to rely on overwhelmed public defenders, but also formally since during preventive prison people with a degree receive different treatment and do not share a cell with uneducated people.

References

Adorno, Theodor W. 2008. *Philosophische Elemente einer Theorie der Gesellschaft*. Frankfurt a. M.: Suhrkamp.

Adorno, Theodor W. 2011. *Philosophie und Soziologie*. Berlin: Suhrkamp.

Arendt, Hannah. 1970. *On Violence*. New York: Harvest Book.

Becker, Howard S. 1967. 'Whose Side Are We On?', *Social Problems*, 14(3): 239–247.

Bourdieu, Pierre. 2005. *The Social Structures of the Economy*. Cambridge: Polity Press.

Bourdieu, Pierre; Boltanski, Luc. 1976. 'La production de l'idéologie dominante', *Actes de la rechercheen sciences sociales*, 2(2–3): 3–73.

Cortina, Adela. 2017. *Aporofobia, el rechazo al pobre. Un desafío para la democracia*. Barcelona: Paidós.

Cospito, Giuseppe. 2016. 'Egemonia/egemonico nei "Quaderni del carcere" (e prima)', *International Gramsci Journal*, 2(1): 49–88.

Damous, Wadih. 2018. 'Josué de Castro, Lula, e a marcha do MST', *Diário do Centro do Mundo*. August 8. www.diariodocentrodomundo.com.br/josue-de-castro-lula-e-a-marcha-do-mst-por-wadih-damous/ (accessed on September 27 2018).

Foucault, Michel. 2008. *The Birth of Biopolitics*. London: Palgrave Macmillan.

Fraser, Nancy; Honneth, Axel. 2003. *Redistribution or Recognition? A Political-Philosophical Exchange*. London: Verso.

Freyre, Gilberto. 1964. *The Masters and the Slaves: A Study in the Development of Brazilian Civilization*. New York: Alfred A. Knopf.

Fricker, Miranda. 1999. 'Epistemic Oppression and Epistemic Privilege', *Canadian Journal of Philosophy*, 29(supl. 1): 191–210.

Gramsci, Antonio. 1992. *Prison Notebooks. Volume I*. New York: Columbia University Press.

Gramsci, Antonio. 1996. *Prison Notebooks. Volume II*. New York: Columbia University Press.

Honneth, Axel. 1996. *The Struggle for Recognition: The Moral Grammar of Social Conflicts*. Cambridge, MA: The MIT Press.

Honneth, Axel. 2014. *Freedom's Right: The Social Foundations of Democratic Life*. New York: Columbia University Press.

Jaeggi, Rahel. 2016. 'What (if Anything) Is Wrong with Capitalism? Dysfunctionality, Exploitation and Alienation: Three Approaches to the Critique of Capitalism', *The Southern Journal of Philosophy*, 54: 44–65.

Jaeggi, Rahel; Celikates, Robin. 2017. *Sozialphilosophie. Eine Einführung*. München: Beck.

Lavinas, Lena (ed.). 2014. *Percepções sobre desigualdade e pobreza. O que pensam os brasileiros da política social?*. Rio de Janeiro: Centro Internacional Celso Furtado.

Leão Rego, Walquíria; Pinzani, Alessandro. 2016. 'Money, Autonomy, Citizenship. Effects of the Programa Bolsa Família on Its Participants', *Philosophy and Public Issues*, 6(3): 115–159.

Leão Rego, Walquíria; Pinzani, Alessandro. 2018. *Money, Autonomy and Citizenship. The Experience of the Brazilian Bolsa Família*. Dordrecht: Springer.

Marins, Mani Tebet A. 2017. *Bolsa Família. Questões de gênero e moralidades*. Rio de Janeiro: Editora da UFRJ.

Michel-Muniz, Jordan. 2018. 'Democracia apresentativa e o apartheid social brasileiro. Crítica da igualdade política', Unpublished Ph.D. dissertation, UFSC.

Mirowski, Philip; Plehwe, Dieter (eds.). 2009. *The Road from Mount Pèlerin. The Making of the Neoliberal Thought Collective*. Cambridge, MA: Harvard University Press.

Pinzani, Alessandro. 2012. 'De objeto de políticas a sujeitos da política: dar voz aos pobres', *ethic@. An International Journal for Moral Philosophy*, 10(3): 83–101.

Schlosser, Markus. 2015. 'Agency', in Edward N. Zalta (ed.), *The Stanford Encyclopedia of Philosophy* (Fall 2015 Edition), https://plato.stanford.edu/archives/fall2015/entries/agency/ (accessed on September 27, 2018).

Scott, James C. 1990. Domination and the Arts of Resistance: Hidden Transcripts. New Haven: Yale University Press.

Simmel, Georg. 2004. *The Philosophy of Money*. London: Routledge.

Smith, Adam. 1976. *An Inquiry into the Nature and Causes of the Wealth of Nations*. Oxford: Oxford University Press.

Stedman Jones, Daniel. 2012. *Masters of the Universe. Hayek, Friedman, and the Birth of Neoliberal Politics*. Princeton: Princeton University Press.

Townsend, Peter. 1987. 'Deprivation', *Journal of Social Policy*, 16(2): 125–146.

Winch, Peter. 2008. *The Idea of a Social Science and its Relation to Philosophy*. London: Routledge.

Zelizer, Viviana. 1989. 'The Social Meaning of Money: "Special Monies"', *American Journal of Sociology*, 95(2): 342–377.

Zurn, Christopher 2011. 'Social Pathologies as Second-Order Disorders', in Danielle Petherbridge (ed.), *Axel Honneth: Critical Essays*, pp. 345–370. Leiden: Brill.

Part II

DIMENSIONS OF EQUALITY

4

REDISTRIBUTION AND RECOGNITION FROM THE POINT OF VIEW OF REAL EQUALITY

Anderson and Honneth through the lens of Babeuf

Jean-Philippe Deranty

There are two ways to understand 'redistribution' in the context of discussions about justice. First, it is simply one of the issues to tackle in relation to justice: What is a fair distribution of the benefits and burdens involved in living together in society, as part of a more encompassing theory of justice? 'Redistribution' also signals a particular approach to define justice in general, based on the idea that the central issue about justice is the issue of fair distribution. That approach, which can be called the 'distributive justice' paradigm, has been the main one in Anglo-American political philosophy in the last four decades, following on from the seminal work of John Rawls. In the following, I will aim to tackle the issues related to redistribution through a critical take on the distributive paradigm. I will draw on the writings of two of the most important critics of this paradigm in contemporary political philosophy, Elizabeth Anderson and Axel Honneth, whose arguments overlap in many ways. Anderson's conception of relational or democratic equality shares a number of key conceptual elements with Honneth's theories of recognition and social freedom. The two authors provide eminent, converging reference points to critically elucidate issues of redistribution in relation to issues of recognition.

However, the angle selected to critically study these issues will be more specific. Despite the overlaps, the two thinkers depart from each other, notably because their fundamental inspirations lie in two separate political traditions. Anderson seeks to retrieve the republican, Honneth the socialist legacy. In both traditions, one of the defining features, and a key point of departure from mainstream liberalism, was the rejection of formal theories of equality and the pursuit instead of 'real equality'. In sections 1 and 2,

I present the two authors from a triple point of view: how their respective theories of recognition overlap and depart from each other; what the implications are for issues of redistribution; and what their conceptions of 'real equality' amount to.

In section 3, I consider the two authors critically, from the point of view of 'real equality', by drawing on the very traditions they refer to in order to mount their respective claims. In the aftermath of the American and French revolutions, in the first half of the nineteenth century, the rejuvenated republican movement and the budding socialist movement were often indiscernible in terms of their main political goals and strategies. One important reference point, whether it was used as inspiration or as an undesirable option, was the movement associated with the name of Babeuf and the "Manifesto of the Equals", which advocated a radical redistribution of wealth to achieve full equality. In her retrieval of 'radical republicanism', Elizabeth Anderson has explicitly contrasted her approach and the strand inspiring her, from this way of framing 'real equality'. I contest her reading of Babeuf and I use him as a foil to raise several critical questions about hers and Honneth's versions of egalitarianism.

1 Elizabeth Anderson's republican conception of 'real equality'

1.1 Anderson's critique of 'distributive justice' and the 'real' concept of equality

The 'distributive justice' paradigm includes the most influential authors in mainstream Anglo-American political philosophy, such as Ronald Dworkin, Richard Arneson, G.A. Cohen, and John Roemer. The fundamental assumption underlying their approaches is that the vagaries of social life, notably the complexity of modern economic systems, as well as the arbitrariness with which natural assets are distributed amongst individuals combine to breach the basic principle of justice that individuals should get what is due to them. Some receive less than they should due to circumstances for which they are not responsible, while others receive more than others, again for no justifiable reason. From this perspective, the problem of justice becomes centrally a problem of fair distribution. The paradigm goods in this approach are economic goods, but other 'goods' are also considered, such as positions of prestige and power, opportunity, or welfare. Indeed, the debates in this paradigm concern precisely which of those 'goods' are the correct 'currency of egalitarian justice' (Cohen 1989). Even with goods that are not economic, however, the primary measure of distributive inequality is in terms of material resources, in terms of property and income, and fair compensation is discussed in terms of financial redistribution through state-run schemes, notably insurance and taxation. Equality is the central normative standard in this approach, as equality of treatment, but it conceives of equality exclusively in a distributive sense and of fair redistribution in material terms.

Elizabeth Anderson's seminal work on equality has developed to a large extent as a critical response to this influential approach to justice. The 'real' concept of equality for her is relational, it refers 'not so much to distributions of goods as to relations between people' (1999: 312). Equality is not first and foremost equality of assets, or opportunities, or welfare, but rather a quality of social relations, one in which every person is able 'to stand up as an equal before others' (1999: 313). The opposite of justice is not primarily unearned advantage or undeserved disadvantage, but unequal relations, in other words oppression of some by others, which manifests itself in relations of violence, domination, discrimination, or exclusion. The ideal of justice therefore is not a state of society where every individual enjoys precisely what they deserve and nothing more, but a society of equals. 'Real' equality therefore can also be defined as 'democratic', since it points to a social ideal where every individual has equal social worth. Full equality means 'to live in a democratic community, as opposed to a hierarchical one'.

The central criterion and medium of justice on this model is the quality of interactions between people. Anderson translates this as a shift from a 'third-person' perspective on justice, which calculates the fairness of social structures from the outside, to a 'second-person' perspective, that looks at the structure of interactions between people: 'a person's due essentially concerns what claims people are entitled to make on others' conduct, with respect to how they treat claimants and their interests' (2010b: 19). As a result, the justice of social arrangements can be specified in communicative terms as a universal capacity to ask for and provide reasons: 'democratic equality regards two people as equal when each accepts the obligation to justify their actions by principles acceptable to the other, and in which they take mutual consultation, reciprocation and recognition for granted'.

The background model of justice is thus a republican ideal of equal participation in social life. We might say that the republican model specifies the very concept of equality. In turn, Anderson transfers these two elements (the republican model of democracy and the concept of equality that befits it) into a methodology that is appropriate to them, namely social contract theory, which she inherits from her teacher John Rawls. Accordingly, the definition of equality reads like a description of a republican political model and can be interpreted as an application of social contract theory: justice as equality means that

> one is entitled to participate, that others recognize an obligation to listen respectfully and respond to one's arguments, that no one need to bow and scrape before others or represent themselves as inferior to others as a condition of having their claims heard.
>
> (1999: 313)

There is thus a circular reinforcement between the central concept, the favoured method, and the social ideal. This is captured in the following statement: 'what citizens owe one another is the social conditions of the freedoms people need to function as equal citizens' (1999: 320).

This model of relational or democratic equality makes room for economic inequality. For Anderson the more 'talented' and the more industrious should be recompensed for their efforts, within the constraints of the difference principle. She objects to luck egalitarians not just because they show disrespect for rich and poor, talented and untalented, by making the state examine life choices to determine whether individuals were responsible for their social fate. It is also important to maintain the possibility of justified inequality because it is part of justice that the deserving get what they deserve. We want to avoid undeserved rewards but we also need to promote talent. This is fair to the better off but for the less well-off as well, since they profit from the higher productivity achieved by the former (1999: 326; 2010b: 20–21). On this model, distribution matters but is not in itself an intrinsic part of 'real' (relational, democratic) equality. Once the less well-off receive the basic resources and opportunities allowing them to 'stand up as equals amongst others', and if the more 'talented' receive their fair reward and indeed are incentivized to be more productive for the benefit of everyone else, distribution is no longer an issue of justice. Indeed, distributive equality in fact is blind to many other aspects of injustice, notably all those aspects that prevent individuals from functioning as equal citizens in the different spheres of social life.

1.2 *Realizing equality*

Elizabeth Anderson's work can also be read as an attempt to rethink justice from the point of view of 'real equality' in a second sense, namely in terms of the actual realization of justice claims. This is one aspect of her advocating a second-person approach to justice. That perspective considers what justifiable demands an individual or group can make on other individuals, in relation to a specific good, in the name of equality. One dimension of this justifiability concern is precisely whether the demand can be satisfied or not, in other words whether the demand for equality, the realization of justice, can actually be fulfilled. This is not just an empirical point but also a conceptual one. It concerns the very notion of justifiability, of what makes a claim a justified claim. As she writes: 'it is unreasonable to demand of agents that they satisfy a principle they are unable to follow. The demands of justice must therefore be tailored to the general cognitive and behavioural capacities of agents' (2010b: 19).

The second sense in which Anderson is concerned about the actual realization of equality relates simply to her many attempts to specify through elaborate, highly informed discussions, how the fundamental principle of relational equality is to be applied on specific policy issues. She has consistently sought to bridge the gap between pure, normative political philosophy, policy, and real politics. For example, her seminal 1999 paper on 'the point of equality' entails precise discussions of the policy implications of her relational conception of autonomy for the compensation owed to people with disabilities or support for people who choose to have children. In several articles (2016a; 2016b), she has made the case for social insurance policies, retracing the historical origins and the normative force of these proposals. She also studied the implications of relational equality for the issue of 'market risks' in contemporary society, that is, what kinds of constraints should be placed upon markets so that unjust outcomes are mitigated (2008). In her recent work on workplace democracy, she has shown the implications of her critical view of the capitalist firm as a space of governance for management and economic policy (2015a).

Finally, a third sense in which Anderson is concerned with equality becoming 'real' relates to methodology. She contrasts her approach with those of moral and political philosophers who develop ideal proposals independent of the historical and sociological facts about human societies (2015b). In contrast, Anderson has sought to anchor her normative claims in thick descriptions of human societies, drawing on economic theory, to discuss technical aspects of distributive justice. She refers to the history of social movements to show how her conceptual model formalizes the actual claims made by individuals and groups seeking justice (Anderson 2014a), and she uses history and sociology to defend her original, republican theory of the firm (2017).

Anderson describes this approach to political philosophy as a form of pragmatism (2014a, 2015b). Crucially, the pragmatist method is consistent with the definition of 'real equality' and republican political theory. On the pragmatist account also, it is only if equality is conceived as the outcome of free, inter-personal interactions, based notably on the exchange of justifications, that it has a chance of being actually realized. In the 2014 Amherst Lectures Anderson closes the circle by arguing that it is precisely by studying how real social movements have enforced more equality that we can learn how equality can become real (2014a). This is a powerful, performative gesture since it relies on a realist, historical account of actual implementation of equality through activities of contestation (and not just moral argumentation), on the basis of which it can be argued what equality as relational entails.

1.3 'Real equality' as historical demand

Finally, another sense of 'real equality' refers to the history of political ideas and the arguments that were raised following the modern revolutions, contrasting merely formal with 'real', or 'actual', or 'full', or 'material' equality.

Anderson explicitly connects her model of justice and equality to the historical tradition of republicanism. Within that tradition, the 'radical' strand, with which Anderson aligns herself (2015a: 51), is characterized by the attempt to 'make equality real', against conservative attempts to limit it, and against merely formal, notably liberal, understandings of it (on the historical roots of 'real equality', see Rosanvallon 2013: 12–74). She also contrasts the radical republican understanding of 'real equality' with socialist alternatives, despite their common roots (Hayat 2018), notably because socialists interpret 'not just formal' conceptions of equality as warranting encroachments upon private property and tend to make stronger claims than republicans about the ethical dispositions required of individuals.

This historical, republican inspiration behind Anderson's work is particularly evident in her work on workplace democracy and racial equality. In Chapter 5 of *The Imperative of Integration* for instance (2010a: 89–110), she retraces the long history of the struggle for full racial equality in the US. The central argument she embraces is the one advanced and fought for by Black abolitionists and radical republicans who attempted to ensure 'full equality', notably by arguing that the latter was analytically entailed in the very idea of a republic. In this view, the notion of 'real' or 'full' equality denotes all the rights individuals have, as citizens, in participating as equals in all the different spheres of social and political life, including at work, on the labour market and in relation to the collective decision-making processes.

2 Honneth's critique of proceduralist political theories

2.1 Honneth's social freedom and relational equality

Honneth would endorse many of the features of Anderson's model of 'relational equality' for his own model of recognition. Like her, he thinks of recognition from the second-person perspective, as a demand individuals make on others, underpinned by the fundamental claim to be able to 'stand as an equal before others' (1995: 112). Indeed, Anderson (1999: 314) explicitly cites Honneth to articulate her relational conception of equality. They both make the point that demands of recognition apply across the different spheres of society. In "What is the Point of Equality?", Anderson draws on Sen's theory of capabilities to extend the demands of equality across all spheres of social life. Demands for equality apply, she claims, to three spheres that roughly map out Honneth's spheres of recognition: functioning as a human being, as a participant in a system of cooperative production, and as a citizen in a democratic state (1999: 317). Conversely, in his remodelling of recognition in *Freedom's Right*, Honneth now presents the model of recognition as a study into 'the social foundations of democratic life'. In other words, he interprets the ideal of recognition as a demand for full democratic life, across all spheres of social life, in the spirit of Anderson's comprehensive model of 'democratic equality'. Both thinkers draw on the historical expansion of rights, from civil to political to social rights, as proof for the pervasiveness of demands for recognition and equality across all areas of social life. Both of them make the point that legal recognition is not sufficient, and ensuring democratic equality in the system of production is also essential for 'real' recognition and 'real' equality. Anderson goes further than Honneth in this respect, as she delves into the structures of domination operating in modern firms. But the general point is shared between them that recognition, or democratic equality, puts constraints on economic organization and that justice requires a lot more in this sphere than just the freedom to contract (Honneth 2012a: 56–75). Finally, both of them connect their theories to real struggles for emancipation. They do this, first, as substantial evidence for the conceptual definitions of justice they advocate. Historical social movements simply illuminate what real justice is about for real people: full equality in social relations. And second, the two thinkers expressly devolve a large part of the 'realization' aspect of their theories to social movements. One dimension of propounding 'democratic' theories of justice is to learn from the public how justice was to be realized in the past, and might be in the future.

Despite these overlaps, however, the concepts of recognition and relational equality formalize justice differently. These differences in turn can be related to differences between republican and socialist conceptions. In Anderson's construal of social relations of equality, the social ideal is inherently political: what measures and ensures equality is the fact that individuals 'live together in a democratic community' (1999: 313). The formula that summarizes her conception of real equality clearly captures the republican slant she puts on it: 'what citizens owe one another is the social conditions of the freedoms people need to function as equal citizens' (1999: 320) By 'social conditions of freedom', Anderson has in mind two specific senses of 'social'. First, she means reciprocal interactions between individuals in terms of justified claims each makes upon the other. The question here is: does each agree to the terms of the relationship? Second, 'social' also means collective, where the collective is conceptualized as the aggregate of all those fictitious encounters between partners in interaction. As said previously, this second-person model of interaction fits with the method of social contract theory she borrows from Rawls and from the republican tradition more broadly.

In this 'republican' sense of 'social', the individual is an autonomous agent whose claims on others derive from her inalienable rights as a free being. Recognition in this sense is reciprocal acknowledgement between autonomous beings that is extrinsic to the individuals. They rely on each other instrumentally for the fulfilment of their claims and in that sense depend on relations of recognition, but individuals are what they are independently of the relationship. In Honneth, by contrast, recognition is intrinsic to the very construction of the individual's identity. In the first model presented in *Struggle for Recognition*, this idea is captured in anthropological and psychological terms: the very process of identity formation relies upon the affirmation of the self by others. The self comes about through the internalization of the attitudes of others towards it. The spheres of recognition are different areas of social life in which selves are 'under the gaze' of others in specific ways. Autonomy in this model is not instrumentally dependent upon others (whether or not they grant me what I need for my freedom to be realized), but intrinsically. I can only relate to myself positively, which is Honneth's initial way of redefining the fundamental norm of freedom as self-determination and self-realization, if the attitudes towards me allow me to do so, at least minimally.

In *Freedom's Right*, the same idea is captured in more formal terms, through the idea of 'social freedom'. Negative conceptions of freedom are only impoverished versions that do not capture the richer sense of freedom as self-determination and self-realization, as they only focus on external obstacles and not on the content and structure of autonomy. A richer sense of autonomy relies upon a 'thick' understanding, which in turn entails a consideration of the 'social' structure of that freedom. This is because the most important ends I might want to achieve to realize myself fully, and thereby achieve full self-determination, only make sense if the others upon whom I relate for the realization of these ends also realize theirs concomitantly, with me. The realization of my ends depends intrinsically, not instrumentally, upon others also being able to realize their own ends. Reciprocal recognition by the individuals involved is here a constitutive condition of each individual's autonomy: 'the reciprocal experience of seeing ourselves confirmed in the desires and aims of the other, because the other's existence represents a condition for fulfilling our own desires and aims' (Honneth, 2014: 45). This is a 'social' conception of freedom because for each particular kind of end realized by each individual, a specific kind of 'we', a specific type of collective is involved: a friendship, a couple, a family, a labour market, a market of commodities, a state, a nation, a culture. The concept of 'social' here goes deeper, as it were, than in the republican conception. That each individual requires social conditions for her or his freedom means: each has to take into account the other's desires and aims in the very formulation of his or her desires and aims, and thereby relates their individual needs, beliefs, and desires to the relevant kind of collective involved. In other words, solidarity, taking the other and the collective into account, becomes an intrinsic condition of the autonomy of each self and guides the ordering of the 'well-ordered society' (2017). In turn, this requires structures of society, both formal institutions and a public culture, that make this possible and entrench such reciprocal mechanisms. This is no longer a republican but a socialist ideal, one that thinks of the just society as an order of cooperation, or as an association of partners who are not just equal in terms of their right for self-realization but co-dependent in this pursuit. The collective on this model arises from the logic of reciprocity animating each individual in relation to the others. Rather than being external to the singular units, the collective underpins individual actions as these are all intrinsically indexed on the well-being of each and all. For all their methodological differences, a similar view of socialism has been defended by G.A Cohen, via his 'principle of community' (2009).

2.2 Honneth's critique of 'distributive justice'

Given these differences between Honneth's and Anderson's models, what are the implications for distribution, both as a problem, and as a paradigm? How does Honneth tackle these issues from the point of view of 'real equality'? Since he aims to address these issues from a 'socialist' perspective, and given the importance of the concern for real equality in that tradition,[1] it seems that the question is justified, even though, as we will see, Honneth does not make 'real equality' a thematic focus of his retrieval of the socialist tradition.

Regarding the distributive justice paradigm, the issue is complicated because Anderson and Honneth occupy different positions in relation to it. Anderson looks at it from within the mainstream, Anglo-American field, in which the paradigm is central, and she pits her approach straightforwardly against it. Crucially, she views her 'relational' approach in the legacy of Rawls. As we saw, she describes Rawls' social contract methodology as a way to instantiate her republican conception of 'real equality', since it aims to ensure that the claims each person would want to make on society could be made from the point of view of anybody else. This can be interpreted, she argues, as equivalent to the idea that justice involves 'what claims people are allowed to make on others'.

Honneth also criticizes the 'distributive justice' paradigm, in terms directly echoing Anderson's. Like her, he makes the point that justice should not be discussed primarily in terms of a fair distribution of goods, but in terms of the quality of social relations. The fundamental issue of justice for him is a thick conception of autonomy, and

> what helps us to acquire autonomy is not cut out of the same cloth as a good that can be distributed; it is fashioned out of living relations of reciprocal recognition that are just to the degree that they allow us to reciprocally value our needs, beliefs and capabilities. (2012a: 41)

And yet Honneth has primarily Rawls in view in his broad criticism of mainstream political philosophy. Indeed a number of important luck egalitarians, notably Cohen, in fact write against Rawls and reject proceduralist accounts. As a disciple of Rawls, Anderson therefore might in fact be a prime target of Honneth's criticisms. The source of the disagreement would be social contract theory and would go back to the difference between the two senses of recognition and what is meant by 'social conditions of freedom'. Because Honneth has a 'thick', constitutive, interpretation of recognition, that is, a view of recognition as that which makes freedom possible in the first place, the proceduralist view of how justice occurs is logically flawed for him. It assumes precisely what it aims to make possible. Despite her rejection of the distribution paradigm of justice, in her embrace of social contract theory Anderson treats the 'social conditions' making freedom possible as if they were goods that citizens with established identities can raise claims about in relation to each other. From Honneth's perspective, the 'second-person' perspective she advocates is not sufficient to escape his criticism, because that perspective thinks of recognition between persons as being external to the very constitution of the personhood of persons.

2.3 Distribution and real equality in Honneth's model of 'social freedom'

Given these differences, how does Honneth discuss distribution and what would be 'real equality' for him?

The contrasting discussion of Honneth's model of 'social freedom' and Anderson's model of 'relational equality' already provides a key element to answer this question. Honneth is never really interested in equality per se. He addresses it only as a dimension of autonomy, which for him is the most fundamental norm (see very explicitly 2014: 15). Justice for him is the equal right each individual has for her or his full autonomy, understood in a 'thick' sense as self-realization. This does not mean that distributional issues are not part of justice, but they are only implications of the view that justice consists in allowing every individual to obtain the social conditions of their self-realization (Deranty 2016a).

One key implication of Honneth's interpretation of the 'social conditions of freedom' in terms of recognition is that it leads to a pluralistic approach to the normative demands individuals can make upon others and the collective. This is because individual self-realization has different axes. In "The Fabric of Justice" for instance, Honneth mentioned 'needs, beliefs and capacities'. These subjective dimensions in turn are developed in different kinds of recognitive relations. The 'spheres of recognition' in his first model, the different institutional spheres in *Freedom's Right*, correspond precisely to the fundamental types of social relations, through which individuals realize different aspects of their identity, welfare, and life plans. This means that recognition is only a generic concept, and that it has different structures depending on the social spheres in question and the kinds of subjective dimensions at stake in them. As a consequence of this pluralistic approach, Honneth's answer to the question of 'real equality' would be that it is impossible to specify one 'true' meaning of equality, except in the very generic sense of equal right to the conditions of full autonomy. Equality in relation to the conditions of autonomy entails different rights and duties between friends, lovers, family members, in the anonymous relations between consumers and producers who meet through market interactions, or between citizens engaging with each other in the public sphere. From this pluralistic point of view, Anderson's equating of 'relational' with 'democratic' looks insufficiently differentiated.

In what ways does Honneth concern himself with the actual realization of 'real equality'? As for Anderson, this question bears directly on his approach. In his case, the virtuous circle he tries to put in place is between the definition of freedom as social freedom, the political 'ism' that he thinks has historically aimed to realize it (socialism), and an approach to political theory that focuses on 'the social conditions of freedom', as he understands them. Such methodological focus means that a realistic social ontology has to form the foundations for the discussion of how the different dimensions of a realization of true freedom would actually unfold. 'Realistic' means that the social ontology grounding the political theory has to be sufficiently detailed, that it needs to make correct distinctions between different social spheres and identify correctly the mechanisms allowing for the different Is to form different Wes. The approach also has to be historically sensitive, so that any claim made by the political theorist regarding what people claim against each other and against society actually has a footing in real modern societies, can be shown to emerge from the real history of social movements for instance. All of these methodological requirements explain Honneth's embrace of his original method of 'normative reconstruction'. The aim behind this method is not just practical, to ensure that normative claims can be shown to have their roots in real societies, but also theoretical.

The implication of the methodological circularity between the definition of freedom (as 'social freedom'), the mode of theory construction (realist social ontology and normative reconstruction), and the favoured political movement (socialism) is that the latter is more than just a subjective preference of the theorist (on the self-reflexivity of Honneth's theory construction, see Deranty 2011). A similar kind of circularity is thus evidenced in Honneth's as in Anderson's work.

It is from these historical-conceptual perspectives that I now want to raise some criticisms of the two thinkers. They retrieve two traditions of political thinking and of real political movements to ground their approaches to justice. They do so positively, to show that their conceptions of justice have actual footing in modern society, and negatively, to demonstrate the abstractness of the 'distributive justice' paradigm. In both the republican and the socialist tradition, a central concern about justice, for activists and thinkers alike, was 'real equality': what equality actually consists of, and how it might be actually realized, against formal conceptions, or only partial realizations of it. I find this method of grounding normative political theory in historical-conceptual arguments very convincing. But there is a sting in the historical tail. There are strands in the very traditions Anderson and Honneth draw on that reflect critically on their theoretical propositions. From the point of view of 'real equality' as a demand made by real, historical actors, their theories might miss crucial considerations.

To make this case, I will refer to the controversial figure of Gracchus Babeuf. Babeuf was active as a journalist, political thinker, and agitator at the time of the French Revolution. He and the companions around him who prepared a "Conspiracy for Equality" in 1796[2] defended the most radical version of equality in modern times, elevating it to the fundamental norm of social and political life. It might seem arbitrary to favour this particular strand of early egalitarian thinking. Two reasons justify the relevance of Babeuf for a critical study of Anderson's and Honneth's versions of egalitarianism. The first reason is that Babeuf is a key representative of the radical tradition of republicanism, which emanated directly from the French Revolution, and which, for the first 50 years of the nineteenth century, until the revolutions of 1848, shared many ideas and political aims with the emerging socialist movement, so much so that it is often difficult to disentangle the two traditions in those crucial formative years. He can thus be used as a critical historical counterpoint for the two contemporary philosophers at the same time. The second reason is that Anderson herself sets up Babeuf as an early proponent of modern socialism and as an explicit foil against which she propounds her American version of radical, egalitarian republicanism (2014b; 2016a).

3 Relational equality and social freedom from the point of view of radical equality

3.1 Two versions of radical republican equality

I will assume here that the basic facts about Babeuf and his 'conspiracy for equality' are known (see Birchall 2016). Anderson focuses on him for several reasons. She wants to question an account of the history of distributive justice that identifies him as the first author in that tradition (Fleischacker 2004: 76–77), in favour of Thomas Paine. This historical point has conceptual and normative significance. Babeuf thought that private property is the root of inequality and thus of injustice. He concluded from this that, in order to achieve justice, private property should be abolished, and the common resources produced by individual workers should be redistributed on a purely egalitarian basis, through a centralized state power. Such vision of justice is wrong and dangerous for Anderson: it justifies tyrannical intervention by the state into people's private affairs; and it leads to an economic levelling that cannot be justified, first on efficiency grounds, and second because those who work more or are more talented should not be prevented from earning more. Paine, on the other hand, in his proposals for social insurance and stakeholder grants, outlines a realistic and fair programme for 'real' equality, ensuring basic support and universal equality of access to material resources.

Anderson's rendering of the ideas of Babeuf and his companions is ungenerous. It is oblivious of the historical location and the literary specificity of the texts she reads. She selects passages to construe Babeuf's doctrine as a direct anticipation of a communist 'totalitarian dictatorship'. But many of the points she presents as programmatic measures are in fact ideal descriptions of what the Equals hoped society *would* look like in the long run following the egalitarian revolution. To cite just one telling example, when Buonarroti writes: 'Nothing in a well-ordered society must stray from the '*esprit du législateur*'' (2016a: 163), '*esprit*' does not mean the prying 'mind' of the legislator, as Anderson reads it, but the spirit of the constitution, in direct reference to Montesquieu and Rousseau.

As a pragmatist, Anderson might have been sensitive to other aspects of the Equals' writings, notably the method by which they arrived at their claims. Their plans for social and political equality were grounded in basic natural law principles, notably the old egalitarian motto repeated through the centuries, that 'the earth belongs to nobody'. But these plans were formulated in negativistic fashion, in direct opposition to a situation of utter injustice. They certainly overreach in some of their conclusions, but they were expressed at a time of extreme political tension, where the opposite positions had no less radical consequences. Despite the situatedness of their arguments, however, and in a certain sense precisely because of it, much can still be gathered from them for egalitarian thinking.

The political arguments are indexed to the social and economic situation, one characterized by appalling deprivation and humiliation for the great majority. Babeuf establishes an explicit link between description and normative principles notably in the most important issue of *Le Tribun du Peuple* (number 35, of 30 November 1795), which features the famous 'manifesto of the plebeians' (Babeuf 2009: 321–336; in Birchall 2016: 195–199). Anderson does not pay attention to the passages that precede the pages in which the manifesto of the Equals is summarized. These pages seem utterly outdated today because of their grandiloquent pathos and eighteenth-century flourishes. The academic reader is tempted to skip straight to the pages that resemble contemporary arguments of political theory the most. But this would be a mistake. The passages describing the suffering of the proletarian population function as a fundamental argumentative layer. This is the first mode in which a negativistic method is used: the factual situation of extreme misery strikes the existing system as invalid *in its very principles*, notably the sacred nature of private property, which prevents the deprived majority from accessing the goods that a minority has in surplus. One might object that precisely because the claim against property is raised at a time of extreme social emergency, it is bound to that situation and no longer holds in a different context. But Babeuf invites us to see the situation of emergency as a litmus test, the historical *reductio ad absurdum* of a social organization based on a principle, private property, that inherently produces injustice. Conversely, the catastrophic social situation is the tragic revelation of the breach of a fundamental principle, that the earth belongs to nobody.

The simple fact of immense inequality is in and of itself an injustice, in a relative and quantitative sense, to the extent namely that it does not seem justifiable that a few could have so much whilst the majority have so little that they can't even survive. This type of injustice is translated by Babeuf into another general principle: that 'no man can justifiably pretend that any other of his *semblables* be less happy than he'.[3] By 'happiness', Babeuf has a minimalist concept in mind: whatever resources are necessary at a given time for an individual to have his or her basic social needs covered. In a fragment of an economic decree written at the same time, we get a concrete sense of what the Equals understood by this: 'healthy, comfortable and decently furnished accommodation; clothing for work and leisure . . . laundry, lighting and heating; a sufficient quantity of food; medical assistance' (Birchall 2016: 202). The principle that 'no man can justifiably pretend that any other of his *semblables* be less happy than he' could be read as the conclusion of a social contract argument. Indeed Babeuf formulates it in reference to Rousseau. But attention should be paid to the exact wording. A social contract argument would focus on the first person: no one would rationally agree to put *themselves* in a position where they would be at a disadvantage in comparison with others. But Babeuf does not refer to self-interested rationality, but rather to moral justification: that it is impossible for me to justify an order in which I know that I would be at an advantage *over others*. This is another implication of the negativistic method, a second argument from injustice. It is clearly an argument that is particularly potent in a situation in which the rich and the powerful are precisely in a situation of extreme advantage, where they enjoy immense wealth whilst the majority starves and sees its children die.

All this alerts us to the need to pause and reflect on the normative force of Babeuf's writings, and what they might teach us today, at a time when inequality is rising and the gap between rich and poor takes on extreme proportions again. Rather than anachronistically looking for the premises of dictatorship in Babeuf, we could instead find inspiration in the way in which he connects the description of a situation of injustice to normative political principles (see Deranty 2016b on a similar method used by Marx in *Capital*). The demand for equality can be justified through natural law and social contract arguments, but it arises first of all as a necessary consequence of the abolition of injustice: if radical inequality is blatantly unjust, then justice demands the suppression of, or at least the significant reduction in, inequality. This is what 'real equality' means first of all. Its urgency arises from the fact that its absolute opposite is the case.

Of course Babeuf's radical inference does not seem to hold at first: the fact that substantial inequality is unjust only means that it should be reduced, not that perfect equality should be established. Rousseau demanded only that 'all have something, and none has too much', indeed Babeuf often quotes this passage. Anderson herself notes that a reduction in economic inequality is needed as it makes real, social and political equality a fiction.

However, the negativistic method underpins another set of considerations that further justify why Babeuf and his companions demanded not just more equality, but a radical implementation of it, why 'real equality' meant perfect equality for them. It is this set of considerations that truly distinguish Babeuf's approach from Anderson's, and as we'll see in the next section, Honneth's.

Babeuf and the Equals do not just denounce unjust inequality as a scandal but also identify its social causes. It is mainly in this light that private property is debated. Babeuf does not deduce the lack of normative validity for private property from positive natural law principles alone, but rather in combination with another negative argument, through the reality and history of injustice. The main problem with private property in the Rousseauian tradition, is that it is the root of inequalities that accumulate over time and harden into structures of social domination producing such large differentials in social power that they end up delivering the kind of extreme injustice Babeuf reports about as a journalist. Other sources of inequality are identified that combine to entrench the inegalitarian effects of private property: the transmission of property through inheritance; how some can acquire property rights over the very person of others through work contracts; how the property of personal attributes, moral or intellectual, that are culturally favoured, translates into higher social benefits for some; how education entrenches social and cultural hierarchies, particularly those relating to the division between intellectual and manual work, by inculcating the younger generations with representations underpinning those hierarchies, and by actively selecting individuals so as to reproduce the distinctions between the elite and the plebs (Babeuf in Birchall: 197–198). The full phenomenon of injustice thus results from a complex combination of social mechanisms centred around property. What we might call 'privatized' wealth (in land, in persons, and even in personal attributes), creates situations of social inequality, which in the long run can translate, and indeed have historically regularly translated, into utter destitution for the majority. From this point of view, even if at particular times inequality is tempered, in societies organized around the privatization of wealth the potential for a serious rise in inequality, leading to destitution for the many, or at least to serious, unjustifiable differences in degrees of 'happiness', that potential remains always present (on the cyclical nature of inequality over long history, see Scheidel 2017).

Significant differentials in 'happiness' are inherently wrong, from the point of view of the positive principle declined earlier, and serious forms of deprivation are an absolute injustice, since they deny individuals the right to live well and in extreme circumstances even to survive. These wrongs are compounded by the breach of another principle that is a derivation of the principle that the earth belongs to no one. This is the idea that general wealth, as it has been produced by everyone, is to be shared by everyone, and that private property from this point of view is social wealth that has been unduly privatized. Such privatization of social wealth occurs precisely through the mechanisms of social inequality whose main sources have been identified previously (inheritance, alienation, meritocracy). The outcome of all these elements (unjustified, domination-inducing privatization, and deprivation-producing inequality) is not just the plain fact that some have too much while others have too little, but that 'some manage to have too much only by *making* others having too little'. The crux is the social dynamic of domination, whose aim is *making* others have too little *so that* one can have too much.

This view of injustice is no longer compatible with Anderson's conception, in which some inequality is defensible on the conditions we have seen previously. For Babeuf, any justification of inequality is normatively impossible because inequality by necessity will lead at some point in time to unjust distribution. *It inevitably means that some, as a matter of fact, will have too little, in relative or absolute terms. It is a social law of which we have abundant historical confirmation that if some have too much, it is by making others have too little.* As soon as inequality is justified, injustice is justified at the same time, as an accepted potentiality of the social organization.

This explains the insistence on *full* equality, without exception, even for those who are more productive or deserving. In terms of natural law, it seems only fair that if everyone has the right to equal access to social wealth, then everyone should have the same amount of it, indexed to what they need for their own 'happiness'. Here we should note the sophistication of Babeuf's argument, in a newspaper article written at a time of extreme political emergency. He directly pre-empts an objection raised by contemporary luck egalitarians: what if my conception of happiness requires that I receive more or more valuable goods than others, so that the principle of equality in 'happiness' in fact leads to material inequality in my favour? Babeuf responds by specifying the definition in a minimalist sense, and by characterizing it in negative terms as 'sufficiency' or the avoidance of misery. In a situation of scarcity, there is no third option between sufficiency for all on the basis of equal redistribution and unequal distribution that leads to deprivation for the many. Adding the condition of scarcity to the 'sufficientarian' argument forces the conclusion to be radically, or at least substantively, egalitarian, since only a condition of indefinite opulence would allow sufficiency for all to translate into unequal parts. This is a direct rejoinder to, for example, the position most famously defended by Harry Frankfurt, against substantive material equality (1987). But the more basic argument, stemming from Rousseau and from social history, remains the negative one: as soon as you justify inequalities, through the right to privatize wealth, you allow the social logics to unfold that lead to unjust inequality. And history shows such inequality ends up producing absolute injustice or at least significant, unjustifiable inequalities in 'happiness'.

It seems difficult to argue against the claim that one cannot justify enjoying more 'happiness' than others, as previously defined in the minimalist sense. But it is also the negative methodology employed by Babeuf that is significant for contemporary discussions, because it signals the need to heighten our sensitivity to any inequality, as being potentially the sign that a social organization is on the way to producing significant or indeed extreme injustice. The negative method also focuses on the many dimensions of inequality that have direct effects on social justice. If the central concern is on the mechanisms by which inequality becomes a social force, leading to situations of injustice, then we have to look at material inequality as well as other forms of inequality, as crucial factors of injustice. In particular, inequality in social representations, notably concerning the hierarchy of professions, becomes problematic from the point of view of social justice. Babeuf argues explicitly that it is wrong to base social and economic inequality on arbitrary representations about the relative values of social contributions.

From the point of view of this link between inequality and injustice through social domination, Anderson's model falls short. As a republican, she is also worried about the mechanisms of social domination (see the taxonomy of forms domination in 2010b: 1–22). But she does not sufficiently consider that unequal property is one of the main ways by which positions of privilege and situations of social domination arise and become entrenched. Anderson is too caught up in discussions with luck egalitarians about the justifiability of equality of resources on the one hand, and on the other hand her relational approach makes her focus exclusively on modalities of social interaction, so that she does not seem to pay attention to the historical and sociological links between private property and domination. She does not thematize this as a problem that political theory needs to address specifically. In the context of the immense concentration of power by the elites, and the undermining of political democracy as a result of social inequality, this lack of attention to the disrupting aspects of large economic inequality should be a central concern for her. A more generous reading of Babeuf would alert her to a worry he inherited from the very tradition of radical republicanism she aims to retrieve herself, namely that democracy is incompatible with large economic inequality. A 'radical republican' stance ought to be wary of providing justifications for any form of inequality and should be particularly concerned to establish the social and political barriers that could effectively interrupt the mechanisms leading to hard structures of domination.

Moreover, as a follower of Rawls and as she is caught up in the framework of 'distributive justice' discussions, Anderson adopts an unproblematic conception of talent, as though there was an objective hierarchy of tasks based on degrees of complexity and differential social value, with only those individuals endowed with superior personal qualities or motivation able to perform them. The notion that 'talents' are social constructions, that some activities, some professions might be privileged in arbitrary ways, is not sufficiently taken seriously by her. Indeed, as Babeuf argues, the part of individual merit involved in particular contributions can also be shown to benefit from substantial social conditions. Individual contributions mobilize resources, material and symbolic, which the individual has not produced but relies upon for her or his own activity (Babeuf in Birchall 2016: 196). Moreover, in cases where some individual achievement does appear particularly valuable and the individual responsible for it therefore worthy of social esteem, if they benefitted from a privileged education, it is highly likely that others might have performed the activity just as well if they had had the chance: an 'equal distribution of knowledge between all would make the individuals roughly equal in capacity and even in talent'. This is not a consideration of moral arbitrariness or luck, as in the distributive justice paradigm, but a substantial claim about the innate equality of intelligences. Babeuf holds a similar theory as the one propounded by fellow revolutionary republican, Joseph Jacotot, whose forgotten name Jacques Rancière revived in *The Ignorant Schoolmaster* (1991). But if all intelligences are equal in principle, and only circumstances allow some to fully develop them or make them fructify, then this significantly reduces the value of individual merit and 'talent'. Such egalitarian theories of intelligence and education are far from the monstrous 'levelling' Anderson reads them as. Asserting the equality of intelligence and the comparable value of social contributions does not translate into bringing down the apparently more deserving individuals. It requires that everyone have access to the knowledge and quality education the privileged individuals enjoyed. Anderson advocates equality of opportunity and equal access to education, not on the basis that this would equalize talents, but only to the extent that some deserving, thus far underprivileged individuals would thereby access occupations and social roles which are objectively superior. We might ask how such meritocratic assumptions fit with an egalitarian ethos. The republican tradition insists on the fact that democracy is more than just an institutional structure, that it should be an ideal for social life as a whole. Anderson fully agrees with this, it is precisely what lies behind her emphasis on equality as a relation. How does such an ideal accommodate the unproblematic assumption that some are intrinsically superior, and some social contributions are obviously more valuable than others?

Babeuf's radical republican claim about the equality of intelligence provides the final plank to his communism: all wealth is socially produced; everyone contributes to social wealth; there is little to distinguish one contribution from another; indeed, even if there are differences in contribution, there is equality in need; therefore everyone should receive equal amounts from the universally produced wealth in proportion to what they need to attain sufficiency in their circumstances. Rather than a dictatorial dystopia, Babeuf's communism can be read as a consistent application of radical republican principles. It anticipates in its main features a consistent contemporary model of justice, the 'contributive' model articulated in recent times by Paul Gomberg (2007).

3.2 Honneth's socialism from the point of view of Babeuf's radical equality

What do Babeuf's challenges entail for Honneth's brand of socialism?

First we can note that the initial way in which Honneth presented his theory of recognition was amenable to aspects of the negative approach delineated previously. In *The Struggle for Recognition*, the overall logic of recognition and the different kinds of recognition claims were established through positive arguments of course, but the ground for these positive descriptions, what provided crucial heuristic orientation for them, was on the one hand the phenomenology of negative reactions demonstrated by individuals and groups exposed to experiences of social suffering and injustice, and on the other hand the history and sociology of collective struggles against injustice. Here, Honneth also employed a method of extracting the normative flashpoints of modern society from the point of view of denials of justice and experiences of social suffering. The more recent model presented in *Freedom's Right*, by contrast, premised upon the institutions of modern society that realize and entrench different spheres of 'social freedom' has lost touch with this negative grounding. Honneth in a number of recent texts has heeded Habermas' methodological edict condemning the alleged genetic fallacy that consists in drawing normative claims from facts about individual and social life. In doing so, he might well have given up on a potent methodological tool.

Regarding the links between social inequality and democratic justice, a similar rupture can be identified. Because of its strong sociological grounding, the initial model of recognition made room for a theory of social domination. Indeed, the very idea of a struggle for recognition put the focus on the social obstacles to full inclusion and equality in self-realization. In his early texts, Honneth focused specifically on the obstacles to social inclusion, including those based on material inequality (2007). This made Honneth's first political model amenable to Babeuf's concerns about inequality being not just a sign but also a vector of injustice. Indeed, despite Honneth's meritocratic assumptions regarding the value of social contributions in the third sphere of recognition, he applied the 'struggle for recognition' directly to the cultural assumptions underpinning value judgements about these contributions. This opened the door for an egalitarian deconstruction of the hierarchy of professions and social activities, notably regarding the division between intellectual and manual labour, or indeed between paid and unpaid work (1995: 129–130). From this point of view, Honneth's first ideal of universal 'self-realization' could fit with the radical republican worry according to which the goal of 'common happiness' necessitates a negativistic focus on the social and political forces acting against it.

In the new model of recognition and the recent work on socialism that prolongs it (Honneth 2017), there is no longer any interest in developing an explicit theory of social domination. The emphasis is on identifying the modern ideal of social freedom, and how different spheres of modern society have gradually realized that ideal and provided specific content to it. This historical, normative reconstruction does entail the reference to social struggles, inasmuch as the latter indicate different ways in which modern individuals have sought to extend and achieve aspects of their individual freedom (for instance 2014: 208). In turn, these references to social struggles point to the antagonistic forces that were obstacles to freedom and thereby prevented social equality. But these struggles for equality and the social forces defending privileges matter only for what they reveal about the content of different aspects of social freedom. They are no longer the focus of the theoretical inquiry. If extensions of social freedom occurred without struggle, for instance through the sheer force of moral progress, then this would be all the same to the new critical model. From the point of view of Babeuf's dynamic view of inequality, as being not just inherently unjust but a main vector of self-perpetuating domination, which potentially entails great deprivation for many, Honneth's indifference to the obstacles to equality seems a theoretical weakness, in light notably of his own political aims.

More worryingly still from a radical egalitarian perspective, the focus on the 'morality of the market', the idea that market interactions are underpinned by moral expectations that make the market itself a sphere of social freedom, means that the Equals' linking of economic inequality with democratic deficit risks being loosened. Honneth would disagree with this, since he claims precisely that those moral expectations with which modern individuals enter market-mediated economic interactions constrain the latter. On the labour market, for instance, historical progress, spurred on by the labour movement, ensured that principles such as fair wages, the right to a meaningful occupation or the right to have a say in economic organization, gradually became established (2014: 223–251). However, in his attempt to make room for market mechanisms as a central plank of a modernized version of socialism, Honneth's political model is close to Anderson's republican one. Like her, Honneth would refuse to view private property as incompatible with social freedom. He states this explicitly in relation to what private property allows the individual to do in relation to others, namely provide a secluded sphere separating her from others, thus allowing her to examine her own life plans (2014: 73–82). But this is not what is at stake here. Babeuf could well accept this sense of 'private' as being part of what 'sufficiency' requires. What is at stake rather is the appropriation of socially produced wealth, both in positive normative terms, from the point of view of the demand that 'happiness' be equally distributed, and negatively, from the point of view of injustice and how undue appropriation is its most potent vector.

Babeuf's egalitarian concern with property is not necessarily as naïve or ill-advised as the two philosophers would think. Babeuf focuses on private property as a productive factor, because ownership of land in his time was the major source of wealth creation. As explained though, his concern with privatization of land is a concern with the privatization of socially produced wealth. As it happens, many contemporary political thinkers today seek to develop alternative economic models that challenge the idea that a modern economy is necessarily based on the privatization of the means of wealth creation. For example, in relation to the theory of the firm, Isabelle Ferreras (2017) shows the fallacy that consists in collapsing the firm, an institution involving multiple constituencies with diverging rationalities, into the corporation, whose sole interest is the maximization of return on investment for the shareholders. It is a historically contingent fact that holding shares in the corporation should have translated into property rights that trump any other rights or interests, placing the workers under the near absolute command of the shareholders and their representatives within the firm, and sacrificing any interests or goals that might be pursued through the firm to the sole financial rewarding of the investors. On efficiency ground, it is not necessarily the case that market interactions require the private property of the means of production. There might be other ways to integrate the different agents involved in production (workers, managers, customers, communities) than through relations of unilateral obedience backed up by untouchable property rights (Borrits 2018). From a more basic critical perspective, Honneth, like Anderson, does not consider the link Babeuf had established between the accumulation of private property and the existence of class structures, which makes the social equality, and with it the equality in self-realization he aims for, impossible.

Notes

1 This might seem controversial, given Marx's famous dislike for equality. However, as Wood (2014) reminds us, Marx' and Engels' rejection of equality was based on the idea that it had *become* an obsolete goal, one that made sense at the time of the bourgeois (French) revolution, but should be replaced by the goal of the abolition of all classes. As Engels wrote: 'The idea of socialist society as the realm of equality is a one-sided French idea resting upon the old "liberty, equality, fraternity" – an idea which was justified as stage of development in its own time and place but which, like all the one-sided ideas of the earlier socialist schools, should now be

overcome' (cited in Wood 2014: 254). This shows that the socialists initially shared the goal of 'real equality' with the republicans. In fact, notwithstanding Marx's reservations, many socialists continuously defended the goals of full equality, G.A. Cohen being one of the most illustrious recent proponents. Marx' description of the first stage of socialism in the Critique of the Gotha Programme is very close to the ideal pursued by Babeuf in the manifesto of the plebeians.

2 This is the title of Philippe Buonarroti's recount of the thought and actions of the insurgents gathered around Babeuf in his *History of Babeuf's Conspiracy for Equality*, London, H. Hetherington, 1836. Buonarroti's book had a great influence on early socialist thinking, including Marx (Hobsbawn 2012: 22–23).

3 '*Semblables*' means 'those who are like me', not in terms of identity, not those who are 'the same as me', but 'similar to me', i.e., equal in terms of rights and duties. On Babeuf's sensitivity to female inequality, especially compared to the Jacobins, see Birchall (2016: 116–161, 184–190).

References

Anderson, Elizabeth. 1999. 'What is the Point of Equality?', *Ethics*, 109: 287–337.

Anderson, Elizabeth. 2008. 'How Should Egalitarians Cope with Market Risks?', *Theoretical Inquiries in Law*, 9(1): 239–270.

Anderson, Elizabeth. 2010a. *The Imperative of Integration*. Princeton: Princeton University Press.

Anderson, Elizabeth. 2010b. 'The Fundamental Disagreement between Luck Egalitarians and Relational Egalitarians', *Canadian Journal of Philosophy*, 36: 1–23.

Anderson, Elizabeth. 2014a. 'The Quest for Free Labor: Pragmatism and Experiments in Emancipation', *The Amherst Lecture in Philosophy*, 9: 1–44.

Anderson, Elizabeth. 2014b. 'A World turned upside down. Social Hierarchies and a New History of Egalitarianism', *Juncture*, 20(4): 258–267.

Anderson, Elizabeth. 2015a. 'Equality and Freedom in the Workplace. Recovering Republican Insights', *Social Philosophy and Policy*, 31(2): 48–69.

Anderson, Elizabeth. 2015b. 'Moral Bias and Corrective Practices: A Pragmatist Perspective', *Proceedings and Addresses of the APA*, 89.

Anderson, Elizabeth. 2016a. 'Thomas Paine's "Agrarian Justice" and the Origins of Social Insurance', in *Ten Neglected Classics of Philosophy*, pp. 55–83. Oxford: Oxford University Press.

Anderson, Elizabeth. 2016b. 'Common Property. How Social Insurance Became Confused with Socialism', *Boston Review*, July 25.

Anderson, Elizabeth. 2017. *Private Government: How Employers Rule Our Lives (And Why We Don't Talk About It)*. Princeton: Princeton University Press.

Babeuf, Gracchus. 2009. *Ecrits*. Pantin: Le Temps des Cerises.

Birchall, Ian. 2016. *The Spectre of Babeuf*. Chicago: Haymarket Books.

Borrits, Benoit. 2018. *Au-delà de la Propriété*. Paris: La Découverte.

Buonarroti, Philippe. 1836. *History of Babeuf's Conspiracy for Equality*, London: H. Hetherington.

Cohen, G.A. 1989. 'On the Currency of Egalitarian Justice', *Ethics*, 99(4): 906–944.

Cohen, G.A. 2009. *Why Not Socialism?* Princeton: Princeton University Press.

Deranty, J.-P. 2011. 'Reflective Critical Theory: A Systematic Reconstruction of Axel Honneth's Social Philosophy', in Danielle Petherbridge (ed.), *Axel Honneth: Critical Essays*, pp. 58–88. Leiden: Brill.

Deranty, J.-P. 2016a. 'Between Honneth and Rancière: Problems and Potentials of Contemporary Critical Theory', in K. Genel and J.-P. Deranty (eds), *Recognition versus Disagreement: A Critical Encounter on the Politics of Freedom, Equality and Identity*, pp. 33–80. New York: Columbia University Press.

Deranty, J.-P. 2016b. 'Exploited: Exploitation as a Subjective Category', *Southern Journal of Philosophy*, 54, 31–43.

Ferreras, Isabelle. 2017. *Firms as Political Entities: Democracy through Economic Bicameralism*. Cambridge: Cambridge University Press.

Fleischacker, Samuel. 2004. *A Short History of Distributive Justice*. London: Harvard University Press.

Frankfurt, Harry. 1987. 'Equality as Moral Ideal', *Ethics*, 98(1): 21–43.

Gomberg, Paul. 2007. *How to Make Opportunity Equal: Race and Contributive Justice*. London: Blackwell.

Hayat, Samuel. 2018. 'Working Class Socialism in France in 1848', in Douglas Moggach and Gareth Stedman-Jones (eds), *The 1848 Revolutions and European Political Thought*, pp. 120–139. Cambridge: Cambridge University Press.

Hobsbawn, Eric. 2012. *How to Change the World: Reflections on Marx and Marxism*. London: Yale University Press.

Honneth, Axel. 1995. *The Struggle for Recognition: The Moral Grammar of Social Conflicts*. Cambridge: Polity.

Honneth, Axel. 2007. 'Moral Consciousness and Class Domination. Some Problems in the Analysis of Hidden Morality', in A. Honneth (ed.), *Disrespect: The Normative Foundations of Critical Theory*, pp. 8–96. London: Wiley.

Honneth, Axel. 2012a. 'Labour and Recognition. A Redefinition', in A. Honneth (ed.), *The I in We*, pp. 56–75. Cambridge: Polity.

Honneth, Axel. 2012b. 'The Fabric of Justice. On the Limits of Contemporary Proceduralism', in A. Honneth (ed.), *The I in We: Studies in the Theory of Recognition*, pp. 35–55. London: Wiley.

Honneth, Axel. 2014. *Freedom's Right: The Social Foundations of Democratic Life*. Cambridge: Polity.

Honneth, Axel. 2017. *The Idea of Socialism: Towards a Renewal*. Cambridge: Polity.

Rancière, Jacques. 1991. *The Ignorant Schoolmaster: Five Lessons on Intellectual Emancipation*. Stanford University Press.

Rosanvallon, Pierre. 2013. *The Society of Equals*. London: Harvard University Press.

Scheidel, Walter. 2017. *The Great Leveller: Violence and the History of Inequality from the Stone Age to the Twenty-First Century*. Princeton University Press.

Wood, Allen. 2014. 'Marx on Equality', in A. Wood (ed.), *The Free Development of Each: Studies on Freedom, Right, and Ethics in Classical German Philosophy*, pp. 252–272. Oxford: Oxford University Press.

5

WORK JUSTICE BEYOND REDISTRIBUTION AND RECOGNITION

Denise Celentano

Neither the paradigm of redistribution nor that of recognition is primarily concerned with issues of labour justice.[1] Yet, it is hard to address work justice in the absence of some sort of economic justice, and without concerns for the quality of social relations. Even if it is not their direct concern, both paradigms convey normative views about work: distributive theories are concerned with unequal opportunities to compete in the labour market, while recognition views focus on social esteem for one's abilities. Whereas distributive views address work mostly in terms of fair conditions of access in occupations, recognition perspectives are concerned with the role of work in individuals' self-realization. Are we able to address objectionable work with the resources that these paradigms provide? How could they help us formulate a conception of labour justice?

In this chapter, I identify and discuss some normative assumptions about work underlying both paradigms, highlighting their strengths and weaknesses in this regard.[2] The discussion points out that if redistribution provides necessary but insufficient conditions of work justice, the recognition-based model does not help us address objectionable relational inequalities in the structures of work. Instead of focusing on only one dimension of justice (goods or recognition) external to work, or of defending an ideal of self-realization through work, I will suggest a multidimensional, deontological, and egalitarian perspective of work justice.

In section 1, I explore how two redistributive models – property-owning democracy and universal basic income – affect work justice, and then identify three common assumptions about work in the distributive paradigm. I conclude that distributive justice constitutes only one dimension of labour justice, consisting of the principle of equal freedom from material need for real free occupational choice, besides equality of opportunity. In section 2, I turn to the recognition paradigm to discuss four normative concepts of work that I identify in Axel Honneth's work: self-transformation, equal social dignity and autonomy, individual achievement, and social integration.

Dwelling in particular on the individual achievement model, in section 3 I argue for a relational perspective of work justice grounded on both a structural and interactional understanding of status inequalities at work, beyond an exclusively psychological account. I conclude that despite providing relevant resources for labour justice, the way distributive and recognition views set the problem of work prevent them from a fully fledged commitment to labour justice: further tools are necessary, distinctively rooted in work and its organization. In section 4, I briefly outline the contributive parity perspective, according to which no one should be prevented from contributing to social cooperation as a peer with regard to multiple dimensions of labour justice. Freely inspired by Nancy Fraser's concept of participatory party and by the relational egalitarian ideal of social equality, this view retains the virtues of both paradigms of redistribution and recognition while overcoming their limitations.[3] Rather than providing a full account of this alternative approach, the aim of this chapter is to explore aspects of the distributive and relational dimension of work justice in that they constitute key aspects of contributive parity.[4]

1 Work and distributive justice

Can labour injustice be adequately addressed in a distributive framework? According to Iris Young (1990), Elizabeth Anderson (1999), and Paul Gomberg (2007), this is not the case. On their view, theories of distributive justice do not account for the essentially relational and processual nature of the division of labour (Young 1990; Anderson 1999) and are grounded on a 'competitive' interpretation of the principle of equality of opportunity, which ends up reserving the less desirable tasks for the worst off, leaving the most desirable ones to a 'privileged class' of workers (Gomberg 2007: 66). Redistribution is said to narrow the focus of justice to the outcomes of production, overlooking the processes of production themselves (Young 1990; 2006). These authors provide crucial insights on the shortcomings of the distributive paradigm, yet it is also important not to lose sight of the relevance of redistribution for work justice.

Before outlining some general normative assumptions about work shared by most distributive views, I consider how two particular realizations of distributive justice, property-owning democracy and universal basic income, would affect work justice. I focus on them because they are among the most discussed distributive models in political philosophy, and authors have made claims about their impact on work.

1.1 How are property-owning democracy and universal basic income supposed to affect labour justice?

Rawls describes the property-owning democracy (POD) as the dispersion of private productive assets (which are not means of production) among the members of society, aimed at preventing their concentration in few hands (Rawls 2001: 139). Whereas welfare-state capitalism 'permits a small class to have a near monopoly of the means of production', POD prevents such monopoly by 'ensuring a widespread ownership of productive assets and human capital (that is, education and trained skills) at the beginning of each period' (Rawls 2001: 139). In *Justice as Fairness*, Rawls asserts that Marx's criticisms to the division of labour under capitalism would no longer be justified in a POD:

> To the objection against the division of labour under capitalism, we reply that the narrowing and demeaning features of the division should be largely overcome once the institutions of property-owning democracy are realized.
>
> (*Theory*, §79). (Rawls 2001: 177)

However, it is not clear how POD's dispersion of economic and human capital would result in the overcoming of the narrowing and demeaning aspects of work. Without specifications in this regard, Rawls seems to assume that, by addressing property, conditions of work will end up spontaneously improved. It can be identified here a typical aspect of distributive approaches: they tend to assume that *fair distribution* entails *fair contribution* (see section 1.3). Yet there is no self-evident connection between them, it should be explained and justified.

Given that Rawls leaves this issue unexplored, I examine two hypotheses that may justify POD's alleged improvements to work. In order not to neglect the different notions of capital used by Rawls when referring to POD, I suggest two possible interpretations of his assertions about the impact of POD on work, which I refer to as 'POD human capital hypothesis' (1) and 'POD economic capital hypothesis' (2).

According to the POD human capital hypothesis (1), the dispersion of human capital would equip individuals with increased skills and educational assets to compete more successfully in the labour market for limitedly available meaningful jobs. This hypothesis connects POD to meaningful work in the classical sense of fair equality of opportunity. However, while providing educational resources to individuals to navigate the labour market, the increase of skills and qualifications would not *in itself* improve the quality of work and of the division of labour. More likely, too many skilled people would be competing for still limitedly available meaningful jobs – which would likely lead most of them to take precisely 'narrowing and demeaning' work. Thus in their work, they would likely be confined to lower positions and perform different tasks than those they are qualified for.[5] The internal characteristics of work would not change for the mere fact that candidates are more skilled or qualified. If this certainly does not make the dispersion of educational opportunities less desirable, still it does not help us justifying Rawls' assertions about POD's alleged impact on the quality of work. Since this hypothesis is not compelling, let us turn to the second hypothesis.

According to the POD economic capital hypothesis (2), by equally providing individuals with economic security and freedom from material need, the dispersion of economic capital would enable real free choice of the occupation, so that people would prefer work characterized by variety, complexity, and self-direction.

This hypothesis reinterprets Rawls' response to Marx's objections on the deadening aspects of the division of labour under capitalism as pointing to what I suggest calling a *principle of equal freedom from material need*. By preventing individuals from taking the first job they find due to economic need, POD's economic capital dispersal would materially provide them with more room for actual choice of the occupation. Which choice would most likely go to various, complex, and self-directed work (Rawls 1999: §79), rather than to narrow and demeaning work – this pattern of preference being justified by the Aristotelian principle, according to which individuals naturally prefer to engage in relatively complex tasks (Rawls 1999: 372 ff.). This hypothesis could substantiate Rawls' statement about the positive effects of POD on the division of labour in so far as in a POD workers would be capital owners themselves and thus would no longer be forced to sell their labour power to capital owners, given that material need constitutes the very ground for accepting deadening working conditions.[6] By substantively increasing workers' room for occupational choice, POD would reinterpret the principle in positive, enabling terms.

Whereas POD involves both economic and human capital, universal basic income (UBI) consists of unconditional, regular cash transfers to individuals above the level of subsistence (Van Parijs and Vanderborght 2017). UBI is usually associated with two typical assumptions concerning labour justice, which can be referred to as the *exit argument* and the *bargaining argument*.[7] According to the former, UBI is expected to provide workers with an 'exit choice' from undesired occupations, since it liberates them from material need and economic insecurity. According to the latter, the decoupling between work and income would provide workers with more bargaining power, thereby indirectly forcing employers to improve the quality of work. For some, UBI is even expected to change the rules of the game of work, bringing about 'cooperative relations' (Block 2013).

However, also in this case one cannot assume that changed material conditions would necessarily lead to an organizational framework instead of another. The view that distributive measures alone suffice to reshape the structures of work can be referred to as a 'ripple effect' conception of labour justice (Celentano 2019a). According to this idea, by intervening on income, improvements on work conditions are expected to follow, even in the absence of any predictable outcome resulting from their connection.

This way, work justice ends up addressed as an *unintended consequence* of distributive justice, with no independent consideration, all the while normatively overburdening UBI. Yet divisions of labour involve practices, norms, habits, and relationships that have to be addressed and negotiated for their own sake: income is only one aspect. Like POD, however, UBI can provide the ground for equal freedom from material need for an enabling reinterpretation of the principle of free occupational choice. Yet unlike POD, it does not include concerns for educational equality of opportunity.

1.2 No contribution without redistribution

I have highlighted that if it is not clear how the wide dispersion of human capital would positively impact the division of labour, POD's economic capital dispersion and UBI would at least provide the material basis for real free occupational choice, which would likely prompt the choice for occupations that are lacking of 'narrowing and demeaning aspects'. Therefore, although it cannot replace work justice, distributive justice can be seen as constituting one necessary dimension of work justice, to be identified in the principle of *equal freedom from material need for real free occupational choice*, against the constraint of economic need in people's access to narrowing and demeaning occupations. To put this idea in a slogan: *no contribution without redistribution*.[8]

If equal freedom from material need is a key condition for work justice in that it substantiates free occupational choice along with equality of opportunity, yet neither POD's capital dispersion nor UBI would entail work justice as such. Redistribution is thus a necessary, and yet insufficient, dimension of work justice. First, socially necessary labour to meet key social needs characterized by monotony and routine would not disappear with the dispersion of economic capital. The question of how to share and organize socially necessary tasks remains unaddressed by POD and UBI – and as a matter of fact, societies respond to this problem through occupational segregation.[9] Second, the very existence of occupations entirely shaped around such tasks is not questioned by distributive justice. The nature itself of these occupations and the shape of the division of labour are taken as a given.[10] How are tasks bundled into occupations? Are there alternative ways to shape and share them across the division of labour? While distributive justice intervenes in the allocation of positions through equality of opportunity, we still need to look at the way these positions themselves are shaped within organizational regimes that create and reproduce relational inequalities (see Tomaskovic-Devey and Avent-Holt 2019). How are tasks bundled into occupations? Are there alternative ways to shape and share them across the division of labour? Third, if work is complex, so should be our approach. Beyond income, too many normatively relevant aspects of work lie out of the distributive scope of justice: issues of power and decision-making processes, labour social relations, the organization of the tasks and the nature of occupations, the social division of labour time. Therefore, a more comprehensive view is necessary.

1.3 Three common distributive views on work

More generally, three common normative assumptions about work – both implicit and explicit – can be distinguished in the distributive paradigm. I suggest to refer to them as the *external justice*, the *derivative* or *one-dimensional*, and the *personal preference* views.

First, the *external justice* view approaches work 'from the outside', restricting its normative concerns to the 'door' of work, as it were. Typically via two principles: *free occupational choice* (FOC) and *equality of opportunity* (EO).[11] The widespread convergence on FOC in the distributive literature goes with an essentially negative interpretation of the principle, according to which individuals enjoy free occupational choice to the extent that they are not legally coerced by an external authority to take a particular occupation.[12] This reading does not point to the positive, *actual* possibilities of choice of the occupation. As for EO, this is perhaps the most frequently evoked principle in distributive debates when it comes to work. In broad terms, the core idea is that people ought to be provided with goods and opportunities to enable them to compete in the labour market on a fair basis. A problem with fair competition is that it does not change the number, shape, and quality of tasks and positions available for which people compete, nor does it affect the organizational aspects of work. It is inherent to the logic of competition that some will lose the race despite their skills and qualifications. If some positions are entirely 'narrowing and demeaning', some parts of the population will be inevitably reserved for them regardless of their abilities.

Overall, what these principles demand is that access into occupations be unconstrained and fairly competitive. To be sure, these are very important requirements, yet they exclusively intervene in the phase that 'precedes' work: once these distributive conditions are ensured, it is implied that what happens in the sphere of work is individuals' business, not a matter of justice. Nothing is said about the internal aspects of work and about how work and the division of labour are to be made fairer. All concerns for equality are confined to opportunities and resources: no equality is envisaged *within* the contexts of work.

A classic example of the external justice perspective can be found in the debate around the 'Malibu surfer' and the duties of reciprocity requiring all to 'do their part' in social cooperation (Rawls 2001: 179). This debate exclusively turns around the problem of whether we have a moral obligation to work in order to be entitled to distributive benefits, without engaging with the internal configurations of work, and, more importantly, overlooking the relevance of the latter to the former. Yet any answer to the should-we-work question should address the how-work-actually-is-and-should-be questions, for relations of domination, meaninglessness, status subordination, occupational segregation, heteronomy, and so on would not be altered by any answer we might give to the should-we-work question alone. In contrast with a purely external approach, a work justice perspective also considers the *internal* structures of work along with work relations, power asymmetries, organizational cultures and norms, and the nature of the occupations.

Second, consider what may be called the *derivative* or *one-dimensional* view, according to which injustices in the division of labour are to be addressed through goods redistribution (i.e., income, opportunities). As seen earlier with regard to POD and UBI, on this view, once distributive justice is ensured, aspects of work are expected to become fair – that is, fair distribution is expected to 'ripple' fair contribution. The *derivative* view tends to see work and the division of labour as mere by-products of income and goods redistribution, it does not see them as discrete realities raising distinct, irreducible normative concerns. Yet even in a perfectly fair distributive world, where no one is forced in any occupation and everyone benefits from equality of opportunity, there would be the problem of socially necessary work. Norms regulating goods allocation are unable to address organizational issues about the fairest way to share socially necessary tasks. For the same reason, providing unconditional income to each does not automatically guarantee that, say, the division of labour in the household ends being gendered.

Finally, what can be referred to as the *personal preference* view dismisses work as a matter of private preferences lying outside of the scope of justice. Intermeshing rationales converge in this view: concerns for value pluralism and its alleged incompatibility with any normative understanding of work (Arneson 1987; Kymlicka 2002), and the idea that justice is essentially a matter of goods redistribution (*external justice* view). Against the idea that work is merely a private matter outside of justice, some observations can be suggested.

First, the division of labour is part of the basic structure (Young 2006), which is, according to Rawls, 'the primary subject of justice'. As a system of 'social institutions that fit together and shape the division of advantages of social cooperation', the basic structure includes, as Rawls says, also the structure of the economy and the family (Rawls 1999, 6 ff.). Not only individuals' lives are profoundly affected by work and the way it is organized, mediating access to other valuable goods – such us income, social esteem, and power – and powerfully affecting their chances to pursue their plans of life. Work is also the core of societies' very functioning, the condition of their existence and reproduction, the precondition of redistribution itself. Workplaces and organizations powerfully create, consolidate, and reproduce economic, social, and power inequalities, making them durable (Tomaskovic-Devey and Avent-Holt 2019; Tilly 1998). Therefore, work exceeds the individualizing account conveyed by distributive views: beyond the private sphere of individuals' conceptions of the good, it is rooted in structures determining the organizational shape of society. Through principles of free occupational choice and equality of opportunity, distributive views do not go beyond the point of access into occupations, after which we are left with a norm-free zone. While the category of 'preference' individualizes the problem of work and reduces it to an exclusively psychological matter, work should be described as first of all a social relation embedded in social structures and a form of participation in the interdependent system of social cooperation. Second, the private preference view presupposes an antithesis between pluralism (at the cost of leaving work outside of justice) and ethical concerns for self-realization through work (which overlook pluralism), which can be overcome by shifting the focus from the ethical desirability of work to concerns for fair social cooperation, in a way compatible with pluralistic understandings of the role of work in a good life (see section 4).

Shared by most distributive accounts – either explicitly or implicitly – the external, derivative, and personal preference views have prevented theories from a full commitment to work justice. Nonetheless, despite the shortcomings of the paradigm, distributive justice should not be dismissed *en bloc*. Work justice cannot be decoupled from distributive justice (recall the principle of equal freedom from material need for real free occupational choice), even though distributive justice ought to be considered as only one dimension of work justice.

In conclusion, despite Rawls' and UBI's advocates allusions about improvements to the division of labour, like most distributive views they provide a partial, essentially external response to work justice. Another perspective, distinctively attentive to the internal configurations of work and its structure, is thus necessary beyond redistribution. The perspective of work justice that I suggest aims to provide a critical-normative framework defining the terms and conditions of fair social cooperation, meaning the way work is conceived of and organized on a plurality of scales. Before outlining some traits of this perspective, I dwell on the recognition view.

2 Work in the recognition paradigm

Theorists of recognition have paid special attention to work, with no equivalent in distributive debates. Loading it with psychological and ethical meanings, they argue that individuals' normative demands at work exceed the scope of the economic discourse: more fundamentally than exploitation, they say, what is at stake is recognition. This view emphasizes the (inter)subjective aspects of work, being primarily interested in individuals' self-realization.

Since Axel Honneth's theoretical perspective is mostly concerned with preventing harms to individuals' positive relation to the self, he tends to address the problem of work as a matter of the *good life* rather than *justice*. Yet, his consideration of work has considerably evolved over the years: from the subject's psychological experience of work, his focus has shifted to the socially integrative function of the division of labour. In what follows, I identify and discuss four main normative concepts of work in Honneth's intellectual path: work as self-transformation (2.1); work as equal social dignity and autonomy (2.2); work as individual achievement (2.3); and work as social integration (2.4). Dwelling on the individual achievement model, I then suggest a sociologically informed alternative perspective freely inspired by Nancy Fraser's status-based concept of recognition and by the relational egalitarian ideal of social equality.

2.1 Work as self-transformation

Inspired by Marx and Hegel, the normative concept of work as self-transformation is developed by Honneth mostly in the 1980s (1982; 1991). Formulated against the prevailing instrumentalist readings of work, this model considers work as an experience of self-transformation, both expressive and formative, through identity formation and learning. It enables Honneth to criticize the capitalist organization of work 'as a socially alienating relationship', in that it separates the worker from the labour process (Honneth 1982 [1980]: 33).[13]

This model presents some problems. First, it is hardly compatible with pluralistic understandings of the meaning of work in the good life co-existing in contemporary society, where the 'work ethic' is increasingly called into question (Weeks 2011).[14] One could value leisure or cultivating friendship more than work as self-transformative experiences, for example. Second, one can identify oneself in one's labour while still suffering from objectionable working conditions. Consider, for instance, certain categories of freelance workers – e.g., the 'entreprecariat' (Lorusso 2016) – particularly exposed to the logic of self-exploitation and 'hope labour', who emotionally over-invest and highly identify in their work. They can express and train themselves through work – as required by the self-transformative model – thus technically speaking they are not 'alienated', yet they experience peculiar forms of self-exploitation that this model does not capture.

Consider also the case of 'dirty work' (Hughes 1951). Most of it is low skilled, and, as for the expressive side, dirty workers struggle to express initiative and creativity in their work (Roca 2010). Even though this would help us to question the ethical desirability of dirty work, since dirty work does not fit the model of self-transformation neither formatively nor expressively, cleaning remains work that has to be done because the social need to live in a clean environment cannot be eliminated. This is the 'somebody's got to do it problem', which distributive views do not address either: how to organize dirty work across society, and thus make sure that the burdens of alienation, as it were, be not reserved for the worst off?

Therefore we have to broaden our perspective beyond the subjective experience of work, emphasized by the self-transformative model of recognition, towards its social organization: that is, beyond concerns for ethical self-realization, to concerns for fairness in social cooperation.

2.2 *Work as equal social dignity and autonomy*

The second normative concept of work points to unequal access to recognition and autonomy in the workplace due to class-related occupational inequalities. In the article 'Moral Consciousness and Class Domination' (1995), Honneth investigates workers' practices of implicit resistance to deprived social dignity. Resistance to the rhythm of work is interpreted as a manifestation of workers' attempt to regain autonomous control over the working process, implicitly pointing to a counterfactual ideal of self-directed work. On this view, conflicts at work should not be reduced to merely distributive disputes over 'quantifiable compensations' (Honneth 1995: 216). Note that the core of the theory of recognition developed later begins to emerge here through concepts such as 'immaterial deprivation', 'unequal distribution of social dignity', and 'asymmetrical distribution of cultural and psychological life chances'.

The focus here is no longer on the psychical experience of work as self-transformation: now Honneth's concerns for workers' subjectivities are conceptualized through class inequalities in essentially two ways. First, the class division of society produces 'different occupational positions', while individualizing success through a system of evaluation focused on individual achievements. Given such strongly individualized ascriptions of respect and intelligence, lower occupational groups see their possibilities of self-respect 'drastically restricted' within 'a lasting inequality in the distribution of chances for social recognition'. Workers respond through 'uncoordinated attempts to gain, or regain, social honor' in order to 'symbolically raise the status of one's own work activity' (Honneth 1995: 218). Second, class society 'codetermines to a great extent the degree of freedom and control of individual work activities'. That is, members of the lower classes in the lowest ranks of the labour hierarchy 'are forced into monotonous work activities which offer little or no opportunity for individual initiative' (Honneth 1995: 219). Overall, in this account low-ranked workers have few chances to experience *autonomy* and *recognition* at work.

Given that it is no longer restricted to the subjective experience of work as in the self-transformation model, but also takes into account class inequalities and occupational hierarchies, this model could have enabled Honneth to develop a relationally sensitive counterfactual ideal of *social equality* at work. Also, since this account does not reduce work to goods and income, it could have allowed him to integrate structural concerns with psychological ones. However, Honneth subsequently leaves aside this focus on class-related occupational hierarchies and their intermeshing with social recognition, turning his attention to universal psychological and ethical demands of recognition. From a potentially multidimensional perspective, where the economic aspects of class are intermeshed with status and recognition dynamics, he later shifts to a one-dimensional view.

2.3 Work as individual achievement

According to Honneth's theory of recognition, in order to have a positive relation to the self, individuals need to experience recognition through love, rights, and esteem the three spheres of recognition. Given its relevance for work, let us give a look at the third one. Whereas in *The Struggle for Recognition* Honneth broadly refers to social esteem for one's 'talents and abilities' without specific reference to work – to 'ways of life' and 'lifestyles' instead – he later explicitly connects it with the meritocratic principle of performance at work, also known as *Leistungsprinzip*. This way, the 'productive citizen' becomes the subject of the third sphere, narrowing esteem to an exclusively labour-mediated concept (Fraser and Honneth 2003: 135–159). This model presents some problems.

First, since modernity has challenged the group-based logic of honour allocation, esteem is to be earned through effort – people *compete* for it (Honneth 1996: 122). The model overlooks the structural impediments to achievement, and tends to attribute any failure to 'achieve' entirely to the individual.[15]

Second, an internal differentiation of the third sphere of recognition between esteem as *individual achievement* and *occupational prestige* would have helped to capture more nuanced dynamics involved in the logic of esteem at work, in a way more suited to a critical perspective. The former refers to the worker's individual performance, whereas the latter points to the social worth attributed to occupational categories (see Kantzara 2007; Hughes 2017 [1958]). In other words, whereas *achieved esteem* tends to rely upon individuals' performance, *ascribed esteem* relies on the prestige already attached to occupations.[16] Occupational prestige is relatively independent from individuals' performances (Dahrendorf 1972: 101): rather than being 'peculiar to the individual; it is historic' (Hughes 2017 [1958]: 57), therefore it reintroduces a pre-modern element of ascription in the modern logic of social worth attribution. Nonetheless, Honneth does not distinguish between them (Fraser and Honneth 2003: 143).

To be sure, these concepts cannot be entirely separated from one another. On the one hand, regardless of one's effort, the low esteem historically 'pre-attributed' to a low prestige occupation is likely to limit chances to get esteem within that occupation. On the other hand, the reverse is also true: workers in high prestige occupations can benefit from 'unearned' recognition regardless of their actual contribution. As the sociologist Everett

Hughes pointed out (2017 [1958]: 71), some professions are rewarded with esteem independently of the internal features of the job and of the quality of individual contributions. It is not much in some inherent excellence of professionals' performances that their esteem is grounded, but in the collective efforts of those who work in such professions to persuade the public of a certain social image of their activity. In their 'journey towards respectability', groups compete with other groups for the social affirmation of their body of work activities – that is, for their professionalization (Hughes 2017 [1958]: 44).

Occupational prestige and esteem are thus intermeshed but distinct. Without differentiating them, one would not be able to grasp the difference between the relative control that individuals exercise over the social outcome of their contribution and the esteem for their abilities, and the social worth already attached to occupations as an outcome of collective struggles for professionalization. From this perspective, to reframe Honneth's own example, the acknowledgement of gendered housework as 'work' (Fraser and Honneth 2003: 148) is better understood in terms of socially ranked worth which resonates women's overall social status, rather than of achievement as individual merit.

Finally, given its intrinsically selective and differential nature, the relation of achievement with equality is certainly complex. Recall that people do not give esteem easily (Brennan and Pettit 2004). Thus in this framework, equality ends up being represented as exclusively a matter of rights and of the formal status of citizens (the second sphere of recognition), while work essentially remains the realm of hierarchies and inequalities. The possibility to think in a more egalitarian way of social relations *within* work seems thus dismissed from the start in this model. While important for individuals' self-relation, esteem for one's abilities does not challenge organizationally embedded status inequalities like occupational segregation, the division between conception and execution, the gendered division of labour. I address this problem in section 4.

2.4 Work as social integration

Inspired by Hegel's and Durkheim's thoughts on the integrative functions of the social division of labour, in 2010 Honneth shifts from concerns for individual achievement to solidaristic cooperation. This model criticizes the social exclusion from being valuable contributors to the division of labour.

In his article 'Work and Recognition: A Redefinition' (2010), Honneth integrates Hegel's view on the market system with Durkheim's insights, according to which a sense of belonging to the community is provided by the social division of labour as an 'organic form of solidarity'. Mutually recognizing their contribution to 'the common good', he points out, 'gives them a sense of being connected to each other' (Honneth 2010). The very idea of collective cooperation is said to have consequences on the nature and the quality of the tasks themselves, which should be complex and demanding enough to enable a 'meaningful connection' with one's work and that of others.

This concept of work presents the advantage of avoiding the shortcomings of a merely subjective reading of work, emphasizing the social interdependence of individual contributions. However, it tends to provide a merely horizontal account of the division of labour. Domination and oppressive organizational inequalities in the division of labour are not represented in the 'organic solidarity' framework, which seems to have expectations of almost philanthropic cooperative motivations in the actors.

2.5 *Normative barriers*

I have examined four normative concepts of work identified in Honneth's intellectual path. The discussion justifies the conclusion that, overall, some 'normative barriers' prevent the paradigm of recognition from providing the resources for a satisfying conception of labour justice.

First, its concerns for the psychological dimension of work do not go with concerns for the structures of work (*structure-blindness* barrier). One can hardly criticize people for esteeming a talented musician or for not esteeming a mediocre performer, but one can and should criticize status-based occupational segregation. As I will argue shortly (3.1), a structural understanding of social relations is necessary besides a merely psychological one, to overcome the shortcomings of the private preference view.

Second, it addresses normative problems of work essentially, if not exclusively, *as* problems of recognition, overlooking the normative specificity of the other dimensions involved – for example, the economic and political dimensions (*one-dimensionality* barrier).

Finally, its strongly perfectionist standpoint makes it hardly compatible with alternative, legitimate interpretations of the role of work in the good life in a pluralist society, like that refusing work as the main source of self-realization emphasized by post-work theorists (*pluralism-blindness* barrier).

In what follows, I provide some critical observations on one-dimensionality, and address the other barriers in the subsequent section.

2.5.1 *The problem with recognition monism*

According to Honneth, social and political demands can be traced back to the common source of recognition, which is supposed to shape not only the sphere of distribution (Fraser and Honneth 2003: 134) but also that of contribution (Fraser and Honneth 2003: 155–156). That is, even 'the social demarcation of professions – indeed, the shape of the social division of labour as a whole' is said to result from the 'cultural valuation of specific capacities for achievement' (Fraser and Honneth 2003: 154). While no doubt the reasons behind pay differentials are not purely economic, and the division between professionals and nonprofessionals is also one of esteem and prestige (Hughes 2017 [1958]; Young 1990), yet in this account the concept of recognition as achievement looks descriptively and normatively overburdened. This principle alone is expected to explain and address too many problems: the exclusion of women from the labour market as well as their devalued contribution in the household; people's pay differentials and inequalities in wealth and income, and even the structuration of the division of labour and the social demarcation of professions.

Yet structures of the capitalist economy and the division of labour are not psychological products. Normative conflicts about work do not merely turn around claims of recognition, the motivational constellation of people at work being rich and various (Kohn and Schooler 1978; Dubet 2013). For instance, it can concern the actual shape of the division of labour in itself. As Andrew Sayer (2011: 92) points out,

> arguments within work teams are often not so much about what each team member gets in terms of pay or other reward, but what each person contributes. . . . There might also be objections if some team members monopolized all the interesting and pleasant tasks, leaving the less attractive ones to others.

Consider the case most cited by Honneth as representative of work misrecognition: gendered domestic labour. Even if recognized as 'real work', this recognition would not make *in itself* the division of housework fairer. Interestingly, the normative remedy that Honneth proposes for the social devaluation of women's domestic work is monetary recognition (Rössler 2007), which is also the remedy suggested by Rawls (2001). Quite surprisingly, distributive and recognition views seem not to differ much in their response to the gendered division of labour. Both accounts lack of tools to make the division of labour fairer beyond considerations of pay or esteem, looking at the division of labour itself.

In his recent reflection, Honneth himself seems to be aware of the relevance of multidimensionality. In *The Idea of Socialism* (2017), he points out that one reason for which the idea of socialism has ended up losing appeal lies in its narrow concerns for the economic sphere. He emphasizes the relevance of the notion of 'functional differentiation' of the spheres inspired by Niklas Luhmann and Michael Walzer: socialism's 'economic fundamentalism' (or 'economic monism'), he says, was a 'fatal misunderstanding' in that it did not acknowledge the 'independent moral logic of other spheres' (Honneth 2017: 76 ff.). However, the same could be applied to Honneth's own views: shouldn't also recognition leave room for other spheres of differentiation, without assuming it as the sole relevant dimension of social reality and normativity – of the division of labour?

3 The relational dimension of labour justice

In contrast with recognition's 'structure-blindness', the status perspective on recognition suggested by Nancy Fraser (2003) looks more promising in that it can enable us to shift from concerns for individuals' psychology to the social structures that make social inequalities at work durable and systemic. Before exploring this point, a look at the sociological research on status can be of help. How do status inequalities and the division of labour intertwine?

3.1 Status inequality and the division of labour: insights from sociology

Status is a belief of assumed competence that works as a normative expectation supported by distinguishing traits or biasing factors (gender, race, class). It propagates through small behaviours that reflect implicit rules about how people should be treated, thereby acquiring the force of a 'shared reality' (Ridgeway 2016). These constitute what the sociologist Tomaskovic-Devey (2014) refers to as the 'interactional basis of systemic social inequalities'. Status-based behaviours' cumulative outcome is that individuals from more advantaged groups are 'systematically tracked into positions of greater resources and power' (Ridgeway 2014). Thus beyond individuals' psychology, status beliefs turn into 'durable inequalities' embedded in social structures and institutions (Tilly 1998; Ridgeway et al. 2009).

Work and organizations crucially participate in the reproduction of status inequalities (Tomaskovic-Devey 2014; Stainback and Tomaskovic-Devey 2012; Tilly 1998). Usually defined as the differential distribution of women and men, black and whites, across different occupations and workplaces (Hinze 2007: 617), occupational segregation is an example of the psychological, interactional, and structural intermeshing of status inequalities and the division of labour. To begin with, when applying for the same jobs, pairs of candidates with identical credentials, skills, recommendations, and professional experience are distinguished by status judgements (Pratto 1999; Sidanius and Pratto 1999; Bendick 2007). The more valued the jobs, the more likely the highest status groups will take them; conversely, the more certain jobs are taken by low status groups, the more they are devalued and deskilled (Tomaskovic-Devey 1993).

Besides hiring processes, status inequalities also shape the very structure of organizations, or 'inequality regimes' (Acker 2006). According to Charles Tilly (1998: 79), pervasive categorical inequalities – men/women, black/white, rich/poor – affect the structures of all sorts of organization, which 'import' 'exterior categories' of inequality (e.g., ritualized gender differences, sex-typed occupations, etc.) and make them match their 'interior categories' (e.g., manager/employee, secretary/director, etc.). For instance, hotels reproduce divisions of labour categorically organized around racial and gender boundaries because they are already familiar to their employees

(Tilly 1998: 96–97). Besides the lower costs of emulating existing organizational models, such inequalities persist in organizations insofar as they facilitate exploitation and opportunity hoarding from the most favoured members of organizations (Tilly 1998: 81–82).

Occupational segregation follows from attempts to prevent 'status dilemmas' as well. Status dilemmas describe the experience of mismatch between the expected traits of a worker's role and her actual traits (Hughes 2017 [1958]: 106 ff.). For instance, a 'black doctor' or a 'woman engineer' typically engender status dilemmas (Hughes 2017 [1958]: 142–149). Societies respond to them, and to the 'status pain' they cause, through segregation, either by putting out of sight individuals who do not comply with status expectations (for instance by preventing customers from coming into contact with them) or by assigning such individuals to occupations that are expected to suit their status (Hughes 2017 [1958]: 50). For example, 'a black sociologist would teach race studies and a woman engineer design household appliances' (Kantzara 2007); likewise, the black doctor will likely have black patients (Hughes 2017 [1958]: 113). Self-selection is a cognitive response of low-status groups to avoid occupations that may bring role conflicts and status inconsistencies as well. An example of the internalization of status hierarchies, which pre-emptively circumscribes even what individuals believe it is legitimate to claim (see Ridgeway and Nakagawa 2017), is that women tend to propose lower starting wages than men (Säve-Söderbergh 2007).

Segregation is not only horizontal but also vertical. The scarce presence of low-status groups in positions of authority and responsibility is a widely documented phenomenon known as the 'glass ceiling' (Federal Glass Ceiling Commission 1995; Cook and Glass 2013). Women are underrepresented in higher-status occupations while being 'overrepresented in traditionally female professions that have also historically been accorded less status' (Hinze 2007; EIGE 2017; Bettio et al. 2009). Furthermore, in occupations where the participation of women is higher, both men and women earn less than in those where men prevail. Note that race is no less segregating, due to 'employer preferences, structural discrimination, job queues, differential access to social networks' (Wingfield and Skeete 2016: 47). Racial minorities are concentrated in badly paid and low status jobs (Acker 1990; Tomaskovic-Devey 1993): they tend to have jobs with fewer responsibilities, and their responsibilities are usually associated with their status, for instance they are asked to supervise other racial minorities or to manage 'diversity programs' (Wingfield and Skeete 2016: 49–52).[17]

It must be clear at this point why, 'if as a society we are to directly challenge sex and racial segregation and the resulting inequalities, we will have to do it in workplaces' (Tomaskovic-Devey 1993: 3). Yet the impact of occupational segregation goes beyond the workplace: besides lowering chances of promotion and career prospects, 'location in occupations with less income, authority, and prestige also decreases the amount of power women hold in both public and private realms' (Hinze 2007: 619).

3.2 Structural and interactional status inequality at work

Labour hierarchies do not merely embody organizational, rational, or efficient responses to cooperative problems. They also reflect socially established scales of worth among people (Tomaskovic-Devey 1993; Branch 2011). Work plays a crucial role in the social distribution of status. Not only our social standing co-determines what occupations and roles we are more likely to get, but our occupation and role tend to shape our social standing as well. In other words, one's social status affects one's access to occupations (as when, for example, a woman is seen as 'more suited' to certain occupational roles, such as secretary or caregiver), and one's occupational position produces effects on one's social status (e.g., occupations associated with low social standing). Therefore, status inequalities are somehow *circularly* involved in labour structures. I suggest referring to this phenomenon as the 'status circle', which emphasizes the circular involvement of social status in the division of labour.[18] As a major system of reproduction of status inequalities, work lies at the core of the status circle.

Given the mutual enhancement between the 'small behaviours' acting on status beliefs and the status-biased shape of the division of labour which perpetuates them, a normative consideration of work in the relational dimension requires that social inequalities be considered as both *interactional* and *structural*.[19] In other words, we cannot restrict our consideration of social relations at work to the psychological dynamics of esteem, as Honneth's achievement model.

Interactional status inequality refers to interactions through which individuals express differential respect to each other, consolidating status beliefs in everyday life. For example, actors in organizations tend to express typical behavioural patterns such as deference towards superiors or scorn, elitism and disdain towards subordinate members (Néron 2015: 13; Fourie 2012; 2015; Runciman 1967: 223). It is at this level of repeated micro-interactions (Ridgeway's 'small behaviors') that status inequalities acquire the force of a 'shared reality' and affect the shape of organizations. For instance, Michael Walzer's 'insolence of office' (1983: 133) is an interactional example of a more general status inequality between 'professionals' and 'nonprofessionals' (Young 1990).

Taken alone, the interactional level is narrow and its critical potential limited. For there can be objectionable social inequalities even in the absence of any explicit one-to-one disrespectful behaviour.[20] One could be treated respectfully by single individuals in the workplace in everyday interactions while remaining occupationally segregated. In other words, one can benefit from interactional status equality all the while suffering from systemic, *structural* status inequality.

Consider the example of eighteenth-century masters and servants. The *interactional* side of inequality points to expressions of deference, scorn, and disrespect, and generally the behavioural apparatus sustaining a superior/inferior relation. However, social inequality embedded in the same relation should be addressed also from another point of view which takes into account their *structural* social inequality, for deference and scorn reflect and strengthen a scale of worth shaping the organizational inequality between people entitled to being served, and people having little choice but serving them.[21]

If status inequalities persist because of the mutual enforcement of micro-interactions and organizational regimes, the latter ensuring their durability over time (Tilly 1998), then a normative perspective concerned with the relational dimension of labour justice should not be restricted to the mere psychological and interactional aspects. Shedding light on what I have referred to as the structural side of social inequality enables us to grasp the socially embedded nature of behavioural status inequality.

Note that the normative models examined earlier are of little help in this framework. Even though all workers should have opportunities for recognition, the achievement model tends to justify social inequalities rather than helping us to address the objectionable ones. Despite being desirable for the positive relation to the self, esteeming individuals for their abilities while leaving them occupationally segregated does not help us breaking the status circle. The achievement model of recognition is ultimately compatible with harsh status inequalities in the division of labour: being concerned with psychological dynamics of social esteem, it overlooks the structural embeddedness of status inequalities. The response is that either we give everyone opportunities to be esteemed, which is not much different from a classic distributive equality of opportunity perspective, or, as I will suggest, we introduce more substantive concerns for equality in social relations of work, which are not present in Honneth's recognition paradigm. In what follows, I explore this alternative.

3.3 Breaking the 'status circle': social equality and status-based recognition

If status inequalities are the reason why inequality is 'inherently wrong' (Rawls 2001: 131; Scanlon 2000) and shape the structure of organizations which mediate people's access to other valuable goods (Tomaskovic-Devey and Avent-Holt 2019), then the 'status circle' cannot be neglected in theories of justice. Nor should status be treated as a by-product of income redistribution, in that it cannot be simply inferred from one's property or income: status follows its own logic and has an 'independent force' (Ridgeway 2014).

While esteem is important to individuals' relation to the self, the relational dimension of labour justice requires to focus also on the structures of work. In order to tackle labour-related social inequalities, I explore two resources alternative to the achievement model of esteem: the relational egalitarian concept of social equality (1) and Nancy Fraser's status-based view of recognition (2).

1 The relational egalitarian ideal of social equality points to 'a society that is not marked by status divisions such that one can place different people in hierarchically ranked categories' (Miller 1998: 23). Taking the idea of the equal moral worth of persons, or of 'universal moral equality' (Anderson 1999: 313) seriously, the ideal of a society of equals looks hardly compatible with a division of labour deeply affected by status inequalities. If one aim of the relational egalitarian project is to examine 'what kinds of institutions and practices a society must put in place if it is to count as a society of equals' (Scheffler 2015: 21), then understanding what forms of work and division of labour better help to realize this ideal is crucial. The issue is usually addressed with regard to distributive patterns. By analogy, a work justice perspective asks: what forms of work help to realize, or undermine, the ideal of a society of equals? What work structures minimize status inequalities while maximizing individuals' chances to get social esteem?
2 Even if Fraser's emphasis is on status *recognition* rather than on *social equality*, the former could be interpreted as a species of the genus 'social equality'. In this interpretation, recognition constitutes a particular dynamic within a more general concern for the quality of egalitarian social relations. Since relational egalitarians are concerned with social status rather than identity-formation, their relatively de-psychologized reading of social relations reveals a potential closeness to Nancy Fraser's status-based notion of recognition. Once the concept of recognition is unburdened from its ethical and psychological load, there is more room for it to get close to concerns for justice and social equality.

Note that in Fraser's account, the ideal of equality is involved to the extent that removing obstacles to recognition is functional to establishing participatory parity. As she points out (2003: 210), the concept of participatory parity refers to a 'radicalization of widely held folk norms of equality' and a '*radical democratic interpretation* of equal autonomy' (2003: 229). In this sense, participatory parity looks like a relational egalitarian concept with a distinctively *enabling* nuance: instead of merely demanding that individuals be *treated* as equals, it demands that they be *enabled to participate* in social life *as peers*. From this perspective, in the sphere of work being treated as equals entails that individuals ought to be enabled to contribute on a peer basis.

If such synthesis between the concept of social equality and participatory parity is sound, then the normative grids that we were seeking for the relational dimension of labour justice can be found here. The ideal of *contributive parity* that I suggest, integrates the virtues of these perspectives by demanding that no one be prevented from contributing to social cooperation as a peer both in the interactions and in the structures of work. With regard to the *interactional* side of status inequality at work, it asserts that status-biased behaviours in interactions are objectionable because they fail to treat workers as equals, misconstruing their position and tasks in the division of labour as indicators of their worth. As for the *structural* side, positions and tasks in the division of labour ought not be reserved for certain people by virtue of their status, and their position, role, and tasks in the division of labour ought not determine their social status. In other words, interactional and structural status inequality are seen in this perspective as mutually reinforcing impediments to individuals' peer contribution to social cooperation, incompatible with the ideal of a society of equals. It is demanded that no one be treated as an inferior because of her role in the division of labour, and that the division of labour does not perpetuate individuals' social inferiority either. It follows that strategies to rethink work and its organization to minimize status inequality are to be implemented. Relational egalitarian accounts mostly focus on workplace democracy as a remedy to relational inequalities in the workplace (Anderson 2017; Néron 2015). However, given the organizational nature of such inequalities, their being rooted in the shape of the division of labour and in the very way we conceive of occupations, further remedies are necessary.

4 Contributive parity: revisiting Nancy Fraser's model

The discussion has shown that, despite their differences, the paradigms of redistribution and recognition share some relevant shortcomings in their approach to work.

First, by confining work to the sphere of particular ethical views about the good life, both paradigms end up excluding work from the scope of justice. They do this in different ways. Distributive theories circumscribe the scope of justice to the 'outside of work', confining their concerns to the principles of free occupational choice and equality of opportunity, work being essentially a matter of private preferences. Recognition theory addresses work in a teleological way, as a matter of subjective self-realization rather than justice. Therefore, in different ways, for different reasons and through different vocabularies, they converge in the *privatization* of work. Either defending an 'external' approach to labour justice (distributive theories) or setting the problem as an ethical matter of the good life (recognition paradigm), both ultimately exclude work from considerations of justice. Further critical-normative tools to distinguish unjust forms of work and division of labour are thus necessary.

Second, in different ways, both distributive and recognition accounts are essentially *one-dimensional*. The resources they provide for labour justice are either distributive *or* recognition-based respectively. Just as distributive theorists consider work fairness as a sort of collateral by-product of redistribution, the recognition paradigm considers the normative issues raised by work as essentially matters of recognition. This way, they overlook the distinct normativity of work and the division of labour. We need a multidimensional account that addresses normative problems risen by the division of labour in themselves, not as redistributive by-products or epiphenomena of recognition. Since labour justice also involves concerns for structural social relations, issues of power and decision-making processes, the nature of tasks and occupations and their organization, other dimensions are to be taken into account.

Finally, neither distributive nor recognition views express concerns for equality at work. At most, equality is conceptualized as a matter of material goods (even in the recognition paradigm) outside of work and its structures. This limits their critical potential with regard to objectionable work structures.

Nancy Fraser's model may offer some resources to overcome these barriers because of its multidimensional, deontological, and egalitarian aspects. Despite these advantages, most attention in the literature has been given to Honneth's conception of work, benefitting of comparatively far less consideration in philosophical reflections on work.

Consider, first, *multidimensionality*. Her model conveys a 'polycentric and multilateral' view of justice (Fraser and Honneth 2003: 209) that rejects the duality between redistribution and recognition as a false antithesis. They are rather seen as 'inextricably intertwined', in a relation of 'mutual irreducibility and co-implication' (2003: 208).[22] To our purpose, this approach can be of help in understanding work as simultaneously involving a number of different, and yet co-essential dimensions – the distributive and the relational dimensions among others.

Second, since in her view social justice consists in participating in social life as peers without economic, social, and political impediments, she provides an enabling and structurally sensitive conception of *equality*. As seen previously, without a structurally sensitive concept of equality, one cannot criticize occupational segregation – for one can be recognized for one's abilities while remaining occupationally segregated.

Third, instead of relying on any 'authoritative ideal of human flourishing', Fraser embraces a *deontological* view of justice. Likewise, I have argued that a conception of work justice should not rely upon an ideal of self-realization nor on a pre-emptively defined intrinsic meaning of work, because competitive interpretations of the role of work in the good life co-exist in society, and favouring one interpretation over another is not only undesirable for pluralism but also unnecessary for work justice. The polarization of the debate between those who deny all normative interest in work, and those who defend it in ethically loaded terms, ends up excluding work from justice. The dichotomy can be avoided by rejecting its underlying premise: that the only way to defend a normative reading of work is by appealing to ethical self-realization. An approach compatible with competing ethics of work should be preferred. Shifting from the ethical to the moral ground, from the ethical desirability of work to concerns for fairness in social cooperation, allows us to accommodate concerns for work in the scope of justice without sacrificing concerns for pluralism. The deontological framework provided by Fraser fits this purpose.

Nonetheless, Fraser is not primarily or specifically interested in developing a normative conception of work, even though her consideration of related issues is rich, particularly with regard to gender (Fraser 1994). Thus I suggest some amendments of her account.

First, reflecting a general tendency in political philosophy, Fraser tends to cast issues of work essentially as matters of redistribution, work being traced back to the realm of economic class subordination. In her account, the distributive paradigm covers a wide range of different issues, such as the property regime, income, welfare provisions, and the division of labour (Fraser and Honneth 2003: 9–26). There is some conceptual indeterminacy over their boundaries. Since in her account no clear line is drawn between class inequalities and the division of labour, problems of labour justice are essentially cast as problems of 'maldistribution'. Yet, in section 1 I pointed out that distributive interventions in economic inequalities do not automatically make the division of labour fair. Even if economic capital dispersion would widen individuals' room for occupational choice, allowing them to avoid narrow and demeaning work, this would not entail the disappearance of this work as such, and would not help us rethinking fairer structures of labour either. Labour justice cannot be entirely subsumed under distributive justice.

Second, from a sociological perspective, the division of labour is a segment of social differentiation not reducible to class or status, even though they overlap (Giddens and Mackenzie 1982). While classes describe economic positions in the market (if one embraces the Weberian view, as Fraser does), the division of labour broadly refers to the social organization of roles and tasks within an interdependent system of cooperation. As a cross-cutting category through class and status inequalities, the division of labour 'refers specifically to the activity of labour itself, and the specific social and institutional relations of that activity', whereas class has to do with the outcomes of labouring activity (Young 1979: 51). Distributive justice is mostly about class, whereas labour justice is primarily concerned with work and the division of labour.

Finally, given the insufficiencies of both redistribution and recognition models in tackling normative problems of work, and the irreducible normative concerns raised by work and its organization, work should be referred to a distinct sphere of justice. Along with redistribution, recognition, and representation (I didn't consider the latter here for space constraints), a further dimension can be referred to as 'contribution'.[23] It would include norms and concerns for work and the division of labour from two main perspectives: the *qualitative* side of work, meaning the 'what' and 'how' of contribution both individually and organizationally, and its *quantitative* side, meaning the 'when' and 'how much' of work. It points to specific forms of injustice rooted in work structures, irreducible to maldistribution and misrecognition. Organizational regimes, the shape of the division of labour, the nature of the occupations, the quality of one's work, and the social division of labour and free time, would be the subject of the contributive paradigm. Exploring in detail this idea goes beyond the aims of this chapter, yet I have clarified why we need further, distinctively contributive resources to tackle work.

5 Conclusion

Once reconceptualized as contributive parity, Fraser's norm of participatory parity is more demanding than the external distributive principles of equal opportunity and free occupational choice, and more compatible with pluralism than the ethically loaded concept of self-realization. Fraser describes this concept in terms of overcoming class, status, and voice obstacles to peer participation in social life. I have reframed it to express more specifically concerns for work justice as contributive parity, meaning overcoming obstacles (of distributive, relational, contributive, and representative nature) to peer contribution. Through this norm, forms of labour organization can be criticized not because they do not allow workers to be self-realized (as in the *self-transformation model*), neither because they prevent workers from getting meritocratic esteem (as in the *achievement model*), nor because they are impeded from being solidaristically integrated through the division of labour (as in the *social integration model*), but because they prevent workers from contributing to social cooperation as peers, thereby treating them in a way inconsistent with the ideal of a society of equals. Unlike distributive views, contributive parity does not stop at the door of work but demands that *internal* structures of work be fair. Unlike recognition views, it is not centred on a perfectionist ideal of self-realization or on a merely psychological account. Among its advantages, it does not prescribe individuals what to think about the ethical meaning of work, it is not grounded in a particular view about work in human nature, still while not renouncing to a normative perspective on work. Unlike both of them, it introduces egalitarian concerns within labour structures. Overall, it expresses egalitarian, multidimensional, and deontological concerns for work justice.

Rather than a positive ideal of just work, this approach aims at providing a critical-normative standard to assess forms of work and division of labour, to help establishing which of them are morally preferable or objectionable.

Even though I have not developed the contributive parity view in detail here, and much more has to be said about how a society satisfying its demands would actually look like, I have discussed some of its key premises by giving a look at existing theories of distributive justice and recognition. Such perspective does not merely dismiss these accounts, but re-conceives and integrates them in a more comprehensive framework: *equal freedom from material need for real free occupational choice* (distributive dimension) and *social equality in the interactions and structures of work* (relational dimension) are the resources for work justice identified through the critical analysis of aspects of both paradigms. To put the distributive and relational premises of contributive parity: *in a slogan no contribution without redistribution and social equality*.[24]

Notes

1 This chapter re-elaborates parts of my PhD dissertation (Celentano 2019b).
2 When considering the distributive paradigm, I have in mind some of the most representative models – namely John Rawls' liberal-egalitarian model, John Roemer's luck egalitarian-socialist model, and Philippe Van Parijs' libertarian approach. When considering the recognition view, I mostly focus on Axel Honneth's theory.
3 I am using a wider notion of work than that of employment in the formal economy. I shall not engage, however, with the problem of the definition of work here. For my purposes it is sufficient to embrace a relatively broad, and still not too large, definition of work as 'a purposeful human activity involving physical or mental exertion that is not undertaken solely for pleasure and that has economic or symbolic value' (Budd 2011: 2). I use the terms 'work' and 'labour' in an interchangeable way.
4 For space constraints, I shall not develop here a complete account of the dimensions of labour justice, leaving aside the very important representative dimension (decision-making processes concerning one's work) and offering only some hints about the contributive dimension.
5 See Brynin (2002).
6 See also DiQuattro (1983); Hsieh (2009).
7 These considerations are presented more extensively in Celentano (2019a).
8 The slogan resonates with Nancy Fraser's 'no redistribution without recognition' (2003). Note that I am confining my attention here to what may be called an *affirmative* remedy to distributive labour injustice, which does not cover all distributive issues involved in labour justice. *Transformative* remedies, to use Nancy Fraser's lexicon (2003), would involve more: the reduction of the wage gap, and workers' fair access to profits and socially produced wealth, to mention a few.
9 See for example Gomberg (2007).
10 On this point, see also Young (2006).
11 For an attempt to apply the difference principle at work, see Arnold (2012).
12 FOC is a pivotal principle in the liberal tradition, even though distributive thinkers of socialist orientation also defend it; see for instance Roemer (1998).
13 Honneth calls it the 'externalization model'.
14 The ethics of the refusal of work does not help us with the 'somebody's got to do it problem' either, and thus raises the same problems.
15 See also Deranty (2009); Smith (2009).

16 I am freely re-adapting Linton's (1936) distinction between achieved and ascribed status (see also Kantzara 2007).
17 Occupational segregation extends also to class (Sayer 2005: 14 ff.; Ridgeway 2014).
18 For objections on normative esteem, see Baker (2015).
19 Of course, insofar as they are embedded in beliefs, they are also cognitively rooted.
20 Unlike Fourie (2012: 117), who claims that social equality 'is focused primarily on relationships, rather than institutions, could be used to highlight the inequalities between individuals which stem from their attitudes and everyday behaviour', on my account institutions also embody social relations and reproduce patterns of social relations.
21 See also Muirhead (2004).
22 This bi-dimensional model is later replaced by Fraser with a tripartite model of justice that includes also the paradigm of representation (2008).
23 I borrow the term from Paul Gomberg (2007), despite using it in an independent way.
24 Affirmative strategies of labour justice intervene in the effects rather than the structures of work relations. Transformative strategies intervene in the structural causes of work injustice, actualizing the classic principle 'from each according to their capacities'.

References

Acker, Joan. 2006. 'Inequality Regimes: Gender, Class, and Race in Organizations'. *Gender & Society*, 20(4), 441–464.

———. 1990. 'Hierarchies, Jobs, Bodies: A Theory of Gendered Organizations'. *Gender & Society*, 4(2): 139–158.

Anderson, Elizabeth. 2017. *Private Government*. Princeton: Princeton University Press.

———. 1999. 'What is the Point of Equality?' *Ethics*, 109(2): 287–337.

Arneson, Richard. 1987. 'Meaningful Work and Market Socialism'. *Ethics*, 97(3): 517–545.

Baker, John. 2015. 'Conceptions and Dimensions of Social Equality'. In Fourie, C., Fabian Schuppert, and Ivo Walliman-Helmer (eds), *Social Equality: On What It Means to Be Equals*. Oxford: Oxford University Press, pp. 65–86.

Bendick, Marc. 2007. 'Situation Testing for Employment Discrimination in the United States of America'. *Horizons stratégiques*, 3: 17–39.

Bettio, Francesca et al. 2009. *Gender Segregation in the Labour Market*. Luxembourg: Publications Office of the European Union.

Block, Fred. 2013. 'The Relevance of Basic Income for Post-Industrial Economies'. In Widerquist, Karl et al. (eds), *Basic Income: An Anthology of Contemporary Research*. Oxford: Wiley Blackwell.

Branch, Enobong. 2011. *Opportunity Denied*. New Brunswick: Rutgers University Press.

Brennan, Geoffrey, and Philip Pettit. 2004. *The Economy of Esteem*. Oxford: Oxford University Press.

Brynin, Malcolm. 2002. 'Overqualification in Employment'. *Work, Employment and Society*, 16(4): 637–654.

Budd, John W. 2011. *The Thought of Work*. Ithaca: Cornell University Press.

Celentano, Denise. 2019a. 'Automation, Labour Justice, and Equality'. *Ethics and Social Welfare*, 13(1): 33–50.
———. 2019b. 'Cooperating as Peers: Labour Justice between Distributive and Relational Equality'. Unpublished PhD dissertation, UNICT/EHESS.
Cook, A., and Christy Glass. 2013. 'Above the Glass Ceiling: When Are Women and Racial/Ethnic Minorities Promoted to CEO?' *Strategic Management Journal*, 35(7): 1080–1089.
Dahrendorf, Ralf. 1972. 'On the Origin of Social Inequality'. in Laslett, P. and W. G. Runciman (eds), *Philosophy, Politics and Society*. Oxford: Basil Blackwell, pp. 88–109.
Deranty, Jean-Philippe. 2009. *Beyond Communication*. Leiden: Brill.
DiQuattro, Arthur. 1983. 'Rawls and Left Criticism'. *Political Theory*, 11(1): 53–78.
Dubet, François. 2013. *Injustices*. Paris: Le Seuil.
European Institute for Gender Equality (EIGE). 2017. *Gender Segregation in Education, Training and the Labour Market*. Review of the Implementation of the Beijing Platform for Action in the EU Member States.
Federal Glass Ceiling Commission. 1995. *Good for Business: Making Full Use of the Nation's Human Capital*. Washington, DC: U.S. Department of Labour.
Fourie, Carina. 2012. 'What is Social Equality? An Analysis of Status Equality as a Strongly Egalitarian Ideal'. *Res Publica*, 18: 107–126.
Fourie, Carina, Fabien Schuppert, and Ivo Wallimann-Helmer (eds). 2015. *Social Equality*. Oxford: Oxford University Press.
Fraser, Nancy. 2008. *Scales of Justice*. Cambridge: Polity Press.
———. 1994. 'After the Family Wage: Gender Equity and the Welfare State'. *Political Theory*, 22(4): 591–618.
Fraser, Nancy, and Axel Honneth. 2003. *Redistribution or Recognition? A Political-Philosophical Exchange*. London: Verso.
Giddens, Anthony, and Gavin Mackenzie, eds. 1982. *Social Class and the Division of Labour*. Cambridge: Cambridge University Press.
Gomberg, Paul. 2007. *How to Make Opportunity Equal*. New York: John Wiley & Sons.
Hinze, Susan Waldoch. 2007. 'Occupational Sex Segregation'. In O'Brien, J. (ed.), *Sage Encyclopedia of Gender and Society*. New York: Sage.
Honneth, Axel. 2017. *The Idea of Socialism*, trans. Joseph Ganahl. New York: Polity Press.
———. 2010. 'Work and Recognition: A Redefinition'. In Schmidt am Busch, H.C., and J. Zurn (eds), *The Philosophy of Recognition*. Lanham, MD: Lexington Books, pp. 223–239.
———. 1996. *The Struggle for Recognition*. Cambridge, MA: MIT Press.
———. 1995[1980]. 'Work and Instrumental Action: On the Normative Basis of Critical Theory'. In C.C. Wright (ed.), *The Fragmented World of the Social*. New York: Suny Press, 15–49.
———. 1995[1982]. 'Moral Consciousness and Class Domination: Some Problems in The Analysis of Hidden Morality'. *The Fragmented World of the Social*, 205–219.
———. 1991[1989]. 'Domination and Moral Struggle'. In C.C. Wright (ed.), *The Fragmented World of the Social*. New York: Suny Press.
Hsieh, Nsieh. 2009. 'Justice at Work: Arguing for Property-Owning Democracy'. *Journal of Social Philosophy*, 40(3): 397–411.
Hughes, Everett C. 2017 [1958]. *Men and their Work*, Toronto: Collier-Macmillan.

———. 1951. 'Work and the Self'. In Rohrer, J.H. and M. Sherif (eds), *Social Psychology at the Crossroads*. New York: Harper & Brothers, pp. 313–323.

Kantzara, Vasiliki. 2007. 'Status'. In *The Blackwell Encyclopedia of Sociology*, pp. 1–4. New York: John Wiley & Sons.

Kohn, Melvin L., and Carmi Schooler. 1978. 'The Reciprocal Effects of the Substantive Complexity of Work and Intellectual Flexibility: A Longitudinal Assessment'. *America Journal of Sociology*, 84(1): 24–52.

Kymlicka, Will. 2002. *Contemporary Political Philosophy. An Introduction* (2nd edition). New York: Oxford University Press.

Linton, Ralph. 1936. *The Study of Man: An Introduction*. New York: Appleton and Co.

Lorusso, Silvio. 2016. 'What is the Entreprecariat?' November 27, 2016. <https://networkcultures.org/entreprecariat/what-is-the-entreprecariat/>

Miller, David. 1998. 'Equality and Justice'. In Mason, A. (ed.), *Ideals of Equality*. Oxford: Blackwell, pp. 21–36.

Muirhead, Russell. 2004. *Just Work*. Cambridge, MA: Harvard University Press.

Néron, Pierre-Yves. 2015. 'Social Equality and Economic Institutions. Arguing for Workplace Democracy'. In Hull, G. (ed.), *The Equal Society*. Lanham, MD: Lexington Books.

Pratto, Felicia. 1999. 'The Puzzle of Continuing Group Inequality: Piecing Together Psychological, Social, and Cultural Forces in Social Dominance Theory'. In *Advances in Experimental Social Psychology*. Cambridge, MA: Academic Press, pp. 191–263.

Rawls, John. 2001. *Justice as Fairness: A Restatement*. Cambridge, MA: Harvard University Press.

———. 1999. *A Theory of Justice* (Revised edition). Cambridge, MA: Harvard University Press.

Roca, Esther. 2010. 'The Exercise of Moral Imagination in Stigmatized Work Groups'. *Journal of Business Ethics*, 96(1): 135–147.

Rössler, Beate. 2007. 'Work, Recognition, Emancipation'. In B. Van Den Brink and D. Owen (eds), *Recognition and Power*. Cambridge: Cambridge University Press.

Ridgeway, Cecilia L. 2016. 'Status Construction Theory'. In *The Blackwell Encyclopedia of Race, Ethnicity, and Nationalism*. Hoboken: John Wiley & Sons.

———. 2014. 'Why Status Matters for Inequality'. *American Sociological Review*, 79(1): 1–16.

Ridgeway, Cecilia L., and Sandra Nakagawa. 2017. 'Is Deference the Price of Being Seen as Reasonable? How Status Hierarchies Incentivize Acceptance of Low Status'. *Social Psychology Quarterly*, 80(2): 132–152.

Ridgeway, Cecilia L. et al. 2009. 'How Easily Does a Social Difference Become a Status Distinction? Gender Matters'. *American Sociological Review*, 74(1): 44–62.

Roemer, John. 1998. *Equality of Opportunity*. Cambridge, MA: Harvard University Press.

Runciman, Walter Garrison. 1967. *Philosophy, Politics and Society*. Oxford: Blackwell.

Säve-Söderbergh, Johan. 2007. 'Are Women Asking for Low Wages? Gender Differences in Wage Bargaining Strategies and Ensuing Bargaining Success'. Working Paper Series, Swedish Institute for Social Research.

Sayer, Andrew. 2011. 'Misrecognition, the Unequal Division of Labour and Contributive Injustice', in Yar, M. and S. Thompson (eds), *The Politics of Misrecognition*. London: Ashgate.

———. 2005. *The Moral Significance of Class*. Cambridge: Cambridge University Press.

Scanlon, Thomas. 2000. 'The Diversity of Objections to Inequality'. In Clayton, Matthew, and Andrew Williams (eds), *The Ideal of Equality*. London: Macmillan, pp. 41–59.

Scheffler, Samuel. 2015. 'The Practice of Equality'. In Fourie, Carina, Fabien Schuppert, and Ivo Wallimann-Helmer (eds), *Social Equality*. Oxford: Oxford University Press, pp. 21–44.

Sidanius, Jim, and Felicia Pratto. 1999. *Social Dominance*. New York: Cambridge University Press.

Smith, Nicolas H. 2009. 'Work and the Struggle for Recognition'. *European Journal of Political Theory*, 8(1): 46–60.

Stainback, Kevin, and Donald Tomaskovic-Devey. 2012. *Documenting Desegregation*. New York: Russell Sage Foundation.

Tilly, Charles. 1998. *Durable Inequality*. Oakland: University of California Press.

Tomaskovic-Devey, Donald. 2014. 'The Relational Generation of Workplace Inequalities'. *Social Currents*, 1(1): 51–73.

———. 1993. *Gender and Racial Inequality at Work*. Ithaca: Cornell University Press.

Tomaskovic-Devey, Donald, and Dustin Avent-Holt. 2019. *Relational Inequalities: An Organizational Approach*. New York: Oxford University Press.

Van Parijs, Philippe, and Yannick Vanderborght. 2017. *Basic Income: A Radical Proposal for a Free Society and a Sane Economy*. Cambridge, MA: Harvard University Press.

Walzer, Michael. 1983. *Spheres of Justice*. New York: Basic Books.

Weeks, Kathi. 2011. *The Problem with Work*. Durham: Duke University Press.

Wingfield, Adia, and Renee Skeete. 2016. 'Maintaining Hierarchies in Predominantly White Organizations: A Theory of Racial Tasks as Invisible Labour'. *Invisible Labour*, 47–67.

Young, Iris M. 2006. 'Taking the Basic Structure Seriously'. *Perspectives on Politics*, 4(1): 91–97.

———. 1990. *Justice and the Politics of Difference*. Princeton: Princeton University Press.

———. 1979. 'Self-Determination as a Principle of Justice'. *The Philosophical Forum*.

6

AFFECTIVE EQUALITY AND SOCIAL JUSTICE

Kathleen Lynch

1 Introduction

The affective care domain of life, arising from human dependencies and interdependencies, constitutes a distinct sphere of social relations. Consequently, affective relations of love, care, and solidarity comprise a relatively autonomous field of social practices, within and through which inequalities and exploitations can occur, just as they can occur in the economic, political, or cultural sphere (Baker et al. 2004; Lynch, Baker and Lyons 2009; Crean 2018).

Affective care relations are not social derivatives and therefore subordinate to economic, political, or cultural relations in matters of social justice. Rather, they are productive, materialist human relations that constitute people mentally, emotionally, physically, and socially. The nurturing work that produces love, care, and solidarity operates under principles of other-centredness, even when it fails in this purpose. Furthermore, neither love nor care are purely personal or intimate matters; care exists as a public practice, be it in terms of health care, environmental care, community care, educational care, or public welfare; solidarity can be regarded as the political expression of such public care (Boltanski and Porter 2012; Lynch and Kalaitzake 2018).

Because the relational realities of nurturing (and their counterpoint, neglect) operate as a distinct set of social practices, love, care, and solidarity relations are sites of political import that need to be examined separately in social justice terms. The lack of appreciation of affective relations leads to a failure to recognize their pivotal role in generating injustices in the production of people in their humanness.

This chapter outlines a framework for thinking about affective relations in structural social justice terms. In so doing, it hopes to contribute to the redistribution, recognition, representation debate about justice by making the case for a fourth dimension, relational justice. The framework is sociologically informed by theoretical work and empirical research undertaken on love, care, and solidarity (Cantillon and Lynch 2017; Grummell, Devine and Lynch 2009; Ivancheva, Lynch and Keating 2019; Lynch 2007; Lynch 2009; Lynch, Baker and Lyons 2009; Lynch, Grummell and Devine 2012; Lolich and Lynch 2016; 2017; Lynch and Kalaitzake 2018).[1] It takes a structural rather than individualist approach to social justice, arguing that equality of conditions matters as it is impossible to have anything but weak forms of equality of opportunity in economically and politically (structurally) unjust societies. In relational terms, one does not just need access to love, care, and solidarity but the experience of love, care, and solidarity in a deep nurturing sense.

The chapter opens with a discussion of how the concept of affective equality is related to, but separate from, conceptions of social justice articulated by Honneth and Fraser. Arising from empirical studies on love, care, and solidarity undertaken over the last ten years, the chapter attempts to advance on Honneth's (1995; 2003) understanding of love and solidarity and Fraser's (2008) three-dimensional theory of justice by proposing a fourth dimension, relational justice. The second section of the chapter outlines a definition of affective equality and explains how affective injustices cannot be examined separately from structural economic, political, and cultural inequalities. It presents an intersectional structural perspective on social justice that recognizes affective relations as a distinct system of nurturing social relations (albeit relations that may fail in their purpose). The chapter concludes by making the case for grounding politics in the ethics of love, care, and solidarity, rather than the ethics of competition and self-interest that underpin neoliberal capitalism.

2 Theories of justice: going beyond Honneth and Fraser

Axel Honneth and Nancy Fraser have undertaken groundbreaking work in advancing the understanding of social justice within political theory. This chapter attempts, albeit in a tentative manner, to advance on their very substantial bodies of work from a sociologically-informed perspective, particularly with respect to the salience of affective care relations within theories of social justice. Given that Fraser gives attention to dimensions of justice beyond that of recognition, notably redistribution and representation, the discussion will focus more on how to advance on her analysis as it is more pertinent to core concerns in this chapter.

2.1 Axel Honneth

Honneth has defined love and solidarity as issues of recognition in social justice terms; in so doing, he has placed issues that are of central concern to women, feminists, and to those who are inevitably dependent, such as young children, at the heart of his theory of justice. This is a welcome development in political theory as it recognizes the salience of love and solidarity for the production and reproduction of humanity.

Honneth identifies, the 'three recognition spheres of love, legal equality, and the achievement principle' as the foundations stones for promoting social justice in modern liberal capitalist societies claiming they have contributed to an 'increase in the social possibilities for individualization as well as a rise in social inclusion' (Honneth 2003: 185).[2]

> Because we live in a social order in which individuals owe the possibility of an intact identity to affective care, legal equality, and social esteem, it seems to me appropriate, in the name of individual autonomy, to make the three corresponding recognition principles the normative core of a conception of social justice.
>
> (Honneth 2003: 181–182)

While he does address affective care in terms of love, the latter is the only type of affective relation that is recognized as such. He also defines love relations in a way that strongly associates them with the family, and treats them as private and, implicitly, apolitical matters. Yet love relations, as with all human relations, have a power dimension; they are public and political issues not private family matters in this respect (Connolly 2010). If the power and related material conflicts within love relations are not recognized as such, there is a danger of psychologizing love in a way the ignores its embeddedness in wider structural relations (McNay 2008). There is related danger of romanticizing family love without looking at its dark side, especially in patriarchal and/or capitalist societies, wherein authoritarianism and abuse can operate in the name of love, thereby creating dispositions that are far from loving in any meaningful nurturing sense of that term. When love relations are psychologized, the potential for political activism for emancipatory social change that lurks deep within the family system can be largely ignored (Connolly 2010). This leads to the situation where there is no political economy language to name the materiality and power dimensions of affective relations, which, in turn, undermines any movement for care-related politics; care consciousness is denied a political voice (Crean 2018).

Honneth defines solidarity as a form of merit or achievement-based recognition. While this is an established way of defining solidarity, it is also a strongly contested view (Lynch and Kalaitzake 2018). An achievement-based recognition interpretation seems to hollow out the affective concept of caring, which is morally led, and is at the heart of solidarity. Defining solidarity in achievement terms is also at variance with much philosophical thought where solidarity is regarded as a disposition of mutual recognition of shared needs and concerns (Rorty 1989: 189), a form of 'benevolent motivation' because 'to feel solidarity is to be morally motivated' (Halldenius 1998: 346).

Finally, Honneth's theory of recognition, as it applies to love and solidarity, does not engage with the materiality of social life and of power itself. The world of recognition is defined in intersubjective terms, detached from an analysis of the social and political relations that mediate and frame recognition (Thompson 2014: 780–781). Lacking a structural analysis, it also underestimates the power of market-led state institutions in framing relations of recognition and care (Garrett 2010). The ways in which capitalist economic systems not only condition power but also frame consciousness and commitment to social (in)justice, through advertising, social media, and living in and through a market-led society (Sennett 1998; Leyva 2018) are not addressed, thereby presenting a very idealized and structurally detached form of recognition and subjectification.

While Honneth's work is rightly respected in terms of providing a profound understanding of recognition, it does not fully recognize the importance of love, care, and solidarity as interconnected affective relational systems that intersect deeply with economic, political, and cultural relations, especially as these are framed within legal and political institutions.

2.2 *Nancy Fraser*

Nancy Fraser has recognized the salience of dependency and care as political issues, both historically and contemporarily (Fraser 1997; 2016). Given this, it is important to examine how she analyzes care and dependency in terms of social justice and how her understanding of social justice relates to affective justice.

In the early 1990s Fraser and Gordon (1994) mapped out the genealogy of conceptions of dependency. They noted that there is no longer any self-evidently valued or approved adult dependency in post-industrial society; independence is 'enjoined upon everyone' but achievable only through paid employment. Fraser and Gordon recognize the problems that this idealization of independence pose: they claim that there is a need to challenge the negative valuations of dependence to enable a more emancipatory vision of society to emerge. However, they do not offer a resolution to the dependency dilemma.

What Fraser (1997) does address, in a separate paper, is the gender equality problem that arises in doing (unpaid) dependency work within family care settings; she recognizes gender-based affective inequality, in the contributive justice sense, although not using this nomenclature. In her 'post-industrial thought experiment' she valourizes caring, outlining an ideal type 'Universal Caregiver' model as a potential resolution of the care/gender equality problem in capitalist societies (Fraser 1997: 59–62). While Fraser (2016: 99–100) does recognize that care is indispensable to the functioning of the economy, politics, and culture of society, care relations are defined as *reproducers rather* than producers of social life. The care crisis is (rightly) defined as a social-reproductive crisis within capitalism, most recently a crisis tendency within contemporary financialized capitalism; however, the role that caring plays relatively independently of capitalism is not explored.

In *Scales of Justice* Fraser moved beyond the perspectival dualism of *redistribution* and *recognition*, that was a defining feature of her earlier work (Fraser 1995). She endorsed a three-dimensional theory of social justice, incorporating issues of political *representation* as social justice matters. She recognized the 'relative autonomy of inequities rooted in the political constitution of society, as opposed to the economic structure or the status order' (Fraser 2008: 6). One of the benefits of this revised framework is that it enables scholars to re-conceive *scale* and *scope* as questions of justice and thereby to move beyond a Keynesian-Westphalian framework that takes the *who* of social justice as being 'the domestic political citizenry' (2008: 30).

Grounded in the view that equality and social justice are principally problems of parity of participation, Fraser claims that social arrangements are just when they 'permit all (adult) members of society to interact with one another as peers' (Fraser 2008: 36). For participatory parity to be upheld, she outlines three key conditions that must be met. These are grounded sociologically in having equality in economic relations, political relations, and cultural relations. 'All three conditions are necessary for participatory parity. None alone is sufficient' (Fraser 2010: 365).

Fraser offers an invaluable three-dimensional theoretical framework for mapping problems of equality and social justice, yet the framework follows a traditional egalitarian theory perspective in relation to care forms of labour. The *who* of social justice is still defined in very particular adult terms (how, if, and when children, and those who are highly dependent on others, experience injustices seems to be outside this frame, as indeed it is in Rawls' theory).[3] The adult experiencing social injustice is the adult of the economy, culture, and politics (the adult of the Marxist/Weberian trilogy of class, status, and power). The framework does not recognize the affective care domain of life as a discrete and relatively autonomous site of social relations. Nor does it address the ways in which the affective relations of the care world operate both independently of, and intersectionally with, economic, political, and cultural relations in promoting injustice. Given that Fraser defines participatory parity as central to her theory of justice this is surprising for two reasons. First, because parity of participation in economic, cultural, and political life is itself dependent on parity of participation in doing unavoidable and inevitable care work, work which women are morally and culturally impelled to do in most societies (Bubeck 1995; Folbre 1994). Second, to become and remain a resourced and enabled adult who can participate fully in society one needs to experience love and care, personally, professionally, and politically, and such needs must be protected and enabled by the state in welfare capitalist societies (Garrett 2010). Without the nurturing resources invested in them, not only as children but also as adults, people would be unable to participate on equal terms with others in social life (Gilbert 2010). They would lack the extensive emotional, ethical, and the intrapersonal and interpersonal intelligences and capacities (see Gardner 1983 on the latter) to do economic, political, and cultural work. They would also lack a sense of *care and love security*, in whatever cultural form that takes. While family, community, and state (welfare and related) caring does *re*produce people for the capitalist economy, it does much more than this; it also produces people in their care relationality, both in its presence and absence.

The primary purpose of love labouring (the nurturing work that is undertaken in the intimate relations of life) is not to serve capitalism (Cantillon and Lynch 2017; Lynch 2007); to reduce love and care work to its indirect market capitalist purposes is to dismiss life outside of the market and economy in terms of relational value. It is to implicitly endorse the very capitalist values one seeks to undermine. Love labour matters because it produces people in their relational humanity: it is the primary element of people's 'humane co-affective relations' through which they make and remake each other (Matheis 2014: 12). The affective relations involved in nurturing people through love, care, and solidarity produce people in their humanness, as sociable beings in-and-of themselves (Oksala 2016: 297); its absence produces neglect, harm, and loss. Love, for its part, enhances the capacity of human lives (Cantillon and Lynch 2017), and it enables moral transformation, in so far as it enables people to think and act other-wise (hooks 2000).

Moreover, given the centrality of affective relations in social life, care consciousness is an empirically observable sociological phenomenon. It is driven by a lay normativity (Sayer 2005) that finds expression in people's 'care relational identities' (Crean 2018: 3), which are connected to, but also separate from, gendered identities (Lynch and Lyons 2009: 54–77). Ironically, there is 'no political economy discourse to articulate the materiality of affective relations and related inequalities' (Crean 2018: 12) that undermine the development of people in their humanity.

A political economy theory of capitalism that ignores the materiality of *human production* is incomplete because it fails to identify the intra-individual distinction between the self that serves the market and the self that serves others outside the market. It fails to recognize the work involved in creating each other through the inevitable interdependencies of life.

3 Affective equality: preliminary remarks

3.1 An equality of condition perspective

In *Equality* colleagues and I distinguished between liberal concepts of equality and the concept of equality of condition (Baker et al. 2004: 21–46). We noted that, while the classical liberal ideal of equality of opportunity matters, there can never be substantive equality economically, politically, culturally, or affectively without a change in the structures that underpin conditions for competitive advantage: the concept of competitive advantage is merely a way of legitimating pre-existing structural injustices. While there is an economically unequal society (especially a neoliberal capitalist one), there cannot be meaningful equality of participation in education (Lynch and Crean 2018) or in society more generally (Wright 2010).

When the principle of equality of condition is applied to affective equality, it implies that having an equal opportunity or chance to have love, care, and solidarity is not enough. As our empirical research on love and care work showed, for people to thrive and not just survive, they need significant amounts of love, care, and solidarity in their personal, professional, civil, and political lives (Lynch and Baker 2009: 216–236). It is pointless to characterize equality in affective relations in terms of having the opportunity to have love and care; what people need is the experience of nurturing through love, care, and solidarity, not just the right to have access to it.

To have equality of condition in affective relations, there must be structural changes in institutions that undermine the practices of love and care, and, as argued elsewhere, that means challenging neoliberal capitalist, patriarchal, racist, disablist, ageist, class-biased, and other unjust practices in the way governments and states organize the distribution of wealth (especially unearned financial wealth), employment relations, care relations, education, and other social institutions (Lynch and Baker 2005; Lynch, Cantillon and Lyons 2007; Lynch and Baker 2009; Cantillon and Lynch 2017).

While the ways in which equality of condition would impact on affective relations cannot be analyzed in-depth in this short chapter, it is a core premise of the work.[4]

3.2 Micro and macro politics

The nature of affective care relations means that affective equality is a micro and highly interpersonal matter, especially in terms of love and care. However, to define affective relations in micro-level terms alone is to miss the central role of wider social relations in determining the capacity of people to care and love each other in a nurturing way.

The nation state, and, increasingly, political institutions such as the EU, play a powerful role in enacting laws regulating political, economic, and cultural relations, that impact on caring relations, be these in families, at work or in wider society. Achieving affective equality is therefore about generating, maintaining, and regulating the social institutions of ownership and control of wealth, and places of employment to ensure that they are enabling and facilitative of loving and caring for all persons regardless of their occupation or employment status, their race, gender, disability, sexuality, or related statuses. It is about promoting education, housing, forms of transport, welfare, health care, and childcare that are legally protected as pro-nurturing. And, it is about ensuring that formal political institutions, at local, national, and global levels are solidaristic in character, so that they enable and facilitate nurturing relations, both in terms of how they operate internally as social institutions but also how and if they exercise political power in the interest of promoting affective equality.

3.3 Gender

Whether affective relations are reciprocal or asymmetrical, whether they are structured by gender, social class, age, race, marital or family status, and/or other abilities, they are always matters of social and affective justice (Duffy 2011; Ehrenreich and Hochschild 2003; Federici 2012; Glenn 2010; Oksala 2016). Most especially, securing equality in the doing of the emotional and material work involved in creating love and care relations is a major gender justice issue, given the unequal distribution of this work over time (Bubeck 1995; Fineman 1995; Folbre 1994; Mies 2014; Oxfam 2020).[5] The gender division of labour in loving and caring is of pre-eminent importance socio-politically, and central to the analysis affective equality in the contributive justice sense (Gomberg 2007; Sayer 2009).

Give the scale and depth of the gender dimensions of affective justice, they cannot be addressed in detail in this short chapter. The focus will be on why love, care, and solidarity are matters of social justice in the more distributive sense, as social goods, while acknowledging that major gender (and classed and racial injustices) arise in the doing of care and love work.

4 Affective equality

As dependency and interdependency are endemic to the human condition (Held 2006; Kittay 1999; Tronto 1993), humans need certain basic forms of care and nurturing to survive and to flourish (Engster 2005). Being emotional as well as intellectual, social as well as individual (Nussbaum 1995), humans also have the capacity for intimacy, attachment, and mutual caring arising from, and lived through, their inter/dependencies. They generally recognize and feel some sense of affiliation and concern for others, and value the various forms of social engagement that emanate from such relations. Bonds of intimacy, friendship, and/or kinship are frequently what bring meaning, warmth, and joy to life, while sustaining intimate relationships, friendships, and trusted community relations, all contribute to human well-being (Layard 2005; Rodríguez-Pose and von Berlepsch 2014). Being deprived of the capacity to develop nurturing affective relations, or of the experience of engaging in them when one has the capacity, is therefore a serious human deprivation and an affective injustice.

Having an affectively egalitarian society in care terms means creating social systems and institutions where people receive as much love, care, and solidarity as is humanly possible. And this means creating the political, economic, cultural, and legal conditions to enable affective egalitarian relationships to happen in a way that the political, economic, cultural, *and* affective needs of carers are fully respected, whether they are paid or not. Affective equality is therefore both an *interpersonal* and a *structural* matter.

Promoting affective equality politically involves securing the safety of nurturing structurally as a social good and ensuring equality in the capacity and resources to nurture. As affective relations operate as a relatively autonomous set of social relations across three major life-worlds, the primary, secondary, and tertiary care spheres (Lynch 2007), affective equality is about maximizing the capacity of peoples *and* societal institutions to create, maintain, and resource the affective relations that produce love, care, and solidarity.

First, it is about protecting and enabling primary care relations at the intimate level to ensure they are as nurturing as possible, including enabling and resourcing the love labouring work that non-substitutable affective relations involve (Lynch 2007; Cantillon and Lynch 2017). Affective equality also involves ensuring that people have the capacity to create nurturing caring relations outside of family, friends, and intimate others. Nurturing needs to be resourced and enabled in secondary sites of caring, including childcare centres, homes for those in need of care, and in other social institutions where the work involved has a care dimension, including education, health care, and welfare particularly. Finally, affective equality is about promoting and sustaining care for strangers in the wider political domains, in one's local community, and at regional, national, and international levels.

Figure 6.1 in what follows presents a visual representation of the three major life-worlds where love, care, and solidarity operate[6]. First, there is the world of primary, intimate relations where there is strong attachment, deep engagement, and intensity. These love relations involve high interdependency and are characterized by strong attachments, intimacy, and responsibility over time. While they vary in form cross-culturally, they arise from inherited or contractual dependencies or interdependencies, and are people's primary care relations. The prototypical relationship in this circle is that between parents and children. Even if little love labour is invested in this intimate world, or if there is abuse or neglect, these relationships retain a high level of personal and social significance.

Secondary care relations are lower order interdependency relations. While they involve care responsibilities and attachments, they do not carry the same depth of moral obligation in terms of meeting dependency needs, especially long-term dependency needs. There is a degree of choice and contingency about secondary care relations that does not apply to primary relations. They characterize outer circles of relatives, friends, neighbours, and work

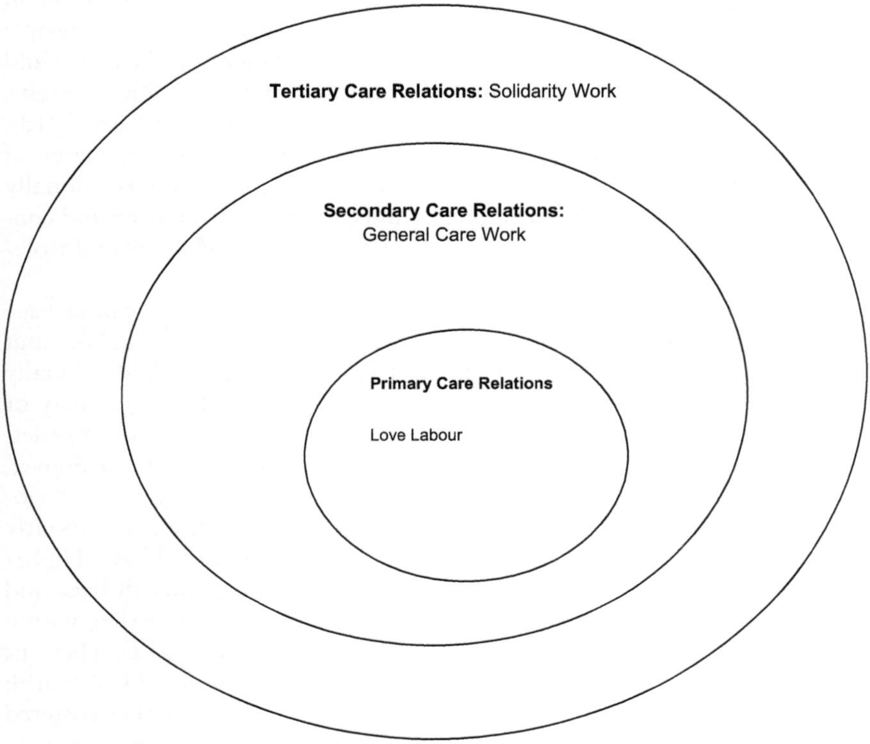

Figure 6.1 Affective relations: love, care, and solidarity
Source: Adapted from Lynch (2007)

colleagues where there are lower order affective engagements in terms of time, responsibility, and commitment.

Solidarity relations generally involve unknown others and do not involve intimacy. They are the political form or social form of love relations (Boltanski and Porter 2012). Sometimes solidarity relations are chosen, such as when individuals or groups work collectively for the well-being of others whose welfare is only partially or not immediately related to their own, or solidarity can be imposed through laws or moral prescriptions that are collectively binding, including taxes to redistribute wealth. Solidarity is both a set of values and a set of public practices. It connotes the work involved in creating and maintaining local communities, neighbourhoods on the one hand, and the advocacy work in formal politics and civil society for social justice at national and global levels on the other. It finds its expression in people's willingness to support vulnerable others within their own country or to support to peoples in other countries who are denied basic rights and livelihoods to live a life of dignity. The levels of solidarity in each society are reflected in everything from the vibrancy of its community activities to the taxes people are willing to pay to fund and support vulnerable members of their own and other societies. It is where the moral, the affective, and the political systems overlap in public life (for a fuller discussion see Lynch and Kalaitzake 2018).

Within each of these circles of care, people live in varying states of dependency and interdependency. And each care reality is intersectionally connected to the other, moving along a fluid continuum from deep and consistent love, care, and solidarity to carelessness, neglect, and abuse and violation (Figure 6.1).

Within primary care relations, labours of abuse and neglect can replace love labouring, not only denying someone the benefits of love labour but damaging the person through abuse and violation (Feeley 2009). Equally in the secondary care relations fields, other-centred care labouring may or may not take place. Highly competitive work environments do not generate cultures of care and concern among colleagues (Ball 2003; Grummell, Devine and Lynch 2009). Neighbourhoods mired by poverty, war, or violence are not likely to produce the kind of trust that underpins neighbourly care; exclusionary forms of social capital persist (Leonard 2004). Higher levels of economic inequality within countries generate greater distrust and less willingness to show solidarity with vulnerable others, either within one's own country or outside of it (Paskov and Dewilde 2012). There is, therefore, nothing inevitable in the love, care, and solidarity (LCS) world; the relational sphere provides contexts where they can be either fostered or destroyed, not least because economic, political, and cultural injustices interpellate with affective relations and frame their character. The higher the levels of economic inequality the lower the trust that exists, and the more uncaring a society becomes (Wilkinson and Pickett 2009, 2018).

5 Why love, care, and solidarity are related concepts

In framing the concept of affective equality, a question that arises is, why are relations of love, care, and solidarity treated as a related family of sociological concepts. The primary reason for locating care and love within the same concept family is because the research literature, both theoretical and empirical, demonstrates that these two dimensions of affective relations are strongly overlapping (Bubeck 1995; Ehrenreich and Hochschild 2003; Finch and Groves 1983; Folbre 2012; Held 2006; Kittay 1999; Mol 2008; Tronto 1987; 1993; 2013). This is not denying that love is distinct from other forms of caring as it is (Ferguson 2014), rather, it is to recognize that the boundaries between love and care cannot always be neatly drawn. Love labour and secondary care work can and do become closely intertwined, with love sometimes emanating from the activity of care (Traustadottir 2000; Folbre 2012; Tronto 2013), while love relations can change, losing their love dimensions.

Solidarity is a moral disposition and commitment to nurture and support vulnerable (albeit generally unknown) others (Rorty 1989). While there are very real tensions between a normative understanding of solidarity as other-centred and inclusive on the one hand, and the self-interested, calculative interpretations of solidarity on the other (Bowles and Gintis 2000; Lynch and Kalaitzak 2018; Stjernø 2004), when solidarity is framed in the positive, inclusive sense of that term, it is clearly aligned with love and care. Solidarity is a macro-level expression of collective caring, a politicized form of love. It is about other-centred work involving the regulation of desires in a way that is focused on the interest of the 'other' (Boltanski and Porter 2012 [1990]: 109–110). Love-as-solidarity can and does find political expression, even among those who are most oppressed (Hardt and Negri 2009: 179–180).

Solidarity can be and is expressed through publicly supported health, education, and welfare programmes, and while this solidarity may be conditional at times, the core principles underpinning it is concern for the welfare of others. If it were solely based on achievements or merit, as Honneth (1995) suggests, it would cease to be solidarity in the sense that it would no longer be driven primarily by the moral motivation to alleviate or prevent the suffering of others (Arnsperger and Varoufakis 2003).

6 Mapping the intersection between relational inequalities, redistribution, recognition, and representational injustices

Affective care injustices are real and have material costs and consequences. Moreover, they do not operate alone but are exacerbated by other structural injustices, notably the unequal re/distribution of resources and wealth, respect and recognition, and lack of parity of representation in the exercise of power. Affective inequality is especially exacerbated by economic inequalities as highly unequal societies (lacking economic solidarity) produce 'socially evaluative threats',[7] leading to anxieties and insecurities that adversely impact on health, including mental health while undermining trust and solidarity (Wilkinson and Pickett 2009, 2018). It is no accident, that those who are in prison are not only disproportionately from very poor households but are also very likely to have suffered severe care deprivations and to have lacked adequate education and other social goods (Feeley 2009; O'Mahony 1997; Wacquant 2009).

Figure 6.2 maps the relationship between affective relations and economic, political, cultural systems, and between each of these and the dimensions of equality/inequality to which they are connected. While affective relations play a key role in framing how people are loved and cared for, economic, cultural, and power structures also impact on the affective domain. As all major politico-economic structures are institutionalized in laws, policies, customs, and conventions to the benefit of the already privileged, they are

Structured social systems where in/equality is generated	**Dimensions of in/equality**				**Processes of acquiring social goods**-sites of in/equality
	Re/distribution (Resources)	**Respect & recognition** (Status)	**Representation** (Power)	**Relationality** (Affective Relations of Love, Care &Solidarity)	
Economic relations	**XX**	X	X	X	Processes of acquiring resources, respect & recognition, representation, love, care & solidarity
Political relations	X	X	**XX**	X	
Cultural relations	X	**XX**	X	X	
Affective relations	X	X	X	**XX**	

Figure 6.2 Four structural systems where in/equality is generated mapped with four key dimensions of in/equality and related processes

Source: Adapted from Baker et al. (2004) *Equality*

The **double XXs** in Figure 6.2 illustrate that this is the site where a given social injustice is generated while a single X indicates an indirect inequality arising simultaneously from the impact of other systems.

very durable (Tilly 1998). It is not possible to address issues of social justice in one social system without addressing those in related systems and structures.[8]

While lack of love, care, and solidarity (LCS) is generated in affective care relations, it has repercussions in economic, cultural, and political relations: those who are uncared for, neglected, or abused do not just experience an affective loss, they also experience indirect costs in economic and political life, often through lack of social confidence or inability to compete and succeed in employment and education.

Not only is injustice generated by the ways in which relations operate within systems, it is also derived from injustices operating in the *processes* that give access to valuable social goods. This is illustrated clearly in how one acquires resources through employment. While paid work gives access to resources, the conditions in which one earns those resources differ considerably, not only in terms of income but also in terms of the burdens and wider benefits of certain forms of work, and in terms of personal autonomy and respect at work (Sayer 2009). The lack of respect for paid care workers is a global phenomenon (Fernandez 2010; Lutz 2011).

Social injustice is not just about what social good one receives; it is also about the processes that operate in determining how one receives it. In the case of economic relations, it is not just the issue of wages that matter, but whether one is always confined to undertaking difficult and/or boring, dirty, or tiring work. As the burden of menial work is generally accompanied by the lowest possible wages and poor working conditions, and as the kind of work people do has a deep impact on the kind of person they can become, and on the quality of their lives, the processes of acquiring social goods is a significant issue of contributive justice (Sayer 2009: 102). In the case of unpaid family care work with vulnerable dependents, the issue is not only that one is without pay but that doing this kind of immanent, and frequently non-transferrable, work also curtails one's ability to contribute to political, economic, and cultural life (Oxfam 2020). Most particularly, it seriously limits the opportunities for many women and carers to exercise their political voice. Primary carers' lack of time and resources to participate and contribute to politics, combined with academic misrecognition of how care consciousness operates separate from but connected to class, gender, and race, leads to silences about the interface between affective inequalities and other injustices in political and sociological discourses (Crean 2018: 13).

7 Affective care relations and values

Because human beings live in affective relational realities, they have emotional ties and bonds that can reinforce their motivation to act as moral agents, to be responsive to others' vulnerabilities (Tronto 1993: 134–135). People are ethical, committed, and caring, as well as economic, political, and cultural: they can and do act other-wise rather than just self-wise. The sets of values that govern people's actions in everyday life and the emotions that accompany them are central to how people live and define themselves (Sayer 2005: 949–952). While interests play a role in framing choices and actions, people are evaluative: they make moral judgements about what matters to them in terms of money, power, and status. Even in a neoliberal capitalist society 'people are "often moved by a quite different set of motives, arising directly out of consideration for the claims of others. They act from a sense of justice, from friendship, loyalty, compassion, gratitude, generosity, sympathy, family affection and the like' (Midgley 1991: 5). Though these latter motives are not necessarily dominant (Sayer 2011: 172), morality exists within people 'as a set of standards of correct behavior that define, orient, and regulate their actions from within' (Vandenberghe 2017: 410); this means that things matter outside of politics and the economy. Moreover, the moral acclaim that comes with being strongly solidaristic impacts on behaviour and directs social action (Stets and McCaffree 2014).

Human vulnerability grounds relationality (Fineman 2004) no matter how complex and conflict-laden these relations may be. Because people have relational nurturing identities (or in some cases unfulfilled nurtured identities), as carers and cared-for persons, their decisions are influenced by their love, care, and solidarity priorities and values, albeit in complex and inconsistent ways (Lynch et al. 2009). To say this is not to deny that people can and do disregard concerns for others; they can and do behave indifferently, neglectfully, and abusively as economic, power, and status concerns intersect with affective relations. The use of brutality and violence as a means of exercising control is, sadly, a global phenomenon, dating back over time (Maleševic 2010). One of the defining struggles in the normative world is the struggle over how to balance concerns and commitment to others with self-interests, tapping into and managing corresponding emotions. But, accounts of human motivation that presume that decisions are made simply in terms of rational self-interest in economic or political terms 'fail to do justice to the . . . ties of sympathy and commitment that bind people to one another in defiance of self-interested calculation' (Nussbaum 1995: 380).

8 Conclusion

Neoliberal capitalism is the dominant political-economic ideology of the twenty-first century. Premised on the primacy of the market in the organization of economic, *and* political and social, life, while it has been contested, it has retained political (Harvey 2005) and cognitive hegemony (Leyva 2018). As it endorses a form of entrepreneurial individualism that is highly competitive and self-interested (Mau 2015), and as it regards these traits as natural and desirable (Friedman 2002), neoliberalism is antithetical to care in deep and profound ways (Federici 2012; Fraser 2016; Oksala 2016). To challenge the values of neoliberal politics, a new language and narrative is required, one that recognizes the sociological reality that humans are moral (as well as self-interested) agents for whom values matter. Affective care relations ground this morality, even if the capacity to act on those values and concerns are delimited by economic, political, and cultural institutions that override them in neoliberal times where self-interest, consumption, and competition have moved from being a common feature of life to being celebrated as social virtues (Bauman 2007; Streeck 2016).

Focusing analytical attention on affective care relations, and the salience of the normative within social scientific and political analysis, offers a different way of thinking about politics and what matters to people in their everyday lives outside of class, status, and power. It opens a political space for new normatively-led modes of political analysis and engagement in a way that challenges many of the core values of neoliberal capitalism. There is scope to intellectually direct political desire towards an admission of vulnerability and other-centredness, to help frame politics relationally and normatively.

Affective relations of love, care, and solidarity matter not only for what they can produce personally (or what their absence or abuse can do negatively to persons, communities, or societies) but for what they might generate politically in terms of heralding different ways of relating beyond hatred, competition, and aggrandizement. Grounding politics in the concerns about love, care, and solidarity, rather than competition and self-interest, has the potential to help generate more egalitarian-driven thinking within public life. It would help restrain the principle of rational economic interest and the politics of fear, both of which are endemic to contemporary capitalism (Beck 1992). It could, over time, create a political discourse that would enable people to think other-wise rather than self-wise. This would help drive public-policy-thinking in a way that is focused on the care-of-the-other in the context of caring of the self, thus breaking the present binary of egoism vs altruism. Recognizing the ethical-political potential of love, care, and solidarity as normative values, therefore, could help change intellectual and public discourse about politics.

To recognize the salience of affective relationality for human choices and actions is not to suggest that relationality is disinterested or driven by simple altruism. Relational beings are simultaneously living in an autonomous space; they are both self-interested and relational simultaneously. People are individuals-in-relation, not separate and soluble persons (England 2005). And being self-interested in the classical economic sense may indeed be what enables people to be other-centred in other spheres of life; autonomy is not the enemy of relationality. Neither is relationality the enemy of autonomy; people who are engaged with the interests of others are more sensitive to their needs and desires and this knowledge of others gives one power to service the other and to be rewarded, in turn, by reciprocal appreciation and action.

A global order that ignores the inevitability of care arising from human inter/dependencies cannot be just (Tronto 2013; Kittay 1999). Ignoring affective relations of nurturing also leads inevitably to a social system that ignores the way women are unable to exercise the kind of parity of participation in the economy, politics, and culture that Fraser (2008) claims is a benchmark of social justice. Affective equality and relational justice are therefore as central to the politics of justice as redistribution, recognition, and representation.

Notes

1 The research for *Affective Equality: Love, Care and Injustice* (Lynch et al. 2009) involved a range of studies on primary and secondary caring for an EU-funded project on which I was the principal investigator. The main Care Conversations'

study involved 21 case studies of care in private households (10 involving care of children and 11 involving care of adults with high care needs). Thirty in-depth conversations were held with carers and care recipients (although some persons held both roles). The households were selected to represent participants from different social classes; they also included disabled people, lone carers, couples (heterosexual and same sex), single people, older and younger carers, people from different ethnic backgrounds, and women and men. Three other related studies are also undertaken for *Affective Equality*: Maeve O'Brien's (2007; 2009) study of the emotional work of 25 mothers with their school-going children – mothers in the study were drawn from a strategically sampled range of different social class, marital status, ethnic, racial, and migrant backgrounds; Maggie Feeley's (2009) study was based on extended interviews with adults aged of those of 28 people aged 40–65 years (15 women and 13 men) who had been in state care, focusing on the relationship between care/lack of care and literacy; Niall Hanlon's (2009) study of eight leaders of men's organizations exploring their views on care and masculinity). The second study investigated the impact of neoliberal policies in the appointment of senior managers in primary, second-level, and higher education institutions, *New Managerialism: Commercialisation, Carelessness and Gender* (Lynch, Grummell and Devine 2012). Fifty people (gender balanced group) were interviewed: 23 senior appointees and 27 chairs and/or key member of the boards of assessors for these appointees. The ways in which care relations interfaced with management in the context of neoliberal reforms was the focus of the study. Finally, a study of solidarity actions during the financial crisis in Ireland was undertaken as part of the SOLIDUS project (EU Horizons 2020 SOLIDUS project). In total, 42 interviews were undertaken with solidarity actors; 25 of these were with leaders of 5 major national organizations involved in organizing solidarity actions against austerity. A further ten individual interviews with leaders of other solidarity movements, and seven more with leaders of women's movements were also undertaken. Data from a focus groups with key national solidarity actors was also collected. This data is currently being analyzed.

2 Whether modern capitalism has contributed to social inclusion is an open question, one that is dependent on empirical verification. It cannot be taken as a given. Data from the OECD (2011; 2015) and work by economists such as Piketty (2014) suggests that while capitalism may have enabled certain social and economic advances, the benefits of these are by no means equally distributed, particularly in an era of neoliberal capitalism.

3 For a critique of the Rawls' (1971) position see Kittay (1999: 75–113).

4 The concept of equality of condition differs from equality of opportunity is discussed in some detail in *Equality: From Theory to Action* (Baker et al. 2004: 21–72).

5 Several studies undertaken by the author also confirm this (Ivancheva, Lynch and Keating 2019; Lynch, Baker and Lyons 2009; Lynch, Grummell and Devine 2012).

6 See Lynch (2007) for a detailed discussion.

7 When inequalities are deep and extensive this provokes anxiety and fear about how one is valued. 'Inequality increases the tendency to regard people at the top of society as hugely important and those near the bottom as almost worthless. The result is that we judge each other more by status and become more anxious about where other people think we fit in' (Wilkinson and Pickett 2018: 28).

8 Inequalities are also intersectional (Crenshaw 1991) because people have multidimensional, structurally framed group-related identities. These must also be recognized in framing theories of justice though it cannot be discussed in detail here (see discussion of this in Baker et al. 2004: 57–72).

References

Arnsperger, C. and Varoufakis, Y. 2003 Toward a Theory of Solidarity. *Erkenntnis*, 59(2): 157–188.

Baker, J. Lynch, K., Cantillon, S. and Walsh, J. 2004. *Equality: From Theory to Action*. Basingstoke: Palgrave Macmillan.

Ball, S. 2003. 'The Teacher's Soul and the Terrors of Performativity', *Journal of Education Policy*, 18(2): 215–228.

Bauman Z. 2007. *Consuming Life*. Oxford: Polity.

Beck, U. 1992. *Risk Society: Towards a New Modernity*. London: Sage.

Boltanski, L. and Porter, C. 2012 [1990]. *Love and Justice as Competences: Three Essays on the Sociology of Action*. Cambridge: Polity Press.

Bowles, S. and Gintis, H. 2000. 'Reciprocity, Self-Interest, and the Welfare State', *Nordic Journal Political Economy*, 26: 33–53.

Bubeck, D. 1995. *Care, Justice and Gender*. Oxford: Oxford University Press.

Cantillon, S. and Lynch, K. 2017. 'Affective Equality: Love Matters', *Hypatia: A Journal of Feminist Philosophy*, 32(1): 169–186.

Connolly, J. 2010. 'Love in the Private: Axel Honneth, Feminism and the Politics of Recognition', *Contemporary Political Theory*, 9: 414–433.

Crean, M. 2018. 'Affective Formations of Class Consciousness: Care Consciousness', *The Sociological Review*, 66(6): 1177–1193. https://doi.org/10.1177/0038026117751341

Crenshaw, K. 1991. 'Mapping the Margins: Intersectionality, Identity Politics, and Violence against Women of Color', *Stanford Law Review*, 43(6): 1241–1299.

Duffy, M. 2011. *Making Care Count: A Century of Gender, Race, and Paid Care Work*. New Brunswick, NJ: Rutgers University Press.

Ehrenreich, B. and Hochschild, A.H. (Eds.) 2003. *Global Women: Nannies, Maids and Sex Workers in the New Economy*. London: Granta.

England, P. 2005. 'Separative and Soluble Selves: Dichotomous Thinking in Economics', in M. Albertson Fineman and T. Doughterty (Eds.), *Feminism Confronts Homo Economicus: Gender, Law and Society*. Cornell: Cornell University Press, pp. 32–56.

Engster, D. 2005. 'Rethinking Care Theory: The Practice of Caring and the Obligation to Care', *Hypatia: A Journal of Feminist Philosophy*, 20(3): 50–74.

Federici, S. 2012. *Revolution at Point Zero: Housework, Reproduction, and Feminist Struggle*. Oakland, CA: PM.

Feeley, M. 2009. 'Living in Care Without Love – The Impact of Affective Inequalities on Learning Literacy', in Lynch et al. (Eds.), *Affective Equality: Love, Care and Injustice*. London: Palgrave Macmillan, pp. 199–215.

Ferguson, A. 2014. 'Feminist Love Politics: Romance, Care, and Solidarity', in A. Ferguson and A.G. Jónasdóttir (Eds.), *Love: A Question for in the Twenty-First Century*. New York: Routledge, pp. 250–264.

Fernandez, B. 2010. 'Cheap and Disposable? The Impact of the Global Economic Crisis on the Migration of Ethiopian Women Domestic Workers to the Gulf', *Gender & Development*, 18(2): 249–262.

Finch, J. and Groves, D. 1983. *A Labour of Love: Women, Work, and Caring*. London, UK: Routledge & Kegan Paul.

Fineman, M.A. 1995. *The Neutered Mother, the Sexual Family, and Other Twentieth Century Tragedies*. New York: Routledge.

Fineman, M.A. 2004. *The Autonomy Myth: A Theory of Dependency*. New York: The Free Press.
Folbre, N. 1994. *Who Pays for the Kids? Gender and the Structures of Constraint*. London: Routledge.
Folbre, N. 2012. *For Love and Money: Care provision in the United States*. New York: Russell Sage Foundation.
Fraser, N. 1995. 'From Redistribution to Recognition: Dilemmas of Justice in a "Post-Socialist" Age', *New Left Review*, 212: 68–93.
Fraser, N. 1997. 'After the Family Wage: A Postindustrial Thought Experiment', in N. Fraser (Ed.), *Justice Interruptus: Critical Reflections on the "Postsocialist" Condition*. New York: Routledge, pp. 41–66.
Fraser, N. 2008. *Scales of Justice: Reimagining Political Space in a Globalizing World*. Cambridge: Polity Press.
Fraser, N. 2010. 'Injustice at Intersecting Scales: On 'Social Exclusion' and the 'Global Poor'. *European Journal of Social Theory*, 13(3): 363–371.
Fraser, N. 2016. 'Contradictions of Capital and Care', *New Left Review*, 100(July/August): 99–117.
Fraser, N. and Gordon, L. 1994. 'A Genealogy of Dependency: Tracing a Keyword of the U.S. Welfare State', *Signs*, 19(2): 309–336.
Friedman, M. 2002. *Capitalism and Freedom*. Chicago: University of Chicago Press.
Gardner, H. 1983. *Frames of Mind: The Theory of Multiple Intelligences*. New York: Basic Books.
Garrett, P.M. 2010. 'Recognizing the Limitations of the Political Theory of Recognition: Axel Honneth, Nancy Fraser and Social Work', *British Journal of Social Work*, 40: 1517–1533.
Gilbert, P. 2010. *The Compassionate Mind*. London: Constable.
Glenn, E.N. 2010. *Forced to Care: Coercion and Caregiving in America*, Cambridge, MA: Harvard University Press.
Gomberg, P. 2007. *How to Make Opportunity Equal: Race and Contributive Justice*. Malden, MA: Blackwell.
Grummell, B., Devine, D. and Lynch, K. 2009. 'The Careless Manager: Gender, Care and New Managerialism in Higher Education', *Gender and Education*, 21(2): 191–208.
Halldenius, L. 1998. 'Non-Domination and Egalitarian Welfare Politics', *Ethical Theory and Moral Practice*, 1(3): 335–353.
Hanlon, N. 2009. 'Caregiving Masculinities: An Exploratory Analysis', in Lynch et al. (Eds.), *Affective Equality. Love, Care and Injustice*. London: Palgrave Macmillan, pp. 180–198.
Hardt, M. and Negri, A. 2009. *Commonwealth*. Cambridge, MA: Harvard University Press.
Harvey, D. 2005. *A Brief History of Neoliberalism*. Oxford: Oxford University Press.
Held, V. 2006. *The Ethics of Care: Personal, Political and Global*. Oxford: Oxford University Press.
Honneth, A. 1995. *The Struggle for Recognition: The Moral Grammar of Social Conflicts*. Translated by J. Anderson. Cambridge, MA: The MIT Press.
Honneth, A. 2003. 'Redistribution as Recognition: A Response to Nancy Fraser', in N. Fraser and A. Honneth (Eds.), *Redistribution or Recognition? A Political-Philosophical Exchange*. London: Verso.
hooks, b. 2000. *All About Love*. New York: William Morrow & Co.

Ivancheva, M., Lynch, K. and Keating, K. 2019. 'Precarity, Gender and Care in the Neoliberal Academy', *Gender, Work and Organization*, 26(4): 448–462. https://onlinelibrary-wiley-com.ucd.idm.oclc.org/doi/pdf/10.1111/gwao.12350

Kittay, E.F. 1999. *Love's Labor*. New York: Routledge.

Layard, P.R.G. 2005. *Happiness: Lessons from a New Science*. London: Allen Lane.

Leonard, M. 2004. 'Bonding and Bridging Social Capital: Reflections from Belfast', *Sociology*, 38(5): 927–944.

Leyva, R. 2018. 'Towards a Cognitive-Sociological Theory of Subjectivity and Habitus Formation in Neoliberal Societies', *European Journal of Social Theory*, 22(2): 250–271. https://doi-org.ucd.idm.oclc.org/10.1177%2F1368431017752909

Lolich, L. and Lynch, K. 2016. 'The Affective Imaginary: Students as Affective Consumers of Risk', *Higher Education Research and Development*, 35(1): 17–30.

Lolich, L. and Lynch, K. 2017. 'No Choice without Care: Palliative Care as a Relational Matter, the Case of Ireland', *Soundings: An Interdisciplinary Journal*, 100(4): 353–374.

Lutz, H. 2011. *The New Maids: Transnational Women and the Care Economy*. London: Zed Books.

Lynch, K. 2007. 'Love Labour as a Distinct and Non-Commodifiable Form of Care Labour', *The Sociological Review*, 54(3): 550–570.

Lynch, K. and Baker, J. 2005. 'Equality in Education: An Equality of Condition Perspective'. *Theory and Research in Education*, 3(2): 131–164.

Lynch, K. 2009. 'Affective Equality: Who Cares?', *Development*, 52(3): 410–415.

Lynch, K. and Baker, J. 2009. 'Conclusion', in K. Lynch, J. Baker and M. Lyons (Eds.), *Affective Equality: Love, Care and Injustice*. London: Palgrave Macmillan, pp. 216–236.

Lynch, K., Baker, J. and Lyons, M. 2009. *Affective Equality: Love, Care and Injustice*. London: Palgrave Macmillan.

Lynch, K. and Crean, M. 2018. Why Equality of Economic Condition is Essential for Equality of Opportunity', in J. Harford (Ed.), *Education for All? The Legacy of Free Post-Primary Education in Ireland*. Oxford: Peter Lang, pp. 139–160.

Lynch, K., Grummell, B. and Devine, D. 2012. *New Managerialism in Education: Commercialization, Carelessness and Gender*. Basingstoke: Palgrave Macmillan.

Lynch, K. and Lyons, M. 2009. 'Love Labouring: Nurturing Rationalities and Relational Identities', in K. Lynch, J. Baker and M. Lyons (Eds.), *Affective Equality: Love, Care and Injustice*. London: Palgrave Macmillan, pp. 54–77.

Lynch, K., Lyons, M. and Cantillon, S. 2007. 'Breaking Silence: Educating Citizens for Love, Care and Solidarity', *International Studies in Sociology of Education*, 17(1–2): 1–19.

Lynch, K. and Kalaitzake, M. 2018. 'Affective and Calculative Solidarity: The Impact of Individualism and Neoliberal Capitalism', *European Journal of Social Theory*, 17(3): 343–358.

Malešević, S. 2010. *The Sociology of War and Violence*. Cambridge: Cambridge University Press.

Matheis, C. 2014. 'On Various Notions of "Relations" in Enrique Dussel's Philosophy of Liberation', *Hispanic/Latino Issues in Philosophy*, 13(2): 9–15.

Mau, S. 2015. *Inequality, Marketization and the Majority Class: Why Did the European Middle Classes Accept Neo-Liberalism*. Basingstoke: Palgrave.

McNay, L. 2008. *Against Recognition*. Cambridge: Polity Press.

Midgley, M. 1991. 'The Origin of Ethics', in P. Singer (Ed.), *A Companion to Ethics*. Oxford: Blackwell, pp. 3–13.

Mies, M. 2014. *Patriarchy and Accumulation on a World Scale: Women in the International Division of Labour*. London: Zed Books.
Mol, A.M. 2008. *The Logic of Care: Health and the Problem of Patient Choice*. New York: Routledge.
Nussbaum, M.C. 1995. 'Emotions and Women's Capabilities', in M. Nussbaum and J. Glover (Eds.), *Women, Culture and Development: A Study of Human Capabilities*. Oxford: Oxford University Press, pp. 360–395.
O'Brien, M. 2007. 'Mothers' Emotional Care Work in Education and its Moral Imperative', *Gender and Education*, 19(2): 159–177.
O'Brien, M. 2009. 'The Impact of Economic, Social, Cultural and Emotional Capital on Mothers' Love and Care Work in Education', in Lynch et al. (Eds.), *Affective Equality: Love, Care and Injustice*. London: Palgrave Macmillan, pp. 158–179.
O'Mahony, P. 1997. *Mountjoy Prisoners: A Sociological and Criminological Profile*. Dublin: Stationery Office, Government Publications.
OECD. 2011. *An Overview of Growing Income Inequalities in OECD Countries*. OECD: Paris.
OECD. 2015. *In It Together: Why Less Inequality Benefits All*. OECD: Paris.
Oksala, J. 2016. 'Affective Labor and Feminist Politics', *Signs*, 41(2): 281–303.
Oxfam. 2020. *Time to Care: Unpaid and Underpaid Care Work and the Global Inequality Crisis*. Oxford: Oxfam International. (Oxfam Briefing paper presented to the World Economic Forum, Davos, Jan.).
Paskov, M. and Dewilde, C. 2012. 'Income Inequality and Solidarity in Europe', *Research in Social Stratification and Mobility*, 30(4): 415–432.
Piketty, T. 2014. *Capital in the Twenty-First Century*. Cambridge, MA: Belknap Press of Harvard University Press.
Rawls, J. 1971. *A Theory of Justice*. Oxford: Oxford University Press.
Rodríguez-Pose, A. and von Berlepsch, V. 2014. 'Social Capital and Individual Happiness in Europe', *Journal of Happiness Studies*, 15(2): 357–386.
Rorty, R. 1989. *Contingency, Irony, and Solidarity*. Cambridge: Cambridge University Press.
Sayer, A. 2005. 'Class, Moral Worth and Recognition', *Sociology*, 39(5): 947–963.
Sayer, A. 2009. 'The Injustice of Unequal Work', *Soundings*, 43: 102–113.
Sayer, A. 2011. *Why Things Matter to People: Social Science, Values and Ethical Life*. Cambridge: Cambridge University Press.
Sennett, R. 1998. *The Corrosion of Character: The Personal Consequences of Work in the New Capitalism*. London/New York: W. W. Norton & Company.
Stets, J. and McCaffree, K. (2014) 'Linking Morality, Altruism and Social Solidarity Using Identity Theory', in V. Jeffries (Ed.), *Palgrave Handbook of Altruism, Morality and Social Solidarity*. Basingstoke: Palgrave, pp. 333–351.
Stjernø, S. 2004. *Solidarity in Europe: The History of an Idea*. Cambridge: Cambridge: University Press.
Streeck, W. 2016. *How Will Capitalism End?* London: Verso.
Thompson, M.J. 2014. 'Axel Honneth and the Neo-Idealist Turn in Critical Theory', *Philosophy and Social Criticism*, 40(8): 779–797.
Tilly, C. 1998. *Durable Inequality*. Berkeley: University of California Press.
Traustadottir, R. 2000. 'Disability Reform and Women's Caring Work', in Madonna Harrington Meyer (Ed.), *Care work: Gender, Class and the Welfare State*. London: Routledge.

Tronto, J.C. 1987. 'Beyond Gender Difference to a Theory of Care', *Signs*, 12(4): 644–663.
Tronto, J.C. 1993. *Moral Boundaries: A Political Argument for an Ethic of Care*. New York: Routledge.
Tronto, J.C. 2013. *Caring Democracy: Markets, Equality and Justice*. New York: New York University Press.
Vandenberghe, F. 2017. 'Sociology as Moral Philosophy (and Vice Versa)', *Canadian Review of Sociology/La Société Canadienne de Sociologie*, 54(4): 405–422.
Wacquant, L. 2009. *Punishing the Poor: The Neoliberal Government of Social Insecurity*. Durham: Duke University Press.
Wilkinson, R.G. and Pickett, K. 2009. *The Spirit Level: Why More Equal Societies Almost Always do Better*. London: Penguin.
Wilkinson, R.G. and Pickett, K. 2018. *The Inner Level: How More Equal Societies Reduce Stress, Restore Sanity and Improve Everybody's Wellbeing*. London: Allen Lane (Penguin).
Wright, E.O. 2010. *Envisioning Real Utopias*. London: Verso.

Part III

RETHINKING GRAMMARS OF OPPRESSION AND INCLUSION

7

VULNERABLE POLITICAL LIFE

Distributive justice, critical theory, and critical care ethics

Naïma Hamrouni

In her influential book *Moral Boundaries* (1993), Joan Tronto drew attention to ways in which the powerful and privileged in society tend to benefit the most from the (underappreciated) care labour provided by others, without being expected to reciprocate. In her more recent book *Caring Democracy* (2013) which appeared 20 years later, Tronto takes up her argument again, developing it further. She explains that the assignment mainly to women and racialized[1] minorities of this invisibilized care labour – conceived of as a labour of love and reproduction but also as the labour required by the mere daily maintenance of life – has enabled the most privileged (in terms of class, gender, race, religion) to maintain its dominant position within political and economic institutions, as well as its monopoly of epistemic privilege in moral and political philosophy.[2] In Tronto's studies and those of her followers, one senses the immense social transformations that a politicizing of care ethics entails, at the very least, as far as the organization of labour and the necessary changes in our patriarchal culture and mentalities are concerned.

The development of a critical care ethics, on the heels of Tronto's vital work, has often focused on a critique of the division of labour and the formal capitalist economy, which significantly impacts the informal care economy. Indeed, many feminist writers who take this approach engage in a project of analyzing and rethinking the ways in which informal care of dependents, including health care, might alternatively be valuated and organized. At present, this type of care operates largely under a neoliberal logic that values efficiency at the expense of good care, which, for its part, solicits the virtues of attentiveness, openness, responsiveness, and concern for others. When proponents of a critical care ethics speak about a 'caring democracy' or 'politics of care', they invite us to imagine a society in which the labour of care is shared more equitably among all citizens (some have even put forward the idea of a 'civic duty of care'), in which this essential work that sees to the support and maintenance of life, and of the environment for living, are given just social recognition and monetary retribution, and in which caregivers have more of a voice when it comes to orienting our public policies and in establishing the values that guide their development. For many sceptics, however, this objective is still far too abstract, unsubstantial, and imprecise. More remains to be said if we are to have a more substantive idea of 1) the specific nature of the criticisms addressed by critical care ethics of the way our organization of labour currently functions under capitalism, as compared, say, with feminist egalitarianism and critical theory, and 2) the concrete ways in which the ideals of critical care ethics are to be deployed.

In this chapter, I aim to provide the beginning of an answer to these questions. I do not purport to offer the best answer, nor even the most ambitious. This answer may not find consensus among critical care ethicists. But the exercise of articulating some possible implications of caring institutions is worthwhile, even if only to determine, in the end, that the answer obtained is not altogether satisfactory. Proponents of care ethics as a critical theory will have at least one, or one more, reference from which to define more clearly what their approach implies, and does not imply, when imagining how a given institution would function. In order to illustrate my point, I will focus, every now and again, on the work culture of political life. This culture has long been denounced by grassroots feminists and antiracist social movements, who believe that still today, political life functions structurally in such a way that women and racialized people are systematically excluded.

I will begin by discussing what both the liberal feminist approach and critical theory consider to be amiss with this organizational and labour culture of political life. I will contrast these two 'classical' analyses with an articulation from the point of view of critical care ethics. I intend to show how a critical care ethics perspective draws attention to something that critical theory does not yet sufficiently highlight, namely, that political life is not just simply invested with a culture that erases and stifles difference in its various manifestations. It also fosters and perpetuates a *denial* or an *epistemic ignorance* (Gilson 2014) of what in my previous works I call 'ordinary vulnerability' (Hamrouni 2015; 2016a), which fundamentally characterizes us as embodied and eminently relational human beings.

1 Political life, underrepresentation of minorities, and the distributive paradigm of justice

The distributive conceptualization of gender inequality, which looks at the gendered division of labour, examines the injustices at the source of, and that have the consequence of perpetuating, the societal assignment of women to caregiving roles, which keeps them out of politics. This conception of distributive justice is essentially articulated around the key concept of inequality of opportunity (which women are subject to, notably) to attain the social positions associated with what the father of the theory of contemporary social justice, philosopher John Rawls (1971) called primary social goods, namely, income and wealth, power and opportunities, and the social bases of self-respect.

Most liberal egalitarian philosophers of the 1970s did not consider the gendered division of labour, or its associated phenomenon of the underrepresentation of women and racialized people in positions of power, as fundamentally raising issues of *justice*. Most saw this as the outcome of free career choices made by individual men and women in accordance with their preferences and conceptions of the good life. Since the publication of Susan Moller Okin's influential *Justice, Gender, and the Family* (1989) however, contemporary egalitarians have tended to take this phenomenon of underrepresentation more seriously. This underrepresentation came to be conceived as the combined effect of persistent forms of discrimination,[3] cultural norms, and socialization that continuously supposes and assigns women to be primary caregivers, which in turn influences their preferences and decisions about family planning and job opportunities. Indeed, gender expectations negatively affect equality of opportunity where women are concerned, to develop apposite skills and to access the occupations in their chosen field available on the job market (whether they anticipate getting married, are married, and also if divorced).

Twenty years after Okin's book, Ingrid Robeyns (2009) and Anca Gheaus (2012) put forward similar arguments from this egalitarian approach. Robeyns argues that the gendered division of labour unjustly undermines women's freedom of choice and translates into unequal opportunities. Gheaus, who also bases her approach on these two same egalitarian liberal principles (equal opportunity and freedom of choice), discusses how gender norms continually orient individuals towards gendered occupations, since adhering to gender roles is less psychologically and socially costly. According to the principle of gender justice that Gheaus puts forward, this gendered division of labour cannot be said to be just so long as the option of defying gender roles is not equally or less costly than adhering to them.

Since the sources of unequal opportunities to advance to positions of power, for example, to hold political office, are multiple and complex, rooted as much in culture, social conventions, and norms as they are in the operations of a market economy, actions taken to remedy this inequality of opportunity that affects women will also necessarily be diverse, from the point of view of egalitarianism and distributive justice. As early as 1989, Okin proposed both legal reforms (essentially civil and labour law) and reforms in public policy, aimed at undoing gender and reversing its adverse effects. Where public policy is concerned, these reforms would aim to abolish gender (understood as power disparities between the sexes) and revise the way labour is organized.[4] Where family law is concerned, these reforms would aim to protect vulnerable parties in a marriage and after a divorce.

She proposes in this vein that 'both partners have equal legal entitlement to all earnings coming into the household' (Okin 1989: 180).

This distributive approach to gender inequality is also predominant among theorists who engage with other disciplines outside philosophy and who approach the issue of the gendered division of labour from their own fields of specialization. For example, in *Why so Slow? The Advancement of Women* (1998) psychologist Virginia Valian examines forms of direct and indirect discrimination and looks at ways to tackle the constraints that prevent women from attaining social positions of power. In so doing, she puts forward the still highly relevant concept of 'gender schemas', which everyone, including employers, marshal in their perceptions of different individuals' abilities, and which negatively influence employers' assessments of female job candidates. These gender schemas lead, unconsciously, to negative evaluations of women who are perceived as 'too feminine' (who, consequently, *are deemed soft, or superficial, and fail to demonstrate the qualities required for the successful performance of power, such as assertiveness*) as well as women who demonstrate these qualities labeled as masculine and so not suited for them. In other words, Valian shows how women who seek to access the spheres of power face a double bind. To take another example, legal scholar Joan C. Williams (2000) discusses the 'maternal wall', pointing out that although the 'glass ceiling' – which she refers to as the legal and official barriers that traditionally block women's access to professional advancement – has been formally broken, one of the main constraints women face in pursuing their careers is connected to the way maternity is treated in the labour market, which still systemically disadvantages mothers. Legal scholar Mary Ann Mason, sociologist Nicholas Wolfinger, and social policy researcher Marc Goulden (2013) have more recently documented this success gap between female and male parents (the baby gap), showing that while having a child slows down women's professional progress towards positions of authority, parenthood has a positive impact on men's career advancement.

The distributive justice approach, which dominated the landscape of social and political philosophy between the seventies and 2000, was able to defend the importance of equal opportunity to access the highest offices of power in our societies, which has long been denied to women and minorities. This approach is guided by the objectives of ensuring equality of opportunity, including equal access to positions in mainstream institutions (education, the labour market, and political office, for instance), and of a more just and equitable distribution of social goods, namely wealth, power, and prestige. It favours anti-discrimination programs and family policies that encourage a more equal share in the childcare between opposite-sex spouses and that financially compensate the losses in opportunity experienced by women taking maternity leave after the birth of a child. But an analysis based in this egalitarian distributive approach of the gendered division of labour and its correlate, the underrepresentation of women in positions of authority, has some serious limitations from the perspective of critical theory, as I will now discuss.

2 Critical theory, structural exclusion, and the oppression of the 'included'

As I wrote together with Pierre-Yves Néron, in *Justice, Gender, and the Corporation* (2017), feminist liberal egalitarianism does not take full measure of how the *ordinary functioning of political institutions*, which have historically been conceived and organized in the absence of women and racialized minorities, disadvantage these groups *by default* and end up *structurally* supporting their exclusion from these milieux. As we have said (2017),

> this distributive approach to gender justice is limited, however, because it assumes that equality will be realized from the moment women are able to access the social positions and roles from which they have traditionally been excluded (due to gender constraints).

This view leaves uncontested the value accorded to these roles, the attitudes required to fulfil them, and the organization of the institution to which women have access. Its advocates could argue that *fair* (Rawlsian) equality of opportunity requires, moreover, that the inequalities that subsist between women and men benefit women, being the 'most disadvantaged' group.[5] Nonetheless, such a scenario, though better than the former, would not address *the injustice of excluding them from the processes by which a) these occupations are defined, b) the skills, competencies, and attitudes to be possessed are predetermined, c) the functions are hierarchically structured, and d) the relations between them are regulated* (Hamrouni and Néron 2017: 210). If we come back to the example of the political life, from the outset, we could say that critical theory better problematizes the masculine, white and ableist culture that has shaped the institution of politics: everything from the human attitudes that are valued and expressed within this milieu, to its rules of operation is put into question by critical theory.

As a great many grassroots feminists activists and critical theoreticians have pointed out, the exercise of political leadership in contemporary political life depends directly on the mastery of masculine, white and ableist attitudes, competencies, and qualities: that is, the capacity of members of a parliament to hold well-reasoned and convincing discourse, to put forward their ideas, and to articulately, eloquently, and competitively debate them in a context that some readily liken to a boxing ring. This analogy is anything but far-fetched and is made explicit with what is commonly called a 'knock-down argument', the final blow that defeats a house member's opponent after a verbal sparring match. Mastering this art of political argumentation, moving easily about in this culture of communication implies, by definition, being mainstream, in the sense that a form of discredit is put on the feminine voice and on the coloured one, from the tone of this voice, to its accent, style, and to the way it is embodied (see also Pateman 1988; Phillips 1995; Young 2000).[6] And while the bellicose culture of political debate disadvantages gender minorities, speaking with an 'accent' or pronunciation that reveals modest social origins or a 'different', stigmatized ethnic origin, also incurs a similar risk of being shut out of the discussion. This is, at least, why egalitarians such as Elizabeth Anderson, in her book *The Imperative of Integration* (Anderson 2010: 35–38), place the emphasis they do on the imperative for racial minorities to raise their educational and 'cultural capital' if we seek integration. Satisfying a dominant majority's expectations generally involves polishing or 'softening' one's accent to mask or erase signs of a socially disadvantaged background or else a past associated with ghettos or suburbs that would cause them prejudice.

From the perspective of critical theory, which starts with the lived experience of oppression, the problem we encounter here is not so much that a command of the quasi-martial discursive attitudes privileged in politics is still denied to women and minorities. Would this be the problem, reducing injustice would simply require that we provide these groups comparable education so they can develop male and white 'skills'. Critical theory argues, to the contrary, that this 'integrative view' put forward by proponents of egalitarian justice actually goes hand in hand with a prior disqualification of the cultures of minoritized social groups (they distinguish between integration and inclusion). This 'integrative view' fails to see and to question the situatedness of the majority culture (its own whiteness and androcentrism) and confuses it with a universal normative standard to be met by all. From a critical theory perspective, if minorities are structurally excluded from political life (and every other sphere associated with power and knowledge), it is because the culture of political life constitutively excludes their own, equally valuable, skills and virtues, so they are excluded even before they are subject to direct discrimination.

Critical theory leads us to reinterpret the problems of the division of labour and of underrepresentation of minorities in politics as one not just of inequality of opportunity but of structural injustice that begets *two distinct phenomena*. The first of these phenomena is a *structural exclusion* of those who do not exhibit the skills and attitudes deemed essential to holding office, while the ensemble of requirements and qualities deemed essential to carrying out official functions has been established by those in positions of power and is based in their own values and interests.

The second phenomenon refers to the perils, for those who nevertheless manage to integrate in these environments, of having to live out the effects of cultural imperialism. They are compelled to submit to a dominant norm against which they, as minorities, are constantly measured, though they can hardly measure up (Young 1990: 59). And they know, they feel, that one's acceptability is not unconditional: it depends on one's ability to conform to the dominant values, interests, and skills. This conditionality compels one to adjust her behaviour and attitudes according to these dominant norms, while scorning and suppressing in herself the tendencies that threaten to disconfirm her qualifications for a given position. The weight of cultural imperialism cannot be experienced without suffering damage, especially psychological damage. Indeed, cultural imperialism (here, androcentrism, whiteness, ableism in the workplace) has the effect of instilling among minorities *a perpetual feeling of being out of place*. In her heavily discussed article, "Changing the Ideology and Culture of Philosophy: Not by Reason (Alone)", feminist philosopher Sally Haslanger confides that being a woman and thus a minority at virtually every major philosophical event, 'often results in [her] feeling tongue-tied and "stupid", even to this day' (Haslanger 2008: 218). While she discusses the underrepresentation of women in academic philosophy, her ideas can clearly be transposed to the issue of minorities in politics or that of a black woman who sits alone among middle- and upper-class white men in parliament, around a business meeting table, or on a board of directors. Haslanger identifies with this feeling of loneliness, of difference and of fundamentally being out of place, which is one reason why, she states, after earning their bachelor's degrees, BIPOC and women philosophy students tend to reorient themselves in other fields that appear more hospitable and where they can feel from the outset that they are in control of their means. That said, it is also of interest here to note the anxiety and loss of resources one experiences as a minority within a larger social group, and the feeling of being alone, exposed, conspicuous. This anxiety and the kind of 'rage' (Haslanger 2008: 210) that such marginalization arouses is reflected in the philosopher's personal account of her experience in her profession.

Some of the most influential critical and recognition theorists, such as Axel Honneth (1996), have for some time now elucidated the damage to the human psyche and identity suffered with the repeated experience of non-recognition and cultural imperialism within a dominant group. From their point of view, our self-being is intersubjectively constituted, dialogically constructed through continual relationship to others, and is thus also intersubjectively vulnerable, fragile. Self-confidence and self-esteem, as well as self-respect, are utterly dependent upon this image of ourselves reflected in our relations with others; our identity is, essentially, always open to the possibility of injury, and its fallibility is susceptible to being exploited from the moment of our encounter with the other. From this point of view, repeatedly being confronted with a deformed or reduced image of oneself, reflected back to oneself in one's relations to the majority, would indeed negatively impact any practical-relationship-to-self one has managed to develop with oneself. Such experiences also compromise the formation of a healthy and integrated identity.

The perspective of a critical care ethics, I suggest, opens the door to a complementary reading of the form of oppression experienced by someone who lives in a context of cultural imperialism. Such a person is not only compelled to relate to herself as inferior or unworthy, through a pattern of negativity. More seriously, she might not be able to relate to oneself, full stop, to feel, and know what she feels – to be authentic, true to herself and others. It is because this is precisely this betrayal of the self that is implicitly expected of minorities presented with the opportunity of obtaining positions of power. And this fundamental betrayal is taught from an early age. Children learn very early on that integration into mainstream institutions is granted on the condition of adjusting and conforming their behaviour and attitudes to the prevailing gender and racial norms, with the consequence that they look down on the inner desires, attitudes, or preferences that would make them unfit to advance in their desired professions.[7] Opening up a broader horizon of possibilities, critical care ethics invites us to imagine what our institutions, from the schools, to the world of politics, and to universities and the businesses would look like if such betrayal of oneself were no longer constantly encouraged by gender, racial, colonial, and ableist norms.

3 Contrasting a critical care ethics with the distributive and critical paradigms of justice

Regarding the gendered and racial division of labour, one might be inclined to think, on the one hand, that critical care ethics would have nothing more to contribute beyond what the arguments of egalitarian distributive justice have brought. It is true that, in a significant way, the critique formulated by care ethics parallels the critique of the gender and racial division of labour that feminist egalitarians have already put forward. Namely, that the assignment of the care labour to subordinate groups leads to their underrepresentation in positions of power. For example, the respective works of Anca Gheaus and Ingrid Robeyns, which draw on the insights of influential thinker Susan Moller Okin, demonstrate how a theory of distributive justice ought also to address the unequal distribution of labour between men and women, both in the family and on the labour market, and also how justice theorists ought to be concerned with various means of countering these gender inequalities.[8] In the realm of politics, indeed, care theorists like Tronto elucidate how the political underrepresentation of racial minorities and women is largely the direct consequence of the unequal division of labour and the assignment of care work to the subordinate. In this respect, theorists from both these camps likely agree to some extent on the probable sources of underrepresentation: the gender socialization, the persistence of gender norms according to which care labour is assigned to women and the division of labour in the family, systemic discrimination, and sexual harassment.

On the other hand, we could also say that precisely where care theorists go further, in offering a structural critique of the gendered and racial division of labour, they converge with critical theorists such as Iris Marion Young. Here, indeed, are where proponents of these two approaches undoubtedly converge as well: the strategy that feminists have criticized as one of 'add and stir' (adding minorities to an existing practice, without changing the practice) leads to an impasse, to a reproduction of the structure that breeds injustices. In this sense, the struggle against oppression is not only about a more equitable distribution of caregiving roles and positions of power (as egalitarians argue), but above all (that is, *even prior to all forms of distribution* within available positions on the market), it must take place through equal democratic participation in restructuring institutions, in decision-making about the organization of labour, in charting various governmental functions and roles, in determining which aptitudes and skills merit being developed and cultivated, and in determining which criteria distinguish success from failure. We are now faced with the question: what is, then, uniquely distinctive about critical care ethics in its approach to the underrepresentation of minorities in politics, or in any other position of power?

Critical care ethics calls for us to recognize, along with critical theorists, the necessity of democratizing institutions and, along with egalitarians, that freedom of choice of a fundamental nature is undermined by the gender norms that govern our social environment, our preferences, our expectations, and our desires. But critical care ethics also goes further in its understanding of the reproduction of injustice. It asks us to pay attention to what is truly being played out with, on the one hand, the relegation of care work to subordinate groups, on the other hand, the concentration of those who are absolved of care work in positions that entail decision-making power. Simply put, the problem, from the point of view of critical care ethics, is not only associated with the fact that women and racialized minorities are denied access to positions of power,[9] or that they have been excluded from participating in defining these institutions of power. The problem arises from the fact that *the powerful classes are themselves cut off from care, lost sight of their own vulnerability and tend to reproduce an institutional culture conceived from this severed point of view.*

This is the argument I present in the following paragraphs, which will allow me to highlight the originality and relevance of critical care ethics for approaching differently a question regularly broached by feminists for some time, namely: 'What's wrong with the division of labour along gendered and racial lines?' A critical care ethics aims at shifting our perspective in order to see behind the scenes: not only is the success of the powerful fueled by an invisible army of care laborers (from women to racialized people, to undocumented immigrants), but also their very ordinary vulnerability is daily supported, repaired, and masked by them. Invisibilizing this dependency upon the marginalized, upon the 'have nots', allows for the subterfuge of meritocracy to persist.

4 Critical care ethics and the denial of ordinary human vulnerability

When we take care as the cornerstone of our critical analysis, the organization of labour shows itself as thought up according to a model of the subject who enjoys the privilege (more exactly, who enjoys what they are encouraged to see as a privilege) of being able to organize their daily life so as to be overworked and loaded down, and, in this same state of being harried and constantly pressed for time, cut off from the substance of caring relations and of ordinary human vulnerability – one's own, that of others. On the one hand, critical care ethics draws attention to a concentration of certain segments of the population in occupations that attend to vulnerability associated with care. On the other hand, it illuminates the norm of invulnerability performed by members of a group who manage to rise to political. Critical care ethics, in other words, points to the fact that the dominant are those who can 1) release themselves from all sorts of care work by delegating these responsibilities to others (for example, by assuming that their partner will take the bulk of the domestic chores and care of the children, and or by hiring a housekeeper to see to the living environment, or a nanny to care for the children), and moreover,[10] 2) receive the care of others without needing to recognize that they benefit from it and depend vitally upon it, since, as it turns out, they are vulnerable subjects too.

Many care theorists have focused their work on the acute or 'special' vulnerabilities of children, the sick, the disabled, or elderly people experiencing a loss of autonomy, as well as on a *derived* vulnerability experienced by caregivers who are answerable to and responsible for the care of others in the informal sphere, without remuneration (Kittay 1999). But the concept of ordinary vulnerability, which I have formulated elsewhere (Hamrouni 2015, 2016a), underscores a vulnerability that characterizes us all by the simple fact that we are embodied and relational beings. Ordinary vulnerability is not just the domain of those who are largely dependent on others. This ordinary vulnerability is not provisional or associated with a phase of normal human development, be it childhood, a temporary loss of function caused by an illness or accident, or old age. Ordinary vulnerability is constant, permanent, and shared by all; it is universal. At no point can we do without the care of others. We would not survive physiologically, and neither would be able to live *well*. This ordinary vulnerability is what makes giving and receiving care, that is, the exchange of care, so vital to each and every person.

This understanding of vulnerability as something ordinary that (also) characterizes the most powerful of humans is central to a critical care ethics. It offers a new angle from which to comprehend the phenomenon by which a class of vulnerable is created and demarcated from the class of those who perform invulnerability. The thesis of this approach is that the fundamental difference between those who purport to be invulnerable and others is the social status that allows the former to absolve themselves of their care responsibilities, while assimilating the care that others provide them, while invisibilizing it. It is this assimilation of care, coupled with its invisibilization, which generates the myth of invulnerability, that also supports the myth of meritocracy.

Since my focus here is on the world of politics, more than on the wider labour market, we could speak, more specifically, of an overworked invulnerable class. Overwork and work schedules that are very demanding of one's time are, to be sure, commonplace throughout our capitalist societies subject to the logic of neoliberalism and economic globalization. I do not want to minimize the pervasiveness of the phenomenon of the overworked American. Only, the political class is also known to be subject to extremely demanding schedules, with little time off and few holidays, and no compassionate or parental leave. Politicians are expected above all to give everything to their work, far beyond the scope of electoral campaigns, which are for their part enormously consuming.

Critical care ethics offers a helpful angle from which we can begin to understand what is at stake with the fact that the people who gain access to political power are more likely to be those who are cut off from care. It does not presume, as well-known philosophers like Simone de Beauvoir and Hannah Arendt have done, that care work is itself always banal, repetitive, unpleasant, trying, something to unburden oneself of, if at all possible.[11] Critical care ethics elucidates, rather, the role that this defiance of care and of human relationality plays in perpetuating divisions and redivisions of labour along lines of gender, race, class, citizenship status, and national origin.

Indeed, a critical care ethics is concerned, at a level of interpretation of the more fundamental social reality, with tracing, in the context of our Western culture, the motivations concealed behind a determination to free oneself of care (via a division of labour which, by the same token, creates social differentiation and relegates care work to minorities). The classification of otherwise undifferentiated human beings into categories assigned to care and categories freed from care certainly works, both economically and politically, to the advantage of the dominant group.

For many men, the performance of manhood ends up cutting themselves off from care (mostly by outsourcing that labour of care). Doing so, they are also prevented from getting in touch with, and cultivating, the part of their humanity that can flourish through caring activities and through the exercise of a caring ethics. In my previous work (2015; 2000), I proposed that, at the individual level, there was an *existential incentive* in being rid of care and in fleeing those practices that involve a relation to the body (especially to fragile or sick bodies), and which inevitably call to the situation our own finitude. Although I am no longer certain of maintaining that kind of perfectionist position concerning the existential incentive in being cut off from care, I will say something else on this point that today seems more likely to be substantiated by empirical studies in neuro and moral psychology: those who cut themselves off from care deny not only themselves, but the whole of society, the moral and psycho-affective capacities for care that they might have developed, and which originate and flourish in caring practices of the kind they do not participate in. These refer to concern, attentiveness, responsiveness, openness to the different other, to being touched, affected, and changed by the other. These capacities merit being mobilized not only within the exchange of care in the family sphere, in loving relationships and friendships, but also in the public sphere of politics.

One could reply here that the overworked invulnerable should be free to choose, from among the set of human capacities, those that they will seek to cultivate – that overwork and invulnerability are conceptions of the good life that individuals in liberal democratic societies, which make pluralism of values possible, should be free to embrace. But this reply is unsatisfactory. That is because the privilege, essentially white and male, of freeing oneself from care and maintaining a denial of human vulnerability deprives society, at the same time, of any possibility of hearing the voices that resist this privilege. At a time when the populist right wing politics is on the rise, when inequalities between the richest and poorest on the planet are growing, when climate change threatens the very future of humanity and all life on Earth, it is no exaggeration to assert that the ruling class, being essentially bereft of activities and time to permit the cultivation of care capacities, puts the very future of humanity in peril. The transformations and actions required by care will not be among the issues figuring on political debate agendas and the electoral platforms proposed by the different parties. They will be relegated to the background, and the political institutional culture will continue to be reproduced by what Joan Tronto has so appropriately called 'the indifference of the privileged' (Tronto 1993).

5 The masterful subjectivity of politicians and epistemic vulnerability

In her book *The Ethics of Vulnerability*, Erinn Gilson devotes a chapter to what she calls the 'masterful subjectivity' performed by those who maintain their ignorance[12] of vulnerability – their own vulnerability. 'Invulnerability as a form of mastery, she writes, is sought at the price of disavowing vulnerability and is sought because it is the paradigmatic characteristic of *an ideal form of subjectivity in present socioeconomic conditions*' (Gilson 2014: 79; emphasis added). The performance of invulnerability, one could add, is almost a prerequisite for integration into the job market, in today's culture of excess and performance. As we saw in the preceding section, citizens who seek to carve out a place within political life, which is extremely competitive and demands a huge investment in time and energy, must conform to exceptionally challenging work schedules that would be simply exhausting for most people.

Socio-economic performance requires the form of 'invulnerability' that Gilson writes about – a form of forgetfulness, even negation, of one's own body and needs (for rest, for exercise, for relaxation). This performance of invulnerability is also revealed in a particularly striking way on the level of communicational interaction among 'workers' and, in the context that interests me here, workers who are also 'politicians'. In what follows, I show that critical care ethics gives a more focused interpretation of what feminists have denounced as the 'male' culture of political life, marked by competitiveness, aggression, and arrogance. Indeed, this approach reveals that the problem is not that this culture is 'masculine', and the remedy cannot be reduced to the 'feminization' of political culture. The communicational culture in politics, especially in a world dominated by medias, sounds like a culture of invulnerability – of being closed off to oneself and to others, of having difficulty being oneself in public, of fearing being touched and transformed by contact with the point of view of a different other (something that is still culturally associated with masculinity, though).

In the following, I suggest that it is more precisely this culture of invulnerability (from an invulnerable, arrogant, and unshakeable voice; and from invulnerable, closed listening) that allows truth to be neither spoken nor heard with care and attention. This culture freezes the partners in the interaction in their respective postures, makes them impermeable to each other. It papers over the loopholes, closes the openings, aims to fend off attacks, possible shocks, and simultaneously it immobilizes interaction, makes it inoperable.

6 The 'different voice': from conventional feminine kindness to 'speaking the truth'

In her book *In a Different Voice*, first published in 1982, pioneer of care ethics Carol Gilligan clearly defined the voice conveying 'conventional feminine kindness' as a type of voice corresponding to the gender expectations that weighed upon girls and women in terms of behaviours and attitudes (that they be sweet, attentive, and concerned with the needs of *others* without listening to their own needs, that they be understanding, showing restraint and humility). In short, they were to reassure and support the speech of others, and they were to know how to stay in the background. This 'voice of conventional feminine kindness' is situated on the spectrum of 'voices articulated in terms of care', but it is not an 'authentic', true voice: it is expressed to satisfy social expectations, to be a 'good girl' – nice, docile, solicitous of others – at the price of swallowing what is really felt. Reaching full maturity in terms of identity and moral development demands, on the contrary, the strength to surpass these 'conventions', to resist the easy option of responding to gender expectations, to assume an authentic 'voice', to be true to oneself. Gilligan refers to this full developmental maturity as the last 'stage of truth', truth and transparency regarding oneself and others, which she distinguishes from the 'stage of conventional kindness' in which thoughts and actions are conditioned by outside expectations, with no critical distance. So, it would be a mistake to think that 'speaking with a different voice' in the sense meant by ethicists such as Gilligan means 'speaking the voice of feminine kindness' and simple concern for others. Speaking with a 'different voice' means speaking your own truth.

Queer feminists and feminists of colour are interested in the way in which the expression of women's anger has been publicly and socially stigmatized in order to contain, domesticate, and subdue it. The figure of the hysteric applied to white women – especially women of power, when they raise their voices – and the figure of the 'black angry woman' or the 'angry feminist' have served, and still serve, as a bogeyman to cast discredit on their speech when it is discordant – that is, when it departs from conventional kindness, disappoints expectations, is a 'killjoy' (Ahmed 2017). Critical theoreticians such as Iris Marion Young affirm the importance of creating spaces of public deliberation that are pluralistic and heterogeneous, where differences can be expressed and heard (Young 2000). A critical care ethics, of course, confirms the importance of creating spaces in which these different voices can resonate, but it adds the following two requirements. First, it is necessary, as I have noted earlier, that speakers can express themselves in such a way that they remain true to themselves. When it comes to political life, this may mean that women and minorities can directly address the topics that they see as important and do so in a way that is faithful to who they are and what they feel, embodying this truth. Second – because it is not because the subaltern is speaking that the dominant will listen – it is important not only to support the 'different' voice of subalterns but also to assure the quality of the context of receptiveness for this voice (Bourgault 2015). It is on this point that I will conclude.

7 Learning how to listen carefully: cultivating epistemic vulnerability

Canadian critical care ethicist Sophie Bourgault writes about how important it is that dominants 'speak less loudly' (Bourgault 2015: 166), cultivate silence – the prerequisite for attentive listening – and be truly concerned with what minorities have to say. 'A fairer way of living together', she writes, 'cannot come to pass simply by including the voices of the excluded; there need to be various measures aiming to lower the volume of dominant discourses' (Bourgault 2015: 166; our translation). The critical care ethics that I am seeking to deploy here would further this reflection by suggesting that it is in fact the performance of invulnerability that tightens the links in a chain of toxic receptiveness, in which those who occupy the dominant positions in the context of the interactions either ignore the voices of others or ridicule them, try to dismantle them, or retaliate.

One might immediately think that these retaliations, or 'defensive moves', reveal the interlocutor's fragility, even though he or she is in a position of power. But this is far from being certain. Looking at interactions between the white majority and racialized minorities in her master piece "White Fragility", Robin DiAngelo speaks specifically about this type of 'fragility', which should be understood, in fact, as an active performance of invulnerability: the 'outward display of emotions such as anger, fear, and guilt, and behaviours such as argumentation, silence, and leaving the stress-inducing situation' are not signs of recognition of vulnerability, in the sense of an opening to how the other and her voice can touch, affect, and move us, can transform not only our ideas but our very identity. On the contrary, this fragility functions as 'a range of defensive moves' that strengthen the protective shell, fend off challenges, leave the individual intact, unaltered, fixed in the posture that was his or hers before the encounter took place (Di Angelo 2011: 54).

Gilson's work proves useful again here, as she precisely identifies five characteristics of an interlocutor who is privileged but who, rather than being closed to the words of the other – and to the other, full stop – can show 'epistemic vulnerability' (Gilson 2014: 94–95). Epistemic vulnerability refers to 'openness to changes in the self in light of coming to perceive what one does not know and has prevented oneself from knowing' (Gilson 2014: 96). Individuals who decide to experience their own epistemic vulnerability, first, recognize that they do not know everything and are open to 'not knowing'. Second, they allow themselves to make mistakes and are ready to doubt what they have up to now taken for granted. Third, they consent to place themselves in situations that are neither familiar nor necessarily easy and comfortable.[13] Fourth, they are open to the idea that a communicational interaction may have the power to touch them emotionally and rationally, to shake up their convictions, perhaps even the deepest ones, which may alter even their sense of self. In fact, epistemic vulnerability means no longer being afraid.

What we might call 'training' for epistemic vulnerability is based on the idea that no, or little, learning happens without discomfort, without immersion in unknown contexts in which the encounter with the other is likely to shake one's sense of identity. The vulnerability training that Gilson talks about is not similar in nature to the philosophical training that develops a critical mind, a capacity to distance oneself from one's own position, and intellectual comprehension of the complexity of the argument put forward by the other. Training for epistemic vulnerability involves learning to create a space of silence to listen to voices that may be experienced as confrontational, intransigent on the affective level but also, on the epistemic level alone, may be heard as incomprehensible or simply inassimilable. Epistemic vulnerability is much more demanding on the identity-related, affective, and psychological levels. It requires constant attention to what plays out within oneself when one listens to the other – to what is expressed in their words and by their body.

8 Conclusion

Confronted with the underrepresentation of minorities in politics, or any sphere of power, critical care ethics does not ask simply that the political landscape be diversified – feminized and colourized – in appearance. Nor does it ask that this diversity 'make itself heard' and find its place. The scope of the transformations that it proposes plays out at a more fundamental level: that of the very identity of citizens, their relationship with themselves, and their relations with others. What it articulates as being necessary today more than ever is the transition from 'masterful subjectivities' to vulnerable subjectivities: the deployment of a vulnerable political life.

Notes

1 The expression 'racialized women' is used here, as Chantal Maillé and I co-wrote in *Le sujet du féminisme est-il blanc?* 'in order to focus on the process of social construction of race as a system of differentiation supporting forms of domination and oppression' (2015: 14).

2 As it will become clear later in the chapter, a critical care ethics understands the 'most privileged' to be those who get to be freed from care labour, without recognizing that they themselves are in constant need of care.

3 This diagnosis is supported by a body neuropsychological research, to which political philosophers frequently refer, on the workings of implicit biases with respect to gender and race. This scientific work tends to show that despite significant gains in minority rights in the second half of the twentieth century, these biases, which lead inter alia to unfair and prejudicial judgements of women and racialized persons, are tenacious, while their effects on equality of opportunity are disastrous (Banaji, Mahzarin and Greenwald 2013).

4 By decreasing the work week to four days or six hours per day, mandating flexible working hours, combatting direct and indirect discrimination and sexual harassment in the workplace, and instituting educational reforms, including gender education from an early age.

5 Following the Rawlsian theory of justice, justice not only requires that we redress the inequalities broached in the 'starting gate theory', namely, in the race to attain socially desirable occupations associated with the best incomes and with prestige and power, by, for example, providing free education and health care. Justice as fairness also requires that the social and economic inequalities that remain, once this race has played out under conditions of equality of opportunity at the starting line, be reduced, in accordance with what he calls the 'difference principle'. This principle states that the inequalities that subsist afterward should operate to the benefit of the least well-off, so as to enhance their incomes, standard of living, power, and status.

6 To take a concrete example from the reality of Quebec, where I come from. As I wrote the first draft of this chapter, in October 2018, the Quebec National Assembly has a female membership of less than 30%, or 27 women out of 125 MNAs. Racialized women make up a mere 0.8% of all elected members. In other words, only one representative out of the 125 members of the house is a racialized woman.

7 It is here that Carol Gilligan's pioneering work In *a Different Voice* (1982), and her more recent reworking of her ideas in *Joining the Resistance* (2011, see also Gilligan 2013) where she presents the voice of care as 'ethically resistant' become indispensable. These works invite us to see that the development of the type of subjectivity that is required by success and aspiration to high positions of power (such as key positions in politics, for example), assumes that people having reached adulthood should cut themselves off from who they once were and abandon their own original voice, to speak the adult language of authority, power, and also of conformism with regard to gender roles imparted to each one. The passages in which Gilligan discusses the moral and identity development of boys are telling in this regard. She shows how boys (who, more so than girls, are socialized to aspire to positions of power) are subject to a sort of ritual, an 'initiation' into patriarchy (Gilligan 2013: 60). Their gendered socialization requires that they give up on heeding the voice of care that calls out from within them, to forge a closed off identity, a 'separate self'. The author refers to research that suggests that on reaching adolescence, boys are compelled to see their friendships with other boys as childish and immature and consider their entry into the adult world as requiring that they distance themselves emotionally from their friends, despite sharing a bond with them. Research shows that girls, at this same time in their lives, also undertake a revision of their deep desires, and come to understand rather quickly that 'success' in this world, marked by a culture that evinces a distaste for relationships, emotions, and the body, especially the female body, requires that they adopt a masculine mode of existence, that they learn to devalue relationships in favour of performance. This 'initiation' to gender roles that occurs in adolescence, creates a 'traumatic break in their relationships, a rupture that is necessary for the establishment of the patriarchal order' (Gilligan 2013: 49). It requires that children, boys and girls both, dissociate from certain vital inclinations they had before being subject to this initiation phase. It demands a rejection of the self that once needed others and wanted to connect with, and care for them. Gilligan identifies this as a 'loss of voice and memory' (Gilligan 2013: 50).

8 In this same line of thinking, feminist philosophers who generally uphold a Universal Basic Income, as a distributive justice strategy, are highly perceptive of gender, racial, and global inequalities. I am also convinced, unlike some classical egalitarians, that it is possible to reformulate a theory of distributive justice that is sensitive to the variables of gender and race. I also believe that contemporary distributive justice theorists are more open than ever to thinking about gender and racial inequalities in terms of injustices not reducible to 'social' or 'class' inequalities. My point here is not to say that distributive justice theorists haven't lived up to expectations yet, but rather to highlight the limits of what this strictly distributive lens can tell us of the injustices that are reproduced within the main social institutions.

9 Moreover, this denial of access to 'positions of power' is seen as problematic to the extent that the functioning of political institutions has not been transformed and that these positions of power have not themselves been redefined. Critical care ethics invites us more fundamentally to revise our very notions of power and our ways of 'exercising' it.

10 Obviously, here it must not be understood that women privileged from their class, race, or citizenship are morally condemnable for employing domestic aids or caregivers/nannies in the present context. I made this very clear in another paper where, in the line of care ethicist Joan Tronto in "The Nanny Question in Feminism" (2002), I aimed to clarify the way feminist theorists are dealing with the question of 'feminist solidarity beyond class and race' (Hamrouni 2016b). Critical care ethics embraces a structural conception of injustice, and what it sheds light on is the structuring of work and political life around a model of the invulnerable and independent agent [not having these constant needs for care, domestic maintenance, emotional and affective support, and so on]. This approach allows to affirm that if women find themselves in the position where they turn towards the hiring of nannies or servants at our time still, it is precisely because (1) their partners do not fulfil their responsibilities, (2) they (and the normative and social gender pressures) assign responsibility for this family dossier to the woman who is responsible for hiring, interacting, negotiating with, and giving instructions to her domestic employees, (3) the cultural and normative as well as the organizational structure in terms of working time are outdated, subject women to excessive pressures, and do not make gender equality possible. Anyhow, most Black Feminists have named this tension (both historical and present) persisting between white women and racialized women. The mainstream (i.e., dominant) feminist movement has not always been capable of representing or including the demands and positions of all the women. Evidently, feminism is heterogeneous. (For a simple example of the classics treating precisely of that question, see also Angela Davis (1983), bell hooks (1982) and Patricia Hill Collins 2000). Contemporary theorists who reflect on care in connection with past and ongoing colonialism also deal with it. For instance, E. Dorlin (2006) in her eloquently entitled article "Dark care". Many books are also devoted to the issue of nannies as a way of managing gender inequality in post-industrialized countries, in the context of globalization, world poverty, and migration (cf. Ehrenreich and Hochschild 2002). Finally, even liberal egalitarian feminists, who generally speak the language of distributive justice, such as Anca Gheaus, recognize that 'feminists who advocate "masculine" lifestyles for women [i.e., equal access of all to traditionally masculine positions of power] have been criticized as compromising the quest for equality by relegating "feminine" work to the often-exploited women whose poverty, race or immigrant status pushes them to the margins of society' (Gheaus 2012). They contend that this is a real problem if all women must be able to claim equality and freedom, and if the 'subject of feminism' is to be truly inclusive and, not simply 'white feminism'.

11 It is worth mentioning, however, that, from their point of view, confinement to the daily labour of care removes us from the possibility of creating, of participating in political life, of pursuing what, in short, distinguishes us as rational and social human beings and sets us apart from other animals.

12 Gilson is referring to epistemological works on ignorance developed for the most part by critical race philosophers (Sullivan and Tuana 2007) to develop the idea of 'epistemic ignorance of vulnerability' in order to emphasize the idea that ignorance or denial of vulnerability is not an 'oversight' or negligence but an outlook supported by different interests: it is important, for the most dominant, that they can continue to conduct their daily affairs as if they were not vulnerable and had nothing to do with the vulnerability of others.

13 It could be added, following the extremely stimulating reflections of Barbara Applebaum (2017), that the individual does not systematically seek to be 'comforted' when he or she experiences discomfort.

References

Ahmed, S. 2017. *Living a Feminist Life*. Durham: Duke University Press.
Anderson, E. 2010. *The Imperative of Integration*. Princeton: Princeton University Press.
Applebaum, B. 2017. 'Comforting Discomfort as Complicity: White Fragility and the Pursuit of Invulnerability', *Hypatia*, 32(4): 862–875.
Banaji, M. R., and A. G. Greenwald. 2013. *Blind Spot: Hidden Biases of Good People*. New York: Delacorte Press.
Bourgault, S. 2015. 'Repenser la 'voix', repenser le silence: l'apport du care', in S. Bourgault and J. Perreault (eds.), *Le care: éthique féministe actuelle*, pp. 63–86. Montreal: remue-ménage.
Davis, A. 1983. *Women, Race, & Class*. New York: Vintage Books.
Di Angelo, R. 2011. 'White Fragility' *International Journal of Critical Pedagogy*, 3(3): 54–70.
Dorlin, E. 2006. 'Dark Care: de la servitude à la solicitude', in P. Paperman and S. Laugier (eds.), *Le Souci des autres. Éthique et politique du care*, pp. 87–97, Paris: Éditions de l'École des Hautes Études en Sciences Sociales.
Ehrenreich, B., and A. Russel Hochschild (eds.). 2002. *Global Woman: Nannies, Maids, and Sex Workers in the New Economy*. New York: Henry Holt and Company.
Gheaus, A. 2012. 'Gender Justice', *Journal of Ethics and Social Philosophy*, 6(1): 1–24.
Gilligan, C. 1982. *In a Different Voice*. Cambridge: Harvard University Press.
Gilligan, C., A. Hochschild, and J. Tronto. 2013. *Contre l'indifférence des privilégiés. À quoi sert le care* (trans. by Marlène Jouan). Paris: Payot.
Gilson, E. 2014. *The Ethics of Vulnerability: A Feminist Analysis of Social Life and Practice*. New York: Routledge.
Hamrouni, N. 2000. 'Towards a Political Theory of Care', in S. Bourgault and F. Vosman (eds.), *In Yet a Different Voice. Francophone Contributions*. Leuven: Peeters.
Hamrouni, N. 2016a. 'Ordinary Vulnerability, Institutional Androgyny and Gender Justice', in C. Straehle (ed.), *Vulnerability, Autonomy, and Applied Ethics*, pp. 69–82. New York: Routledge.
Hamrouni, N. 2016b. 'Repenser la question des nounous par-delà le moralisme et le "tout au marché"', in E.-M. Mbonda and T. Ngosso (eds.), *Théories de la justice: justice globale, agents de la justice et justice de genre*, pp. 247–260. Louvain: Presses Universitaires de Louvain.
Hamrouni, N., and C. Maillé (eds.). 2015. *Le sujet du féminisme est-il blanc? Femmes racisées et recherche féministe*. Montreal: remue-ménage.
Hamrouni, N., and P.-Y. Néron. 2017. 'Justice, Gender, and Corporations: Outline of a Feminist Political Philosophy of the Corporation', *World Political Science Review*, 13(2): 193–219.
Haslanger, S. 2008. 'Changing the Ideology and Culture of Philosophy Not by Reason (Alone)', *Hypatia*, 23(2): 210–23.
Hill Collins, P. 2017[2000]. *La pensée féministe noire: Savoir, conscience et politique de l'empowerment* (trans. by Diane Lamoureux). Montreal: remue-ménage.
Honneth, A. 1996. *The Struggle for Recognition: The Moral Grammar of Social Conflicts*. Cambridge, MA: MIT Press.
hooks, b. 1982. *Ain't I a Woman: Black Women and Feminism*. London: Pluto Press.
Kittay, Eva Feder. 1999. *Love's Labor. Essays on Women, Equality and Dependency*. New York: Routledge.

Mason, M. A., N. H. Wolfinger, and M. Goulden. 2013. *Do Babies Matter? Gender and Family in the Ivory Tower*. London: Rutgers University Press.
Okin, S. M. 1989. *Justice, Gender and the Family*. New York: Basic Books.
Pateman, C. 1988. *The Sexual Contract*. Cambridge: Polity Press.
Phillips, A. 1995. *The Politics of Presence*. Oxford: Clarendon Press.
Rawls, J. 1971. *A Theory of Justice*. Cambridge, MA: Harvard University Press.
Robeyns, I. 2009. 'When Will Society be Gender Just?', in J. Browne (ed.), *The Future of Gender*, pp. 54–74. Cambridge: Cambridge University Press.
Sullivan, S., and N. Tuana (eds.). 2007. *Race and Epistemologies of Ignorance*. Albany: State University of New York Press.
Tronto, J. 1993. *Moral Boundaries: A Political Argument for an Ethic of Care*. New York: Routledge.
Tronto, J. 2002. 'The "Nanny Question" in Feminism', *Hypatia*, 17(2): 34–51.
Tronto, J. 2013. *Caring Democracy. Markets, Equality, and Justice*. New York: New York University Press.
Valian, V. 1998. *Why So Slow? The Advancement of Women*. Cambridge, MA: MIT Press.
Williams, J. 2000. *Unbending Gender: Why Family and Work Conflict and What to Do about It*. New York: Oxford University Press.
Young, I. M. 1990. *Justice and the Politics of Difference*. Princeton: Princeton University Press.
Young, I. M. 2000. *Inclusion and Democracy*. Oxford: Oxford University Press.

8

REDISTRIBUTION, RECOGNITION, AND PLURALISM

a Rawlsian criticism of Fraser[1]

Luigi Caranti and Nunzio Alì

One of the central theses defended in the by now classic philosophical exchange between Nancy Fraser and Axel Honneth (Fraser and Honneth 2003) is that the mainstream, broadly Rawlsian-inspired, distributive paradigm of justice is unable to capture all dimensions of injustice in advanced capitalist societies, a defect that the alternative or (according to Fraser) complementary recognition paradigm is meant to remedy. The central aim of this chapter is to criticize this thesis, at least if understood in the sense that no version of the redistributive paradigm is capable of capturing the dimensions of injustice highlighted by the recognition paradigm. To prove our point, we start from three main assumptions that we take as relatively non-controversial. To begin with, we hold (1) that the recognition paradigm needs to prove that its insufficiency thesis remains valid even if the strongest exponents of the redistributive paradigm are elected as intellectual adversaries. Since very few would hold today that justice concerns itself *only* with the questions of wealth distribution, the focus should be with approaches that by and large fit the redistribution paradigm but are not so simplistic as to fall into that reduction. We further assume (2) that Rawls is still the best example of redistributive approaches that does not commit this mistake. The reason why we are confident in making this assumption can be explained by referring to the distinction between allocative-distributive conceptions of justice in contraposition with relational conceptions – what Forst (2014) calls the two pictures of justice. The former adopts a distribution-centred and a recipient-oriented point of view, and thus the basic question is what 'goods' you have, while the latter focuses on intersubjective relations and structures and its basic question is not 'what you have but how you are treated' (Forst 2014: 20). While the allocative-distributive model, of which Dworkin (2000) can be considered a representative, is perhaps unable to account for injustices of misrecognition,[2] things are quite different with the relational model. Built into this model is a preoccupation with the extent to which you are recognized as a citizen with equal status, which is not considered as entirely dependent on the amount of resources you are given. For our concerns, the question thus becomes whether Rawls belongs to the first or to the second model. Now, although Rawls emphasizes distribution of 'primary goods', this is always and explicitly considered as functional and subordinate to the ultimate goal of designing a society in which one's rights, expectations and status are not arbitrarily sacrificed to the advantage of someone else. This is precisely what fairness means, as it becomes evident in Rawls' criticism of utilitarianism and perfectionism. In Rawls, the point of justice seems to be relational from the very beginning.[3] For this reason, Rawls seems to be the 'redistributivist' that the defenders of the recognition model should target, if they want to take the hard, but most rewarding path. Finally, we assume (3) that the recognition paradigm, especially in the deontological version defended by Fraser, wants to remain faithful to the Kantian distinction between what concerns justice and what concerns ethics. In other words, we think that the non-teleological version of the recognition paradigm makes room for a class of merely ethical duties (e.g., being faithful in a relationship) that should not be turned into legal duties whose compliance can be coercively enforced.[4]

Starting from these assumptions, the paper defends three main theses: 1) Fraser lacks a clear distinction between practices that, on the one hand, generate misrecognition but merely concern the ethical substratum of our societies, not its institutions, and, on the other hand, practices that generate misrecognition but do concern justice, 2) most, if not all, of the misrecognition generating practices that concern justice are captured by Rawls, 3) Fraser's participatory democracy does not leave enough room for pluralism of comprehensive doctrines, of the radical yet reasonable kind that Rawls takes very seriously from *Political Liberalism* onwards. Our analysis is articulated accordingly. First, we introduce Fraser's insufficiency thesis in the context of the redistribution vs recognition debate (section 1). The second section shows how Rawls' account of justice as fairness has resources to capture most of the dimensions of misrecognition dear to Fraser, why it remains silent on the remaining dimensions, and why it has good reasons for doing so. This leads us to the third section where we suggest that Fraser's model does not make enough room for reasonable pluralism, an essential and welcome feature of our societies.

1 Fraser's insufficiency thesis

Started by the 2003 philosophical exchange between Nancy Fraser and Axel Honneth (Fraser and Honneth 2003), the debate between redistribution and recognition has flourished during the last two decades and its intensity shows no sign of decline. The paradigm of redistribution is usually associated with the liberal egalitarian tradition, and in particular with contemporary Anglo-American analytic philosophy. For instance, according to Rawls (1971: 4), a conception of social justice should provide a way of assigning rights and duties to citizens and define the appropriate distribution of the benefits and burdens of social cooperation. More specifically, 'all social values – liberty and opportunity, income and wealth, and the bases of self-respect – are to be distributed equally unless an unequal distribution of any, or all, of these values is to everyone's advantage' (Rawls 1971: 62). From this perspective, it seems to be evident that justice requires redistribution of a certain kind, and, conversely, that injustice is basically a question of maldistribution. By contrast, those who advocate the paradigm of recognition believe that the redistributive paradigm is unable to adequately capture other dimensions of social injustice, in particular those related to gender or race discrimination and to disrespect of individual or group identity. From this point of view, the redistribution paradigm would be unable to capture the injustice of being denied recognition. Noticing the redistribution insufficiency, however, is not the same as claiming that one dimension has priority over the other, let alone that one could be reduced to the other. This reduction is what characterizes Axel Honneth's approach. In fact, Honneth (1992) proposes a normative monistic account of recognition and seeks to subsume under it all issues traditionally framed as questions of redistribution. To use his words, 'even distributional injustice must be understood as the institutional expression of social disrespect – or, better said, of unjustified relations of recognition' (Fraser and Honneth 2003: 114). Between the two extreme positions, a meritorious midway point is taken by Nancy Fraser (1995; 1996) who tries to integrate the paradigm of recognition with the paradigm of redistribution. In her 'perspective dualist' analysis, the two categories are seen as 'co-fundamental and mutually irreducible dimensions of justice' (Fraser and Honneth 2003: 3).[5] The core meaning of Fraser's theory is the parity of participation. According to this principle, 'justice requires social arrangements that permit all to participate as peers in social life. Conversely, overcoming injustice means dismantling institutionalized obstacles that prevent some people from participating on a par with others, as full partners in social interaction' (Fraser 2010: 16). And 'participatory parity' could be undermined either by maldistribution or misrecognition (or both).[6]

Independently of whether one accepts Fraser's definition of a just society as one in which social arrangements permit all 'to participate as peers in social life'(Fraser and Honneth 2003: 47), she is certainly right in identifying seriously problematic practices that escape a conception of justice centred on the idea of distributing wealth (or material goods). However, the point is to know when and how a society generates injustice because of misrecognition. In particular, what is it that must be recognized to avoid injustice? To correctly answer this question, we need to recall the most important theoretical and normative shift within the recognition paradigm endorsed by Fraser, namely the 'status model of recognition'. Fraser (2000; 2001; 2003 with Honneth) rejects what she calls the 'identity model' which, conceiving recognition as a matter of self-realization, would fall within the domain of ethics.[7] By contrast, she formulates recognition as a matter of the social status that institutions attribute to citizens. As she puts it:

> To be misrecognized, accordingly, is not to suffer distorted identity or impaired subjectivity as a result of being depreciated by others. It is rather to be constituted by *institutionalized* patterns of cultural value in ways that prevent one from participating as a peer in social life. On the status model, then, misrecognition is relayed not through deprecatory attitudes or free-standing discourses, but rather through social institutions.
>
> (Fraser and Honneth 2003: 29, our emphasis)

This reformulation allows Fraser to focus on social institutions as the main, if not the sole, source of misrecognition. She is not after private 'deprecatory attitudes'. Misrecognition that concerns justice only happens when social institutions impact individual lives and impede parity of participation through choices inspired by diminishing cultural patterns. At this point the question obviously becomes: what does Fraser mean by 'social institutions'? Clearly, she does not conceive of them narrowly. Conceiving of social institutions in the restricted, formal way dear to liberals, according to Fraser, leads to a failure to grasp certain kinds of misrecognition that should be considered genuine injustices, such as the common practice not to pay for or acknowledge women's housework in some form. Thus, institutions include not only government and its branches but also firms, associations, the family, and perhaps even rituals. The hallmark seems to be the capacity for a social entity to influence directly or indirectly the prospects of individuals' participation in social life.[8]

For Fraser it thus becomes crucial to distinguish clearly between acts of misrecognition that we could call 'merely private' and institutionalized ones. This leads to our first point of criticism.[9] As Zurn (2008: 162) notes, Fraser does not detail 'what it means for patterns of cultural interpretations, social norms, and attitudinal dispositions to be "institutionally anchored"', and it is not clear whether her account leaves room for a compelling distinction between 'unacceptably institutionalized and acceptably episodic and "free-floating" patterns of misrecognition' (Zurn 2008: 163).[10] In fact, we doubt that she provides any theoretical and normative criterion to achieve this distinction, which is, however, absolutely crucial for her reinterpretation of the recognition paradigm. Let us take a fresh look at one of the most famous passages in Fraser's work. In the context of her example of discrimination against homosexuals, Fraser writes:

> the social division between heterosexuals and homosexuals is not grounded in the political economy . . . rather, in the status order of society, as *institutionalized patterns of cultural value* construct heterosexuality as natural and normative, homosexuality as perverse and despised. Pervasively institutionalized, such heteronormative value patterns structure broad swaths of social interaction. Expressly codified in many areas of law (including family law and criminal law), they inform legal constructions of family, intimacy, privacy, and equality. They are also entrenched in many areas of government policy (including immigration, naturalization and asylum policy) and in standard professional practices (including medicine and psychotherapy). Heteronormative value patterns also pervade popular culture and everyday interaction. The effect is to construct gays and lesbians as a despised sexuality, subject to sexually specific forms of status subordination. The latter include shaming and assault, exclusion from the rights and privileges of marriage and parenthood, curbs on rights of expression and association, demeaning stereotypical depictions in the media, harassment and disparagement in everyday life, and denial of the full rights and equal protections of citizenship. These harms are injustices of misrecognition.
>
> (Fraser and Honneth 2003: 18, our emphasis)

Fraser shows here that discriminations in advanced societies are not all related to the 'how rich' and 'how poor' citizens are. You may comfortably be in the upper percentile of society and yet suffer from discrimination related to your race, sexuality, gender. This shows, among other things, that misrecognition cannot be redressed or cured by a more egalitarian redistribution. Even if you are an acclaimed and relatively well-off scientist in a society, you may suffer serious forms of injustice because you are gay, as the biography of Alan Turing, made widely known by the recent movie devoted to him, made crystal clear. But it seems to us that only some of the cited ways in which misrecognition takes place concern social *institutions*, even if we understand them in the enlarged sense indicated previously.

This seems to be in tension with Fraser's point that her status model approach is not interested in 'deprecatory attitudes or free-standing discourses'. As we saw, she refuses to construe misrecognition as 'impaired subjectivity' in turn caused by others' depreciation. Rather she insists on the *institutionalized* patterns of misrecognition thereby admitting – perhaps not explicitly enough – that for her misrecognition happens only when social or political structures bigger and more powerful than the individual, and endowed with some coercive powers (in the highest degree, obviously, the state) exercise their negative influences on the life prospects of citizens considered inferior in status.[11] Now the question becomes: do all the instances of misrecognition cited in the passage fall into this qualified category?

Institutionalized instances are certainly those that concern family law (if inspired by patriarchy) and criminal law. We assume Fraser has certain countries in mind where homosexuality is a crime or where they are discriminated for access to certain professions but also government policies related to immigration, naturalization, and asylum policy. Less clear are the other cases mentioned. It is reasonable to assume that discriminatory practices in the workplace become institutionally relevant in cases similar to the one made famous by the movie *Philadelphia*.[12] But, one may wonder, to what extent does the decision by a homophobic son not to hire gay caregivers for his father concern justice? Even less clear are cultural habits responsible for 'stereotypical depictions in the media, harassment and disparagement in everyday life'. Such habits, at least prima facie, seem to concern ethics, not justice. Though most of us would agree that they violate some rule of morality, very few would say that they call for state intervention. Using state coercion to ban depictions of homosexuality that are disrespectful and yet short of hate speech in privately owned TV media channels or – even more problematically – in 'everyday life' would strike many as, among other things, a questionable limitation of the individual right of expression.

Thus one easy reply to the insufficiency thesis open to supporters of the redistribution paradigm is to say that most if not all the unfortunate phenomena of misrecognition indicated by Fraser concern questionable aspects of the ethical life of the society but do not concern justice. Let's focus on another of Fraser's favourite examples, 'The case of the African-American Wall Street banker who cannot get a taxi to pick him up'. Fraser says that 'to handle such cases, a theory of justice must reach beyond the distribution of rights and goods to examine institutionalized patterns of cultural value; it must ask whether such patterns impede parity of participation in social life' (Fraser and Honneth 2003: 34). The easy reply would go roughly as follows: Cab drivers adopt a more or less conscious discriminatory choice when it comes to offering their service, and that is clearly a bad thing. Yet, this calls into question the individual morality of cab drivers, not the institutional structure of the society. And perhaps the easy answer would add that if government were to enforce rules that aim to avoid these forms of misrecognition, it would soon degenerate into paternalism. Put in general terms, if the problem is a 'cultural' one, it seems reasonable to say that the state has no business in advancing the 'right' culture. The cure should be a free confrontation of ideas in the public sphere, not the repression of politically incorrect opinions through public coercive means.

This line of defence seems to be promising, and in fact comes close to what we will be arguing, but it is hardly defensible without further qualification. There are many examples of positive actions taken by governments to avoid similar cases of 'private misrecognition' which few would find problematic. After all, hate speech – a conduct by now considered as a crime by most liberal democracies – is nothing but a case of private misrecognition. Similarly, very few would say that the police should not remove racist banners when they appear in sporting events like soccer matches. Also, we believe that it is not left to the freedom of spectators to boo an athlete playing for the adversary team using the colour of his or her skin as a target. These examples cut even deeper than more famous anti-discriminatory policies adopted by the US federal government such as the *voting act*.[13] It will be recalled that the voting act, one of the most effective pieces of legislation against racial discrimination ever passed in US history, outlawed all the arrangements – like the imposition of a fee for voting – through which Southern states made voting for blacks practically impossible. They cut deeper because the voting act targeted arrangements that in theory did not affect the equal rights of blacks but in practice gave an indirect *institutional* backing to misrecognition. In the cases cited previously, however, the institutional side seems to be missing altogether. It is not that local authorities encouraged racist boos at the stadium or the like. These are cases in which private individuals are targeted for their racist or homophobic *expressions*.

This shows that even private behaviour expressing and causing misrecognition may trigger legitimate coercion. And yet when we enter the terrain of private misrecognition, that is, private bits of behaviour, clearly resulting from a cultural pattern in a society, and yet mainly consisting in a verbal offence without immediate and clearly identifiable consequences for the victim's status as a citizen, things get immediately complicated. Take the prohibition – enforced in the US but not in Europe – disallowing a landlord to discriminate among prospective tenants based on things like race, religion, or sex. Recently in Italy the candid reply of a woman who respectfully refused to rent her house to an openly gay couple caught the attention of the media. Though a backlash of moral reprobation was expressed publicly against the woman, nobody argued that there should be a law of tenant-rights to protect homosexuals or punitive consequences for discriminatory landlords. Another example is a recent conservative campaign against the possibility for gays to adopt kids based on the slogan 'two men do not make a mother'. The slogan was perceived as offensive by many Italians and yet very few advance the argument that it was a crime.

Later we will be arguing that some forms of private misrecognition should be strictly confined to the realm of ethical offences because the cost to make them crimes would be too high in terms of loss of individual freedom. In that context, we will also try to understand whether Fraser and more generally the recognition model has a principled way of identifying cases in which state power can be legitimately used against cultural forms of discrimination, as discerned from other cases relevant only from the point of view of ethics.[14] Remember that we are assuming that the deontological, hence Kant-inspired approach *à la* Fraser is willing to draw that line. If, as Fraser says, 'in the recognition paradigm . . . the remedy for injustice is cultural or symbolic change' (Fraser and Honneth 2003: 13), then it is an open question how we make sure that the remedy does not come close to some authoritarian measures. Postponing this point to the last section, let us focus now on how much institutional misrecognition is captured by non-reductivist, redistributive approaches, such as that of Rawls.

2 Misrecognizing Rawls

We acknowledged previously that the recognition model in general and Fraser in particular sheds light on dimensions of injustice that have very little to do with bad redistribution of material resources, and perhaps of primary goods in general. And yet we want to ask: who precisely is Fraser's intellectual adversary? We assume that the redistribution model does not wish to target a straw man or pick easy fights with approaches that reduce justice to a distribution of wealth. In fact, it is even difficult to find examples of this reductivism. Perhaps one could quote radical versions of sufficientarism or luck-egalitarianism. Certainly other redistributivist approaches, among which most importantly Rawls', are far from endorsing this simple-minded reductivism. Our question thus becomes whether Fraser's criticism applies to Rawls' *justice as fairness*. Fraser seems to think that it does[15], but is it really so?[16]

First of all, let us recall that Rawls' first principle of justice already takes care of most of the cases of misrecognition listed in the excerpt from Fraser quoted previously. Thus, discriminations in family law, let alone criminal law, are clear violations of the first principle of justice. The case of the family is difficult but a charitable interpretation of Rawls, doing justice to his liberal, hence individualistic, orientation, would let the first principle rule out cases of discriminations related to marriage and inheritance law for gays. Unless an argument is provided to show that, in adopting children, gays are violating the equal and most extended sphere of freedom of some other citizens, it is hard to understand how on Rawlsian grounds such a prohibition could be permitted.

Second, and less obviously, since the basic structure encompasses a society's major political and social institutions, including 'the political constitution, the legally recognized forms of property, and the organization of the economy, and the nature of the family' (Rawls 2005: 258), there is room for arguing that discrimination against women, gays, non-whites in the workplace (chiefly, unjustified lower compensation than straight white men) can be easily considered a violation of the first principle of justice. Differentiation of salaries or opportunities depending on gender or sexual orientation, no matter how confined to the established patterns of the economic sector of the society as opposed to explicitly introduced in the legal system, would call for redress on Rawls' own terms.

Third, it is reasonable to consider as part of the Rawlsian 'basic structure' aspects of the society that Rawls does not explicitly mention, such as established patterns of behaviour or habits that make social relations and in general cooperation particularly burdensome for some citizens. Among those a clear example is the set of *real* opportunities women enjoy, independently of whether they suffer no discrimination in their status as citizens. If women, for all sorts of reasons, from patriarchal traditions to adaptive preferences, have less opportunities than men in the job market, receive a lesser pay for equal performances, have to work harder to have their talent recognized in a dominantly male work environment, this *is* part of the 'organization of the economy' that determines the distribution of burdens and advantages to members of a society. In short, it is part of the basic structure. As such, the discriminations or diminished opportunities suffered by women call for institutional action. They cannot be passively considered as an unfortunate historical circumstance to be overcome through a spontaneous moral improvement unassisted by the state.[17]

Fourth, the 'basic structure' includes all gender biased circumstances that surround marriage, no matter how equally and fairly the law treats the spouses. In other words, it is not sufficient that marriage law does not allow formal inequality and that the legal system provides some particular juridical protection for women, as in the case of Brazilian legislation (*Lei Maria da Penha*[18]). Taking seriously the circumstances of justice means to evaluate whether marriage in a certain society can be truly seen as a 'free', 'voluntary', and 'parity' relationship between partners or whether, on the contrary, women are de facto not as free as men in the relationship. Thus, it means to evaluate whether women have a fair opportunity to enter in the labour market and receive adequate payment, whether they have the same chances as men to get out of marriage or other kinds of familial relationships and so on.[19]

Finally, on our reading the basic structure also includes firms. In this sense, unlike Rawls[20], we do not consider a firm a simple private 'association' for which the criteria of justice cannot be applied in its internal rules and procedures. If a private firm decides to pay a woman, a homosexual, or a person of colour less than a straight white man at the same level of responsibility, just because she is a woman, a homosexual, or a person of colour, then this *is* a violation of the principles of justice.[21] This does not mean, however, that we intend to make all social relations part of the basic structure. Things that remain outside are, for example, how teachers should grade their pupils, how parents should educate their children or allocate resources towards the education of their children, how partners treat each other in a private and intimate relationship, how members of a private association should distribute their own resources, etc.[22] In these spheres of social life, we have moral obligations that concern our personal conduct or character, but they remain confined to the domain of social virtues and their specific requirements, which include, to quote O'Neill, 'rejection of direct indifference to others: sympathy, beneficence, love, care and concern, solidarity, etc.; and rejection of indirect indifference to the social fabric and to the material basis of life' (O'Neill 1996: 205).[23]

This broad conception of the basic structure, very much in the spirit of the late Rawls, already covers many dimensions of misrecognition that the redistribution paradigm was supposed to leave unchallenged. But we can go a bit further. It is important to recall that Rawls' inclusion of the 'social bases of self-respect' in the list of primary goods, actually his inclination to consider it as the most important one (Rawls 1971: 440), bears witness to his full appreciation of dimensions of justice that can be captured neither by shares of material goods nor by the instrumental value of liberties.[24] As Rawls clearly puts it:

> the basis for self-esteem in a just society is not then one's income share but the *publicly affirmed* distribution of fundamental rights and liberties. . . . [We seek] to eliminate the significance of relative economic and social advantages as supports for men's self-confidence.
>
> (Rawls 1971: 545, our emphasis)[25]

Distributing equally fundamental rights and liberties is not only important to enable people to choose their preferred pattern of life. It is also important because it counts as a public affirmation of equality of status among citizens, which in turn is taken by Rawls as a precondition of self-respect and as a powerful defence against threats to our self-image that may come from other inequalities in the society.[26] According to Rawls' perhaps over-optimistic intuition, once institutions recognize citizens as equals in terms of status, their inequality in material goods will not impact too negatively on their self-respect, provided that one can show that inequalities are primarily at the advantage of the worst-off.[27]

The significance of this is that institutions seem to have a direct duty to eliminate all forms of symbolic and cultural discrimination that could negatively affect individuals' self-respect. This may come in two different versions, a weak and a strong one. The weak, unproblematic version is to say that institutions (not only governmental, but also major economic and social ones) should make some effort to remove entrenched patterns of symbolic and cultural misrecognition. An example would be using public money to launch a campaign in public schools against homophobia. The strong version would be that political institutions have to use their monopoly of force to sanction public expressions, by individuals or groups, of misrecognition. In the last section, we will show why it is advisable to endorse the weak while rejecting the strong form.

Finally, the lexicographical priority of the first principle reinforces the idea that there is room for capturing misrecognition within justice as fairness and it does so in two ways. Directly, it shows that for Rawls the most serious injustice has nothing to do with the distribution of material goods; it has rather to do with what Fraser would call misrecognition, as it becomes evident if one keeps in mind the non-instrumental value of liberties we just highlighted. Indirectly, the same priority is introduced as functional to self-respect to which the major threat is relational. The most important social basis for self-respect, thinks Rawls (rightly or wrongly), is an exceptionless implementation of the first principle of justice. In other words, the lexical priority of the first principle is justified because equal and most extended liberties are the most solid social basis of the allegedly most important basic good, that is self-respect.

If most discriminations denounced by Fraser are captured by justice as fairness and Rawls can*not* be charged for focusing exclusively on material goods, how could misrecognition still be used to criticize Rawls? One could argue that what is left out – despite all we said previously – is the disparagement certain minorities suffer for a discriminatory attitude initiated by a) private individuals and b) in forms that merely remain at the level of a cultural/symbolic offence. For example, naming a gay person a faggot, making jokes that reproduce racial stereotypes, or, in an ascending order of seriousness and yet well within the non-institutional private-symbolic, having a patriarchal attitude in personal relations, holding public speeches in complacent media in which homosexuals are portrayed as perverse and so on. As we saw, Fraser herself alludes to these forms of discrimination, as quoted previously on section 2 (Fraser and Honneth 2003: 18). And it does look like Rawls' model has no resources to counter *them*. This leads us to our final and most important point about the recognition model, in the deontological form endorsed by Fraser. The relation between recognition and pluralism.[28]

3 Recognition and reasonable pluralism

Let us go back to the problem we mentioned before. Is it permissible or desirable to consider private symbolic offences that misrecognize individuals in virtue of their belonging to some groups (again, homosexuals, people of colour, women, and so on) as concerning not only morality but also justice? What should government do with cultural patterns that encourage stereotypes about Jews, tolerate homophobic expressions, stigmatize homosexuality as a kind of sickness or the like? What should government (not us as private individuals or associations) do about sexist jokes, Islamophobic speeches – publicly broadcasted through private TV channels or in the net – supremacist theories, holocaust denials?

This is a controversial issue and the different lines drawn by liberal democracies about what is permissible and what is a crime bear witness to the fact that even within the same political family there is reasonable disagreement. We mentioned before the different treatment in Italy and in the US regarding discriminatory selection of tenants on the part of landlords. In that case, it seems that the United States is more ready to sacrifice the full exercise of private property (surprising no?) for the sake of protecting people from misrecognition. Allow us to offer another example that goes in the opposite direction. While denying the holocaust in a public speech (including academia) is not a criminal offence in the United States, and human rights activists have opposed attempts to criminalize denial with the argument that it would unduly restrict freedom of speech, it is a crime in 16 European countries. Similar differences occur in the legislation related to endorsement of patriarchy, racism, and so on.

Prima facie, it would seem that all these symbolic assaults, short of institutional backing and performed with no intention to be translated into discriminations carried out through legislation, neatly fall within what Rawls would consider reasonable pluralism. After all, the great appeal of the freestanding nature of justice as fairness, as reformulated in *Political Liberalism*, is that it has the resources for gaining the approval (for the right reasons) even of illiberal comprehensive worldviews. What political liberalism asks from adherents to illiberal views is not that they renounce their beliefs, but that they abstain from attempting to translate them into laws that would make the sphere of freedom of some individuals or groups smaller than that enjoyed by others. In other words, one of the virtues of *Political Liberalism* is its ability to make room for illiberal and in this sense discriminatory comprehensive doctrines without any prejudice to the strictness of political obligations of liberal justice. Famously, one can be a strict religious believer, thus being fully convinced that being gay is a serious crime against the natural/divine order and yet not only tolerate but be willing to uphold a political system in which absolutely *no* discrimination against gays, in the legal and economic system, is allowed. In other words, one can adopt Rawls' conception of justice and fairness and yet still be free to express, in one's private or associative life (not through a political party though) views that on Fraser's account would clearly count as symbolic assault. By the standards of *Political Liberalism* one can preach on the streets that homosexuals are a social plague and perhaps also that people of colour are inferior without being fined or imprisoned by the public authority.

The point in fact cuts even deeper. Rawls' grounded hope is that these people would not *want* to live in a state in which homosexuals are discriminated against or punished. Being reasonable, they realize the existence of the burdens of judgement and tolerate other religious or moral standpoints that, with equal right, profess profoundly different worldviews. In short, they are illiberal in their comprehensive doctrine, but liberal in their political views. We take that Fraser does not want a society in which calling someone a 'faggot' is a crime or perhaps simply using that expression in the privacy of one's house entitles the police to fine you or worse. But if this is not what she wants, then Rawls seems to be in a better position to avoid similar counterintuitive conclusions.

Things, however, are not as simple as this quick defence of Rawls suggests. The boundaries between what counts as an immoral assault short of legal relevance and a crime, even for Rawls, are not easy to draw. We already recalled how liberal democracies, even those in which sovereignty over one's own property is taken very seriously, have already adopted laws in which coercive measures discourage a use of property in the market inspired by misrecognition (not renting to people of colour, for example). Also illuminating is the case of racism. Most liberal democracies now have crimes against the mere uttering of a racist creed. A 1993 Italian law (*Legge Mancino*) punishes with 6 to 12 months of jail or with a fine of up to €6000 to those who spread racist ideologies. And similar punishments are foreseen for the fact of belonging to private associations with that kind of ideology.

But here one must notice an important nuance. The law – at least the *Legge Mancino* under consideration – makes an effort to say that the crime lies not so much in having or expressing these ideologies but in 'spreading' them and/or in participating in associations whose goal is that of promoting them. Thus it seems that the problem is the transformation of a private belief, that may also be expressed without fear of sanction, into an ideology with political impact. Rawls would say that this is precisely the moment in which an illiberal yet reasonable position becomes a non-reasonable one.[29] Illiberalism and discrimination are OK to the extent in which they remain within the sphere of the private, thus not infecting the political. They are not to be tolerated if they trespass that boundary. The problem is that drawing the line between holding and expressing, or between expressing with or without the intention to *spread* the belief expressed, or in general between acts that fall within the realm of the private, and as such deserve no sanction, and acts that have a public/political resonance is difficult, if not impossible to do in a non-arbitrary way. Habermas (1990;1995; 1996) would say that there is no principled way of drawing that distinction before a decision is made by citizens in a democratic discussion possibly carried out in ideal circumstances. We think Fraser would agree with this solution, which nevertheless is itself quite problematic. In fact, it leaves us with two options: either we assume that all citizens agree on the point where the line should be drawn, which comes close to denying the fact of pluralism, or we take seriously the existence of pluralism but consider all ideologies that violate recognition as deserving the attention of coercive powers. While the former is intellectually unsatisfactory – it stubbornly denies an undisputed and easily verifiable fact – the latter is a moral disaster: it opens the door for state power to enter even into the household of comprehensive illiberals to make sure that they do not utter discriminatory statements, a sort of recognition Gestapo. Even if we are well aware that Rawls' attempt to secure a space of freedom for non-liberals with the trick that they are obliged to remain 'reasonable' is not free of difficulties, still we want to side with this option to avoid the risk of an authoritarian alternative. We want to be able to fight racist, homophobic, patriarchal ideologies on the terrain of moral confrontation, without having the police on our side.

We are not suggesting that Fraser would be indifferent to this intellectual desideratum. We are saying that holding participatory parity as the sole criterion of justice, perhaps the sole political value worthy of consideration in the normative realm of politics, combined with her failure to specify with precision what makes patterns of cultural misrecognition more or less institutional (admittedly, not an easy distinction to draw) leads Fraser to paternalistic outcomes that she would herself despise.

4 Conclusion

After a decade and a half, the debate between redistribution and recognition remains particularly rich and the dispute between which of the two paradigms best capture all dimensions of injustice in advanced capitalist societies still promises to illuminate the strengths and weaknesses of each model. Although in this chapter our aim was limited, we tried to rephrase the current controversy of redistribution vs recognition in light of the fundamental point, usually overlooked, that justice concerns what public and political authority (and more generally the state intervention) may and should do. In doing so, our intent was to issue a warning about the risk of paternal authoritarianism in the recognition paradigm, even in the deontological version defended by Fraser against Honneth. In this way, we have been able to evaluate the extent, if any, to which the limits of the paradigm of redistribution, denounced by the alternative recognition paradigm, are valid, at least when Rawls' political conception of justice is taken into account. Our conclusion is that Rawls' conception captures all the misrecognition practices that concern justice and is in a better position than Fraser's model to deal with the reasonable pluralism that characterizes our societies. In the end, Fraser is right when she shows us, perhaps better than Rawls, that not all injustice is misdistribution; though it is equally important to remember the other side of the coin, namely that not all misrecognition is injustice.

Notes

1 This project has received funding from the European Union's Horizon 2020 research and innovation programme under the Marie Skłodowska-Curie grant

agreement No 777786 and from the Grant #2018/04606-4 of the São Paulo Research Foundation (FAPESP).

2 For a defence of Dworkin on this point see Heath (2008).

3 We thus agree with Rainer Forst that 'Rawls does not share the first [allocative-distributive] but the second [relational] picture of justice, the one which accords priority to social structures and relations and the social status of the individual' (Forst 2014: 31). On this reading Rawls can be considered a 'relational egalitarian'. For the debate about relational egalitarianism, see also: Anderson (1999); O'Neill (2008).

4 Kant, The Metaphysics of Morals [239] – [242], 1996, p. 64–67. Other authors (O'Neill 1996; Pogge 2000; Forst 2014) defend the distinction between the obligations of justice and obligations of social virtues such as sympathy, beneficence, love, care, solidarity.

5 Some authors suggest that Fraser take into consideration a third dimension of justice – the political one – which is analytically distinct from redistribution and recognition (see: Zurn 2008: 147; Feldman 2008). It follows that we should be talking about a three-dimensional theory of justice: redistribution, recognition, and representation, with each dimension considered as not reducible to the others. Other authors hold that Fraser should assign to the political dimension a priority over the other two (see: Olson 2008; Forst 2008, reprinted in 2014).

6 The redistribution vs recognition opposition however may be deeper than Fraser herself recognizes and, for this reason, less easy to overcome through her two-dimensionality (or even three-dimensionality). Indeed, the contrast seems to rest on the opposition between two different moral languages. As De Vita notes, the moral language characteristic of egalitarian liberalism interprets every form of injustice as an infringement on the principle of equal rights for all. The moral language of the paradigm of redistribution, by contrast, does not seem to be content with a focus on equal legal rights, in turn considered as core guarantors of equal status. That language seems to consider private cultural assaults against the equal status of citizens, even if neither originated nor remediable by institutions, as equally problematic for justice as discriminations in legal rights (de Vita 2014: 112).

7 Fraser (Fraser and Honneth 2003: 10) mentions Taylor and Honneth as two champions of the identity model.

8 Fraser moves this critique not only against mainstream liberalism and the standard theories of distributive justice but also against the so-called second generation of critical theorists represented by Habermas (see in particular Habermas 1984; 1987). According to Fraser (1985), Habermas excessively substantialized the distinction between system and life-world, thereby leaving out certain dimensions of symbolic injustice. To use Fraser's famous example, women suffer not only because their domestic work is unpaid but also because the same is not properly recognized as a valuable occupation.

9 Our critique is consonant with Scheuerman's recent comments on Fraser (Scheuerman 2017). According to Scheuerman, 'Fraser has little to say about the law, in part because the foundations of her theory, despite their many virtues, probably do not provide her with enough room for doing so'. Fraser – he continues – endorses an approach in 'which law and rights too often remain fundamentally an impediment to autonomy rather than something indispensable to its realization' (Scheuerman 2017: 123). We agree with Scheuerman about the active and positive role of the law and of coercion, for instance to avoid some important forms of misrecognition, but exactly for this reason we think the limits of the law's reach should be clearly defined. Fraser's

underestimation of the law, as rightly observed by Scheuerman, prevents her from doing so.

10 Zurn (2008) argues that a substantive theory of social institutions like the one defended by Fraser cannot be simply deontological but should also include some teleological considerations. He believes that not all misrecognition can be accounted for by Fraser's status model. Some misrecognition can only be captured through the intellectual arsenal of critical social theory of the teleological kind Honneth defends. Zurn's point is interesting for our purposes. In fact, we agree that there are instances of misrecognition that remain outside of a deontologically inspired conception of justice. But we argue that we have *moral* duties to eradicate, mitigate, or overcome them while rejecting the view that coercive force and, more generally, state intervention can be used for that purpose.

11 Here 'coercive powers' are not only those of the state. For us, each of the institutions part of the basic structure – thus the family and the economic system as well – exercise coercive powers over individual lives. On this see more in what follows when we discuss firms as part of the basic structure.

12 The movie centres on the story of a lawyer fired by a law firm because of his homosexuality.

13 It was signed into law by President Lyndon B. Johnson on August 6, 1965.

14 Drawing a principled distinction between misrecognition that should be the business of the law and misrecognition that is and should remain the business of ethics is difficult even if one assumes Honneth's monistic principle of recognition (Honneth 1992). Honneth distinguishes three spheres of recognition – Love, Law, Achievement – and claims that they are governed by the normative principle of Love (or Care), Equal Rights, and Social Esteem. On his account, all three seem to concern 'justice' in the sense that if someone does not receive enough love in his or her life, this becomes a problem for institutions. Adultery is a very important form of disrespect in marital relationships. It can represent a serious humiliation for the betrayed partner. Surely, adultery is a violation of the principle of care and yet it would be odd, to say the least, that the betrayed partner is to receive some form of compensation from institutions and that the betrayer should face some legal charge. In his later *Freedom's Right* (Honneth 2014) the problem is not solved and if anything it becomes more serious. There Honneth defends institutionalization of the value of social freedom in the personal relationships such as friendship, intimate relationships, and families. Many agree that realizing social freedom in personal relationships contributes significantly to the worth of our lives, but are we really to think that, say, a friendship in which one partner is manipulated and lacks 'social freedom' should trigger some form of state intervention?

15 See: Fraser and Honneth 2003: 34 and note 34.

16 Fraser affirms that the standard theories of distributive justice cannot satisfactorily subsume questions of misrecognition without providing much evidence besides the examples of misrecognition that have nothing to do with material resources (Fraser and Honneth 2003: 34; 1996: 27–28). She includes Marx, Rawls, Sen, and Dworkin into this insufficient distributive model (Fraser 1996: note 26; 2001: note 8; 1995: 71 note 3). Moreover, Fraser (1996) only mentions as exception Kymlicka's account (1989), while ignoring Okin's (1989) and Phillips's (1999) works. Even more surprisingly, not many adherents to a distributive approach to justice have engaged with Fraser's critique. We can mention Robeyns (2008) and Healt (2008) who defend respectively Sen's and Dworkin's accounts, as well as Lægaard (2005) for a defence of Rawls' theory. For a general criticism from an egalitarian perspective of the recognition approach in its identity version (the one Fraser does not like) see: Barry (2001).

17 This enlarged interpretation of the basic structure, among other things, allows Rawlsians to defend themselves better from feminist criticisms *à la* Susan Okin (1989). In fact, it makes the gendered biased structure of the society subject to the criticism of the principles of justice. Not accidentally, Rawls himself adopts it in his reply to Okin: 'if we say the gender system includes whatever social arrangements adversely affect the equal basic liberties and opportunities of women, as well as of those of their children as future citizens, then surely that system is subject to critique by the principles of justice' (Rawls 2001: 167).

18 Law number 11.340–07/08/2006.

19 We are obviously siding here for that orientation in the feminist criticism of Rawls that sees justice as fairness as a model that has implicit potential for advancing typical feminist claims, as opposed to one helplessly imbued with gender-biased prejudices. For an overview of the various feminist interpretations of John Rawls see Abbey (2013).

20 See: Rawls 2005: 468.

21 Recently Anderson (2017) argued about the several forms of injustice that may occur in the internal structure of a firm. For a forceful reading that makes firms part of the basic structure see Celentano (2019). A similar reading was also defended by Alì (2018). Though most of the time those who argue for the inclusion of firms within the basic structure have big firms in mind, one may wonder whether small firms or family-run businesses should also be included in the basic structure and therefore made subject to the principle of justice. For example, shouldn't a homophobic entrepreneur with a firm whose dependents are all family members be free to hire only heterosexual employees? We have mixed intuitions here and we do not feel confident to defend either side. To solve the impasse one could be tempted to apply the Kant-inspired Rawlsian criterion of 'publicity' ['The publicity of the rules of an institution ensures that those engaged in it know what limitations on conduct to expect of one another and what kinds of actions are permissible. There is a common basis for determining mutual expectations' (Rawls1971: 56)]. As Lægaard (2005: 343) observes: 'if the social factors affecting self-respect are to be within the scope of justice according to this publicity constraint, they must be connected to behaviour describable as realizing rules that are public in this way'. But in the case at hand it is not clear to us how making homophobic selection criteria public would not impact negatively on gays' and lesbians' self-respect. At the same time, we resist endorsing a society in which the owner of a family-run, small business is not fully free to choose his and her employees.

22 In this sense, we think that we offer a more adequate interpretation of Rawls' idea of society 'neither as community nor association' (Rawls 2005: 40–43).

23 In contrast to obligations of social virtues, O'Neill conceives requirements of justice as 'rejection of direct injury to others: no systematic or gratuitous violence, coercion etc. [and] rejection of indirect injury: (a) rejection of damage to the social fabric and (b) rejection of damage to the material basis of life' (O'Neill 1996: 205).

24 Even Fraser acknowledges the social bases of self-respect as a resource in Rawls' theory 'for dealing with issues of cultural justice as well' (Fraser 1995: 71 note 3; see also Fraser and Honneth 2003: 34 nota 34). Moreover, many authors mentioned Rawls' social bases of self-respect as the best element to deal with injustices of misrecognition. See: Kymlicka 1989; Weinstock 1994; 1999; Tully 1995; Galeotti 2002; Lægaard 2005; Werle 2014. Warner and Zink (2016) point to Rousseau's influence on Rawls as evidence of how justice as fairness extends

beyond distributional questions and reaches the realm of political culture and psychology.

25 Rawls initially treated the terms 'self-respect' and 'self-esteem' as interchangeable. Famously, however, some authors (Sachs 1981: 346–347; Thomas 1978: 259 note 5; Darwall 1977: 48 note 18; Eyal 2005: 201–202) showed that by self-respect and self-esteem we usually mean two different things that sometimes are even in tension with one another. Subsequently, Rawls acknowledged this difference, and opted for the expression 'social bases of self-respect' (Rawls 2005: 404 note 39). For a comprehensive discussion of the different roles of self-respect and self-esteem in Rawls see: Shue (1975); Joshua Cohen (1989); Zink (2011).

26 Lægaard (2005: 338) argues that

> Rawls . . . tells two somewhat different stories about what the social bases of self-respect are. On the one hand . . . self-respect merely requires that a limited number of other persons affirm the value of one's conception of the good in a private association. In other places, however, Rawls makes self-respect depend, not on the affirmation of the value of one's conception of the good, but on respect for or recognition of one's status as an equal citizen and a fully cooperating member of society. This respect is to be expressed, not by other individual citizens in private associations, but by the public conception of justice and the basic structure which it regulates, especially by the equal basic liberties accorded to all members of society.

According to Lægaard, this second understanding of the social bases of self-respect connects very well with Fraser's status model, a view we readily share. Lægaard however seems to think that Fraser's model of recognition is able to avoid excesses in state intervention for the sake of recognition, as a liberal approach should do. We doubt that.

27 Doppelt (1981) argued that in advanced capitalist societies self-respect is so powerfully influenced by our share of material resources that it is hard to accept Rawls' suggestion that public affirmation of citizens' equal status is a sufficiently strong basis for their self-respect.

28 Note that this is also Fraser's concern. Indeed, Fraser affirms also that her approach is compatible with a plurality of reasonable views of the good life (Fraser and Honneth 2003: 228–229).

29 For an accurate discussion on this point, see Freeman (2007).

References

Abbey, Ruth. 2013. 'Introduction: Biography of a Bibliography: Three Decades of Feminist Response to Rawls', in Ruth Abbey (ed.), *Feminist Interpretations of John Rawls*, pp. 1–23. Pennsylvania: Pennsylvania State University Press.

Alì, Nunzio. 2018. 'Economic Inequality and Proportionality. How Rich Should the 1% Be?', Ph.D. dissertation, Universidade Federal de Santa Catarina.

Anderson, Elizabeth. 1999. 'What Is the Point of Equality?', *Ethics*, 109(2): 287–337.

———. 2017. *Private Government: How Employers Rule Our Lives (And Why We Don't Talk About It)*. Princeton: Princeton University Press.

Barry, Brian. 2001. *Culture and Equality: An Egalitarian Critique of Multiculturalism*. Cambridge: Polity Press.

Celentano, Denise. 2019. 'Cooperating as Peers: Labor Justice Between Distributive and Relational Equality', Unpublished Ph.D. dissertation, UNICT/EHESS.
Cohen, Joshua. 1989. 'Democratic Equality', *Ethics*, 99(4): 727–751.
Darwall, Stephen L. 1977. 'Two Kinds of Respect', *Ethics*, 88(1): 36–49.
de Vita, Àlvaro. 2014. 'Critical Theory and Social Justice', *Brazilian Political Science Review*, 8(1): 109–126.
Doppelt, Gerald. 1981. 'Rawls' System of Justice: A Criticism from the Left', *Nous*, 15(3): 259–307.
Dworkin, Ronald. 2000. *Sovereign Virtue: The Theory and Practice of Equality*. Cambridge, MA: Harvard University Press.
Eyal, Nir. 2005. '"Perhaps the Most Important Primary Good": Self-Respect and Rawls's Principles of Justice', *Politics, Philosophy & Economics*, 4(2): 195–219.
Feldman, Leonard. 2008. 'Status Injustice: The Role of the State', in Kevin Olson (ed.), *Adding Insult to Injury. Nancy Fraser Debates Her Critics*, pp. 221–245. London: Verso.
Forst, Rainer. 2008. 'Thing First Thing: Redistribution, Recognition and Justification', in Kevin Olson (ed.), *Adding Insult to Injury. Nancy Fraser Debates Her Critics*, pp. 310–326. London: Verso.
———. 2014. *Justification and Critique: Towards a Critical Theory of Politics*. Translated by Ciaran Cronin. Cambridge: Polity Press.
Fraser, Nancy. 1985. 'What's Critical about Critical Theory? The Case of Habermas and Gender', *New German Critique*, 35: 97–131.
———. 1995. 'From Redistribution to Recognition? Dilemmas of Justice in a "Post-Socialist" Age', *New Left Review*, I/212 (July–August): 68–93.
———. 1996. 'Social Justice in the Age of Identity Politics: Redistribution, Recognition, and Participation', *The Tanner Lectures on Human Value*, Stanford University April 30-May 2: 1–67.
———. 2000. 'Rethinking Recognition', *New Left Review*, 3 (May–Jun): 107–120.
———. 2001. 'Recognition without Ethics', *Theory, Culture & Society*, 18(2–3): 21–42.
———. 2010. *Scales of Justice: Reimagining Political Space in a Globalizing World*. New York: Columbia University Press.
Fraser, Nancy and Axel Honneth. 2003. *Redistribution or Recognition? A Political-Philosophical Exchange*. London: Verso.
Freeman, Samuel. 2007. 'Public Reason and Political Justification', in Samuel Freeman (ed.), *Justice and the Social Contract: Essays on Rawlsian Political Philosophy*, pp. 215–225, Oxford: Oxford University Press.
Galeotti, Anna Elisabetta. 2002. *Toleration as Recognition*. Cambridge: Cambridge University Press.
Habermas, Jürgen. 1984 and 1987. *The Theory of Communicative Action – Vol. I and Vol. II*. Translated by Thomas McCarthy. Boston: Bacon Press.
———. 1990. *Moral Consciousness and Communicative Action*. Translated by Christian Lenhardt. Cambridge, MA: MIT Press.
———. 1995. 'Reconciliation Through the Public use of Reason: Remarks on John Rawls's Political Liberalism', *The Journal of Philosophy*, 92(3): 109–131.
———. 1996. *Between Facts and Norms. Contributions to a Discourse Theory of Law and Democracy*. Translated by William Regh. Cambridge, MA: MIT Press.

Heath, Joseph. 2008. 'Resource Egalitarianism and the Politics of Recognition', in Kevin Olson (ed.), *Adding Insult to Injury. Nancy Fraser Debates Her Critics*, pp. 196–218. London: Verso.

Honneth, Axel. 1992. *The Struggle for Recognition: The Moral Grammar of Social Conflicts*. Translated by Joel Anderson. Cambridge: Polity Press.

———. 2014. *Freedom's Right. The Social Foundations of Democratic Life*. Translated by Joseph Ganahl. New York: Columbia University Press.

Kant, Immanuel. 1996. *The Metaphysics of Morals*. Translated by Mary Gregor. Cambridge: Cambridge University Press.

Kymlicka, Will. 1989. *Liberalism, Community, and Culture*. Oxford: Clarendon Press.

Lægaard, Sune. 2005. 'On the Prospects for a Liberal Theory of Recognition', *Res Publica*, 11: 325–348.

Okin, Susan Moller. 1989. *Justice, Gender, and Family*. New York: Basic Books.

Olson, Kevin. 2008. 'Participatory Parity and Democratic Justice', in Kevin Olson (ed.), *Adding Insult to Injury: Nancy Fraser Debates Her Critics*, pp. 246–272. London: Verso.

O'Neill, Martin. 2008. 'What Should Egalitarians Believe?', *Philosophy & Public Affairs*, 36(2): 119–156.

O'Neill, Onora. 1996. *Towards Justice and Virtue: A Constructive Account of Practical Reasoning*. Cambridge: Cambridge University Press.

Phillips, Anne. 1999. *Which Equalities Matters*. Cambridge: Polity.

Pogge, Thomas W. 2000. 'On the Site of Distributive Justice', *Philosophy and Public Affairs*, 29(2): 137–169.

Rawls, John. 1971. *A Theory of Justice*. Cambridge, MA: Harvard University Press.

———. 2001. *Justice as Fairness: A Restatement*. Cambridge, MA: Harvard University Press.

———. 2005. *Political Liberalism: Expanded Edition*. New York: Columbia University Press.

Robeyns, Ingrid. 2008. 'Is Nancy Fraser's Critique of Theories of Distributive Justice Justified?', in Kevin Olson (ed.), *Adding Insult to Injury: Nancy Fraser Debates Her Critics*, pp. 176–195. London: Verso.

Sachs, David. 1981. 'How to Distinguish Self-Respect from Self-Esteem', *Philosophy & Public Affairs*, 10(4): 346–360.

Scheuerman, William E. 2017. 'Recent Frankfurt Critical Theory: Down on Law?', *Constellations*, 24(1): 113–125.

Shue, Henry. 1975. 'Liberty and Self-Respect', *Ethics*, 85(3): 195–203.

Thomas, Larry L. 1978. 'Morality and Our Self-Concept', *The Journal of Value Inquiry*, 12(4): 258–268.

Tully, James. 1995. *Strange Multiplicity*. Cambridge: Cambridge University Press.

Warner, John M. and James R. Zink. 2016. 'Therapeutic Politics: Rawls's Respect for Rousseau', *The Review of Politics*, 78: 117–140.

Weinstock, Daniel M. 1994. 'The Political Theory of Strong Evaluation', in James Tully (ed.), *Philosophy in an Age of Pluralism: The Philosophy of Charles Taylor in Question*, pp. 171–193. Cambridge: Cambridge University Press.

———. 1999. 'How Can Collective Rights and Liberalism Be Reconciled?', in Rainer Bauböck and John Rundell (eds), *Blurred Boundaries: Migration, Ethnicity, Citizenship* (Chapter 11). Aldershot: Ashgate.

Werle, Denilson Luís. 2014. 'Justice, Basic Liberties and Social Bases of Self-Respect', *Ethic@*, 13(1): 74–90.

Zink James R. 2011. 'Reconsidering the Role of Self-Respect in Rawls's: A Theory of Justice', *The Journal of Politics*, 73(2): 331–344.

Zurn, Christopher F. 2008. 'Arguing Over Participatory Parity: Nancy Fraser's Conception of Social Justice', in Kevin Olson (ed.), *Adding Insult to Injury: Nancy Fraser Debates Her Critics*, pp. 142–163. London: Verso.

9

THE POLITICS OF WHITE MISRECOGNITION AND PRACTICES OF RACIAL INEQUALITY

Sarah Bufkin

1 Introduction

The Great Recession cracked the neoliberal settlement and revealed the weak underpinnings of its push towards privatization, market deregulation, and the overextension of easy credit. Austerity has strained the welfare state's promissory note towards its citizens, and the rise of financial capitalism has fuelled a dramatic rise in economic inequality as stock investments have skyrocketed and wages have remained flat. In 2020, capitalism feels anything but tame. The past two decades have also seen growing disillusion among progressives over multiculturalism's emancipatory potential. Two obstacles in particular have provoked serious concern about the viability of recognition as a normative framework. First, neoliberal capitalism has, in many instances, appropriated cultural and racial difference (Gilroy 2000). Corporate diversity schemes have neutralized the force of identity claims by tokenizing visibly different bodies to boost their brand's aesthetic. And companies have found that they can exploit the consumer market segments that identity markers provide. Second, reactionary groups peddling White nationalism and xenophobia have weaponized identity-driven political logics. Racialized fears over immigration, refugees, and crime have pushed far-right parties back into the political mainstream and, increasingly, into the halls of electoral power.

Today, many political commentators and theorists advocate for the end of identity politics.[1] Focusing on cultural and racial difference has only balkanized political resistance, they argue. What the Left needs is a robust class politics aimed at toppling the wealthy and revitalizing the social-democratic vision of the post-war period. At their most naïve, these critics offer a return to a reductive economism that is as crude as the excess of culturalism that they decry. Even more nuanced observers are in danger of jettisoning the most salient and important insights of the antiracist, feminist, and indigenous movements: that social hierarchies often work *through* difference to exploit, oppress, and marginalize vulnerable groups. The problem of identity – understood as an 'embodied politics of location' rather than as a form of racial or cultural essentialism – is irrevocably entangled with both the practices of inequality and the kind of political mobilization required to transform those hierarchies (Rich 1986: 210). As Black feminists have long argued, recognizing racial differences is not a barrier to political organizing but often provides the necessary bridge across diverse social positions. Naïve multiculturalism might be dead, but understanding the relationship between social positionality, embodied subjectivity, and material hierarchies remains just as important today as it did 20 years ago. The contemporary political conjuncture calls not for the jettisoning of recognition as an analytical framework but instead for renewed attention to how best to think the relation between recognition and redistribution.

This is particularly true when it comes to understanding how racial hierarchies function in the contemporary United States. Racial inequalities remain rampant, affecting almost every index of social functioning and opportunity (Alexander 2010; Hero and Levy 2016; Massey 2007; Oliver and Shapiro 2006; Rohde and Guest 2013; Wacquant 2002; Western and Pettit 2005). The persistence of racial domination too is more than just a historical legacy of chattel slavery and Jim Crow. These racial hierarchies are actively reproduced through racialized practices. Perry writes, 'In contexts such as employment, health care, education, law enforcement, housing, and more, the evidence demonstrates that, in aggregate, people make choices that tend to advantage Whites' (Perry 2011: 31). The state uses racial classifications to discipline and manage populations it deems dangerous and disposable (Gilroy 2018). The police survey, stop, search, and arrest (sometimes violently) Black Americans at much higher rates than Whites; the courts, in turn, are more likely to charge, prosecute, and convict racial minorities (Cole 1999; Wacquant 2002). The labour markets use racial classifications to separate the employable from the expendable (Hall 1986: 24); Black employment, wages, and career advancement continue to lag behind Whites, even those of comparable educational levels (Perry 2011; Western and Pettit 2005). Financial lenders have consistently targeted Black home buyers for subprime mortgages and more expensive forms of credit (Wang 2018). At the interpersonal level, anti-Blackness continues to cathect even the most mundane of interactions and judgements. Racial orders operate through classifications that have become naturalized and self-evident – inert markers of difference and desert marked on the body (Mbembe 2017). Antiracist theory and politics, therefore, must be carefully attuned to the complex ways in which maldistribution and symbolic domination are articulated together.

In this chapter, I seek to rethink the relationship between economic maldistribution and cultural (mis)recognition when it comes to analyzing the reproduction of the contemporary US racial order. Black political thought has a rather complicated, often times antagonistic, relationship to the paradigm of recognition as a mode of thinking racial justice. Cultural recognition of Black subjects is always overdetermined from the outside by a racial imaginary constructed by Whites. As thinkers like Frantz Fanon, James Baldwin, and Raoul Peck make clear, the act of interracial recognition often does more to confirm the authority and legitimacy of White imaginaries than it does to free Black subjects. I will argue that critical theorists Axel Honneth and Nancy Fraser prove too optimistic about the role that cultural recognition can play in redressing social injustice, albeit in different ways. Neither thinker is equipped to deal with the ways in which White-dominated social imaginaries – and the forms of life they regulate – can provide forms of ostensibly 'healthy' social recognition for White subjects while also legitimating unjust practices and racial inequality. Nor is the symbolic revaluation of Blackness enough to unmake the racialized institutions that centuries of White supremacy have left in their wake. Today's corporate celebration of ethnic diversity, at best, exists alongside and, at worst, helps to obscure the racialized market segmentation that separates out those communities ripe for investment from those vulnerable to economic predation. As Baldwin and Peck demonstrate, there was – and remains – an internal relation between practices of White capital accumulation and zones of Black economic neglect.

2 Axel Honneth, Nancy Fraser, and the critique of late capitalism

In *Redistribution or recognition?*, Fraser and Honneth frame the relationship between recognition and redistribution in divergent ways. Fraser advocates for what she describes as a perspectival dualism in which recognition and redistribution pose two analytically distinctive but practically entangled paradigms of social justice. Neither framework ought to be subsumed into the other or seen as secondary, she argues. Each paradigm helps to isolate distinctive sources of injustice and to point the way towards practical strategies for redress. In contrast, Honneth offers a normative monism centred around intersubjective relations of mutual recognition. While economic injustice is also of serious import for Honneth, he argues that claims of exploitation or maldistribution are in fact a subsection of recognition claims. In order for individuals to experience economic inequality as a moral wrong, he reasons, they must see it as a violation of their normative expectations regarding the kinds of recognition they are owed.

Neither Honneth nor Fraser provides a satisfactory framework through which to think racial injustice and the reproduction of White hegemony, albeit for different reasons. Honneth's singular fixation on recognition forces him into diagnostic trouble when it comes to racial injustice. At the sociological level, this means that he is left providing an analytically unsatisfactory account of today's racialized capitalism (Zurn 2005). Fraser, in turn, offers a more promising account of the relationship between misrecognition and maldistribution. By adopting a dualist framework, she is capable of critiquing both hierarchical patterns of symbolic value and the systemic logic of late capitalism, without reducing one to the other. Yet for all its normative advantages over Honneth's theory, Fraser's approach reduces the problem of recognition to the thin problem of status subordination in ways that limit her diagnostic acumen in critiquing racial hierarchies.

At first look, it might seem that Honneth's theoretical claim – that economic maldistribution results from practices of social misrecognition – might prove more accurate when it comes to thinking racial discrimination in capitalist markets. After all, individuals and institutions continue to make racialized decisions about who to employ and who to fire, who to grant loans to and who to deny, who to invest in and who to pass over. At a systemic level, these everyday judgements reproduce Black un- and underemployment, consolidate White wealth, and conserve certain sectors of the labour market for White communities (Perry 2011). Yet it would be just as reductive to assume that all instances of racial inequality stem from anti-Black discrimination as it would be to assume that all forms of poverty and wage exploitation stem from a lack of social esteem for certain groups. 'Racist maldistribution is not simply a by-product of status hierarchy; nor is racist misrecognition wholly a by-product of economic structure' (Fraser and Honneth 2003: 23). Racialized advantages compound over time, in the form of capital, practical know-how and proximity to resources. And once they do, they can reproduce inequalities in ways that do not draw directly on racialized imaginaries or anti-Black stigma.

Part of the problem here is Honneth's conceptualization of the relationship between capitalism and racism. Honneth sees the capitalist market as a community where individuals are valued as contributors to the collective good (Honneth 2001, 2004). That normative reconstruction stands in stark contrast to the picture of racial capitalism that emerges from more genealogical accounts. 'The plantation regime, and later, the colonial regime presented a problem by making race a principle of the exercise of power, a rule of sociability, and a mechanism for training people in behaviours aimed at the growth of economic profitability' (Mbembe 2017: 81). In a conceptual framework in which racism is seen as a moral aberration from the norm of mutual cooperation in the market, then perhaps diagnosing all racial inequality as the result of discriminatory decisions and value hierarchies would make more sense. But when we situate contemporary racial inequalities within a genealogical critique of the capitalist market as a fundamentally racist and racialized institution, from its outset in the United States through to today, then the picture becomes much more complex (Robinson 2000). Racial inequalities are sedimented into the market system itself, whether that involves looking at the wealth that different racial groups have accumulated, the capital that they can access, the social networks upon which they can draw, the educational institutions whose credentials are available to them, or the protections afforded by the social environments in which they live (Oliver and Shapiro 2006). Honneth's commitment to a monist framework prevents him from offering a more analytically robust interrogation of global capitalism and its racialized projects of extraction and underdevelopment.

Fraser's participatory dualism avoids this shortcoming. She insists that social justice involves two analytically distinctive but practically entangled paradigms – that of recognition and redistribution. Incidents of misrecognition arise out of the social imaginary, particularly from the symbolic hierarchies that devalue or stigmatize certain groups. Patterns of maldistribution, in contrast, are best diagnosed by looking at the systemic imperatives of late capitalism, its priorities and functional norms. 'Each dimension has some relative independence from the other. Neither can be redressed indirectly, therefore, through remedies addressed exclusively to the other' (Fraser and Honneth 2003: 23). Not all instances of economic maldistribution can be explained through, or redressed by dismantling, pathological patterns of cultural value. Fraser acknowledges that global capital flows are largely driven by systemic imperatives – the availability of cheap labour across national borders, the rise and risks of financial speculation, and the consolidation of certain markets behind a few mega-firms. And yet she also refuses to assimilate all instances of injustice to either one form of injustice or the other. For oppressed minorities, the problems of symbolic devaluation and economic maldistribution are often mutually reinforcing. This leaves Fraser much better positioned to analyze the multiple sources of Black oppression in the United States. Her dualistic framework offers more granular analyses of political conjunctures than does Honneth's Hegelian reconstruction.

Yet Fraser's account of misrecognition too falls short when it comes to critiquing racial stratification. In contrast to Honneth's focus on the lived experience of intersubjective affirmation, she argues that recognition should be thought of in more objectivist terms – as a matter of status hierarchies (Dahl et al. 2004). Critical theorists shouldn't care about the recognition of social differences for difference's sake, but because certain identity-driven differences make a difference in how people are treated (Fraser 1995). Fraser therefore avoids falling back into the same sort of uncritical subjectivism that Honneth does by linking recognition back up to institutionalized hierarchies of value. Narrowing her analytical gaze to the thin problem of status devaluation, however, overlooks the complex and emergent ways in which racialized imaginaries (mis)recognize Black subjects and naturalize White hegemony. At an abstract level, racism does often involve a form of insidious inferiorization, one that Fraser likely has in mind when she discusses exclusionary cultural hierarchies. But in racial orders, there are more subtle and complex ways to tell people to stay where they are, to accept their racialized positionality, than through prejudice alone (Fanon 2008).

Fraser too neglects the internally related problem of status exaggeration, which drives many exclusionary forms of White ethno-nationalism (Mills 1997). And such a framework obscures all the ways in which racialized imaginaries naturalize Black suffering without explicitly stigmatizing Black people. As Baldwin and Fanon will make clear, racialized norms of recognition are not only problematic when they actively subordinate or devalue Black personhood. In complicated ways, White racial imaginaries can still appropriate narratives of Black skill or desirability to further justify oppressive practices. White subjects are capable too of deflecting their own accountability by misrecognizing the role that their seemingly racially-neutral practices play in upholding oppressive hierarchies (Shelby 2014). In turn, many White liberals deflect moral responsibility onto readily identifiable 'White racists' in ways that undercut their support for antiracist policies.

Reading the racialized encounter through a more negativist understanding of White mystification, I argue, will allow for a more productive reckoning with how social imaginaries contribute to distributive injustice. This is particularly helpful when it comes to understanding how individuals – even those White and Black subjects that cognitively accept the propositional claims of Black personhood and racial equality – can participate in the reproduction of oppressive hierarchies (Hall 1986). The road to racial justice is thornier than either Honneth or Fraser allows.

3 Frantz Fanon and the ambivalence of racialized recognition

Antiracist activism has long been at the forefront of political struggles for recognition, respect, and inclusion within the US political community. And yet many Black intellectuals and political theorists have taken a more guarded stance towards the theories of social recognition that gained traction in the 1990s and early 2000s. Black political thought has remained more sceptical of the emancipatory potential that recognition theorists like Taylor or Honneth have been quick to ascribe to this conceptual framework. This hesitancy, in large part, stems from political concerns over the paradigm's conservatism and from the sense that the phenomenology of interracial recognition is much more fraught than they allow. I argue that Frantz Fanon gives us a more accurate starting point for social criticism in rigidly stratified racial orders. By focusing on the ways in which social hierarchies corrode the possibilities of mutual recognition, Fanon is able to isolate the differential conditions under which the 'master subject' and the 'subordinated subject' are positioned – and to critique how those asymmetrical acts of reification contribute to the reproduction of racial inequalities (Fanon 2001, 2008).

Building a politics centred around claims for the recognition of Black racial identities is much more fraught than much of the 1990s multiculturalist rhetoric would have it. Similarly to Fraser's concerns with identitarian approaches to recognition, many critics have warned that crude versions of multiculturalism can essentialize racial identities in misleading, unstable, and at times even dangerous ways. Grounding the politics of difference in pre-set social identities can lead to exclusionary logics that often reinforce other symbolic hierarchies, like heteronormativity or misogyny (Phillips 2007; Thomas 1998). At its worst, such a rarefied focus on identity-driven collectivities could lend itself to authoritarian movements that policed internal dissent and coercively regulated their constituents' self-expression and ethical commitments. Paul Gilroy even argued for getting rid of what he termed 'raciological' thinking altogether as a basis for diagnosing social harms and organizing political collectivities (Gilroy 2000). Even the sorts of racial solidarities and counter-publics that oppressed groups have formed in order to insulate themselves and resist White supremacy can fall back into essentialist logics of Us-Them. No matter how resistant their impulses, these raciological commitments can fuel attempts to ontologize racial difference in ways that legitimate racialized exploitation and violence. Adopting simplistic views of social justice qua racial recognition, then, can lead to similar kinds of theoretical and political closure. The difficulty with theorizing 'race' is to acknowledge its social and political facticity without rendering it into a metaphysical, transhistorical, or stable ground for thinking human difference.

Critics also worry that the recognition of marginalized groups ends up supporting existing power hierarchies rather than dismantling them. Demands for recognition within hierarchical social orders can force marginalized and oppressed groups to seek acknowledgement from their oppressors – and on their oppressors' terms (Coulthard 2014). Granting recognition, then, becomes an act of beneficence from the master subject that only further confirms his authority, rather than challenging or escaping from it. 'The need to demand recognition from the dominant culture or group is a symptom of the pathology of oppression' (Oliver 2001: 9). bell hooks argues that Black Americans should not preoccupy themselves with seeking recognition from White America (hooks 1990). True emancipation involves Black individuals' creative capacity for self-definition. Some thinkers also worry that the politics of recognition forces Black subjects to perform their own victimhood in ways that do little to destabilize the status quo. Adopting the posture of the Black victim may be strategically necessary to unlock certain forms of rights and state support, yet it can re-inscribe anti-Black stigma and deflect from broader claims of systemic injustice (Crenshaw 1997). It can also feed into practices of White voyeurism. Historically, the visibility of Black bodies in pain has been a key source for the enactment of White power and pleasure (Weheliye 2014). A politics that fixates too much on racist degradation as the grounds for White empathy comes close to reproducing those self-same structures of White spectatorship – without any guarantees of real political change.

This scepticism towards recognition makes sense if we look to a different phenomenological model than the notion of mutual affirmation that Honneth gives. Frantz Fanon's existentialist account of the racialized encounter provides a better diagnostic framework. He reinserts the interracial encounter back into the asymmetrical structural context that overdetermined White-Black social relations. European colonial orders give rise to a 'Manichean delirium' that splits the human into White and Black, settler and native, civilized and barbaric (Fanon 2001). 'The fierce colonial desire to divide and classify, to create hierarchies and produce difference, leaves behind wounds and scars. Worse, it created a fault line that lives on' (Mbembe 2017: 7). Within this racialized ontology, there are two kinds of subjects – a White European subject granted the formal status of personhood and all its incumbent rights, and a Black or native subject whose foundational Otherness and deficiency sets them out for domination. The two subject positions might not have any true metaphysical ground, but they have become existentially co-constitutive within racial formations.

In these fiercely partitioned social orders, Whites have little exposure to Black communities. The sorts of interactions they do have are fiercely constrained by a White racial imaginary that constructs the Black Other as little more than a caricature. The interracial encounter is always-already overdetermined from the outside. Fanon offers a well-known account of the traumatic experience of confronting the White gaze in *Black Skin, White Masks*. While he is travelling on a French train, a White child pointed to him and called out, 'Look, a Nègre!' (Fanon 2008: 89). Fanon is reified, fixed in place by the White Other who displaces his personhood and his individuality with a mythic Blackness. He now sees himself as the White child does: 'I cast an objective gaze over myself, discovered my blackness, my ethnic features: deafened by cannibalism, backwardness, fetishism, racial stigmas, slave traders, and above all, use, above all the grinning Y a bon Banania' (Fanon 2008: 92). Fanon is at one and the same time recognized and misrecognized. His capacity for individual self-determination has been constitutively elided in the face of the Negro, whose phantasmagoric character replaces and displaces every Black subject. The child's identification renders Fanon into the essentially Other and inferior. 'I sense, I see in this White gaze that it's the arrival not of a new man, but of a new type of man, a new species. A Negro, in fact!' (Fanon 2008: 95).

These racialized encounters are much more complicated than the kind of Other-regarding mutuality that Honneth touts as the basis for intersubjective sociality. There is no straightforward affirmation of the Other here, even when the child's mother attempts to compliment Fanon – 'Look at how handsome that Negro is' (Fanon 2008: 94). Neither the White child nor his mother could actually see Fanon as an individual, as a person with a biographical history and a point of view. Instead, their gaze was obscured by the veil that they had forced him to wear. In racialized encounters, 'no amount of visibility will alter the ways in which one is perceived' (Rankine 2014: 24). This is presence as erasure, sight as blindness. We have the White subject whose gaze reifies the Black subject into little more than an object, who depersonalizes the Black subjectivity into little more than the visual marker of an absolute difference (Mbembe 2017). And we have the Black subject who is doubled, who wears both the mask that the White racial imaginary has provided for him and peers out at the White world that has revealed so much about itself in the process of dehumanizing him. Fanon's existential phenomenology, then, draws attention to two specific ethical critiques that help to explain how racial hierarchies are maintained. On the one hand, he analyzes what he describes as the state of Black alienation under White supremacy. On the other, he explores how the practices of White misrecognition help to stabilize the status quo and its power asymmetries. I will sketch each briefly.

Black subjects suffer from a profound alienation under racial colonialism (Fanon 2008). The systemic nature of these racist reifications effectively conditions how Black subjects experience themselves, their identities, and their relationships to others. It is not necessarily that Black subjects are so fixed by racial and racist discourses that they believe themselves to be inferior or less than human. In fact, as Fanon stresses, Black subjects know that they are not what the Other stereotypes them to be (Fanon 2008). Yet that doesn't mean that their embodied subjectivity is free from the corrosive influences – whether interpretative, affective, or practical – of hierarchical racialization. At a foundational level, these forms of racialized ascription represent more than just symbolic harms to Black self-worth. Racialized imaginaries opens Black bodies up to discrimination, domination, silencing, and violence. '[R]acism is a visceral experience . . . it dislodges brains, blocks airways, rips muscle, extracts organs, cracks bones, breaks teeth' (Coates 2015). To inhabit a Black body in racial orders is to subject oneself, daily, without respite, to the threat of White racism. It is stressful, exhausting, oppressive. Black subjects learn to manage their visibility in White spaces, to make themselves appear less threatening and more trustworthy. Their habits and practices become racialized and distorted, not rightly their own. 'The worst injury is feeling that you do not belong so much/to you' (Rankine 2014: 146). Constantly navigating projections of Black inferiority displaces Black subjects from a right relation to their own embodied subjectivity.

White subjects, in contrast, are the producers of these racist knowledges, yet they remain in the dark. In constructing this historical-racial schema, they blind themselves. This racialized imaginary says more about White knowers, their fears and desires, their ignorance and their empathetic failures, than it does about Black people. 'The Other, the White man . . . had woven me out of a thousand details, anecdotes, and stories' (Fanon 2008: 91). White subjects are trapped by myths of their own making – phantasms that they have cathected with their existential anxieties and their (often legitimate) concerns over how Black people will respond to centuries of domination (Baldwin and Peck 2017). For all that the gaze appears to go one way – showing the Black subject into an object or a kind of subhuman being – it is the White subject who is the one who is truly revealed in that encounter (Baldwin and Peck 2017: 103). In turn, White subjects often know little about the natives or the Black people that they construct as inferior and dangerous Others. 'The racist subject sees the humanity in himself not by accounting for what makes him similar to others but by accounting for what makes him different' (Mbembe 2017: 36). What appears to them to be a moment of Black recognition is always-already the site of White misrecognition.

White knowers obscure not just the specificity of Black subjectivities but also the oppressive conditions that Black communities are subjected to *and* their role in the active reproduction of those oppressions. This is where the critical element of Fanon's diagnosis becomes unavoidable. White subjects dehumanize Black people while at the same time denying that they have done so. He saw Whiteness not as an aspirational ideal but as an ideological and ethical trap that prevented people from relating to themselves or to their own actions with anything like reflexive responsibility. 'The Negro enslaved by his inferiority, the White man enslaved by his superiority alike behave in accordance with a neurotic orientation' (Fanon 2008: 60). Within racialized orders, then, the oppressed's desire to be recognized by the oppressor subject is not a claim for social justice; it further entrenches the symbolic hierarchy that allows White people to dictate the terms of inclusion, esteem, and ultimately personhood that they deem intelligible and legitimate.

Neither Honneth's account of intersubjective affirmation nor Fraser's attention to objective status hierarchies can fully capture the agential and epistemic failures that Fanon's work on Black alienation and White mystification points to. 'Recognition, like capital, is essential to the economy of domination, which is not to say that oppressed people should not fight for both capital and recognition' (Oliver 2001: 23). Simply valourizing Blackness or reallocating social esteem to Black people will do little to dismantle these broader racial imaginaries in which White hegemony is seen as both normal and natural rather than as oppressive, exploitative, and contradictory to its own stated moral commitments. Achieving racial justice in the United States would never be a matter of simply including Black folks within White ways of life (or at the very least, within the formal remit of their social and legal institutions). It would involve dismantling Whiteness as a regulative norm, along with the material and symbolic hierarchies that Whiteness continued to shore up (Du Bois 1940). In the next section, I turn to James Baldwin and Raoul Peck to further analyse the ideological work that these practices of White misrecognition do to reproduce racial inequality.

4 James Baldwin, Raoul Peck, and White mystification

Raoul Peck's documentary, *I Am Not Your Negro*, reconstructs the critical aspects of James Baldwin's work for contemporary US audiences. Peck wanted to make a film on the book that Baldwin started but never finished. In these writings, Baldwin attempted to stand in witness of the lives and struggles of three Black men: Medgar Evers, Malcolm X, and Martin Luther King Jr. (Baldwin and Peck 2017: 5). All were murdered young, within five years of each other during the 1960s. Like its wellspring, Peck's documentary wants to say something about a bigger unfinished project – that of dismantling White hegemony in the United States. Released one month after the inauguration of a president who had openly courted White supremacists, this film offered a serious conversation about America's racial pathologies at a time when White liberals were desperately in need of someone, anyone, to say something substantive about how we had ended up where we were. What I am interested in is how Peck uses his curatorial agency in *I Am Not Your Negro* to de-naturalize the White racial imaginary and the moments of misrecognition that it encodes. His reading undercuts the tacit presumption that White American bodies, their cultural praxis and their imagined world are enlightened and ethically neutral, if not outright desirable. The film discloses how practices of White mystification – both of the Black Other and of the White world – legitimate rampant inequalities. By dramatizing how White Americans neglect systemic and spectacular forms of racial oppression, Peck reminds us that, in the United States at least, it is the face of racial injustice that works so hard to remain blind.

Peck's documentary attempts to provoke in White viewers what Stuart Hall might have called an oppositional decoding of their racial common sense (Hall 1980a). 'Sociality or intersubjectivity is . . . essentially imaginary. Individuals enter society with conceptions and images of themselves and of others, though often enough these are distorted, fortuitous, and misleading' (Saar 2015: 121). For many Whites, the White world is simply the world. This colours their understanding of dominant social institutions and of themselves. The liberal state is a neutral arbitrator that enforces laws equally, protects spheres of individual autonomy and assures social order for all. The capitalist markets provide opportunities for individual self-development and wealth accumulation for those who apply themselves, regardless of skin colour. The United States is interpreted as a place of freedom and opportunity (Mills 1997). In this pastoral vision, the problem of 'race' becomes the problem of Black and brown people. Whites are, in turn, almost race-less. They are individuals, human beings, mothers and daughters, fathers and sons, professionals and workers. In this race-neutral liberal view, if anyone is responsible for the ongoing racial inequalities in America, it is either minorities who don't take responsibility for their own lives or those White racists who haven't gotten with the times.

As Fanon reminds us, master subjects under rigidly racialized regimes are structurally and interpretatively predisposed to misrecognition. They cannot see the world that they themselves have made. Peck's documentary sets about correcting some of those cultivated blind spots. Black subjects, he reminds us, live in a very different America than the one that forms the imaginative backdrop for White communities. *I Am Not Your Negro* pushes this contradiction to the fore. Peck pulls an excerpt from a 1960s propaganda film in which a voiceover outlines all the bountiful advantages to the American way of life. Images of White bodies jumping into a pool, of a Ferris wheel spinning, of White bodies playing baseball, now football, unspool across the screen as a voice declaims, 'There's unending scenic beauty and there's freedom' (Peck and Jackson 2017). The video reel switches to brutal shots from the 1965 Watts protests in Los Angeles. White officers are beating Black bodies to the pavement. The voice over continues, 'For all of us, there's all of America, all of its scenic beauty, all of its heritage of history, all of its limitless opportunity'. Peck's documentary reveals the lie behind that inclusive rhetoric with its visual register of racial violence. By foregrounding both police brutality and the White mob, he sets out one of the key existential conditions confronting Black subjects in America – that of precarity. Baldwin says, 'it is not a figure of speech, the corpses of your brothers and your sisters pile up around you. And not for anything they have done. They were too young to have done anything' (Baldwin and Peck 2017: 49). A series of faces parades across the screen, Black children killed in 2012, 2014, 2015, 2016. Their names are a litany: Tamir Rice, Trayvon Martin, Aiyana Stanley-Jones, Christopher McCray. Baldwin's words are still not a figure of speech.

Peck manages to confront racial violence without glorifying it for the White viewer. He refuses to limit depictions of Black communities to their shared experiences of dehumanization – to the typical roles in through which White people are accustomed to seeing Black people. Instead, the film gives the viewer image after image, reel after reel, of Black people being human in both mundane and remarkable ways. There are scenes with Martin and Malcolm and Medgar, leading marches and giving speeches and rallying people and standing stoically before White cops (Peck and Jackson 2017). And we see them smiling, with their arms around families and friends. We see Black women shopping, Black children playing in the fire hydrant spray. Baldwin's words spill out, 'I missed the way, when a dark face opens a light seems to go everywhere' (Baldwin and Peck 2017: 14). Yet the film wants to do more than simply provide a new recognitive frame for Black subjects. Peck turns the White gaze back on itself and shows the White viewer how White America appears to the Black people that it exploits and dominates.

I Am Not Your Negro reserves its most trenchant critique for Whiteness and the White subject. Throughout his oeuvre, Baldwin took aim at White Americans' spurious innocence. What he identifies is not a simple lack of knowledge, but an actively cultivated and morally bankrupt refusal to know about the extent of Black suffering or White complicity (Baldwin 1963). He argued that White Americans had adopted habits of epistemic denial and empathetic closure to insulate themselves from demands for seismic changes to the status quo. If White knowers accepted the extent of systemic and structural racism, those disclosures would be hugely destabilizing to Whites' material security, their moral standing, and their collective self-image. When they couldn't ignore Black suffering, they had to find ways to deflect it or explain it away – often through the scapegoating of White Others, the sorts of racists who lived far from White liberal America. 'White people are endlessly demanding to be reassured that Birmingham is really on Mars. They don't want to believe, still less to act on the belief, that what is happening in Birmingham is happening all over the country' (Baldwin and Kenan 2010: 96).

Neither Baldwin nor Peck are content to indict only the easy and expected White actors – the men who beat and arrest and throw Black bodies to the ground, the White women who spit on Black children integrating a school, the White children carrying Confederate flags. Against the backdrop of this outright violence and this institutionalized racial domination, there is no room for White ignorance. To cling to the performance of innocence when you are complicit in systems and practices that oppress entire communities is a morally culpable act. What both Baldwin and Peck disclose as ethically suspect, then, is White normalcy. Juxtaposed against Baldwin's indictments of White America – and against images of Black bodies involved in serious and urgent struggle – are a cascade of images of White bodies revelling in their own consumption, wreathed in smiles and caught up in the whirlwind of their own entertainment. The scenes depicted here are the most remarkable for their very banality: White people in sweaters, laughing and taking photos by the fireplace; White people having picnics in green parks; White families picking tin can after tin can off the shelves in the grocery stores; White women dancing on TV programs, smiling and shimmying and confident of their own desirability (Peck and Jackson 2017).

In *I Am Not Your Negro*, however, these White bodies are anything but normal. The documentary re-presents these dancing White figures as strange and repugnant. Their smiles are just rows and rows of gaping teeth. The coordinated tap-dancing and arm flailing seem robotic, the limbs moving of their own accord. It is as if the archival footage has itself been transmogrified – in place of the White people are a series of zombie-like figures. They are pure desire, insatiety. They run across the grass in a giant horde. They have human form, but there is nothing human behind the eyes. At its most destabilizing, Peck's film tells White viewers, this is how you appear to Black people – as so morally destitute as to be verging on the dead (Peck and Jackson 2017). All of these White bodies consuming luxury goods, consuming television programs, consuming, consuming, as Black people are exploited, neglected, dominated, and oppressed by the very same institutions and practices that allow White America to keep consuming. 'No other country in the world has been so fat and so sleek, and so safe, and so happy, and so irresponsible, and so dead', Baldwin writes. 'A great many people do not live this way and cannot imagine it, and do not know that when we talk about "democracy", this is what we mean' (Baldwin and Kenan 2010: 12).

In this oppositional decoding of moral personhood, it is White subjects' ethical vacuity that renders them both inhumane and inhuman. Peck forces the viewer to re-encounter White cultural praxis, the erotic investments in White femininity and even the forms of White middle-class consumption and entertainment against the backdrop of systemic racism. This throws into sharp ethical relief forms of White bourgeois life under late capitalism that may seem far from Black pain and yet are constitutively entangled with it. As Black playwright Lorraine Hansberry told Bobby Kennedy in 1963, 'I am worried about the state of a civilization which produced that photograph of the White cop standing on that Negro woman's neck in Birmingham' (Baldwin and Kenan 2010: 138). Within racial regimes, the moment of White misrecognition fuels and obscures practices of racial maldistribution.

Peck – like Baldwin before him, and Fanon before him – dramatizes the internal relation between Whiteness and Blackness in racial orders. Whiteness and Blackness do not mark out any stable metaphysical differentiations in the human but instead are socio-political constructions whose origins are radically entangled with one another. 'The black man is not. No more than the White man' (Fanon 2008: 206). This relation can, of course, can and has been read as an existentialist claim about intersubjective recognition: the White subject comes to be only through its antagonistic struggle with the Black Other, whose irreducible difference becomes the foil against which the autonomous, rational, and self-determining individual agent is defined. But I contend that Fanon's claim can also be construed in a more materialist sense – as a kind of genealogical argument about the role that Black people have played in the consolidation of racial capitalism within Euromodernity.[2] This is what Peck is arguing in his documentary. In his telling, it is systemic Black suffering that makes possible White middle class forms of life in the United States.

5 Thinking Whiteness and Blackness in today's racialized markets

From a historical standpoint, this sort of internal relation between White affluence and Black oppression is easy to trace. Historians and critical race theorists alike have demonstrated that, in the New World colonies, the White person and the Black subperson emerged in tandem as distinctive juridical categories (Wolfe 2016; Harris 1993). This hierarchical division that was justified through a presumed metaphysical difference between Europeans, on the one hand, and African and indigenous peoples on the other. This legal schema too was compounded with more everyday discourses 'whose goal was to produce the Black man as a racial subject and site of savage exteriority who was therefore set up for moral disqualification and practical instrumentalisation' (Mbembe 2017: 28). Chattel slavery laid the groundwork for industrial capitalism, both in Europe and in the United States (Blackburn 2013; Johnson 2013; Solow and Engerman 1987; Williams 1944).[3] This is true both in the sense that enslaved Black Africans were exploited for their labour to extract raw materials for the manufacturing sectors and in that their bodies themselves became commodities whose value circulated through European financial markets.

White settlers created the stereotyped figure of the Black slave. The presence of Black unfree labour – and later the threat of non-European immigrants – consolidated Whiteness into a meaningful (and, historically, heavily policed) political category (Haney Lopez 1996; Wolfe 2016). From its inception, White supremacy required the consent of poor and working-class Whites if it were to function. W.E.B. Du Bois demonstrated that, while the White working class might have been exploited by White capital, they also reaped substantive symbolic advantages from the presence of enslaved and free Black labour. The racial divide provided even property-less Whites with a status differentiation; they might be poor, but at least they weren't Black (Du Bois 2014). 'White workers could, and did, define and accept their class position by fashioning identities as "not slaves" and as "not Blacks"' (Roediger 2007). But the White working class also benefitted materially from the compromise that they had struck with White capital. They too enjoyed privileged positions in the labour market and differential access to other sources of wealth, particularly with regard to housing and credit (Katznelson 2005).[4] When Fanon writes, 'the settler owes the fact of his very existence, that is his property, to the colonial system', he isn't just talking about the White planter or the White capitalist (Fanon 2001: 28).

Yet the United States is no longer best understood through the lens of chattel slavery or the Jim Crow South; this is no longer Baldwin's America or Fanon's settler colonial state. To assert that all racisms stand in a similar relation to material practices of capital extraction and accumulation is to fall back into an essentialist analysis. At the abstract level of moral indictment, all racisms are 'deeply anti-human and anti-social' practices (Hall 1986: 23). At the concrete level of sociological analysis, contemporary structures of racialization function differently than they did at the height of Jim Crow segregation. '[Racism] has no natural and universal law of development. It does not always assume the same shape' (Hall 2017: 146). The real task is assessing the nature of this determining and determined relation between the economic order and the racial structure within specific social formations. This sort of analysis is particularly important now, in this post-post-racial era in American politics, when mainstream liberal politicians are responding to calls for reparations for Black Americans. Such demands require a nuanced understanding of how Whiteness and Blackness, as symbolic status distinctions and ascribed racial identifications, relate to both past and *present* practices of material inequality. Otherwise, these substantive programs of material redistribution might fail to dismantle racial hierarchies in any radical way. They might leave the roots of White hegemony intact.

The past 40 years has altered the racial order on its economic, political, and cultural fronts. The most striking developments have been the rise of the Black middle class and the emergence of a certain subsection of Black elites. Contrary to the mid-century United States in which Black workers were isolated in certain low-paying jobs and denied access to certain forms of wealth, particularly gainful homeownership, the United States economic order has made room for a small section of Black professionals in conventionally 'White' industries (Durant Jr. and Louden 1986). Median Black wealth grew at a faster rate than median White wealth between 1982 and 2006 – although White households still possessed ten times the net worth of their Black counterparts (Kochhar and Fry 2014; Wolff 2014). Politically speaking, Black Americans are much more formally integrated into American democracy than they were during the 1960s in which they were systematically disenfranchized and dominated by White political parties. While Black elected officials remain a persistent minority in legislatures across the country, the Democratic Party in particular is now basing its electoral strategy around reaching Black voters in many of its key races.[5] Within the cultural sphere, 'race' no longer provides the strict boundary between inclusion and exclusion, esteem and disregard, that it used to. Whiteness has become more porous in twenty-first-century America; many bodies can become 'White' if they can possess the right sort of class and educational background (Perry 2011). Today's America not only tolerates but celebrates the racially ambiguous body and the aesthetics of ethnic diversity that it symbolizes (Gilroy 2004; Perry 2011). The era of corporate multiculturalism has turned the performance of cultural difference into a kind of social capital. 'Race' too can become part of a brand; Blackness sells.

Yet neither the emergence of the Black elite nor the rearticulation of Blackness as a site of cultural esteem has done much to challenge underlying market mechanisms that continue to evaluate White bodies and White spaces as worthy of investment. Fraser is correct, therefore, in her intuition that 'race' cannot be read as a pathology that stems simply or directly from the symbolic order of status hierarchies (Fraser and Honneth 2003); it remains entangled with the economic relations between capital and labour in historically distinctive ways. Many Black Americans certainly are better integrated into the United States' political and economic institutions today than they were 50 years ago, but that does not mean that either the Black working class or the Black middle class stand on equal footing with their White counterparts. Many more Black peoples are unemployed and underemployed, regardless of their educational attainment, than Whites from similar socio-economic backgrounds (Wang 2018; Western and Pettit 2005). Black workers are the first to be let go when employers face economic downturns, and they often have less wealth in reserve to tide them over until the labour market tightens again (Crouch and Fairlie 2010). This dynamic became particularly evident during the Great Recession of the late 2000s when Black households were particularly hard hit. Mean Black wealth declined in real terms by 33% between 2007 and 2010, compared to only 12% for White households. This differential is driven by the fact that Black households had more of their assets tied up in housing and greater degrees of mortgage debt in relation to their home values – a phenomenon directly linked to the rise of predatory lending in the subprime mortgage market (Austin 2012; Wolff 2014; Wolff 2018). Wealth differentials between the average White household and the average Black household remain stark. In 2013, mean White net worth was, at $141,000, 13 times that of Black net worth (Kochhar and Fry 2014).

Markets today remain a key driver of racial inequality. They continue to aggregate collective practices of racial evaluation that advantage White Americans. It is not as if racist decision-making ceased with the advent of the post-civil-rights era in the US. Now individuals need only justify their actions through ostensibly race-neutral proxy norms. Welfare recipients, inner-city residents, single-parent households, juvenile delinquents – all of these categorizations became overcoded as 'Black', even when many of the people who fall into those categories are in fact White (Massey and Denton 1993; Perry 2011). Neoliberal capitalism and its fetishization of individual choice, in turn, displaces these race-conscious practices from political reckoning. Where a parent decides to send their children to school, where a homeowner decides to purchase a home, which neighbourhoods a utility company expands to, which businesses a consumer frequents, where a teacher decides to take a job – all of these actions are shuttled into the protected realm of individual preferences, even if they contribute to ongoing structures of racialization that deprive Black children of educational resources or Black businesses of capital. 'By making the marketplace the final arbiter of all social relations', Patricia Hill Collins notes, 'the segregation and hierarchy that does remain can be attributed to the good and bad qualities of people who compete in the marketplace' (Collins 2006: 7).

The Black and White working classes are distinguished from one another by more than racial prejudice. The same is true of middle class professionals in the US today. Even when Black Americans are employed in similar professions and bring home similar incomes to their White co-workers, they don't stand in the same relation to capital – whether economic or political (Hall 1980b). White wealth far outstrips Black wealth, on personal terms, but also members of the White middle class and working class alike are generally better positioned to draw on social networks, community resources, and institutional benefits that elude their Black counterparts (Oliver and Shapiro 2006). Being able to appropriate capital involves both questions of social standing but also of physical access to the sites in which it is produced and circulated (Bourdieu 1999). In the US racial order, generations of White supremacy have sedimented investment and opportunity within particular environments – spatial zones that are coded White and which continue to be largely populated by White citizens. In the second-half of the twentieth century, this involved the subsidized growth of the White American suburbs (Massey and Denton 1993); today, it is the growth of mixed-use development projects in the urban neighbourhoods that White flight abandoned decades before – and the White affluence that this new retail and housing attracts. In this sense, proximity to Whiteness doesn't just grant an individual a certain degree of esteem or status inflation; it also puts them closer to the mechanisms of capital accumulation.[6]

The housing market – and the debt economy that finances it – provides an obvious example (Conley 1999). The Federal Housing Authority in the United States famously underwrote the growth of suburban White homeownership during the 1930s, 40s, and 50s in ways that excluded Black Americans and contributed to segregation (Aalbers 2011). It did so through redlining, or the practice of denying government-backed mortgages and other forms of credit to people buying homes in Black neighbourhoods. 'By manipulating market incentives, the federal government drew middle class Whites to the suburbs and, in effect, trapped blacks in the inner cities' (Wilson 1996: 46). After the Fair Housing Act of 1968 was passed (and then strengthened in 1988), housing discrimination on the basis of race was formally outlawed, but residential segregation patterns in urban areas remain highly stratified along White-Black lines, with Blacks living in more segregated and concentrated urban enclaves than other racial minorities (Schuetz 2017). Black families continue still face greater obstacles to homeownership (Aalbers 2011; Perry 2011). This owes both to the persistence of anti-Black prejudice among White homeowners and to institutional market actors who see Black spaces and Black applicants as bad investments. Real estate agents have continued to give White homebuyers better treatment, showing them more units located in mostly White areas (Korver-Glenn 2018; Massey and Denton 1993). Even when they do grant loans to Black Americans in diverse areas, banks regularly give less favourable terms and require higher interest rates before extending credit (Wang 2018). For financial institutions, 'race' still remains a 'rational' way to separate out those applicants who can be trusted with good-value mortgages and those who are ripe targets for subprime lending, its higher mortgages and its higher risk of foreclosures (Aalbers 2011; Brown et al. 2003). The deregulation of the mortgage securities market only accelerated these racialized practices of extraction. 'Although restrictive covenants, redevelopment, redlining and subprime lending appear to be distinct and separate processes, local geography links them as one intergenerational practice that racializes market outcomes', Jesus Hernandez writes. 'Hence, race plays a historical as well as a contemporary role in the way housing markets shape cities' (Hernandez 2009: 309).

Homeownership, or even just the ability to secure a pay for a rental, in a 'good' neighbourhood, in turn, provides a set of crucial supports when it comes to individual wealth accumulation. Owning one's own home has long proven the gateway to middle class status and material security (Shapiro 2004). Even when Black homeowners do everything right and secure access to credit, the neighbourhood that they purchase property in could shift under their feet – either because too many White people move in, gentrifying the area and sending property values skyrocketing in ways that price them out; or because too many White people move out, and property values fall (Brown et al. 2003; Massey and Denton 1993). When it comes to the American housing market, Whiteness isn't just a proxy for desirability; it becomes valuable in and of itself. It makes land valuable, and it heralds increased forms of public and private investment. What becomes clear is that racialization isn't just about 'racing' certain kinds of bodies in order to distinguish degrees of political and economic incorporation; it is also about setting up racialized worlds – segregated environments where practices of development and investment, on the one hand, and projects of underdevelopment and extraction, on the other, are constitutively intertwined.

Fanon's insights once again prove instructive. He describes the spatialized nature of force in White settler colonialism thusly:

> The settler's town is a strongly built town. . . . It is a brightly lit town; the streets are covered with asphalt, and the garbage cans swallow all the leadings, unseen, unknown, and hardly thought about. . . . The settler's town is a well-fed town, an easy-going town; its belly is always full of good things. The settler's town is a town full of White people, of foreigners. The town belonging to the colonized people, or at least the native town, the Negro village, the medina, the reservation, is a place of ill fame, peopled by men of evil repute. They are born there, it matters little where or how; they die there, it matters not where, nor how. . . . The native town is a hungry town, starved of bread, of meat, of shoes, of coal, of light.
>
> (Fanon 2001: 30)

Fanon's description of this 'world cut into two', bears structural resemblances to the zones of racialized poverty that still dot American cities (and increasingly, their suburbs) (Wilson 1987). Where one owns property in America matters. Having a home in a 'White' middle class area makes an individual all the more likely to have access to high-performing schools, well-paying jobs, good infrastructure, safe green space, affordable food, clean drinking water, better hospitals, and a responsive but not intrusive police force. Whereas many 'Black' urban enclaves in the United States continue to suffer from public neglect and private disinvestment in ways that render their inhabitants more vulnerable to violence, environmental harm, poor schooling, and police harassment (Perry 2011). Private capital invests in gentrifying (i.e., increasingly White) neighbourhoods – bringing both businesses and their jobs, the demand for public infrastructure and its benefits. Commercial lenders assessing the viability of redevelopment projects see in Whiteness a safe bet (Wang 2018). An altogether separate economic logic regulates capital's relationship to poor and minority neighbourhoods – one aimed at extracting money and assets from these communities while keeping them in states of economic dependency. This is the terrain of predatory industries like payday lenders, rent-to-own schemes, and other sources of 'bad-faith credit' that make being poor expensive (Wang 2018).

But private capital is not alone here in seeing poor communities as ripe for the picking; local police and judicial systems too have made a regular practice of surveying, charging and fining the Black poor and working classes for petty crimes in order to make up funding shortfalls.[7] 'While in the private sector the extension of subprime credit is often deployed as a racialized form of expropriation, in the public sector municipal governments . . . use the police to loot residents of primarily black jurisdictions' (Wang 2018: 77). Compounding this differential rate of investment and disinvestment is the fact that the state too often neglects Black communities in order to divert resources to the White middle class. Where municipalities extend utility lines and sewage service, where they build their landfills and deposit hazardous waste, where they provide clean water, where they bulldoze homes for new highways – many of these decisions reflect racialized evaluations of concern that exclude historically Black neighbourhoods (Taylor 2014). Notably too, another key driver of economic redistribution – the public education system – is funded at a residential level by the taxpayers living in the surrounding area, which leads to a resource gap that states have often failed to offset (Baker, Farrie, and Sciarra 2016). In this sense, the housing market – along with the institutional apparatuses that rely on residential logics to determine who they serve and who falls outside the bounds of responsibility – continues to serve as a key gatekeeper to the White middle class that Peck exposes as ethically fraught in his documentary.

'Race' first got its start as a regulative segmentation that could separate out free from unfree labour in colonial capitalism. And it continues to play a role in the institutions and practices that reproduce material inequalities above and beyond that which we can attribute to the presence of anti-black prejudice. As Fanon noted, 'Europe is literally the creation of the Third World. The wealth which smothers her is that which was stolen from underdeveloped peoples' (Fanon 2001: 81). This is the same kind of claim that anchors Black activists' demands for reparations in the United States. In recent years, Anglo-American political philosophers too have begun to debate whether governments ought to redistribute material resources to communities that they have harmed in an egregious way in the near or distant past (Butt 2008). Under certain conditions, individuals who have benefitted from historical injustice might have certain normative obligations to those people who have been disadvantaged by these same wrongs. Thinking about the sedimentation of ill-gotten gains that have contributed to existing forms of racial inequality is certainly an important piece of the puzzle that explains ongoing Black disadvantage and White wealth.

Yet not all demands for reparations for Black Americans are as progressive as they might seem at first glance. Framing this redistributive burden narrowly in terms of the long-past-due compensation for slavery and Jim Crow situates this debt firmly within the White America's immoral past. It obscures the ways in which 'race' continues to regulate how markets distribute advantage, investment, and opportunities. Reparations, in this view, are designed as a response to a static picture of racial inequality, one whose roots lie in chattel slavery and the Jim Crow era's reign of White terror over freed slaves. In a similar respect, Iris Marion Young critiqued narrowly redistributive paradigms to social justice for failing to address the practices and institutional apparatuses that produce and reproduce these inequalities in the first place. 'Many aspects of social structure and institutional context cannot be brought into view without examining social processes and the unintended cumulative consequences of individual actions', she writes (Young 2011). Without paying close attention to the ongoing mechanisms by which White communities consolidate their economic, social and political capital, political theorists will not go nearly far enough towards dismantling unjust social hierarchies. Dismantling that racialized schema, in turn, will take far more than simply reallocating social esteem or increased status to Black subjects. As Fanon saw all too clearly, the entire racial edifice will need to fall.

6 Conclusion

We might no longer unreservedly affirm social struggles for recognition today as social critics did in the 1990s. But it is crucial for political theorists to understand how identity claims relate to and determine broader struggles over capital, state resources, and the regulatory apparatuses that delimit both distributive schemas. White ethno-nationalism and the postures of racial resentment that it mobilizes have renewed political currency. The commodification of Blackness in the winds of global capitalism is changing what Blackness signifies while often doing little to shift resources or power to Black communities. Advocates of egalitarian politics neglect the analytical framework that an 'embodied politics of location' could provide at their own peril. What is required instead is a re-evaluation of how cultural patterns of value, and the statuses and identities they regulate, can be critically deployed to challenge power hierarchies rather than to entrench them.

Political theory will need a more complicated analysis of the relation between cultural misrecognition and economic maldistribution than what either Honneth or Fraser offered in their 2003 dialogue. We can find this a better account by looking to the work of Black radicals like Fanon, Baldwin, and Peck. In particular, they stress that the moment of interracial encounter is structured by imaginaries, architectures, and practices that all too often render the Black person into little more than a Black body. The ambivalence of the recognitive moment in racial regimes reminds us that social critics must do more than simply indict the obvious racist and the clearly malicious acts of anti-Black prejudice. Racial hierarchies reproduce themselves through far more insidious mechanisms than simply outright racial discrimination and exclusion, although of course those practices still play a substantive part. On the one hand, we must look too to the narratives, norms, and affective postures that naturalize White hegemony and racialized markets. On the other, social critique should not lose sight of how capital flows intersect with and mobilize racial divides in White settler states to better pursue its systemic imperatives – the search for cheap labour, new markets of segmented consumers, and new sites for investment and speculation.

In their critiques, Baldwin and Peck took aim both at White racists and at the sorts of White people who might very well consider themselves 'allies' – liberals (or today's progressives) who stand on the right side of US history. In the 1960s, Baldwin thought that America needed to have a serious conversation about the fact that 'there is not one step, morally or actually, between Birmingham and Los Angeles' (Baldwin and Kenan 2010: 96–97). After Trump's election, the progressive establishment would do well to remember that.

Notes

1 Much of the recent commentary centred around an opinion piece that Mark Lilla wrote for *The New York Times* on November 18, 2016 and his later, rather controversial book, *The once and future liberal: After identity politics* (Lilla 2016, 2017).

2 Paul Gilroy makes a similar argument for the essential role that Blackness and the construction of the biopolitical Other has played in the consolidation of liberal democratic projects in Europe and in North America (Gilroy 2000).

3 Eric Williams first made a powerful argument about the internal relation between Caribbean slavery and British industrial capitalism in his 1944 book, *Capitalism and Slavery*. More than half a century later, Robin Blackburn defends and expands on Williams' argument in his book, *American Crucible*. 'The broader construction of the argument looks not just at profits, or the slave trade, but at the way that slavery in the Americas and the Atlantic slave trade furnished markets, capital or credit and raw materials for the industrialising economy', he notes in a separate essay (Blackburn 2014).

4 For a nuanced discussion of this differential positioning of the White working class and the Black working class in settler colonial orders, see Stuart Hall (1980).

5 For more on this electoral strategy shift for 2020, see "African-Americans are the Democrats' most loyal constituency", *The Economist*, 7 March 2019, for example.
6 Of course, not all forms of intimate exposure to White communities are positive; White people too have used the closeness of physical space to dominate, exploit, and abuse Black people. The terms of this access matter; a Black woman benefits from owning a home in a well-resourced White neighbourhood, not from working as domestic help in a White home.
7 The Department of Justice report on the Ferguson Police Department details these practices. See United States Department of Justice – Civil Rights Division, "Investigation of the Ferguson Police Department", 4 March 2015, accessed at www.justice.gov/sites/default/files/opa/press-releases/attachments/2015/03/04/ferguson_police_department_report.pdf. (accessed 21/4/2020).

References

Aalbers, Manuel B. 2011. Place, Exclusion and Mortgage Markets. Malden, MA: Wiley-Blackwell.
Alexander, Michelle. 2010. The New Jim Crow: Mass Incarceration in the Age of Colorblindness. New York: New Press.
Austin, Algernon. 2012. 'A Good Credit Score Did Not Protect Latino and Black Borrowers', Economic Policy Institute.
Baker, Bruce D., Danielle Farrie, and David G. Sciarra. 2016. 'Mind the Gap: 20 Years of Progress and Retrenchment in School Funding and Achievement Gaps', ETS Research Report Series 1: 1–37.
Baldwin, James. 1963. The Fire Next Time. New York: Dial Press.
Baldwin, James, and Randall Kenan. 2010. The Cross of Redemption: Uncollected Writings. New York: Pantheon Books.
Baldwin, James, and Raoul Peck. 2017. I am not your negro. London: Penguin.
Blackburn, Robin. 2013. The American Crucible. London: Verso.
Blackburn, Robin. 2014. 'The Scope of Accumulation and the Reach of Moral Perception: Slavery, Market Revolution and Atlantic Capitalism', in Hall et al. (eds.), Emancipation and the Remaking of the British Imperial World. Manchester: Manchester University Press.
Bourdieu, P. et al. 1999. The Weight of the World: Social Suffering in Contemporary Society. Stanford: Stanford University Press.
Brown, Michael K. et al. 2003. Whitewashing Race: The Myth of a Color Blind Society. Berkeley: University of California Press.
Butt, Daniel. 2008. Rectifying International Injustice: Principles of Compensation and Restitution Between Nations. Oxford: Oxford University Press.
Coates, Ta-Nehisi. 2015. Between the World and Me. New York: Random House.
Cole, David. 1999. No Equal Justice: Race and Class in the American Criminal Justice System. New York: New Press.
Collins, Patricia Hill. 2006. From Black Power to Hip Hop. Philadelphia: Temple University Press.
Conley, Dalton. 1999. Being Black Living in the Red: Race, Wealth, and Social Policy in America. Berkeley: University of California Press.
Coulthard, Glen Sean. 2014. Red Skin, White Masks: Rejecting the Colonial Politics of Recognition. Minneapolis, MN: University of Minnesota Press.

Crenshaw, Kimberlé Williams. 1997. 'Color Blindness, History, and the Law', in Lubiano, W. (ed.), The House that Race Built: Black Americans, U.S. Terrain. New York: Pantheon Books.
Crouch, Kenneth A., and Robert Fairlie. 2010. 'Last Hired, First Fired? Black-White Unemployment and the Business Cycle', Demography 47(1): 227–247.
Dahl, H., P. Stoltz, and R. Willig. 2004. 'Recognition, Redistribution and Representation in Capitalist Global Society: An Interview with Nancy Fraser', Acta Sociologica 47(4): 374–382.
Du Bois, W.E.B. 1940. Dusk of Dawn: An Essay Toward an Autobiography of a Race Concept. New York: Harcourt, Brace & co.
Du Bois, W.E.B. 2014. Black Reconstruction in America: An Essay towards a History of the Part which Black Folk Played in the Attempt to Reconstruct Democracy in America, 1860–1880. New York: Oxford University Press.
Durant Jr., Thomas J., and Joyce S. Louden. 1986. 'The Black Middle Class in America: Historical and Contemporary Perspectives', Phylon 47(4): 253–263.
Fanon, Frantz. 2008. Black Skin, White Masks. London: Pluto.
Fanon, Frantz. 2001. The Wretched of the Earth. London: Penguin.
Fraser, Nancy. 1995. 'From Redistribution to Recognition? Dilemmas of Justice in a "Post-Socialist" Age', New Left Review 212: 68–93.
Fraser, Nancy, and Axel Honneth. 2003. Redistribution or Recognition? A Political-Philosophical Exchange. London: Verso.
Gilroy, Paul. 2000. Against Race: Imagining Political Culture beyond the Color Line. Cambridge, MA: Belknap Press of Harvard University Press.
Gilroy, Paul. 2004. After Empire: Melancholia or Convivial Culture? Abingdon: Routledge.
Gilroy, Paul. 2018. '"Where Every Breeze Speaks of Courage and Liberty": Offshore Humanism and Marine Xenology, or, Racism and the Problem of Critique at Sea Level', Antipode 50(1): 3–22.
Hall, Stuart. 1980a. 'Encoding/Decoding,' in Hall, S., D. Hobson, A. Love, and P. Willis (eds.), Culture, Media, Language. London: Hutchinson.
Hall, Stuart. 1980b. 'Race, Articulation and Societies Structured in Dominance', in Sociological Theories: Race and Colonialism. Paris: UNESCO.
Hall, Stuart. 1986. 'Gramsci's Relevance for the Study of Race and Ethnicity', Journal of Communication Inquiry 10(2): 5–27.
Hall, Stuart. 2017. Selected Political Writings: The Great Moving Right Show and Other Essays. London: Lawrence and Wishart.
Haney Lopez, Ian. 1996. White by Law: The Legal Construction of Race. New York: New York University Press.
Harris, Cheryl I. 1993. 'Whiteness as Property', Harvard Law Review 106(8): 1707–1791.
Hernandez, Jesus. 2009. 'Redlining Revisited: Mortgage Lending Patterns in Sacramento, 1930–2004', International Journal of Urban and Regional Research 33(2): 291–313.
Hero, Rodney E., and Morris E. Levy. 2016. 'The Racial Structure of Economic Inequality in the United States: Understanding Change and Continuity in an Era of "Great Divergence"', Social Science Quarterly 97(3): 491–505.
Honneth, Axel. 2001. 'Recognition or Redistribution? Changing Perspectives on the Moral Order of Society', Theory, Culture & Society 18(2–3): 43–55.

Honneth, Axel. 2004. 'Recognition and Justice: Outline of a Plural Theory of Justice', Acta Sociologica 47(4): 351–364.
hooks, bell. 1990. Yearning: Race, Gender, and Cultural Politics. Boston: South End Press.
Johnson, Walter. 2013. River of Dark Dreams: Slavery and Empire in the Cotton Kingdom. Cambridge, MA: Harvard University Press.
Katznelson, Ira. 2005. When Affirmative Action Was White: An Untold History of Racial Inequality in Twentieth-Century American. New York: W.W. Norton.
Kochhar, Rakesh, and Richard Fry. 2014. 'Wealth Inequality Has Widened Along Racial, Ethnic Lines Since End of Great Recession', Pew Research Center.
Korver-Glenn, Elizabeth. 2018. 'Compounding Inequalities: How Racial Stereotypes and Discrimination Accumulate across the Stages of Housing Exchange', American Sociological Review 83(4): 627–656.
Lilla, Mark. 2016. 'The End of Identity Liberalism', The New York Times, 18 November, online. Accessed 10 Sept. 2018.
Lilla, Mark. 2017. The Once and Future Liberal: After Identity Politics. London: Hurst & co.
Massey, Douglas. 2007. Categorical Inequality. New York: Russell Sage Foundation.
Massey, Douglas, and Nancy Denton. 1993. American Apartheid: Segregation and the Making of the Underclass. Cambridge, MA: Harvard University Press.
Mbembe, Achille. 2017. Critique of Black Reason. Durham: Duke University Press.
Mills, Charles. 1997. The Racial Contract. Ithaca, NY: Cornell University Press.
Oliver, Kelly. 2001. Witnessing: Beyond Recognition. Minneapolis, MN: University of Minnesota Press.
Oliver, Melvin and Thomas Shapiro. 2006. Black Wealth/White Wealth: A New Perspective on Racial Inequality, 2nd ed. New York: Routledge.
Peck, Raoul, and S. Jackson. 2017. I Am Not Your Negro. [video-recording]. London.
Perry, Imani. 2011. More Beautiful and More Terrible: The Embrace and Transcendence of Racial Inequality in the United States. New York: New York University Press.
Phillips, Anne. 2007. Multiculturalism Without Culture. Princeton: Princeton University Press.
Rankine, Claudia. 2014. Citizen: An American Lyric. Minneapolis: Graywolf Press.
Rich, Adrienne. 1986. Blood, Bread and Poetry: Selected Prose, 1979–1985. London: Virago.
Robinson, Cedric. 2000. Black Marxism: The Making of the Black Radical Tradition. Chapel Hill, NC: University of North Carolina Press.
Roediger, David. 2007. The Wages of Whiteness: Race and the Making of the American Working Class. London: Verso.
Rohde, Nicholas, and Ross Guest. 2013. 'Multidimensional Racial Inequality in the United States', Social Indicators Research 114(2): 591–605.
Saar, Martin. 2015. 'Spinoza and the Political Imaginary', Qui Parle: Critical Humanities and Social Sciences 23(2): 115–133.
Schuetz, Jenny. 2017. 'Metro Areas Are Still Racially Segregated, But it's More Complicated than "Chocolate City, Vanilla Suburbs"', Brookings Institution.
Shapiro, Thomas. 2004. The Hidden Cost of Being African American: How Wealth Perpetuates Inequality. New York: Oxford University Press.
Shelby, Tommie. 2014. 'Racism, Moralism, and Social Criticism', Du Bois Review: Social Science Research on Race 11(1): 57–74.

Solow, Barbara L., and Stanley L. Engerman (eds.). 1987. British Capitalism and Caribbean Slavery: The Legacy of Eric Williams. New York: Cambridge University Press.

Taylor, Dorceta E. 2014. Toxic Communities: Environmental Racism, Industrial Pollution, and Residential Mobility. New York: New York University Press.

Thomas, Kendall. 1998. '"Ain't Nothin' Like the Real Thing": Black Masculinity, Gay Sexuality, and the Jargon of Authenticity', in Lubiano, W. (ed.), The House that Race Built: Black Americans, U.S. Terrain. New York: Pantheon Books.

Wacquant, Loic. 2002. 'From Slavery to Mass Incarceration, Rethinking the "Race Question" in the U.S.', New Left Review 13: 41–60.

Wang, Jackie. 2018. Carceral Capitalism. Pasadena, CA: Semiotext(e).

Weheliye, Alexander. 2014. Habeas viscus: Racializing Assemblages, Biopolitics, and Black Feminist Theories of the Human. Durham: Duke University Press.

Western, B., and B. Pettit. 2005. 'Black-White Wage Inequality, Employment Rates, and Incarceration', American Journal of Sociology 111(2): 553–578.

Williams, Eric. 1944. Capitalism and Slavery. London: The University of North Carolina Press.

Wilson, William Julius. 1987. The Truly Disadvantaged: The Inner City, the Underclass, and Public Policy. Chicago: University of Chicago Press.

Wilson, William Julius. 1996. When Work Disappears: The World of the New Urban Poor. New York: Knopf.

Wolfe, Patrick. 2016. Traces of History: Elementary Structures of Race. London: Verso.

Wolff, Edward. 2014. 'Household Wealth Trends in the United States, 1962–2013: What Happened over the Great Recession?', National Bureau of Economic Research, Working Paper No. w20733.

Wolff, Edward. 2018. 'The Decline of African-American and Hispanic Wealth since the Great Recession', National Bureau of Economic Research, Working Paper No. 25198.

Young, Iris Marion. 2011. Justice and the Politics of Difference. Princeton: Princeton University Press.

Zurn, Christopher. 2005. 'Recognition, Redistribution, and Democracy: Dilemmas of Honneth's Critical Social Theory', European Journal of Philosophy 13(1): 89–126.

Part IV

MORAL ECONOMIES OF RESPECT AND ESTEEM

10

A MORAL ECONOMY?

Honneth, recognition, and the capitalist market

Renante Pilapil

1 Introduction

Following the end of the Cold War and the collapse of the socialist bloc, the capitalist market economy triumphed together with liberal democracy. Market capitalism is an economic system in which capital goods are privately owned by individuals and corporations that are engaged in free economic exchange, the motive of which is the maximization of profit or utility (see also McMurtry 1997: 645). Also, in the capitalist market, the production of goods and services is based on the law of supply and demand, including market competition, and not on an external or regulating agency. According to Karl Polanyi (2001: 71), the market economy is an economic system 'controlled, regulated, and directed by markets alone'. The state is reduced into what Robert Nozick calls a 'night watchman' because markets by themselves are perceived to lead to efficient allocation of resources (Friedman 1962: 22–36). Market deficiencies, such as unemployment, or a high inflation rate, are left to the market mechanisms to be corrected. In today's world, deregulated markets may be hard to find. States have in one way or another intervened in the market in many ways such as incentivizing strategic sectors and de-incentivizing others, counter-cyclical economic policies, safety nets for firms and workers, the role of central banks, among others.

The German philosopher Axel Honneth, a representative of the third generation of critical theory, calls into question the view that the capitalist market should be normatively conceived in terms of profit-maximization. In his recent work *Freedom's Right*, Honneth draws upon Hegel and Durkheim in arguing that an explanation of the capitalist market has to take into account its inherent moral dimension, more particularly the 'pre-contract' norm of solidarity among subjects. For Honneth, the capitalist market can be normatively considered as a 'relational' institution of social freedom in which market participants recognize their dependence on one another. In turn,

Honneth uses this inherent normative dimension as a basis for what he calls his 'immanent' criticism of the capitalist market. Drawing upon his theory of recognition and moving away from the Marxist lens in social analysis, he demonstrates tellingly how the injustices of market capitalism are best analyzed as injustices of recognition. More precisely, he describes how the economization of the three spheres of recognition such as love, respect, and esteem produces deleterious effects on the person's self-relations. In these respects, it can be said that Honneth rehabilitates and puts at the centre the moral conditions of the market, particularly the ways the market economy serves as an important medium of social integration. Applying this insight to his social theory, Honneth consequently rejects the view that the economic system is norm-free. For him, the latter cannot be adequately explained in terms of the functionalist perspective of economic efficiency as if it had a logic on its own.

The chapter explores the critical potential of Honneth's views on the capitalist market and the economy. It raises three concerns as regards their plausibility. Firstly, the chapter argues that the idea of the markets as spheres of social freedom and social integration might have been expressed in an overly optimistic and simplistic fashion. Secondly, the chapter calls into question the sufficiency of Honneth's experiential approach in exposing the injustices of market capitalism and that it needs to be complemented with a structural approach. And thirdly, contrary to Honneth, the chapter argues that it might be possible to speak of a relative autonomy of the economic sphere. In the end, the chapter argues that while Honneth's views on the capitalist market and the economy are promising, they are not entirely adequate.

The chapter will proceed in five steps. Firstly, Honneth's notion of the market economy as a medium of social freedom as well as his analysis of the pathologies of market capitalism as fundamentally injustices of recognition will be discussed. In view of this, the succeeding second, third, and fourth sections will respectively raise three arguments, namely, 1) that the idea of capitalist markets as spheres of social is problematic, 2) that the experiential approach to criticizing the capitalist market has to be complemented by the structural approach, and 3) that it might be possible to speak of a relative autonomy of the economic sphere. The last section will present a brief conclusion.

2 The market economy as sphere of social freedom

According to Honneth (2010: 228), the market cannot be explained merely in terms of the functionalist perspective of economic efficiency. To do so would be equivalent to assuming that the market is an autonomous self-regulating system where an 'invisible hand' operates behind the backs of the agents governed by profit motive and the law of supply and demand. Honneth argues that to effectively explain the market economy requires taking into account its moral dimension most particularly in the way it satisfies individuals' normative expectations. Drawing upon Hegel and Durkheim, Honneth (2014: 181) contends that market efficiency where decisions and behaviours of economic agents are well-coordinated could not have been achieved without a pre-contract moral rule. Honneth (2014: 192) argues that implicit in market relations is the mutual recognition of subjects not only *legally*, that is, as agents participating in a contract, but, more importantly, *morally* or *ethically*, that is, as members of a cooperative community (which he calls the 'we' of market economy). The market economy is grounded in an 'antecedent' sense of solidarity which occurs *before* members recognize the right of each one to maximize his/her self-interest. Without such antecedent feelings of solidarity, Honneth insists that market economy could not have functioned in an 'orderly fashion'. Questions arise here: What does Honneth mean by 'solidarity' here? What is the basis of this solidarity? In *The Struggle for Recognition*, Honneth (1995: 129) speaks of solidarity not in terms of shared feelings of sympathy but in terms of some shared or reciprocal concern, interest, or value. Solidarity is achieved when individuals are given the equal chance to contribute to the realization of communal goals. In *Freedom's Right* (2014), however, Honneth does not specifically define solidarity but refers to it in a much more general sense, particularly in terms of individuals' membership in a cooperative community. Such solidarity also involves a 'beneficent and trusting attitude' towards one's co-members, which, is a necessary condition for the market.

According to Honneth, the justification of the market economy lies in the fact that market is a fertile ground for reciprocal relations among agents as members of a cooperative community. It is in the market where individuals recognize their obligations towards one another as cooperative partners. In other words, what justifies the market economy is that it serves as a medium for the realization of social freedom (Honneth 2014: 192). The integration of individual interests, which occurs anonymously in the market, enables the freedom of one individual to become the condition for the realization of another's freedom. This idea of freedom tends to de-emphasize the usual individualistic conception of freedom and highlights its social dimension. That is to say, the condition for the possibility of one's freedom is essentially connected to others' freedom (or the other way around). Or, to put it differently, the concern is less of how I realize my freedom at the expense of others, but more of how I realize my freedom because of others (and vice-versa). In the market sphere, this would mean that my freedom to sell shoes depends on the freedom of others to buy them. Yet, even as this whole process is fully impersonal – the producers and the buyers of the shoes do not personally know each other – there must have been a prior recognition that took place. When producing shoes, the shoemaker has in mind a potential buyer or user; meanwhile, when buying shoes, the shoe-buyer knows that the shoes were made by someone. I never know the producers of the shoes I buy in the same way that I do not know the buyers of the shoes I make. Honneth notes that even the negative, legal conception of freedom (the idea of freedom as *absence of obstacles or interference*) continues to have a space in the idea of social freedom, but such has to be adjusted within the requirements of mutual recognition of cooperating partners. Conceived in this way, freedom, just as rights, is fundamentally relational. In his latest work on *The Idea of Socialism*, Honneth reiterates the notion of social freedom. Honneth (2017: 27–28) writes:

> According to this principle [of social freedom], human beings cannot realize their individual freedom in the matters most important to them on their own. The satisfaction of generally shared needs depends on intersubjective relationships that are only "free" under certain normative conditions – the most important of which is the mutual sympathy found only in communities of solidarity. . . . The members of society must not only act "with each other", but also "for each other", for this is the only way they can satisfy their shared needs freely.

Interestingly, Honneth conceives the notion of social freedom in the context of the market economy where the interests of individuals, no matter their diversity and even apparent incompatibility, are harmoniously integrated. For him, the behaviours of market participants (whether consumer, seller, or producer) are fundamentally characterized by an antecedent sense of mutual recognition as members of a cooperative community. He writes: 'Expressed in terms of recognition, this means that economic actors must have recognized each other as members of a cooperative community before they can grant each other the right to maximize individual utility' (Honneth 2014: 192). Honneth (2014: 199–253) illustrates this both in the sphere of consumption and the in the sphere of production. When consumers buy a good, they do so not merely to satisfy their need but also to contribute to the realization of the producers' interest, say enabling them to earn a living. Conversely, when producers produce a good, they do so not merely to maximize their profits but also to satisfy the needs of the consumers. The same implicit mutual recognition in market relations is manifested in haggling commonly practised in public markets. Buyers cannot just demand for too low a price for the goods they want to buy without taking into account the potential economic loss on the part of the trader.

Likewise, according to Honneth, labour contracts concretize the idea of mutual recognition in market relations. Taking his cue from Parsons, Honneth (2014: 188) says that labour contracts do not only specify the obligations derived from the company's or society's generally accepted value system. They serve as proof that workers' activities are recognized as worthwhile and through which employers can expect loyalty and responsibility from workers. The pre-contract rules of mutual recognition are further institutionalized in compensation schemes that normatively determine the social value of work, the legal system establishing and controlling private property, among others (Zurn 2005: 112). For instance, the level of earned income or the prices of goods in the market serve as a function of cultural assumptions regarding the social value of paid work. Unfortunately, in the current capitalist system an ideological basis lurks behind how social usefulness of work is determined, favouring not only those types of work undertaken by 'independent, middle class, male bourgeois'. Sometimes, the market also dictates the social value of certain jobs.

The idea of the capitalist market as a sphere of social freedom has important consequences. Beyond the egoistic view of market relations in which what matters is only the individual's self-interest, market competition in which two agents want to outdo each other is a secondary phenomenon. Market relation is *first of all* a form of cooperation where the interests of 'all' are taken into account. Individual self-interests are regarded as 'means for the complementary realization of . . . individual aims or purposes' (Honneth 2014: 192). This would further imply that the individual interests of market participants are not regarded as fixed once and for all. They are, instead, characterized by plasticity, constantly adjusted on the basis of the participants' greater or lesser concern for others' interests (Honneth 2014: 193). As active participants in social cooperation, individual members of the community work together harmoniously in order to achieve their respective ends.

According to Honneth (2014: 191), the pre-contract moral norms of solidarity and social freedom are not simply normative additions to the nature of the free market. There is an 'intrinsic connection' between the market mechanism and these pre-market norms because without the latter economic processes of exchange cannot be viewed by subjects as legitimate and justified (Honneth 2014: 191). Without them, the market participants would no longer be interested to actively participate in the economy. As such, much more than the concern of how to maximize utility, questions about 'feelings of injustice' and 'norms of justice' are more important in market relations (Honneth 2014: 197). It is only from this ideal of justice and fairness that the market economy is considered as justified in the eyes of economic agents.

Given the explanation and justification of the market as a sphere of social freedom and solidarity, this becomes the basis of Honneth's criticism of market capitalism. Drawing upon his theory of recognition, Honneth demonstrates tellingly how the injustices of the market are best analyzed and normatively judged as injustices of recognition (see also Sandel 2012). More precisely, he describes how the economization of the three spheres of recognition namely love, respect, and esteem produces deleterious effects on person's self-relations. Let me start with the sphere of love.

Drawing upon the work of the sociologist Eva Illouz (1997: 26), Honneth, together with Hartmann (2006: 55) says that although love or intimate relations had been increasingly 'reified and commercialized', subjects are still able to enter into a 'pure' relationship in which the primary reason for entering into an intimate relationship is because of its emotional value (Giddens 1994: 58). However, in the last two decades the unstable integration of consumption and feeling is threatened by a new form of consumer rationality. According to Honneth and Hartmann (2006: 49–56), intimate relationships are exposed to pressure by career demands that require individuals to be in constant move and flexible in terms of location, time, and activity. Today one reason as to whether or not couples must continue their relationship is largely determined by the compatibility or the ability of their relationship to cope with the demands of their work. The normative value of love has been diminished, held hostage by prudential or practical concerns. This arrangement is potentially disastrous because it threatens to empty out all intimate relationships with feelings, the reason for entering into the relationship in the first place. Consequently, our quest for meaning concerning our relationships becomes even more elusive (Illouz 1997: 152).

Meanwhile, capitalism does not only threaten the sphere of love and intimate relationships but also the sphere of rights, most particularly social rights such as welfare rights. For Honneth, social rights are not only prerequisites for civil and political participation but they are also testaments of the community's solidarity for the less fortunate. That is, they have an 'empowering and unburdening status' (Honneth and Hartmann 2006: 51). However, the picture has dramatically changed due to the economization of social services. A growing emphasis on individual responsibility – one's success or failure is understood to be dependent on one's choices alone – looms large (Honneth and Hartmann 2006: 51–52). What worries Honneth in this turn of events is that social solidarity is threatened. A capitalistic framework of individual responsibility (largely a product of the Enlightenment and the Reformation's focus on autonomy and conscience) unjustly ignores the necessary connection between the misfortune of the worse off and the good fortune of the better off. This condition of individualization which grants individuals 'precarious freedoms' (Beck and Beck-Gersheim 2002: 4) creates a potentially dangerous psychological effect. Being left on their own devices to meet the excessive demands of individual responsibility people become more susceptible to emptiness, depression, and other forms of mental illness particularly when failure befalls them (Honneth 2004a: 475; Honneth and Hartmann 2006: 52). As the demands of responsibility increase, the chances of feelings of dissatisfaction also increase (Honneth 2004a: 475).

Finally, with the entry of capitalism, the principle of achievement has been transformed particularly on how to determine whether or not a particular activity can be considered an achievement. Although the criteria for what can be considered a genuine contribution or achievement have been universalized and democratized, the entry of capitalism puts at risk the practical content of the principle of achievement by tying the latter largely to the market forces. Because the capitalist market is now governed by profit motive, individuals' activities that cannot be converted into profits are in danger of being unilaterally dismissed as no achievement at all (Honneth and Hartmann 2006: 54). Moreover, the meritocratic system that depends on market success as the only basis for granting achievement does not take into account factors such as accident, inheritance, and luck in the distribution of material and symbolic goods. This change in the practical content of achievement is politically dangerous. The principle of achievement is no longer taken as a means for political emancipation but as a tool that compromises social welfare and wrongly suggests 'the possibility of partaking of status where it in fact does not exist' (Honneth and Hartmann 2006: 54).

Now, against Honneth's views on the capitalist market, I would like to raise three arguments: 1) the idea of the capitalist market as sphere of social freedom and solidarity is not that straightforward, 2) the experiential approach in criticizing the capitalist market has to be complemented by the structural approach, and 3) it might be possible to speak of a relative autonomy of market capitalism.

3 From integration to disintegration

Honneth believes that the market is a medium of social integration in that the latter gives individuals the opportunity to make positive contributions to the common good. Borrowing from Durkheim, he writes:

> market-mediated relations give rise to social relations in which members of the society are able to form a particular, "organic" form of solidarity, because the reciprocal recognition of their respective contributions to the common good gives them a sense of connectedness.
> (Honneth 2010: 224)

Notice that one way through which Honneth arrives at the idea of the social integrative character of the market relations is his notion of work in which one is given the opportunity to contribute to the common good. Work provides an opportunity for creating social relations through which a sense of connectedness can arise.

Nonetheless, one worry is that the notion of the market's social integrative function might have been expressed in an overly simplistic and optimistic manner. A meticulous analysis of what actually happens in market transactions appears to be neglected in favour of his moralist agenda. There might be some truth in the view that, echoing Amartya Sen (1999, 6), to participate in the market is 'part and parcel' of people's basic liberties akin to the freedom of exchange of words, goods, or gifts; in other words, doing so is 'part of the way human beings in society live and interact with each other'. As Honneth (2014: 192) puts it: the capitalist market 'can be considered [as] a relational institution of social freedom'; 'economic actors must have recognized each other as members of a cooperative community before they can grant each other the right to maximize individual utility'. Yet, the view that market relations inherently promote social integration seems to be counterintuitive, if not contrary to our experience as economic agents that participate in market transactions. As economic agents, we want to satisfy, first and foremost, our individual interests and this is done not necessarily within the background of mutual recognition of others as members of a cooperative community. In fact, in economic relationships, we often see the other not as a 'partner' but as a competitor. Although there is the possibility of the social motivations of our actions, like being appreciated by others or fulfilling the expectations of others including our friends and fellow citizens, the latter seems to be more of a derivative than primary. When I buy a pair of rubber shoes, I do so primarily because it feels good on my feet, or because I need it for my sports activities. Of course, the case might be different in small-scale market relations where a one-to-one relation between me and the seller/producer exists. There could be a sense of feelings of solidarity in this context especially when the economic agents recognize each other's rights and that without the exercise of the other's rights one cannot pursue his/her interests. Sometimes (and this maybe beyond the intentions of Honneth's sense of solidarity) economic agents are willing to revise their interests for mutual advantage. However, empirical evidence would show otherwise. On a bigger scale, the idea of mutual recognition of economic agents as members of a cooperative community is difficult to sustain, if not make sense of, especially in the context of capitalist market.

Elizabeth Anderson (1993: 141–167), for example, argues that capitalist market relations are 'impersonal, egoistic, exclusive, want-regarding, and oriented to exit rather than voice'. The (capitalist) market is impersonal because access to commodities is solely based on money income. As Michael Sandel (2012: 14) points out, the market reasoning is impersonal to values in that it does not distinguish between admirable preferences and base ones. What matters is only the question of how much one is willing to pay, regardless of the good in question. Moreover, the capitalist market is egoistic because individuals mainly pursue their interests without regard to other's interest. Related to this issue is the fact that the market economy has pushed individuals to the consumption of material rather than nonmaterial resources (Fromm 1976), which consequently has contributed to the overconsumption of natural resources and various environmental problems (see Wright 2011).

Meanwhile, the capitalist market is also characterized by brutal competition. True, competition in the market might be good especially when we talk about the improvement of products and services, or when we talk about social productivity. But market competition has a bad side as well which could potentially outweigh its good side. This especially happens when those competing are not competing on equal footing, say for instance, between a large multinational company and a small medium enterprise. As Rawls (1999a: 240) says, there is no perfect competition. In principle, the winners could compensate the losers but in practice this almost never happens (Stiglitz 2006: 63). It is no wonder that although the market transactions can be the appropriate basis for allocation of resources because it is efficient, they cannot be the basis of distributive justice (Rawls 1999a: 241). Market transactions could allow any distributive scheme even if only a tiny minority enjoys the benefits while the rest shoulder the burdens. Because capitalist markets do not produce just results, the need to regulate them becomes an imperative. Given these features of the capitalist market, it is difficult to imagine how it can become a medium of social integration.

Interestingly, Honneth is not unaware of this difficulty. As pointed out previously, he makes explicit the paradoxical character of the achievement principle. While it favours universalistic criteria by trumping esteem on the basis of birth or origin, it can lead to 'achievement insecurity' when the capitalist liberal market is used as the authority for evaluating the social usefulness of work. The market, he says, does not take into account luck, accident, and inheritance in the distribution of material or symbolic goods. Moreover, in agreement with Marx, Honneth says that the capitalist market economy can be a potential source of 'desolidarization' in that it 'prevents fraternal social relationships' and opens the gates for unbridled private egotism where individuals – acting either as consumers or producers – are only concerned with the satisfaction or maximization of their utility (Honneth 2017: 16–17). This desolidarization is further manifested in what Honneth (2014: 251 & 247–248) calls the 'individualization of responsibility' and the 'privatization of resistance' as is the case in the service sector where workers are left on their own to succeed and survive in their 'occupational destiny'. Elsewhere, he explicitly describes the capitalist market as not a sphere of social freedom: 'It is not anchored in role obligations to which all could agree, and which interweave with each other in a way that would enable subjects to view each other's freedom as the condition of their own freedom' (Honneth 2014: 176). Clearly, the market in this context cannot be considered as a social institution for which everyone shares a responsibility as members of a cooperating community.

So given that Honneth is indeed aware of this seemingly contradictory nature of the market, how would he negotiate the potential tension between the social integrative and the fragmenting character of the market? Unfortunately, this paradox has been left as it is. Honneth does not offer an explanation for the cause of this 'shift' or 'change of attitudes' either, offering instead his doubt whether or not there is indeed some shift (Honneth 2014: 250). He writes:

> It is certainly too soon to pass judgment on whether this general change of attitudes about the concept of the market really has

> taken place over the last few decades. And the mere consideration of such a shift probably belongs to precisely that class of sociological hypotheses about which we will never attain true clarity because they cannot ultimately be empirically proven.
>
> (Honneth 2014: 250)

Perhaps, in defence of Honneth, one can say that there is really no paradox here. While market capitalism has the potential for de-solidarization, that is not really its essential nature. Similar to a phenomenological leap, it can be said that before de-solidarization, the primordial condition of market relations is that there is an antecedent sense of solidarity or mutual recognition of subjects. As such, the latter becomes the immanent normative criterion through which capitalist markets are judged.

However, the problem with this reasoning is that it is difficult to make sense especially when applied to the current context of market transactions and economic globalization. Firstly, when the goods to be traded are morally questionable, for instance, sex, votes, or human organs, the notion of social freedom and solidarity would not make sense at all. Indeed, Honneth's focus in justifying the capitalist market is its implications for human relations particularly in the way it demonstrates (or promotes?) a sense of mutual recognition among economic agents. But his view seems to be incomplete or too narrow in that it excludes another important component of the equation – the goods to be traded or exchanged in the market economy. This point cannot just be easily dismissed especially that, as Sandel (2012: 15) and even Honneth point out, market reasoning has infiltrated our social life, human relationships, and everyday lives. Secondly, although social freedom and solidarity could hold true in traditional or smaller markets, they appear to be unrealistic if not irrelevant in the phenomenon of globalization. This is because in the latter transactions between economic agents, which include multinational corporations, have become anonymous and ever more complex. I will return to this matter in the next section. In the final analysis, it is difficult to imagine the capitalist market as a social institution for social freedom and social integration.

4 From experiential to structural approach

Drawing upon his theory of recognition, Honneth's critique of market capitalism revolves around its impact on the capacity of individuals to achieve self-realization, particularly in terms of its effect on individual's personal identity. His approach is characterized as 'experiential' in contrast to the structural approach of criticizing the capitalist market. This focus on subjective identity – whether it is in the sphere of love, respect, and esteem – relative to criticizing market capitalism appears to be attractive. It provides us with a fresh perspective in that it does not recycle the hackneyed Marxist analysis of the bourgeois-proletariat relation. Additionally, the experiential approach avoids slipping into the oftentimes anonymous, faceless critical discourses on the structural problems of market capitalism. It makes the evils of capitalism concrete by directly associating the latter with the negative effects on individuals' emotional lives, for example, the way feelings of love are diminished because of economic rationality, the loss of feelings of social solidarity due to emphasis on individual responsibility, and the loss of self-esteem when unprofitable work is not considered as achievement.

More recently, Honneth uses the same experiential approach in exposing the pathologies of current labour relations. In his normative discourse on work, Honneth (2010: 223–239), quoting Pierre Bourdieu (1999: 257–320), points to the moral suffering of workers – including factory workers, farmers, artisans, teachers, police, and white-collar clerks – who are denied of a socially dignified existence because of too low, hard to swallow wages and unpaid overtime. The current German sociology of work follows the same lead in its emphasis on concepts of subjectivity, identity, and recognition. As Stephan Voswinkel (2012: 23) puts it, work 'means more for the life context than the mere creation of the means for reproduction associated with it'. Because what is emphasized are the meaning of work and the worker's contribution at work, it could be said that the decades-old domination of the paradigm of interest has been displaced by the paradigm of recognition.

Honneth's experiential approach in criticizing market and labour relations is consistent with his theory of 'recognitive' justice which pins down the issues of justice to the victims' subjective experience of injustice, particularly the moral-psychological effects of misrecognition or nonrecognition to their sense of self (see Honneth 2004b; Honneth 2002). For Honneth, the issue of social justice is not simply about equal access to material and non-material resources necessary for the pursuit of the good life, as in Rawls (1999a), nor is it about providing equal opportunities to participate as a peer in social life as in Fraser (2003). The goal of social justice, according to Honneth (2003: 259), is the creation of social relations through which all individuals are given the chance to realize their personality in that they 'can publicly uphold and practice their lifestyle without shame or humiliation'.

However, despite its attractiveness, how far can the experiential approach in criticizing the capitalist market actually work? There might be good reasons to suspend our enthusiasm here. Immediately, following Fraser's (2003: 31) critique, it can be raised that the exclusive focus on the experiential approach might be prone to 'psychologization' of the evils of the capitalist market. This would imply that if the capitalist market does not produce any negative impact on individual's sense of self – whether it is in the sphere of love, respect, and esteem – then, one can say that there is nothing wrong with it. True, the experiential approach makes the evil of neoliberal capitalism concrete – that is, not faceless, subject-less, or empty. But it would appear that determining whether or not capitalism is wrong depends on how far individuals are able to manage its impact on individuals' subjectivity. This is problematic because it is one step closer to blaming the victim and it unnecessarily ignores the contributions of other agents to the unjust conditions suffered by the victim. More so, the psychologizing strategy could find itself in hornet's nest in terms of its normative validity. The evils of market capitalism emotionally experienced by individuals could be erroneously regarded as mere products of their imagination.

Given the inherent problems of the experiential approach, there is, therefore, a need to complement it with the structural approach of criticizing the capitalist market. Along with the effects of the capitalist market to the personal or emotional lives of individuals, the ways it unjustly operates as a structure (or system) have to be exposed. Here, I am referring primarily to the evil of the capitalist system, including its institutions like the multinational corporations (MNCs). True, through the global capitalist markets foreign investments and trade have yielded substantial economic benefits in the form of higher economic growth as well as greater productive efficiency at the global level (Beitz 1999: 145). According to the World Bank (2004), in 2002 the world's total export value amounted to $6,455 billion and, based on OECD (2014) statistics, in 2013 the total amount of foreign direct investment at the global level amounted to $1.3 trillion. However, it is mostly the rich countries most particularly their MNCs which benefit most this huge economic leap while the poor players yoke the burdens. Oftentimes, MNCs fix prices in excess of competitive levels to the detriment of local industries in developing nations just because they have more capital, technological monopoly, and greater capacity to transfer production from country to country. MNCs also evade paying taxes on domestic profits as required by law by wielding political power along with their capacity to transfer profits from country to country. With the international economic order, vulnerable poor nations that want to improve their standard of living had to 'compete over access to the same heavily protected markets of the affluent countries' (Pogge 2002: 219).

More tellingly, while market capitalism has produced so much wealth unprecedented in modern history, it has aggravated the problem of poverty and inequality. Participation in global trading and investment has increased the internal inequality between the rich and the poor in the domestic country. MNC's investments in vulnerable countries may have opened up new job opportunities offering high salaries but oftentimes these jobs are taken on by highly skilled workers, mostly the educated upper class. More so, the entry of new capital investments has brought a sharp rise in the price of basic goods making them unaffordable to the poor. Indeed, the poor are still excluded from the market despite the rosy picture of economic development. In India, for example, it was reported that only 0.01% of its population, mainly the rich, has disproportionately taken advantage of the economic globalization in the last decades (Banerjee and Piketty 2005; see also Basu 2006: 1364). In this condition, the poor are not just poorer compared to the richest but also their absolute welfare may decline (Basu 2006: 1364).

Moreover, other than internal inequality, market capitalism has coincidentally produced obscene global inequality of resources between a few industrialized countries and poor nations. Guy Standing (2016) puts it succinctly: 'Corporations and financiers have used their growing influence to induce governments and international organizations to construct a global framework of institutions and regulations that enable elites to maximize their rental income'. One of such schemes is the 'international resource privilege' in which leaders of natural resource-rich but poor countries are given the privilege to transfer rights of ownership of the country's natural resources to foreign corporations. According to Pogge (2002: 115), the international resource privilege is morally questionable because it disregards the fact that leaders and governments of these poor countries are corrupt, inefficient, brutal, authoritarian, undemocratic, and repressive. Regardless of how the leaders of these countries come to power and of how they exercise such power, they are conferred with such privilege by multinational corporations and developed countries that have their own vested interests. For example, multinational oil companies like Shell and some foreign governments have been accused of supporting and maintaining the repressive Nigerian government led before by Sani Abacha in order to benefit from the rich oil-deposits in the Niger Delta. To use liberally Standing's (2014) word, this arrangement has coincidentally produced a new evolving mass class called 'precariat' who are in constant anxiety and insecurity.

The issue of global inequality is morally important because inequality opens the floodgates for economic and political exploitation, coercion, and deception of the poor (O'Neill 2000: 95). For example, poor countries are forced to lift trade barriers on imported products from developed countries or they are forced to accept terms of trade that put at risk their domestic economies. According to Onora O'neill (2000: 95), what makes coercion possible is

> the *relative weakness* of their intended victims. It is not their absolute lack of capabilities and resources that constitutes vulnerability to coercion; rather it is that they possess *fewer* capabilities, powers, or resources than others, and specifically than their coercers [my emphases].

At the global level, this unequal condition is made concrete through the fact of 'differential power relations' between rich and poor countries. Decisions that have political and economic repercussions to vulnerable countries are controlled by a few rich countries (Tan 2004: 119). For example, in the

International Monetary Fund (IMF) a country's vote is measured according to its financial contribution to the organization, a condition which is, obviously, more favourable to wealthier countries.

Sensing the need for structural approach to criticizing the capitalist market, Honneth in his later work *Freedom's Right* embarks on a project that focuses precisely on institutions and the historization of recognition patterns (see Marcelo 2013), one of which is in the market economy. For example, Honneth has mentioned how the pressure of economic globalization leads to lower taxes, less-regulated financial markets, power imbalance between large and small investors in the stock market, lower wages, and preference for company executives possessing 'purely objective financial knowledge'. More interestingly, describing the market as essentially a medium for social freedom, he shows how in the sphere of consumption and labour relations there exists an inherent dynamics of mutual recognition – the 'we' of the capitalist market economy (Honneth 2014: 176–255). In turn, this becomes the basis of Honneth's criticism of the latter, arguing that the 'we-consciousness' has given way to a greater concern for individualization as manifested in private consumption and individual responsibility. However, notwithstanding Honneth's intentions, his project to focus on the historicization of recognition patterns proves to be wanting.

True, the emphasis on individualism has practically wiped out the notion of we-consciousness among market participants. Yet, the relevance of the concept of we-consciousness when we speak of the dynamics of global market capitalism in which the main players are big MNCs, including the financial market is not entirely clear. The concept of we-consciousness which seems to be a normative description for relations between persons does not necessarily apply to global institutions such as multinational corporations (MNCs) and states. We cannot speak of mutual relations of recognition between global structures or institutions whether it is between MNCs and persons, or between MNCs and states, or between MNCs themselves, or between states themselves, in the same way that we speak of mutual relations between persons. One might say that the mutual relations of recognition could apply at least *indirectly* to the dynamics of market capitalism if its institutions were conceived primarily as rules promulgated by individuals as is the case of labour relations between workers and corporations. However, inasmuch as this is an attractive step to make, it is potentially problematic. Ontologically speaking, persons and institutions are not identical. The latter, like states, have no subjective feelings, a crucial fact of the mutual aspect of the social relations of recognition. More so, global economic institutions like MNCs are not fundamentally concerned with this 'we-consciousness' and instead treat each other as competitors. Also, they treat individuals not really as subjects to be respected but as 'objects' – faceless and anonymous – to be manipulated and utilized for the maximization of profit. Let me now proceed to my third and last argument.

5 Relative autonomy of the economic sphere

Meanwhile, dismissing systemic and functionalist arguments in his social theory, Honneth passionately argues that the economic sphere is not free from normative conditions or moral constraints. A nonnormative logic of the market that occurs behind the backs of participants in economic processes is strongly rejected. To him, market laws are not laws of nature but rather reflective of institutional arrangements. This suggests that, for Honneth, the economic sphere has no logic or life of its own, and that it is completely determined by normative preconditions. Indeed, this could be interpreted as a positive step in contrast to Habermas' substantive separation of the economic sphere from the cultural sphere. It might be the case that behind economic laws – such as the law of supply and demand, law of diminishing returns, and others – are different determinants such as a social logic, or political interests. In that sense, capitalist markets are not natural phenomena but are a system of rules (as well as conventions, norms, values, and customs) – both constitutive and regulative (see Searle 1995: 27) – organized by states, firms, and other agents. As a basic feature of social reality, capitalist markets are products of and dependent on human agreement or in the words of Searle 'collective intentionality' (see Searle 1995: 23).

Nevertheless, it seems that Honneth has unnecessarily overemphasized the normative character of markets, most particularly the capitalist market. This leads him to reject any amount of independence of the capitalist market (a stance which he appears to soften later on in his work *Freedom's Right*). Yes, it can be granted that market mechanisms are morally and culturally embedded. As Fraser (1989: 118) puts it:

> In the capitalist marketplace, for example, strategic, utility-maximizing exchanges occur against a horizon of intersubjectively shared meanings and norms; agents normally subscribe at least tacitly to some commonly held notions of reciprocity and to some shared conceptions about social meanings of objects, including what sorts of things are considered exchangeable. Similarly, in the capitalist workplace, managers and subordinates, as well as co-workers, normally coordinate their actions to some extent consensually and with some explicit or implicit reference to normative assumption.

Yet, the question is: Is it really the case that all operations of the capitalist market, particularly the present global capitalist market, are completely determined by normative preconditions as Honneth seems to suppose? Are all economic processes in this age of economic globalization planned, intended, designed, or willed? There are good reasons to suspend our enthusiasm at this point. Firstly, the previous view seems to run contrary to the erratic and sometimes inexplicable character of unintended consequences of market relations especially in the current international trade. Take the case of the recent global financial crisis. Granted that it might have been caused by different economic rules and policies of the banking and other financial sectors mainly in the US, for instance reduced interest rates, easy credit especially to finance housing, subprime lending,[1] and incorrect pricing of risk. But who could have thought that these would lead to liquidity problems of the US banking system, a collapse of large financial institutions, a decline in stock markets all over the world, and failure of key businesses all over the world, that is, a complete global economic meltdown?

The point here is that even if it can be granted that markets are a system of rules promulgated by different market agents, such rules may not always produce the results they intend to have. Why is this so? From the viewpoint of structuralism, it has something to do with the basic nature of systems/structures that occur behind the back of people, have a life of their own, and are reproduced without anyone intending them (see also Habermas 1987). Ferdinand de Saussure (see Ricoeur 1976) cites the example of structural linguistics in which languages composed of signs, codes, and meanings, that is, structures, reproduce themselves and we unwittingly participate in them. When we speak we are not aware of the grammar; there are structures out there independent from us and which shape how we think about the world. In the reading of Anthony Giddens (1984: 16), for the structuralists, 'structure' is usually understood as 'some kind of patterning of social relations or social phenomena' 'akin to the skeleton, morphology of an organism or the girders of a building'.

Despite the attractiveness of this view, this is not what I intend to defend. The main problem with structuralism is its apparent extreme position of treating structures and social objects as completely independent from the social agent, external and superior to human action. Structures are considered to have primacy over human actions and are regarded as constraints, so that the person's choices are made to conform to the structures outside of him/her. That leaves the agency of human beings completely irrelevant and toothless in the face of structures. In this condition called 'pure structural determinism' (Hays 1994: 61) where there is an absence or derogation of human agency, structures are neither intentional nor meaningful (King 2000: 369). When individuals follow rules, for example, there is no meaningful negotiation between the individuals and the rule. What happens is simply an individualistic implementation of an 'objective structure' to ensure that individuals act appropriately according to the rule.

Against this view, I would argue that rules do not necessarily produce the results they intend to have largely due to the unpredictability of human actions or human choices that interact with the rules in question. Rules do not exist independently by themselves but they are procedures of human action for the enactment or reproduction of social life (Giddens 1984: 21–22). In the words of Rawls (1999b: 37–38), rules are rules of a social practice that specify a form of action or a move so that they constitute the condition for the possibility of actions and the background for any action to be meaningful at all. So when rules interact with human choices, it might be the case that unintended consequences could result. Human beings, as part their agency, may engage in intentional acts where they know fully well the consequences or outcomes of their actions. However, there are particular moments in our social life where, despite the intentional conduct, say when an individual follows the rules of an institutionalized practice, unintended consequences could ensue (Giddens 1984: 12). Consider the so-called accordion effect of human action. A person turns on the switch of his room and sees a burglar who escapes down the road. The latter is caught by a policeman and spends a year in jail after being convicted of burglary. Although turning on the light was an intentional act, the rest of the cumulative consequences arising from the single intentional act are unintended (see Merton 1963).

On the bigger scale of social life, the situation is even more complicated as individuals' actions are varied and they happen to interact with one another beyond our consciousness. There is a complex of individual activities, say a mother buying milk in the grocery shop, a farmer taking care of his cows in the dairy farm, a street vendor selling agricultural products, a manager of an agricultural company attending a meeting, among others. Obviously, these are different individual activities undertaken separately by individual actors. Yet, it may not be difficult to imagine that they interact with one another, especially when they all occur in the same sphere like the economic. More so, in the process of their interaction, there could be an unintended pattern resulting from an aggregate of courses of intentional and 'regularized behavior' (Giddens 1984: 13–14), say, an increase in the prices of baby's milk. Another classic example of similar case would be the ways ethnic segregation might develop due to the desire of members not to live in a neighbourhood where they are ethnically a minority (see Schelling 1971; Boudon 1982; Giddens 1984: 10).

Applied to the capitalist markets, this suggests that it might well be the case that their operations are not completely determined by normative preconditions. In other words, they may have a certain degree of *relative autonomy* that is way beyond the control of economic agents. This is not necessarily equivalent to 'market triumphalism' in which markets are left on their own, correcting themselves through some kind of logic or invisible hand like a closed system. The point is that while markets, especially capitalist markets, still have to be planned or regulated by economic actors like governments, there has to be some consciousness that that capitalist markets can only be planned, willed, or intended by economic actors up to some extent. This is because the consequences of market operations cannot be fully predicted in advance especially when the consequences of the choices of economic agents within the markets may produce unintended consequences. Again, the global financial crisis in 2008 is a perfect of example of this. Because of reduced interest rates in the housing market, hundreds of Americans opted to take up housing loans in banks, but this consequently led to liquidity problems of the US banking system which led further to the collapse of large financial institutions globally.

6 Conclusion

I have discussed Honneth's notion of the market economy as a medium of social freedom and his analysis of the pathologies of market capitalism which he anchors in the latter's effects on the person's emotional life. I have shown how these have consequently influenced Honneth's social theory, most particularly his views of the economic sphere as not norm-free in contrast to Habermas's functionalist perspective of economic efficiency. Given these views of Honneth, I have raised three arguments. Firstly, I have argued that the idea of capitalist markets as spheres of social freedom might have been expressed too optimistically. Secondly, I have argued that the experiential approach to criticizing the capitalist market has to be complemented by the structural approach. Although Honneth has attempted to do just this in his later works, it has failed to capture precisely the evils of market capitalism. And thirdly, contrary to Honneth's social theory, it might be possible to speak of a relative autonomy of the economy given the reality of unintended consequences on the interaction between human action and rules. In the final analysis, I have argued that while Honneth's views on capitalist market are promising, they are not entirely convincing.

Note

1 Subprime refers to the credit quality of particular borrowers who have weak credit histories and greater risk of credit default than prime borrowers.

References

Anderson, Elizabeth. 1993. Value in Ethics and Economics. Cambridge, MA: Harvard University Press.

Banerjee, Abhijit and Thomas Piketty. 2005. 'Top Indian Incomes, 1922–2000', The World Bank Economic Review, 19(1): 1–20.

Basu, Kaushik. 2006. 'Globalization, Poverty and Inequality: What Is the Relationship? What Can Be Done?', World Development, 34(8): 1361–1373.

Beck, Ulrich and Elizabeth Beck-Gersheim. 2002. Individualization: Institutionlized Individualism and its Social-Political Consequences. London: Sage Publications.

Beitz, Charles. 1999. Political Theory and International Relations with New Afterword. Princeton: Princeton University Press.

Boudon, Raymund. 1982. The Unintended Consequences of Social Action. London: Macmillan.

Bourdieu, Pierre. 1999. The Weight of the World: Social Suffering in Contemporary Society, trans. Priscilla Parkhurst Ferguson et al. Cambridge: Polity Press.

Fraser, Nancy. 1989. Unruly Practices: Power, Discourse and Gender in Contemporary Social Theory. Minneapolis: University of Minnesota Press.

Fraser, Nancy. 2003. 'Social Justice in the Age of Identity Politics: Redistribution, Recognition, and Participation', in Redistribution or Recognition: A Politico-Philosophical Exchange, pp. 7–111. New York: Verso.

Friedman, Milton. 1962. Capitalism and Freedom. Chicago: Chicago University Press.

Fromm, Erich. 1976. To Have or To Be. New York: Harper & Row.

Giddens, Anthony. 1984. The Constitution of Society: Outline of the Theory of Structuration. Cambridge: Polity Press.

Giddens, Anthony. 1994. The Transformation of Intimacy: Love, Sexuality and Eroticism in Modern Societies. Stanford: Stanford University Press.

Habermas, Juergen. 1987. Theory of Communicative Action Vol. II, Lifeworld and System: A Critique of Functionalist Reason. Boston: Beacon Press.

Hays, Sharon. 1994. 'Structure and Agency and the Sticky Problem of Culture', Sociological Theory 3(1): 57–72.

Honneth, Axel. 1995. The Struggle for Recognition: The Moral Grammar of Social Conflicts, trans. Joel Anderson. Cambridge: Polity Press.

Honneth, Axel. 2003. 'Redistribution as Recognition', and 'The Point of Recognition: A Rejoinder to the Rejoinder', in Redistribution or Recognition: A Political-Philosophical Debate, pp. 110–197; pp. 237–268. New York: Verso.

Honneth, Axel. 2004a. 'Organized Self-Realization: Some Paradoxes of Individualization', European Journal of Social Theory, 7(4): 463–478.

Honneth, Axel. 2004b. 'Recognition and Justice: Outline of a Plural Theory of Justice', Acta Sociologica, 47(4): 351–364.

Honneth, Axel. 2010. 'Work and Recognition: A Redefinition', in Hans-Christoph Schmidt am Busch and Christopher F. Zurn (eds), The Philosophy of Recognition: Historical and Contemporary Perspectives, pp. 233–239. Plymouth: Lexington Books.

Honneth, Axel. 2014. Freedom's Right: The Social Foundations of Democratic Life, trans. Joseph Ganahl. New York: Columbia University Press.

Honneth, Axel. 2017. The Idea of Socialism: Towards a Renewal, trans. Joseph Ganahl. Cambridge: Polity Press.

Honneth, Axel and Martin Hartmann. 2006. 'Paradoxes of Capitalism', Constellations, 13(1): 41–58.

Illouz, Eva. 1997. Consuming the Romantic Utopia: Love and the Cultural Contradictions of Capitalism. Berkeley: University of California Press.

King, Anthony. 2000. 'The Accidental Derogation of the Lay Actor: A Critique of Gidden's Concept of Structure', Philosophy of the Social Sciences, 30(30): 362–383.

Marcelo, Goncalo. 2013. Recognition and Critical Theory Today: An Interview with Axel Honneth. Philosophy and Social Criticism, 39(13): 209–221.

McMurtry, John. 1997. 'The Contradictions of Free Market Doctrine: Is there a solution?', Journal of Business Ethics, 16(7): 645–662.

Merton, R.K. 1963. "Manifest and Latent Functions', in Social Theory and Social Structure. Glencoe: Free Press.

OECD. 2014. OECD International Direct Investment Statistics 2014. OECD Publishing.
O'Neill, Onora. 2000. Bounds of Justice. Cambridge: Cambridge University Press.
Pogge, Thomas. 2002. World Poverty and Human Rights: Cosmopolitan Responsibilities and Reforms. Cambridge: Polity Press.
Polanyi, Karl. 2001. The Great Transformation: The Political and Economic Origins of Our Time. Boston: Beacon Press.
Rawls, John. 1999a. A Theory of Justice. Cambridge, MA: Harvard University Press.
Rawls, John. 1999b. John Rawls: Collected Papers, ed. Samuel Freeman. Cambridge, MA: Harvard University Press.
Ricoeur, Paul. 1976. Interpretation Theory: Discourse and the Surplus of Meaning. Fort Worth: Texas Christian University Press.
Sandel, Michael J. 2012. What Markets Can't Buy: The Moral Limits of Markets. New York: Farrar, Straus and Giroux.
Schelling, Thomas. 1971. 'Dynamics Models of Segregation', Journal of Mathematical Sociology, 4(2): 143–186.
Searle, John. 1995. The Construction of Social Reality. London: The Penguin Press.
Sen Amartya. 1999. Development as Freedom. Oxford: Oxford University Press.
Standing, Guy. 2014. 'The Precariat and Class Struggle', Revisita Critica de Ciências Sociais, 103: 9–24.
Standing, Guy. 2016. The 5 Biggest Lies of Global Capitalism. From www.weforum.org/agenda/2016/12/lies-of-global-capitalism-guy-standing/. Retrieved on 23 July 2018.
Stiglitz, Joseph E. 2006. Making Globalization Work. London: Penguin.
Tan, Kok-Chor. 2004. Justice Without Borders: Cosmopolitanism, Patriotism, and Nationalism. Cambridge: Cambridge University Press.
Voswinkel, Stephan. 2012. 'Recognition and Interest: A Multidimensional Concept in the Sociology of Work', Distinktion: Scandinavian Journal of Social Theory, 13(1): 21–41.
World Bank. 2004. World Development Report 2004. New York: World Bank Publications.
Wright, Glen. 2011. 'Conceptualising and Combatting Transnational Environmental Crime', Trends in Organized Crime, 14(4): 332–346.
Zurn, Christopher. 2005. 'Recognition, Redistribution and Democracy', European Journal of Philosophy, 13(1): 89–126.

11

SOCIAL ESTEEM BETWEEN RECOGNITION AND REDISTRIBUTION[1]

Christian Lazzeri

In this chapter I aim to revisit the debate between Nancy Fraser and Axel Honneth around the issue of redistribution and recognition published mostly in the volume *Redistribution or Recognition: A philosophical exchange* in 2003. The concept of social esteem that this contribution deals with is of particular importance for both authors: for Honneth, it is at the heart of the sphere of work and exchanges; for Fraser, it refers to the differentiated evaluation of the agents' participation in a multiplicity of social activities and it has an indirect relationship with the economic sphere. If social esteem falls within the generic concept of recognition, then what is its relationship with redistribution and more broadly with the sphere of work and exchanges within the capitalist system? In an article written in 2013 entitled: "Des luttes perdues dans le capital: essai de correction normative de la critique marxienne de l'économie" (Honneth 2013), Honneth questions a theoretical failure of Marx's economic analysis and more generally of his social theory. He summarizes it as follows: what lacks in Marx and the Marxist tradition's analysis of the structures and dynamics of the capitalist society, is what Honneth calls 'moral economy': *i.e.*, the fact that economic relations are never reducible to pure relations of production, exchange, and circulation based solely on an economic rationality that aims at promoting the agents' interests. Economic relations are in fact underpinned by moral and social norms (Honneth 2013: 238). It is only by incorporating morality into the economy that we can see another dimension of social conflict emerging within the capitalist market economy itself. These moral norms, as Honneth argues, are precisely those of mutual recognition in a cooperative context, a mutual recognition which is here called social esteem. For him, this does not mean that we should return to the earlier phase of the history of capitalism described by Polanyi in *The Great Transformation*, when economic relations were embedded in social relations. It rather means that economic relations are *always* embedded in *moral* relations and cannot be approached without taking this dimension into account if one is to avoid the theoretical and practical errors of the economic and social conflicts of the last century.

Nancy Fraser would not disagree with the idea that Marxism has tended towards economic monism and neglected as a result the importance of struggles for recognition, ignoring or reducing them to variations of economic demands. But she also insists on another and equally damaging form of monism. This monism, of which Honneth is, in her eyes, one of the representatives *par excellence*, emphasizes on the contrary the supremacy of the concept of recognition, here conceived in terms of social esteem. It imposes culture as the dominant social factor of all social criticism and therefore of all claims and conflicts, obfuscating their economic dimension while claiming to absorb it. This may lead to treat economic conflicts and transformations are first and foremost moral and cultural, and to miss their very economic nature. Here are the two opposed positions that I would like to compare and confront. By doing so, I wish to address three questions that are relevant to contemporary social theories. The first concerns the object of conflicts of recognition. One can agree with Honneth and Fraser that these conflicts are not limited to simple problems of social representation or categorization between social groups. They do not only aim at changing the 'gaze' or 'consciousness': they concern class and social status relationships and only really produce effects by building on these social relationships to transform them. The second question concerns the nature of conflicts of recognition and redistribution and reverses the perspective: an analysis of the objective structure of social relations such as the one offered by classical Marxism proves insufficient to understand the nature of conflicts of recognition and redistribution. One could agree with Honneth and Fraser, in their (re)constructive criticism of Marxism, that the relations of production and the relations between social classes cannot directly account for social conflicts; we must also take into account the identities and status that overdetermine class membership. Regarding these two questions, it will however be objected to both Honneth and Fraser that their conception of the relations between economic structures, class, status, identity, and recognition, face multiple theoretical and practical difficulties that imply to reshape more or less extendedly their theoretical framework. The third question is normative: Fraser and Honneth are social justice theorists who argue that offers and claims for recognition must be evaluated by reference to normative principles. These principles should allow us to clearly state the difference between those which are righteous and those which are not. It will be asked, then, whether these principles of justice are convincingly established and whether they prove to be effective as critical normative principles of social relations within capitalist society.

1 The Honnethian concept of social esteem

One could begin by stating some general characteristics of the Honnethian theory of recognition before coming to the definition of his concept of social esteem. The Honnethian theory belongs to the family of interactionist theories, and it is more specifically a moral interactionism. It was first built as a theory of recognition and then expanded into a theory of social cooperation which was gradually inserted in a functionalist theoretical framework. This theory argues that attitudes and acts of recognition are essentially intersubjective relationships in which the partners confirm 'reciprocally and in an unconstrained way specific aspects of their personality which always depend on the mode of social interaction' (Honneth 2008, 88). These intersubjective relationships, which are expressed in three spheres of recognition of emotional, civic, and social nature, possess a *normative* dimension. Indeed, mutual recognition is a precondition of partners' access to autonomy and implies a self-limitation of each partner's desires, in the Kantian sense of the term, in order to avoid an asymmetric enjoyment of recognition that would destroy their access to autonomy (Honneth 2006: 237–238, 257, 261; 2014: 45–53; 2015b: 238; 2017: 24–25). For recognition to achieve its goal, it must be expressed as a *specific intention*, and as intentionally addressed to one or more partners:

> Whether they be gestures, speech acts, or institutional policies, such expressions or attitudes are always cases of recognition if their primary purpose is somehow to affirm the existence of another person or group. This basic conceptual choice means that we won't define as forms of recognition *positive attitudes that inevitably go hand in hand with the pursuit of other interests in the context of interaction.*
> (Honneth 2007b: 253, my emphasis)

Recognition interactions thus provide partners with a reciprocal confirmation of their identity, but this identity is a *practical* one, an identity already structured by moral norms, since, in each sphere of recognition, partners are precisely defined by their differentiated normative recognition capability. This type of recognition leads to Honneth's conception of justice as reciprocal recognition. While recognition cannot be equally distributed in all spheres, it is at least *mutual* if these conditions are met: it must be ethical in its purpose and normative in its means. These conditions allow to discriminate between offers and claims for recognition that do not meet this requirement, nor use the appropriate means to achieve it. There are fair offers and claims for recognition, as there are unfair ones.

1.1 Contributive recognition

With these premises in mind, we can come to the Honnethian definition of social esteem. It has two aspects, which refer to different stages in the construction of the concept. Both have been preserved in the last state of Honneth's theory, that can be found in *Freedom's right: The Social Foundations of Democratic Life*, but they are not on the same level. The oldest definition of the concept of social esteem – its first aspect – is elaborated in a series of texts that defend what might be called for convenience (although the expression is not from Honneth) a 'contributivist' principle of esteem based on a meritocratic model: in *The Struggle for Recognition*, Honneth begins by defining social esteem in relatively broad terms:

> In modern societies, relations of social esteem are subject to a permanent struggle, in which different groups attempt, by means of symbolic force and with reference to general goals, to raise the value of the abilities associated with their way of life.
>
> (Honneth 1995b: 127)

This concept, however, acquires a more precise content with the emphasis on work and the sphere of exchange. This significantly limits its scope in the context of capitalist society, which brings about a double reversal: on the one hand, capitalist societies establish an equality of rights typical of the exercise of democratic citizenship; on the other hand, they value a principle of 'social achievement' (*Leistungsprinzip*) based on economic performance, which is collectively recognized as socially useful and for the monopolization of which social groups begin to compete (Honneth 2003: 218; 2001, 154; Honneth & Fraser 2003: 145, 148, 152). This principle, although it has been historically promoted and mobilized as a '*sociodicée*' of the bourgeois classes, nevertheless appears as a moral progress since it represents a norm of social justice that extends the process of social integration to a larger number of individuals and groups by diversifying the qualities and abilities that are being recognized (Honneth & Fraser 2003: 184). Insofar as this principle first works as a class legitimization, it begins by excluding from its application any form of recognition devolved to the workers, thus creating a statutory difference that duplicates the difference in economic resources and class position. Secondly, it combines with the old social hierarchies that value male wage labour and discriminate women's work and in general despise domestic work (Honneth & Fraser 2003: 48; Honneth 2003: 218, 221). This is a typical case of 'social pathology' engendered by a restrictive distortion in the application of a social norm. However, since the distribution of social esteem is governed by a principle of mutual recognition justice, the meritocratic principle interpreted in its strict universality should lead to consider all forms of contribution to social utility, regardless of their degree of achievement, of the area of activity they take place in and of the characteristics of the individuals who perform them. To put it another way, the principle of reciprocal recognition which governs the distribution of social esteem contains a universal normative claim that can be used critically, as a *surplus of validity*, or as a *semantic surplus*, against all restrictions which put the principle in contradiction with itself and weaken its legitimacy and scope (Honneth 2002: 7; 2003: 211). Conflicts of recognition in the sphere of distribution of social esteem happen in relation with its implementation. They concern the practical identity of the agents since they concern the value of the capacities people want to be recognized in relation with their achievements.

Such conflicts can essentially take two forms: first, people can claim a reassessment of their own social contribution, even if it is not of major importance; by so doing, they make an explicit demand for social integration through the recognition of the value of their contribution. A large part of the conflicts of recognition in the sphere of work and exchanges are thus conflicting demands of re-evaluation: of the value of the profession, more generally of the value of the services performed, as in the case of domestic work, of the value of the performances in different types of work, or of the value of the qualities and abilities expressed in the work. They aim at changing social representations about the value of contributions and at incorporating these changes into practices and the law. The second form of conflicts of recognition that raise the question of the distribution of social esteem concerns more specifically workers temporarily or permanently located outside the labour market and whose contribution can no longer be directly assessed. Here, the contributivist principle is coupled with the principle of civic equality that intervenes to support the recognition of their social value. The principle of civic equality can be formulated as follows: the principle of citizenship requires the mutual recognition of the citizens' capacities of judgement and deliberation to solve collective problems in the political sphere; as such, it implies that this type of activity can be performed only if one has a minimum of economic resources. To value the contribution of these workers, the social state secures the distribution of a minimum income outside work thus ensuring 'a minimum of social esteem and economic welfare' (Honneth & Fraser 2003: 149; Honneth 2003: 221). In their two forms, conflicts of recognition affect the redistribution of resources and aim at social integration.

If so, the distribution principle of social esteem on a contributivist basis changes: it refers to a reproductive contribution, not in the narrow sense of capitalist society, but of society as a whole; moreover, it does not rely on a narrow interpretation of the meritocratic success principle identified with economic success, but on a broader interpretation that takes into account contributive performance to social utility. This one, finally, is defined in a more extensive way than the production of goods or supplies services: work is eminently a cooperative activity that values teamwork and the development of professional skills through the mutual recognition workers give to each other; it values the acquisition of technical skills and know-how, investment in effort, and is a source of performance and innovation in terms of technical devices (Honneth 2012: 64). These norms and practices become socially shareable and inform the broader social values that structure social bonds.

If we combine these different forms of work, we will then say that work, in a broad sense, refers, as Honneth writes, to a 'professional status . . . connected to skills and talents of value to society'; individuals should be able to receive social esteem as citizens 'holding a job, and according to the nature of [their] achievements' (Honneth 2003: 217). The qualities and abilities that contribute to economic success are thus socially valued and create differences in statutory positions, if and only if they contribute in a variable way to the collective utility and its social reproduction.

In defending the principle of a distributive justice of recognition based on a meritocratic norm, Honneth proceeds to a critical correction of the restrictions and distortions of this principle of distribution. But he does not dispute its essentially *unequal* character. This principle can only be readjusted through conflicts and public deliberations and the inequality it generates can be limited by minimal benefits in terms of economic resources and social esteem (Honneth 2014: 338, sqq).

1.2 Recognition in the exchange

The second aspect of the concept of social esteem refers to another form of recognition, this time derived from the Honnethian rereading of the paragraphs 182–199 of Hegel's *Principles of Philosophy of Right*, in the light of Durkheim's and Parsons functionalism: the one that is relevant to the exchange of goods and services. If this concept of exchange was not subsumed under that of social esteem, what kind of recognition would it be? This concept, external to any contributivist model, can be inferred from direct and horizontal economic cooperation between agents who, when exchanging goods and services, reciprocally recognize their complementarity in the exchange and the value of the standards their exchange must respect in the name of a principle of justice also based on reciprocity. This is what could be called for convenience (although the term is not of Honneth) a principle of 'commutative' justice. According to Hegel, whom Honneth follows here, this conception of mutual recognition in economic exchange is based, first of all, on the way the contractors perceive themselves as legal subjects, possessing capacities and able to conclude cooperative agreements while mutually respecting their equal legal status (Honneth 2007a: 107–110; 2014: 181). Second, as each of them satisfies his own needs (self-subsistence) and those of his partners through his activity and develops for this purpose professional skills, each demonstrates to the other his autonomy, which value is also reciprocally recognized in this exchange relationship (Honneth 2012: 64). Third, as each of the partners satisfies the needs of the other, each recognizes the value of the partner's needs and interests as a condition of the exchange and tends to satisfy them by an appropriate and acceptable remuneration principle which is not limited to the consumer goods market but also applies to the labour market. It thus constitutes 'a social institution that offers everybody the opportunity to satisfy their interests in free reciprocity' (Honneth 2014: 250).

From this threefold dimension of reciprocal recognition follows the achievement, for each partner, of a form of freedom which is distinct from the negative liberty of liberalism. This freedom is understood as an intersubjective social freedom based on the affirmation of each partner's value as a legal subject, an autonomous subject, and on the affirmation of the value of his needs and interests. The exchange so conceived creates a form of 'solidarity' between partners since they work towards the achievement of a common goal which lies in the mutual satisfaction of their needs and expectations of recognition through the exchange.

All these 'precontractual conditions' of exchange define, within the capitalist system, the existence of a 'moral economism'. That's why Honneth can say, following Durkheim, that 'justice and fairness are not normative ideals externally imposed on the capitalist organization of labour, but constitute, within it, functionally necessary presuppositions that must imperatively be applied *for a consciousness of social cohesion to develop*' (Honneth 2012: 69). As the contributivist principle, this moral economism can be used from a 'counterfactual' point of view in order to criticize the economic relations which deviate from the definition that makes their *raison d'être*, thereby helping to legitimize the moral protests of the social movements, including the workers' movement, against the pathologies of exchange. From there, one can turn to the Honneth-Fraser debate and to Fraser's objections, while presenting her own understanding of the relationship between recognition and redistribution.

2 The perspectivist dualism of Nancy Fraser

Nancy Fraser's criticism of Honneth's theoretical construction lies in the frontal challenge of the possibility of directly solving redistribution problems from recognition claims or recognition problems directly from distributive claims. Redistribution and recognition come, in fact, under different logics that cannot be reversed: a request for redistribution implies that we change the organization of work, obtain a right to control investment to a certain extent, demand the correction of inequalities of resources, abolish purely and simply exploitation. It also involves giving access to social assistance, and to do so, changing the distribution of resources. Thus, the accumulation and redistribution of resources concern, on the one hand, economic agents simply considered as productive forces and mobilize no other social property than this. That's why a white worker fired because of a merger only suffers an economic injustice (Fraser 1997: 17, 19, 1999: 36–37; 2003: 30). But redistribution concerns, on the other hand, social agents who can receive public aid. We can therefore act within the sphere of production and social assistance only through specific actions that directly produce effects in this sphere: these actions imply that we modify the redistributive practices of material resources.

Conversely, a demand for recognition consists in demanding the end of an inequality of status, by transforming the cultural conditions of the depreciation of identities in terms of gender or ethnicity, in order to escape the social contempt that leads to unequal participation in the most diverse social activities. What characterizes requests for recognition is that they may affect cultural, ethnic, racial, or sexual minorities, regardless of their economic situation. For example, gender domination is precisely 'transclassist': it occurs whatever the position of economic agents in the circuit of production, and whatever their level of resources. In this case, we can only act to change the social value of the different groups considered by relying mainly on the transformation of collective beliefs and social practices that affect the value of these groups: it is these actions that directly produce effects in this sphere (Fraser 2001: 27; 1999: 28; Honneth & Fraser 2003: 13–14, 79–83). When, on the contrary, the denial of recognition combines with class domination, they reinforce each other.

2.1 Class and status

Such a difference, in Fraser's approach, between redistributive practices and attitudes of recognition is grounded in a distinction borrowed from Max Weber's sociology, namely, the distinction between class and status. The concept of class oscillates, however, according to the texts, between the Marxist definition and the Weberian definition that Fraser considers compatible. It is thus defined from the position of the economic agents within the structures of production, according to their possession or not of the means of production (or the grabbing of the direction of the means of production) which, according to the allocation of differentiated resources and the possibility of exploitation, defines the chances (or lack thereof) of using surpluses to take advantage of market opportunities in terms of acquisition of goods (Fraser 2003: 293, n. 2; 1997: 17; 1999: 28; Honneth & Fraser 2003: 49, 68, 96, n.10). The relations between the classes of possession and non-possession are relations of economic subordination and although Fraser states that it is not necessary to define classes in strictly economic terms but to broaden this definition by adding cultural properties to them, one does nevertheless find no traces of this enriched class dimension, which reduces it to its economic properties (Fraser 1997: 17). With regard to social status, it is defined as the position of power that agents occupy within the social structure according to the esteem, honour, or prestige attributed to them. Unlike Honneth, for whom status – if translated in terms of social esteem – is closely related to the social position defined by the economic parameters of social achievement, the concept of status for Fraser refers to the general position of different social groups in the social hierarchy, a position defined by gender, race, or ethnicity properties that do not fall within the economic sphere, which avoids a form of reductionism in the conception of social esteem. This social position is defined in terms of collective beliefs, cultural values, and social and institutional assignments that organize this hierarchy and that characterize pre-capitalist as well as capitalist societies. For example, gender is a source of statutory differentiation, just as ethnicity or race create relationships of power and subordination between social groups that result in the difficulty or impossibility for members of the dominated groups to participate on a par in a multitude of social activities (Fraser 2003: 293, n. 10; 1997: 17; 1999: 28; 2003: 27; Honneth & Fraser 2003: 12, 48–50, 68). In short, for Fraser, the statutory differentiation unfavourable to the dominated can be understood essentially in terms of *discriminatory* subordination and not in terms of subordination *tout court* which could be produced solely by economic relations in the strict sense of the word, but which does not fall within the concept of recognition. This explains why class and status can only be combined *externally* (Fraser 1999: 36; 2013: 94; Honneth & Fraser 2003: 23–24). As a result, some agents, such as white workers, for example, find themselves economically exploited, while enjoying a higher status in terms of social esteem, than members of discriminated ethnic groups who may have in some cases superior economic resources, such as black businessmen who are discriminated in everyday life (Fraser 1999: 36). Thus, the class oppression suffered by the white worker cannot be carried back to the class identity of the proletariat and to a statutory dimension. Similarly, in an almost Marxian sense, when exploitation is translated directly into the power of the owners of capital over the organization of work, by excluding any possibility for workers to decide about their working conditions and the organization of work, by the power of employers to unilaterally decide about the type of investment to be made in the enterprise, this is not a question of statutory subordination, but of a 'political' one only representing a deficit of democracy in the workplace and about the control of economy in general (Honneth & Fraser 2003: 68–69). On the other hand, it is quite possible that certain attitudes of statutory reassessment (i.e., recognition) of women and ethnic minorities against discrimination co-exist with the radicalization of precariousness and exploitation, characteristic of the neoliberal turn of the contemporary economy. Such unilateral demands can be supported by the 'cultural feminism' criticized by Fraser as a type of identity politics that gives up the social critique of capitalism. It is a way for Fraser to anchor feminism into socialism (Fraser 2013: 160–161, 177, 219; 2017: 59).

Finally, if status constitutes the essential parameter of the definition of social esteem, this one is understood, contrary to Honneth, as a recognition obtained from participation in various social activities (political, cultural, sexual, professional . . .). By definition, and contrary to respect, the social esteem allocated is essentially variable and depends on the value of the performances achieved, which gives it a meritocratic and therefore inegalitarian aspect. The result, according to Fraser, is that Honneth makes a mistake when he claims that the legal interference of public institutions in the distribution of esteem can correct its unfair allocation by means of social benefits that produce 'a minimum of social esteem' for non-market workers. One thus loses the sense of the definition of esteem by confounding it with respect.

2.2 Perspectivist dualism

These positions lead Fraser to simultaneously reject two conceptions of distributive justice that are characterized by the fact that redistribution and recognition issues are dealt with from only one perspective. For example, some redistributive theorists such as Rawls, Sen, or Dworkin, according to Fraser, opt for the reduction of recognition to redistribution by arguing that redistributing rights and resources is enough to solve recognition problems (Fraser 2001: 28; Honneth & Fraser 2003: 34, 99–100). Conversely, Honneth attempts to reduce the paradigm of redistribution to that of recognition, arguing that the unequal economic relations of capitalist societies can be analyzed by reference to a cultural model of meritocratic achievement or, more broadly, by reference to a contributivist model of justice. In short, these social justice theorists reduce the injustices of status to class injustices or class injustices to injustices of status (Fraser 2001: 29; 2013: 164). Against this kind of reductionism Fraser supports a model of sociological analysis and normative theory which is defined as a 'perspectivist dualism'. This dualism is primarily a *dualism* because it admits, as we have just seen, the irreducibility of redistributive actions to attitudes of recognition and attitudes of recognition to redistributive actions: we must act within each category by mobilizing appropriate actions or attitudes convenient to the specific properties of the type of practice considered. However, this dualism, unlike an 'ontological' dualism which would separate class from status, is *perspectivist* because it admits that:

> Treating every practice as simultaneously economic and cultural, albeit not necessarily in equal proportions, it must assess each of them from two different perspectives. It must assume both the standpoint of distribution and the standpoint of recognition, without reducing either one of these perspectives to the other
>
> (Fraser 1999: 45)

and that it is possible to combine the effects of each of the two categories so that each produces *indirect* effects on the other (Fraser 1999: 45, sqq; Honneth & Fraser 2003: 35).

Gender injustices, for example (but it is the same for race or ethnicity), can be read in a two-dimensional way: on the side of inequities of distribution, gender appears as a principle of organization of the division of labour which makes a fundamental distinction between industrial paid productive work of dominant male and non (or less) paid reproductive and domestic work dominated female. Even within paid work of the industrial or service type, female jobs are subject to unequal pay for equal work, which generates a second type of economic injustice. This institutionalization, in a broad sense, which contributes to the naturalization of this division of labour, results in exploitation and inequality of power and decision-making within the family structure, as well as within companies and organizations. On the side of the injustices of recognition, gender must be understood from the point of view of a differentiation of status that refers to codified, more or less institutionalized, collective beliefs which assign to women subordinate social positions with regard to masculinity. This results in social categorization attitudes based mainly on the use of stereotypes of inferiority that prepare or accompany practices of domestic violence, moral and sexual harassment, stigmatizing collective representations, exclusion of positions of responsibility, unequal remunerations, difficulties in participating in collective deliberations in different public spaces. This institutionalization, in a broad sense, leads to the difficulty or the impossibility of an effective participation in the most varied social spheres (Fraser 2013: 162, 215; Honneth & Fraser 2003: 19, sqq; 2008: ch. III & IV). From Fraser's point of view, we can conceive of a programme of political and social reform, more or less important (which cannot be discussed here) that extends from reformism to socialism, combining the two dimensions of perspectivist dualism that can strengthen each other.

2.3 Parity of participation

It remains to be wondered, since Fraser is a social justice theorist, what is the principle of justice to which she refers in order to justify legitimate demands for recognition and redistribution? It is on this point that she makes a second criticism of Honneth's theses, and the principle of this criticism is that the Honnethian theory of justice, entirely based on the paradigm of recognition, is impracticable to the extent that it is essentially grounded on the confirmation or the repair of *identity*. For Fraser, a theory of recognition which expects principles of justice to repair symbolic injuries that affect individual or collective identity is a 'psychologist' and cannot produce the desired effects (Fraser 2013: 167 sqq; 2001: 26; 1999: 35). It is not possible to measure to what extent an individual is wronged in his identity by a denial of recognition, and it is not possible to know whether two individuals, stigmatized in the same way, experience the same damages: we cannot know if their claim for compensation are comparable and require the same measures. How can recognition policies respond to heterogeneous demands by means of general measures necessarily inappropriate to the variety of individual or social demands? There is no principle of justice capable of responding to such situations.

Therefore, according to Fraser, what is to be recognized is not the identity of an individual or a group. We must be able to build a politics of recognition that is not a politics of identity. Since recognition refers, as we have seen, to the statutory position of discriminated individuals or social groups, it is on discrimination that a politics of recognition must focus. On the other hand, redistribution concerns the level of resources, which indirectly defines status. Now, in the culture of democratic societies there is a commonly shared norm of equality that postulates the equal moral value of individuals and justifies their freedom to interact equally with others in the different social activities they participate in. Thus, it becomes possible to ground a principle of justice on equality of participation or on what Fraser calls 'parity of participation'. Parity of participation implies an equality of political and civil rights, the opportunity to participate equally in political deliberations but also equality with reference to work from the point of view of its gendered organization and remuneration. It also has implication in the family where it means equitable distribution of domestic work between the sexes. Finally it is works in the context of society as a whole, since cultures, as well as sexual orientations, are a priori considered of equal value (Fraser 2001: 33, 37; 2003: 27; 2013: 164, sqq; Honneth & Fraser 2003: 229). Parity of participation is, if one wants, an extension of the value of equality as it exists in the political democratic sphere to the different domains of social life.

3 Sociological concepts and normative principles

Honneth and Fraser, as we just saw, are social philosophers who defend a number of theses in social theory, and they are, at the same time, normative philosophers who refer to principles of social justice to justify and resolve claims for recognition and redistribution. It is these two dimensions of their theory that we must now submit to a close analysis. We will raise some difficulties that, among many others, deserve discussion.

3.1 A double reduction

Let's start with the strictly sociological dimension of their social theory and with Fraser's theses, which face several difficulties. By taking up the Weberian concept of status and distinguishing it from class, Fraser *reduces* its meaning: for her, the concept refers to subordinate social positions defined by gender, ethnicity, or race, that must be corrected in the light of the principle of parity of participation. But this raises a clear problem: in the first place, can one simply claim that because a white male worker has a higher status position than his female colleagues or foreign workers, he, too, does not occupy a subordinate statutory position? Obviously Fraser seems to hesitate on this point and she says in *Justice interruptus* 'To be sure, its members also suffer serious cultural injustices, the 'hidden (and not so hidden) injuries of class'. But far from being rooted directly in an autonomously unjust cultural structure, these derive from the political economy, as ideologies of class inferiority proliferate to justify exploitation. 'The remedy for the injustice, consequently, is redistribution, not recognition'. (Fraser 1997: 17). Fraser suggests that class inferiority, which is based on an asymmetry in the access to the means of production, can lead to a statutory inferiority and thus indirectly generate a deficit in terms of recognition. But why not go to the end of the argument? The principle of individual success which justifies economic success can be used and is used as a way to justify exploitation. Under these conditions, irrespective of the market constraints, if the ideological justification for exploitation is based on an alleged class inferiority, it will not be possible to oppose exploitation without at the same time rejecting the justification it is based on. Exploitation is justified by reference to the alleged inferior cognitive, technical, organizational, and decision-making capacities of the wage-earners. Their inferiority justifies their subordination in the production process for the benefit of the employers, who, on the contrary, are called to the functions of production management and the appropriation of the surplus product of work because of the eminence of their capacities. In this case, 'class wounds' do not stem from an autonomous cultural structure, but from cultural and social representations connected to an inequality in *economic* power. These injuries stem from the legitimization of exploitation and from the affirmation of social differentiation based on capacities and performances which confirm the success of economically dominant groups seeking to monopolize social recognition. In this case, the rejection of inferiority as a justification for exploitation necessarily implies the existence of a struggle for recognition and for redistribution in the context of work to jointly correct the inequalities of recognition and the distribution of resources. Thus, the two forms of struggle merge without rest and the struggle for recognition is *inseparable* from the struggle against exploitation: exploitation will be delegitimized if social inferiority is contested. Secondly, the indissolubility of the relationship between class and status can also be seen in the systematic mobilization of the 'false recognition' attitudes used by management of companies and organizations as incentives to increase labour productivity, or incentives to assume the occupational risks associated with precarious employment. The rejection of these forms of inauthentic recognition is also a way of fighting exploitation, of which they constitute an instrument. Thirdly, if the capitalists have the power of command over the organization of work and its conditions, as well as over the economic strategy of the enterprise, why would this subordination be 'political' only? Why would not it be a statutory subordination, producing a denial of recognition that sanctions subordinate positions of power? As a result, conflicts of recognition and political conflicts are strictly inseparable and there is no privileged entry into the conflict such as parity of participation. Fourthly, even the most 'economic' conflicts have a dimension of recognition that is inherent to them. Why does the dismissal of employees after years of professional investment in their company produce reactions of indignation which do not only lead employees to attempt to raise the 'bidding' of severance pay? This comes from the fact that the truth of work is not reducible to the concept of 'simple work' exchanged for remuneration (its objective truth) and that investment in work as a means of self-realization and investment in professional relations of recognition within a work collective (its subjective truth) foster a form of self-exploitation often perceived as a gift unrecognized in return by dismissal ('after all that I did for them!').

If we now turn to the concept of class, Fraser's thesis presents a risk of reducing the properties of the concept of class to the position occupied by social agents within the relations of production (Marx) or on the income scale (Weber). However, the properties related to class membership are both more varied and of a more qualitative nature. To put it in Bourdieu's terms, we can define objective social class by means of principal and secondary properties that govern the behaviour of social agents and their perception of the social world. Secondary properties such as prestige, distinction, social capital, and gender – status attributes – strongly overdetermine the occupational category and add determinants which are invisible for statistics but remain very important to account for the attractiveness of the position and its perception by social agents. Thus, the secondary characteristics do matter in the construction of class, because they add distinctive features to its fundamental properties and affect the practice and perception of agents; by so doing, they can reinforce the effect of class subordination, mark or not the decline of the class, as for example, the status of the female sex that always refers to a lower and negative function, or celibacy, which affects the decline of the French peasantry. As for the essential properties, they reside in the volume and the structure of the capital in relation to the position of production. The structure of class is thus defined by the system of relations between these main properties and the secondary properties. It is defined by the 'structure of the relations between all the relevant properties which confer to each of them and to the effects that it exercises on the practices, their own value' (Bourdieu 1979: 118; 1966: 201–223). The fundamental importance of the volume and structure of capital must always be connected to its overdeterminations by sexual, national, and ethnic factors, and to the representations of the position – representations that are also determined by other classes' representations, to which one reacts by investing specifically in all the properties of the class. This is inherent to the logic of the construction of the social identity of the class.

3.2 *Parity of participation and identity*

If we now come to the examination of conflicts of recognition and look at the thesis of the priority of parity of participation over identity, we can make a last objection concerning the relationship established by Fraser between parity of participation and social identity: social identity, as we have seen, cannot be the primary goal of social mobilizations for demands of recognition since its valuation is only a derived effect from the parity of participation, produced itself by the transformation of social beliefs and their possible public expression in the law. But this thesis is vulnerable to a double criticism: first, parity of participation may be insufficient, by itself, to correct statutory inequality and repair identity; second, parity of participation turns out to be dependent on this same repair. Indeed, offering opportunities for participation in terms of voting, deliberation capacity or power within an organization is not enough, by itself, to lead to *effective* parity of participation; for social groups in situation of vulnerability and with very unfavourable access to the linguistic market may simply have adapted their preferences to their chances of success. The cost of the participation requirement, as the exercise of participation itself, can thus be high and dissuasive for the dominated (Lazzeri 2009: 221–224). Third, since the refusal of parity of participation is legitimized in the framework of redistribution as in that of recognition by the social inferiority of the dominated, it becomes difficult to obtain parity of participation without having first questioned this assignment of inferiority. In other words, it will be necessary to first transform, through conflicts of recognition, the negative representation of the identity of the dominated so that parity of participation can become effective and reinforce, in return, their social legitimacy. This is the first condition for the achievement of parity of participation, the implementation of which depends, moreover, on the ability of collective mobilization to succeed in overcoming the adaptation of the preferences of the dominated.

3.3 A restriction of the concept of social esteem

The conclusion of these objections concerning the role of identity and the relations between class and status is that we must agree with Honneth that conflicts of recognition can contribute directly to the transformation of economic relations between social agents, through demands of social esteem that challenge the statutory subordination of wage labour. The objection to Fraser, therefore, is that if class and status are at times distinguishable, they are not necessarily distinct; they refer to two principles of social stratification that can merge from *outside* only: the Fraserian concept of status is thus *too narrow*; status can refer not only to gender and ethnicity; it must also describe *all* subordinate social positions, including those stemming from class membership and which produce relations of subordination, in this case also that of the 'white worker'. Honneth's position thus forces us to broaden the concept of status and this weakens the separation between the two domains that perspectivist dualism refers to. Social relations that come under the contributory principle are *inevitably and intrinsically* economic relationships and relationships of recognition.

However, on the other hand, the objection to Fraser also turns against Honneth's position. The concept of social esteem that he defends is entirely circumscribed to the practice of work and exchange. Why should we accept such a restriction? Honneth provides no consistent justification for it. There is in fact a multiplicity of practices external to the formally organized work that also contribute to social reproduction and which are structured by expectations, conflicts, and distributions of recognition. These practices are generally organized according to principles that are different from those of the economic sphere, even if they can present at the most formal level some similarities with it, concerning for example the value of performances or services: this is true, besides those already mentioned by Fraser, for artistic, sporting, military, scientific, and political practices (Bowness 1989; Joyeux-Prunel 2015; Bourdieu 1992; Ehrenberg 2011; Bowman 2006). This is even more true for all associative sociability practices that contribute to the construction of distinct social groups with different status, offers, and demands for recognition, as well as conflicts of recognition linked to the social visibility of a large number of practices and groups (Goode 1978). From this point of view, the plural forms of recognition described and advocated by Fraser correspond better than Honneth's monism to the real social pluralism of contemporary societies. Moreover, Honneth's monism also raises several difficulties.

The first concerns the justification of the *reduction* of social esteem to cooperation within the sphere of work and exchanges, or the exclusion of other social spheres from the scope of the concept. Why should social esteem be limited to this set of practices? Why would the denial of social esteem essentially occur in production and exchange? Why should the 'principle of achievement' be limited to work, even if it is understood in a broad sense, exceeding its valuation in the market to which economic elites restrict it? If one wishes to ask the question historically, has the progressive construction of the capitalist mode of production led, on the part of the bourgeois classes, to the localization of social esteem in the framework of work and exchanges alone?

To answer these questions in order, one could – defending the Honnethian point of view – begin by invoking the thesis of the 'centrality of work'. But this would not be useful, since it is not clear why – despite the importance of work – the centrality of work would result in denying the role of social esteem in other social spheres considered insignificant or second-rate. Is exclusion justified by the fact that normative recognition in terms of contributive or commutative justice would only apply to economic cooperation because of the ease of evaluation of the relationship between contribution and distribution or between value of goods and services traded? Even from the normative perspective of Honneth none of these propositions would not be true, both in the context of interactions and in terms of the distributive logic of the institutions: we do not see *a priori* what the structural obstacles for such an evaluation would be, since each social sphere has performance evaluation rules that can, in some cases, be as precise as those in the economic sphere. Finally, on the historical level, the nascent capitalist society represents a social formation in which social spheres are increasingly differentiated: beyond the economic, political, and religious fields, the artistic, sporting, scientific, and educational fields gradually affirm their relative autonomy and the distribution of recognition operates according to specific rules often framed and guaranteed by the State. It is thus not proved historically that, even for the bourgeois society under construction, the principle of distribution of esteem and success is restricted to the economic sphere alone.

This arbitrary reduction raises a second difficulty, which is that exchange and distribution of social esteem outside the economic sphere, as well as the specific conflicts of recognition they give rise to, could, because of this reduction, become a 'terra incognita' for social theory. Forms of domination that are encountered outside the economic sphere, expectations and conflicts of recognition that occur there would be arbitrarily ignored and would receive neither attention nor principled solution.

The third difficulty is that such exclusion leads to a normative limitation. It has already been pointed out earlier that the Honnethian conception of the just distribution of social esteem in its contributive aspect is meritocratic and tolerates distributional inequality when it is considered legitimate. Nevertheless, Honneth himself, not only in his debate with Fraser but also in others contributions argues that bourgeois classes inevitably tend to capitalize the social esteem they draw from their economic achievement because it has been the historical driving force behind their social and political importance (Honneth 1995a: 201; 2003: 216–218; Honneth & Fraser 2003: 141). This capitalization is accompanied by a tendency to restrict the application of the universal principle of recognition of the value of work in order to create forms of monopolization of recognition for their benefit. It follows that, on one hand, the unequal distribution of social esteem could be the basis of a symbolic domination of the ruling classes that should be corrected by appealing to the same principle of justice as regarding transfer incomes. As long as we remain in the economic sphere, the principle would compensate the distributive distortions that it could generate through the allocation of transfer revenues. The whole problem, on the other hand, is that the social elites use this symbolic capital outside the sphere of economy; so denials of recognition that find their source in this 'ethnocentrism' of class, affect the culture, lifestyle, hygiene, or morality of the popular classes or ethnic minorities as indistinct collective entities regarding which the production of social boundaries and spatial boundaries often overlap, imposing significant obstacles to their social mobility (Paugam et al., 2017). This is what Honneth observes, in his critical discussion of Bourdieu's *Distinction*:

> Economically powerful groups do have a considerably greater chance of institutionally generalizing their own value conceptions in society and thereby increasing the social recognition of their own conduct

> of life, but they achieve this not by the accumulation of cultural goods, but only the enforcement of a particular life-style which has conditional social approval.
>
> (Honneth 1995a: 201)

The problem is that this observation has no effect in Honneth on the tendency to monopolize social esteem in different social universes, as well as the study of its multiple consequences. Therefore, what, from the point of view of a normative theory of social esteem, could compensate or correct these general distortions of the contributory principle in diverse social spheres? Without a clear reorientation of the theory, there can be no answer to this question.

3.4 Recognition in exchange

The fourth difficulty concerns, this time, the economic exchange itself in its 'commutative' dimension. Can we argue that there is a form of mutual recognition at the heart of market exchange in its different forms? The difficulty here concerns the possibility of perceiving the immanence of recognition within the exchange interactions. The discussion can be initiated from an earlier observation by Honneth about the conditions of the distribution of recognition. For recognition to be effective, it must be *intentional* on the part of the partners, who must be free from 'the pursuit of other interests of the interaction' (see earlier). Can one consider, on the basis of this 'condition of intentionality', formulated generally when Honneth analyzes the 'false recognition' of the entrepreneurial management, that reciprocal recognition is *internal* in economic cooperation? This recognition rightly applies to the formal freedom of the partners which constitute the condition of contractual exchange and it could be described as a statutory parity. But it is not in fact 'internal' to the economic transaction because it is based on the very general phenomenon of historical social constitution of the value of formal individual freedom, transversal to all social spheres (Lazzeri 2016: 35–44). This explains why the freedom of the partners in the exchange can be recognized *per se* beyond the 'other interests of the interaction'. On the other hand, if we want to say that the integration of an employee in a work collective is the condition of recognition of the quality of his skills and the value of his performances with a non-instrumental objective, we have case, rightly so, to one of the dimensions of recognition at work, widely studied by sociologists and social psychologists of work and which can be considered valid (Linhart 2009: 35, sqq; 2015, III; Dejours 2009: 295, sqq; Woswinkel 2007: 59–87; Kocyba 2007: 103–118). However, beyond this specific dimension of exchange, we do not see in which sense we can be confirmed 'in the desires and aims of the other, because the other's existence represents a condition for fulfilling our own desires and aims' (Honneth 2014: 75). The structure of economic exchange is essentially oriented by the expected utility of the partners without which the exchange would be that of a gift and a counter-gift. In this context, the value of the partners' respective goals is taken into account only if it satisfies each other's interest which is the *raison d'être* of the exchange. The self-limitation of the interest of the economic agents mentioned by Hegel is only the condition of the realization of the exchange. It is true that the partners must exhibit some essential properties for this to happen: their reciprocal solvency, their execution of contracts, the punctuality thereof, the quality of products or services . . . the qualities and capabilities that these properties express are the object of social esteem in terms of the *reputation* of the agents. It directs their pre-cooperative engagement, in the same way as the Protestantism of Weber's bankers guarantees, as a 'moral principle', the confidence of their prospective depositors. We are dealing here with a form of *instrumental* esteem attached to the abilities that have a market value, but which value is non-existent for the partner whose transaction is not necessary (or weakly needed). This kind of esteem show no more 'authentic' value than the one distributed by managers to their subordinates in the practices of evaluation that are typical of 'late capitalism' (Honneth 2012: 89–94). This explains at the same time that these abilities are not estimated independently of the market demand and that no constraint internal to the exchange forces agents to do so. This instrumental esteem is thus strictly conditioned by the needs of the partners. It is not a pathology of exchange but its operating principle, as Marx observes in the *Grundrisse* (Marx 1993: 243–244).

Therefore, if the driving force behind the exchange is the expected utility of the partners, the recognition which envelops it, when it is the case, will have to overdetermine it normatively by the gift, the 'social debt', the 'quasi-contract' of solidarity, the legal norms that guarantee the execution of contracts, the belonging to the same social group that creates an identity between partners and overcomes distrust. The exchange is thus *embedded* in social norms that correct it from the outside. The 'moral economy' of which Honneth speaks refers precisely to a situation of this type in traditional societies and can be updated to a certain extent today within the social economy. In this case, it is difficult to argue, consistently with Honneth's condition of intentionality, that a reciprocal internal recognition *valid for itself*, could be derived from the structure of the exchange of goods, a recognition that the action of the Hegelian or Durkheimian corporation (or that of the State) would make possible to restore by correcting the pathologies of the exchange (Thompson 1993, chap. IV–V; Polanyi 2001: 65, sqq). No doubt his conception of recognition in exchange is intended to justify or reinforce the 'market socialism' that he defends, but it can be argued that socialism, even if it must make room for market, probably rests on other foundations. This is an opportunity for social theory to enrich its conceptual framework by extending its investigations around the concept of social esteem.

Note

1 Translated from French by Marie Garrau.

References

Bourdieu, Pierre, 1966, "Condition de classe et position de classe", *Archives Européennes de Sociologie/Europäisches Archiv für Soziologie*, 7(2): 201–223.
———, 1979, *La distinction. Critique sociale du jugement*, Paris, les éditions de Minuit.
———, 1992, *Les règles de l'art. Genèse et structures du champ littéraire*, Paris, éditions du Seuil.
Bowman, James, 2006, *Honor: A History*, New York, Encounter Books.
Bowness, Alan, 1989, *The Condition of Success*, London, Thames and Hudson Ltd.
Dejours, Christophe, 2009, "Entre inégalités individuelles et coopération collective: la question de l'autorité", in *Comment penser l'autonomie ? Entre compétences et dépendances*, edited by Marlène Jouan & Sandra Laugier, Paris, Presses Universitaires de France, pp. 291–313.
Ehrenberg, Alain, 2011, *Le culte de la performance*, Paris, éditions Fayard.
Fraser, Nancy, 1997, *Justice interruptus. Critical Reflections on "Postsocialist Condition"*, New York and London, Routledge.
———, 1999, "Social Justice in the Age of Identity Politics: Redistribution, Recognition, and Participation", in *Culture and Economy after the Cultural Turn*, edited by Larry Ray & Andrew Sayer, London, Sage Publication, pp. 25–52.
———, 2001, "Recognition without Ethics", *Theory, Culture & Society*, 18(2–3): 21–42.
———, 2003, "Rethinking Recognition: Overcoming Displacement and Reification in Cultural Politics", in *Recognition, Struggles and Social Movements, Contested Identities, Agency and Power*, edited by Barbara Hobson, Cambridge, Cambridge University Press, pp. 21–35.
———, 2008, *Scales of Justice: Reimagining Political Space in a Globalizing World*, Cambridge, Polity Press.
———, 2013, *Fortunes of Feminism: From State-Managed Capitalism to Neoliberal Crisis*, London, Verso.
———, 2017, "Néolibéralisme progressiste contre populisme réactionnaire: un choix qui n'en est pas un", in *L'âge de la régression*, edited by Heinrich Geiselberger, Paris, Éditions Premiers Parallèles, pp. 55–68.
Goode William J. 1978, *The Celebration of Heroes. Prestige as a Social Control System*, Berkeley & Los Angeles, University of California Press.
Honneth, Axel, 1995a, *The Fragmented World of the Social: Essays in Social and Political Philosophy*, edited by Charles W. Wright, New York, State University of New York Press.
———, 1995b, *The Struggle for Recognition: The Moral Grammar of Social Conflicts*, Cambridge, MA, The MIT Press.
———, 2001, "Recognition or Redistribution? Changing Perspectives on the Moral Order of Society", *Theory, Culture & Society*, 18(2–3): 43–55.
———, 2002, "Reconnaissances et justice. Esquisse d'une théorie pluraliste de la justice", *Le passant ordinaire*, n° 38 janvier–février (www.passant ordinaire.org/revue/print.asp?id=349 handwritten pagination) (accessed on 26 February 2019).

———, 2003, "La reconnaissance: une piste pour la théorie sociale contemporaine", in *Identités et démocraties, diversité culturelle et mondialisation: repenser la démocratie*, edited by Ronald Le Coadic, Presses universitaires de Rennes, pp. 205–221.
———, 2006, *La société du mépris Vers une nouvelle théorie critique*, Paris, éditions La Découverte.
———, 2007a, *La Réification. Petit traité de théorie critique*, Paris, éditions Gallimard.
———, 2007b, "Recognition as Ideology", in *Recognition and Power: Axel Honneth and the Tradition of Critical Social Theory*, edited by Bert van den Brink & David Owen, Cambridge, Cambridge University Press, pp. 323–347.
———, 2007c, *Disrespect: The Social Foundations of Critical Theory*, Cambridge, Polity Press.
———, 2008, *Les pathologies de la liberté*, Paris éditions La Découverte.
———, 2012, "Labour and Recognition: A Redefinition", in *The I in We: Studies in the Theory of Recognition*, Cambridge, Polity Press, pp. 56–74.
———, 2013, "Des luttes perdues dans le capital: essai de correction normative de la critique marxienne de l'économie", in *L'injustice sociale. Quelles voies pour la critique ?*, edited by Julia Christ & Florian Nicodème, Paris, Presses Universitaires de France, pp. 225–242.
———, 2014, *Freedom's Right: The Social Foundation of Democratic Life*, Cambridge, Polity Press.
———, 2015b, *Ce que social veut dire. II. Les pathologies de la raison*, Paris, éditions Gallimard.
———, 2017, *The Idea of Socialism. Towards a Renewal*, Cambridge, Polity Press.
———, & Nancy Fraser, 2003, *Redistribution or Recognition: A Philosophical Exchange*, London, Verso.
Joyeux-Prunel, Béatrice, 2015, *Les avant-gardes artistiques 1848–1918. Une histoire transnationale*, Paris, éditions Gallimard.
Kocyba, Hermann, 2007, "Reconnaissance, subjectivisation, singularité", *Travailler*, 18: 103–118.
Lazzeri, Christian, 2009, "Recognition and Redistribution: Rethinking Nancy Fraser's Dualistic Model", *Critical Horizons: A Journal of Philosophy and Social Theory*, 10(3), December: 307–340.
———, 2016, "Quelques prémisses pour une théorie de l'estime sociale", *Terrains/Théories*, n° 4: 35–44 (http://journals.openedition.org/teth/679; DOI: 10.4000/teth.679).
Linhart, Danièle, 2009, *Travailler sans les autres?* Paris, éditions du Seuil.
———, 2015, *La comédie du travail. De la déshumanisation taylorienne à la surhumanisation managériale*, Paris, éditions Eres.
Marx, Karl, 1993, *Grundrisse, Foundations of the Critique of Political Economy* (Rough Draft), London, Penguin Books, in association with *New Lelt Review*.
Paugam Serge, et al., 2017, *Ce que les riches pensent des pauvres*, Paris, éditions du Seuil.
Polanyi, Karl, 2001, *The Great Transformation: The Political and Economic Origins of Our Time*, Boston, MA: Beacon Press Books.
Thompson, Edward P., 1993, *Customs in Common*, London, Penguin Books.
Woswinkel, Stephan, 2007, "L'admiration sans appréciation. Les paradoxes de la double reconnaissance du travail subjectivé", *Travailler*, 18: 59–87.

12

RECOGNITION VS REDISTRIBUTION

The case of self-respect

Caroline Guibet Lafaye

The starting point of my reflection is Rawls' description of self-respect as 'the most important primary good' (Rawls 1987: 577), that is, the first good necessary for the exercise and development of the two specific powers of moral personality: the capacity for a conception of the good and the capacity for justice as well.[1] Universal rights declarations on which our democracies stand, and many international declarations as well, state and aim to guarantee basic liberties for all, along with equal treatment, access to primary goods, capabilities, and basic functionings[2] but also equal dignity. These principles involve the public protection of dignity and people's self-respect, especially in situations of social vulnerability.

Turning now from political declarations to moral and political philosophy, the debate over redistribution tends to give way to reflections on recognition, namely its means and conditions. However, the interest for recognition cannot dismiss redistributive concerns, since 'reforms concerning recognition cannot succeed unless they are associated to struggles for redistribution' (Fraser 2005: 68). Rather, the main political issue of our times should be that of knowing 'how to develop a consistent program capable of integrating redistribution and recognition' (Fraser 2005: 69). In particular, the issue of self-respect reflects the interdependence between recognition and redistribution in the field of social justice. For example, the lack of self-worth and of one's capacity to do something worthwhile is exacerbated by the experience of a contrast between oneself and others (i.e., between social and economic positions) which is perceived as humiliating, especially when this disparity is made visible by the social structure and by societies' life standards. In this sense, self-respect raises distributive questions as well.

My contribution to the debate, which tends to represent redistributive and recognition approaches in a conflicting way, will be to show that a theory of social justice which refers to well-chosen 'achievements' opens the way to a conciliation of redistribution and recognition perspectives. The need for this conciliation is even more evident as we deal with self-respect. For this purpose, I will proceed, first, to highlight the social relevance of the notion of self-respect or self-esteem; then, I will address the role of social institutions in the construction and preservation of self-respect; finally, I'll identify the most suitable redistributive procedures and measures to ensure the consolidation of self-respect.

1 What is self-esteem or self-respect?

Unlike other goods such as income and leisure, self-respect presents a specific problem of definition. When can one say that self-esteem has been acquired? Is it a contribution to society? Does it have something to do with the satisfaction of specific needs or with the worth of individuals as such? Although Rawls points out the importance of self-respect, considered 'perhaps' (as he frequently says in *A Theory of Justice*) as the most important primary good, he suggests a relatively rough definition of it. As a first step, I will devote my attention to a preliminary definition.

1.1 Self-confidence, self-respect, and self-esteem

1.1.1 Self-respect involves a number of interactions

'*To a certain extent, self-respect acquires a perceptible mass only in a negative form* – specifically, only when subjects visibly suffer from a lack of it' (Honneth 2000: 146). In this sense, self-respect may be difficult to define in positive terms.[3] However, in order to specify its content, it is useful to refer to the works of Axel Honneth on recognition. Honneth identifies three essential strands of integrity corresponding to three identifiable forms of recognition, first providing qualities inherent to the notions of self-respect and self-esteem (Honneth 2000: 114). They are:

- the ability to meet one's own physical and psychological basic needs by means of *self-confidence* provided by the affection of relatives and friends;
- the ability to develop oneself as a subject capable of judgement by means of *self-respect* provided by the guarantee of fundamental rights;
- the ability to contribute to social life by means of *self-esteem* provided by social esteem, that is, the social confirmation of our skills and good capacities by others.[4]

The *identity-formation* as *positive relation-to-self* thus implies self-confidence, self-respect, and self-esteem.

1.1.2 *Self-respect requires self-confidence*

(α) Self-confidence – identified by Rawls as a specific dimension of self-respect – can be described as the sense of one's self-worth; it translates into the deep belief that one's own conception of the good and plan of life are worth fulfilling (see Rawls 1987: § 29).

(β) Broadening its meaning beyond the legal sense, self-respect requires self-confidence (i.e., the belief of one's self-worth) as well as the confidence in one's ability to achieve his/her intentions, within the limited means at one's disposal (Rawls 1987: 479–480).[5]

(γ) Finally, self-esteem in Rawls' terminology translates the fact and the feeling of being sure of the worth of one's plan of life as well as the capability to carry it out. It adds a condition to 'self-respect' which, in Rawls' account, basically represents a condition of meaningful perseverance in life. Instead, I'll point out that the lack of self-esteem would follow (1) a lack of self-confidence or self-worth, (2) a lack of confidence in one's capability to do something worthwhile, (3) a sense of impotence associated to these two elements (Rawls 1987: 577). We will see further that these elements justify the possibility that the lack of self-esteem could lead to a social claim.

1.1.3 *Self-respect requires respect from others*

Self-respect is also based on a certain relation with others in a wide range of spheres. Three essential relational dimensions of recognition are at stake: the dimension of primary relations, especially concerning the family (where the individual experiences love and friendship); the dimension of legal relations which determines the individual's status and recognizes his/her capability as a subject of law as well as a person; finally, the social community and its role in recognizing the worth of one's participation to the group and the related skills.

In this way, instead of thinking quite naïvely that self-respect and self-esteem would merely refer to a relation-to-self – unlike the notion of recognition, which directly refers to otherness – it seems that these two notions equally rely on respect from others. Insofar as self-esteem needs recognition by the other, it requires intersubjectivity and presents an important social dimension. Thus, for example, if we feel that our actions do not inspire respect from others, it would be difficult, and indeed impossible, to maintain that our purposes are worth pursuing (see Rawls 1987: § 67).

The dimension of otherness, which is a component of self-respect and self-esteem, justifies their social consideration. Nevertheless, the nature and the limits of social claims immediately present in a problematic way: when does a subject really esteem oneself, when does one feel really respected? We face here a difficulty that Paul Ricœur describes as the temptation of 'a new form of "unhappy consciousness", under the species of an incurable feeling of victimization and of a relentless representation of ideals out of reach' (Ricœur 2005: 316). However, this is not to justify that a painful state of mind would motivate a legitimate social claim. Instead, my aim will be to identify the *social conditions necessary to the constitution (to the formation) of self-respect and self-esteem.*

1.2 *Social pertinence of the notion of self-esteem*

1.2.1 *The lack of self-esteem: a matter of justice rather than psychology*

In order to understand the social relevance of self-esteem, we must first justify that respect and self-esteem have a meaning which is not merely psychological but also social. This shift from a psychological meaning to a social one raises a normative concern insofar as we are to justify it. In short, we must determine that self-respect or self-esteem are not only a matter of self-realization but rather a matter of justice.

1.2.1.1 THE ESSENTIAL INDIVIDUAL VALUE OF SELF-RESPECT

The essential conveyor of this interpretation is given by Rawls who sees in the social bases of self-respect *the most important primary good.* Indeed, self-respect is what provides the individual with a feeling of self-worth. Self-respect allows one to find value and confers it on one's own existence as well as on one's own plans. From its value for the individual, Rawls is able to conclude that 'the parties would wish to avoid at almost any cost the social conditions that undermine self-respect' (Rawls 1987: 480) and that 'they would not agree to count this sort of subjective loss as irrelevant' (Rawls 1987: 577).

As we have seen, the lack of self-esteem is attributable to a lack of self-worth along with a lack of self-confidence in one's capacity to do anything worthwhile, or also to a sense of impotence associated with these two elements (see Rawls 1987: 577). Compared to this lack of self-esteem, many conditions enable the feeling of self-worth, which is to say the first element of self-respect. In particular, I consider (a) *having a rational plan of life* and, more precisely, a plan that meets the Aristotelian Principle, that is, a plan where the agent is able to develop his/her talents in a challenging way.[6] In fact, the more one's skills are fully attained and organized in a complex and refined way, the more one's confidence in one's self-worth. (b) The second condition is that *our person and our acts are appreciated and valued by others* that we equally esteem. The question then becomes that of knowing how a society can guarantee the 'social bases of self-respect' to everyone. We will see that these two dimensions can legitimately be taken into account by society in order to ensure their fulfilment for everyone.

1.2.1.2 THE INTERSUBJECTIVE DIMENSION OF SELF-RESPECT

The dimension of intersubjectivity, which is essential for self-respect, justifies the social relevance of the latter. This dimension is crucial since without the appreciation of our peers, it would be impossible for us to maintain that the things we do are worthwhile. Since self-respect rests in part upon recognition by the ones we recognize, it requires otherness and intersubjectivity: that's why it can be legitimately considered as a matter of social concern.[7] Intersubjectivity turns recognition into a *reciprocal need* and embeds this issue into the context of face-to-face relations: the universal need of seeing one's own existence and uniqueness confirmed by another is fed by a principle of reciprocity. This requires the creation of intersubjective conditions conducive to personal integrity, respect, and self-esteem.[8] Let's clarify this.

1.2.2 The lack of self-esteem as a matter for social claims

The loss of self-esteem can thus become a matter for social claims. Indeed, as soon as the question of self-esteem can be interpreted in terms of justice, we are able to (α) take into account the social conditions needed for a positive relation-to-self – as we shall see, through the universal guarantee of a list of primary goods; (β) to consider the question of self-esteem in terms of rights, namely legal status; (γ) to finally consider the question of self-respect with reference to the denial of recognition based on *status*, that is, within the field of social relations and not psychology. Let's analyze these elements in detail.

Concerning the intersubjective constitution of the self, the formation of the practical Self depends on the reciprocal recognition between the subjects. Being confirmed by the other in one's activity, an individual comes to understand oneself as a practical Self, i.e., as an individualized and autonomous subject. In this sense, there is a morally constraining dimension of claims in terms of self-respect. The struggle for recognition and self-respect involves normative expectations. More precisely, the disillusionment of normative expectations, whose fulfilment is considered essential for one's identity or group (that is, the *moral* experience of contempt), leads to claims – by individuals or groups – aimed at achieving the social conditions for a positive self-relation. These social struggles are motivated by the intersubjective nature of practical subjectivity and self-respect: they feed on the relation – of recognition – to others.

Likewise, self-esteem is very frequently undermined by the social status of people and their situation, namely by their relative social positions, particularly when they are assumed as having subordinated status. This is the case when people are not considered as fully-fledged partners of social interaction and consequently suffer from a denial of recognition and of status subordination. They don't take part in this interaction as equals. Yet, when an individual is affected by the 'lack of social esteem', he/she is negatively affected in his/her chance to develop a positive relation-to-self, due to the absence of recognition. Involving both individuals and groups, the correction of this subordinate status hindering self-esteem consists in ensuring an equal political status and a 'participatory parity to social life' (Fraser 2005: 82).[9]

1.2.3 Self-esteem as a 'primary outcome'

The consideration of self-esteem as a matter of social claims expressed in terms of *rights* gives me an opportunity to mark my difference of opinion with Nancy Fraser. According to Fraser, 'approaching the problem of recognition from the perspective of justice prevents from supposing a right to social esteem for all' (Fraser 2005: 51.[10] In her view, this position is indefensible as it could undermine the meaning of esteem. Fraser embraces a minimalist position, maintaining that 'everyone has a right to pursue social esteem under fair conditions of equal opportunity' (Fraser 2005: 51). Yet it seems to me that we cannot merely provide individuals with 'opportunities' of social achievement or self-esteem without taking into account their situation 'at the end' of distribution of opportunities, or the outcome they achieve by means of the opportunities initially allocated.

Indeed, the exclusive focus on resources or opportunities in spite of achievements, of the 'fundamental social achievements' (Fleurbaey), is not justified. For what counts is not so much what people have, but what they can achieve with their resources.[11] For this reason, self-esteem cannot be merely considered as a primary good or an initial resource, but rather as a fundamental achievement, a 'primary outcome' enjoyable by everyone. It is a 'primary functioning',[12] meaning a state achieved by the individual. In this sense, respect and self-esteem not only take part in (being also a condition of) *the accomplishment of normal human functions*, but they also result from it.

As basic dimensions of human flourishing, respect and self-esteem don't rest merely on subjective well-being: rather, they justify a social consideration. Some objective fulfilments – i.e., in the field of education – are equally important. This attention is justified also by their relation to essential outcomes in terms of *social, rather than merely individual, conditions* (see Fleurbaey 1995). The social consideration of the 'fundamental social achievements' seems to respond to the needs of contemporary moral philosophers to reconcile the concern for redistribution with that for recognition. Indeed, theories of recognition have drawn attention to the fact that some aspects of social life – related to issues of social justice – cannot be fully understood when considered as things. This awareness has entailed, for some authors like A. Honneth, a break with the distributive paradigm, giving priority to the intersubjective dimension of recognition. In the following, my aim will be that of showing that the distributive approach is in a position to meet the concerns for self-respect, provided that it takes into account not merely the distribution of *initial opportunities* but the distribution of 'primary outcomes'.

2 Social institutions and self-respect

2.1 (Objective) social conditions of self-respect

Concerning the determination of self-esteem suggested previously, it is by no means clear that it requires, either negatively or not, some social conditions. For this reason, social institutions have a role to play in respect and self-esteem. In particular, participation in social life as a fully-fledged member of the community – what Fraser refers to as 'participatory parity' – requires specific economic and institutional conditions. In the first case, the *distribution of material resources* should be such that participants are able to enjoy independence as well as the opportunity to express themselves.

Put another way, 'participatory parity' in interaction is equally jeopardized when some actors lack the minimal economic resources for interacting with others as peers. As a consequence, forms of material inequality and economic dependence impeding this participatory parity must be revised. This should also be the case with social dispositions contributing to the persistence of deprivation, exploitation, and great disparity of opportunities, along with income, leisure time, and in the distribution of primary goods, resulting in depriving people of the means and opportunities necessary to interact as peers with others.[13]

Similarly, it is questionable that there is such a thing as a real 'independence' between social positions and self-esteem.[14] Indeed, the social inferiority of a person, measured in terms of the *index of primary goods*, can be so overwhelming that it would undermine one's self-respect (Guibet Lafaye 2006: 178). Likewise, esteem and self-respect are harmed when the social position of the most disadvantaged doesn't seem to be able to provide a constructive opportunity to address the favourable situation of the most advantaged. Finally, the lack of self-esteem, especially the lack of confidence in one's self-worth and capacity to do something worthwhile, is strengthened when the contrast between oneself and others is made (too) visible by social structures. The situation of the less advantaged is frequently recalled, which may lead to even less esteem for themselves and their own way of life.

Furthermore, participatory parity isn't merely guaranteed by objective or distributive conditions but also by institutional and social obligations, in that institutionalized models of interpretation and evaluation structuring social action must express equal respect for all participants and ensure at least equality of opportunities in the search for social esteem. In what follows I shall focus on the economic conditions of respect and self-esteem and on the fact that an unfair distribution of resources and 'primary outcomes' is a key impediment to participatory parity to social life, bringing about social subordination and injustice.

2.2 Social stigmatization and 'transformative remedies'

My first challenge is that very often the existing redistributive practices entail institutionalized models of interpretation and evaluation that diminish people's self-respect. Indeed, the distributive means provided to guarantee individuals with access to self-respect frequently entail a social stigmatization, preventing the possibility itself of self-respect. That is the case, for example, of all means-testing social assistance, which provides targeted support to the unemployed and underemployed. Likewise, many welfare policies stigmatize single mothers as sexually irresponsible parasites. In these examples, interaction is mediated by institutionalized models of cultural values, which forge some social categories as normative models, while representing others as inferior or deficient. Providing material assistance, these welfare programs maintain social inequalities and strengthen high economic and social differences – in short, they leave untouched the socio-economic structure, creating the kind of inequality they claim to repair. They contribute, in particular, to representing the least advantaged as a defective and needy class. In this way, these social measures, even though they aim at providing people with primary goods, end up preventing the minimal conditions for self-esteem.

These measures of corrective justice, which generally rest upon a universalistic account of equal moral worth, thereby meeting one of the vital requirements of self-respect, end up contradicting this principle of equal moral worth in the very *practice* itself of corrective redistribution, especially when controlling recipients' lives. These tests thrive on stigmatizing dynamics which are at odds with the official engagement in the respect of equal moral worth of people. Therefore the focus should be on identifying the redistributive measures that don't undermine either recognition nor self-esteem of the recipients, thereby providing an answer in terms of corrective justice to Fraser's claim that 'justice today requires both redistribution and recognition, none of them being sufficient alone' (Fraser 2005: 94).

So how can redistributive measures, meeting the (negative) condition of self-respect of non-stigmatization of recipients, be implemented? With reference to the previous examples, the first avenue would be that of removing conditionality from social welfare. Likewise, the guarantee of a 'basket' of minimal social goods or fundamental social achievements may take another path. These sorts of measures would fall within what Fraser refers to as 'transformative remedies' as distinguished from the 'affirmative remedies' (Fraser 2005: 31). These 'transformative remedies' generally combine universal welfare systems, progressive taxation, wide public sector, considerable public or collective property, and a process of democratic decision-making over the priorities of development. They try to ensure access to employment for all, having the effect of reducing social inequality without creating stigmatized classes of vulnerable people, guilty of freeriding on public charity. In other words, these measures allow reparation of distributive injustices without undermining recipients' self-esteem. And even better, they contribute to redressing certain injustices of recognition: in so doing, they are conducive to generating self-respect for those who were previously deprived of it. These measures don't rest only upon the *principle* of equal moral worth of people: unlike conditional remedies of justice, in addition, their *implementation* doesn't comply with self-respect.

Therefore, in my view, this measure is crucially important as it tends to *guarantee self-respect, fostering solidarity* and *reciprocity* in social relations and social justice. It avoids undesirable forms of stigmatization and prevents a doubling of the injury of deprivation suffered by the most disadvantaged because of misrecognition. 'Transformative remedies' foster solidarity and contribute to guarantee the conditions of self-respect for all, avoiding stigmatization on the one hand, and answering to some forms of misrecognition on the other. Thus the next step is to identify a number of 'transformative remedies' (Fraser), namely distributive justice measures that are likely to meet the conditions of self-respect, as well as contributing to the deployment of strong solidarity among the members of society.

3 The social bases of self-respect

What role should social institutions play in order to *positively* contribute and ensure at least the access for all to conditions of respect and self-esteem? The answer to this question will lead to the distributive configuration and to the allocation of available resources ensuring equal self-respect for all. From this perspective, should we favour Rawls' theory of primary goods? Thus what role would remain for 'opportunities' (i.e., of initial resources) in building self-respect? Is universal basic income the best answer that can be given for equal self-respect? I can already say that I agree with Rawls and Fraser in that social institutions are to ensure access to conditions of self-respect for all. Nevertheless, my purpose is to determine that they are to provide not only the *conditions* of self-respect – comprising, on the one hand, the condition of non-stigmatization and, on the other hand, the resources needed in order to make the enjoyment of self-respect possible – but also self-respect as such, as well as a sense of self-worth for all. In fact, self-respect is a primary good and we cannot accept that some are deprived of it.

3.1 Institutional conditions for self-esteem

Measures of Rawls' theory of justice may be considered as 'transformative remedies' to the extent that they have an effect on the 'basic structure of society'. Given that 'self-respect is the most important primary good', Rawls points out that 'the parties [in an originary equal position] would not agree to count this sort of subjective loss [that of self-respect] as irrelevant' (Rawls 1987: 577). Consequently, the social structure and its principles of justice are to be in such a way that they don't lead to a loss of self-esteem – if so, they need to be revised.

A society based on the principles of justice as fairness,[15] namely a 'well-ordered society', provides its members with the conditions of equal self-respect. It answers to the causes of loss of self-esteem that I have previously underlined. (1) With reference to the first condition of self-esteem (i.e., the sense of one's own self-worth), the concept of justice as fairness requires that everyone have equal basic rights. Accordingly, Rawls concludes that 'for all these reasons the less fortunate have no cause to consider themselves inferior. . . . The disparities between themselves and others, whether absolute or relative, should be easier for them to accept than in other forms of polity' (Rawls 1987: 579). In addition, he suggests the need for measures enabling the least fortunate not to feel themselves inherently inferior to others. Finally, in a well-ordered society, members of the community have a common sense of justice and they are bound by ties of civic friendship, contributing to self-respect for all in a positive way (see Rawls 1987: § 75–76).

(2) Turning now to the second condition and to the relation between self-esteem and social positions, according to Rawls *the income and wealth gap* shouldn't be too large in a well-ordered society; in other words, in the application of the difference principle – although the latter allows, in theory, inequalities and gaps of individual situations as wide as you like (see Rawls 1987: § 26). Here the measure provides that a well-ordered society should limit the occasions in which the least advantaged may feel their condition as impoverished and humiliating (see Rawls 1987: 580).

In addition, 'the plurality of associations in a well-ordered society, each with its secure internal life, tends to reduce the visibility, or at least the painful visibility, of variations in men's prospects' (Rawls 1987: 579). In this sense, a well-ordered society fosters a certain degree of ignorance about the differences of wealth and individual circumstance. This ignorance is facilitated by the general recognition of the principles of justice by all citizens, at least when they meet each other for public affairs. Everyone in the public arena is seen as a sovereign and equal person being treated with equal respect. Thus 'the public recognition of the two principles gives greater support to men's self-respect' (Rawls 1987: 208–209) in the context described by Rawls. Therefore, his conception of justice as fairness would publicly state people's reciprocal respect and thereby guarantee their sense of self-worth.

3.2 *Political conditions of self-esteem*

3.2.1 *Public affirmation of fundamental rights and liberties*

What can be retained of Rawls' theory is that the affirmation of equal political rights for all citizens is crucial for protecting and perhaps enforcing one's self-respect. Equality of rights and public attitudes of mutual respect have a major place in enhancing the sense of citizens' self-worth, for a subordinate status would actually be humiliating and damaging of self-respect. Self-respect thus requires the recognition of the equal *status* as peers in the political community. In a society grounded on the principles of justice as fairness, the need for status is met by the public recognition of fair institutions, along with 'the full and diverse internal life of the many free communities of interests that the equal liberties allow' (Rawls 1987: 587). Rawls concludes that the base of self-respect in a fair society wouldn't be the share of income, but the publicly recognized distribution of rights and fundamental liberties.

Dividing the social order into two parts (political and not political), Rawls considers the equal political status of citizens to be the main source of self-respect. For example, he shows that the priority of liberty leads to the equality of social bases of self-respect.[16] However, I argue that the equal distribution of rights and fundamental liberties isn't sufficient to guarantee self-respect for all, as the material and moral situation of homeless people in our liberal societies can easily show. Political status alone isn't able either to 'ensure the least fortunate the sense of their own value' (Rawls 1987: 137) nor to limit the hierarchies that place some at the bottom, into indecent life conditions. Equal liberty and the commonality of political status are certainly a necessary condition (a 'base') of self-respect, but yet not a sufficient one.

3.2.2 *The principle of participation*

Self-esteem equally rests upon political participation, that is, the possibility of attaining the subject's 'excellences' – namely, individual qualities and talents that it is rational for everyone to aim (Rawls 1987: 483). Thus both equal political liberties and participation to political life enhance people's sense of self-worth. This participation contributes to the political competence of each citizen, increases his/her moral and intellectual sensitivity and provides the base of his/her conscience of duties and obligations, on which the stability of fair institutions relies.

If the recognition of a political status is a primary good and a resource to be ensured to everyone in order for them to get self-respect, political participation is by contrast a fundamental achievement that does not end in the possible (guaranteed by constitutional rights) access to the public arena. Likewise, the participation to 'communities of interests' (especially the economic ones as emphasized by Rawls), while necessary, does not in itself support that the economic difference of positions might be neglected.[17] In *A Theory of Justice*, Rawls certainly underestimates the role of economic and social differences among the sectors of society. I believe by contrast that this shouldn't be the case. Participatory parity isn't ensured by equality of political rights alone. Political participation is a fundamental social achievement requiring that the conditions of *actual* (real) political participatory parity are guaranteed. Yet, the nature of these conditions is not merely legal, institutional, or formal. It is not sufficient that people *formally* have the same basic rights in terms of basic political liberties.

Whether political, economic, or cultural, participatory parity depends on material and social conditions, which are conditions of self-esteem as well. Rawls points this out in his work of 1993, highlighting that 'below a certain level of material and social well-being, formation and education as well, it is out of the question that people can participate in society as citizens, and as equal citizens' (Rawls 2001: 208) – but he deals with these elements only in terms of constitutional claims (Rawls 2001: 208). My focus here will be on some economic and social conditions (i.e., not exclusively political or constitutional[18]) drawing 'a conception of justice that seeks to eliminate the significance of relative economic and social advantages as supports for men's self-confidence' (Rawls 1987: 587).

3.3 Economic conditions of self-esteem

3.3.1 Guaranteeing a 'basket' of primary goods

As I have pointed out, a loss of self-esteem is possible when society allows great discrepancies in the allocation of primary goods. Rawls' difference principle recommends – provided respect of fundamental liberties and fair equality of opportunities[19] – to ensure everyone a basic 'basket' of goods in terms of wealth, power and self-respect. The difference principle comprises a *maximin* criterion concerning some basic goods, namely liberties and individual rights, some conditions of security, self-esteem, and the satisfaction of basic material needs equally guaranteed for all. As it is well known, the principle of a guaranteed minimum doesn't end in giving priority to the most deprived but, essentially, to the extremely poor whose basic needs for food, shelter, health, and self-esteem are not met. Such a principle stems from the idea that everyone owes a decent treatment to others as well as *a limited care for the basic conditions of a decent existence*.

Nonetheless, such a *maximin* shouldn't end in merely guaranteeing this 'basket' of primary goods to the least fortunate, stigmatizing them as such (cf. supra 2.2), but rather to *all* members of society. Beyond policies of public health care, education, etc., one way to ensure the satisfaction of basic material needs would be that of attributing a universal basic income to all, a citizenship or subsistence income. This has the advantage of offering to all some of the material means essential to the formation of a rational plan of life and to ensure the greatest real freedom to all. That is already expressed by the consideration of social primary goods, on which the social bases of self-respect rely.

3.3.2 Universal income, real freedom, and self-esteem

Admitted that self-respect means that individuals have a solid sense of self-worth and self-confidence, which is essential to the pursuit of their goals, an unconditionally guaranteed basic income to all (which would contribute to the maximization of real freedom for all, especially in terms of income) is conducive to self-respect. The principle of maximization of real freedom for all suggests that we legitimately expect that society provides, to the greatest possible extent, the objective means for happiness.[20] It takes into account self-respect as it meets the need for unconditionality, it dismisses means-test procedures and control of personal life,[21] it avoids all sense of stigmatization and humiliation to its recipients. To that extent, the principle of maximization of real freedom for all, based on the universal income that ensures a certain standard of living to all, would be preferable not only to the difference principle but also to the whole hierarchy stemming from it, i.e., the principle of equal liberty and the principle of equality of opportunities (see Van Parijs 1991: 188).

Considering unconditionality, universal income falls within the scope of transformative redistributions – as in Fraser's distinction – that give priority to the universal right to social benefits specifically targeted at the poor. For this reason, universal income is more conducive to guarantee self-respect. Insofar as it avoids the stigmatization of the needy, it fosters social solidarity, which also contributes to self-respect providing recognition and social values to all. 'Non-reformist reforms' (see Gorz 1964) like that of universal income (midway between affirmative and transformative strategies) can have cumulative effects over time that will allow not only to repair the unjust distribution of goods but also to create real social conditions of self-respect. This would be true both individually (by avoiding stigmatization of the least fortunate) and intersubjectively or socially (by developing social solidarity).

3.4 Social conditions of self-esteem

3.4.1 Rejection of the principle of perfection and participation to associations

From a social point of view, several dimensions are to be considered in order to guarantee the social bases of self-respect. The participation of people in various associations or activities they deem rational and which are publicly appreciated by others can be regarded as a measure allowing the most disadvantaged not to feel themselves as inherently inferior to others (Rawls 1987: 481).[22]

Indeed, this participation contributes to individuals' sense of self-worth and to the valourization of these daily activities. In addition, these associative bonds enhance the second aspect of self-esteem, as they tend to lower the risk of failure by providing a response over doubts about oneself in case of difficulties. Where the internal life of these associations suitably fits its members' talents and desires, it provides a solid base to the feeling of self-worth. In fact, our plan of life determines what we are ashamed of.[23] The feeling of shame is *related to our aspirations*, to what we try to do, to those we wish to be associated with (see James 1890: 309 *sq.*). Consequently, it is essential to create adequate associations on the grounds of a multiplicity of interests, in order for them to fit the ideals linked to the aspirations and talents of everyone.

Thus the rejection of the principle of perfection by the parties involved in the interaction makes possible the recognition of a variety of conceptions of the good in all activities that comply with the Aristotelian principle (and that are, of course, compatible with the principles of justice). All meritocratic bias would be avoided as well. Thus *this democratic way of reciprocally learning and assessing purposes is the foundation of self-esteem*. In public life, this allows citizens to mutually respect their purposes as well as arbitrating their political claims in such a way that doesn't destroy their self-esteem. Therefore the guarantee of the social bases of self-respect entails that everyone is able to take part in at least one community sharing his/her interests, where his/her undertakings can be appreciated by others.

3.4.2 Guaranteeing primary social outcomes, 'fundamental social achievements'

Regardless of whether the approach is inspired by Rawls or Philippe van Parijs (through real freedom), the effective protection of equal liberties is expected to guarantee self-respect. Nonetheless, the approaches involving a concern over resources or opportunities for all are insufficient, especially if we aim to establish a lasting basis for self-respect. Thus for example it is not sufficient to assure everyone the 'chances to acquire cultural knowledge and skills' (Rawls 1987: 104), equal opportunities of 'education and cultural knowledge' (Rawls 1987: 315) or access to political life as well as various forms of social interaction (i.e., associations), as it is necessary to take into account the outcome and the situations resulting from opportunities.

Thus an approach that gives priority to 'fundamental achievements' has the advantage of taking into account the possibility of individuals' misuse of resources or opportunities of which they previously benefitted. In fact, caring only about opportunities may lead to the idea that individuals with low fulfilment who benefitted from equal opportunities are to be deemed responsible for their own situations. Theories of equality of resources[24] as well as theories of equality of opportunities[25] don't exclude – neither do they suggest a remedy to – the possibility of a misuse of resources or opportunities by recipients. By assessing individual situations in terms of resources or opportunities, these theories don't provide any safety net in terms of individual fulfilment.

It seems therefore necessary to identify some achievements, some 'social outcomes' (Fleurbaey) or essential 'primary *functionings*' that should be socially guaranteed to all and that contribute to the real conditions of self-respect.[26] These fundamental achievements are defined with reference to the basic dimensions of human flourishing. As Rawls suggests, 'excellences'[27] represent the conditions of human flourishing and self-respect. The fact of holding them feeds the confidence of our self-worth.[28] These achievements involve in particular the main outcomes relevant to the individual's social status and relations. Suggested by the works of M. Fleurbaey, this approach creates a sphere of responsibility still respecting agents' freedom,[29] their preferences and life choices – within a pluralistic democracy – yet without compromising their fundamental interests nor strengthening the questionable principle of meritocratic inequalities (Fleurbaey 2004: 16–17).

Individual outcomes which are deemed merely private – i.e., the feeling of subjective satisfaction – are neglected. By contrast, individuals are entitled to social benefits when they don't succeed in the chosen dimensions of fulfilment. The concern for 'social outcomes' allows thereby that no one would ever be left at bay, respecting the principle of autonomy.[30] This approach is grounded on a certain definition of the extension of social responsibility, given that its limits are determined through duties and mutual rights of solidarity and autonomy. Principles of solidarity partly entail that it is not decent to let others live in inferior (or mediocre) conditions, whatever their moral responsibility may be, and they tend towards a sort of *basic social equality*. With time, social institutions will contribute to reduce high inequalities *with reference to these fulfilments* – thereby responding to the problem of disparity of relative and absolute social positions, which is a vector of self-esteem.

In the field of education, for example, it is then required not only to provide equal opportunities 'of education and cultural knowledge' (Rawls) to all, but to ensure that everyone has a common culture, a basic education and culture. The idea is not to distribute educational resources by assessing the agents according to productivity criteria but rather to take into account the *value of enrichment* of citizens' personal and social life, especially that of the most disadvantaged (Rawls 1987: 137). It would be appropriate for example to define what compulsory school should ensure to all students, to identify the basic capacities (reading, writing, counting, etc.), the general knowledge and the cognitive skills essential for living in our societies, as well as the practical skills that all students must have attained once they have finished school. Indeed, school plays a specific role in the formation of individuals as subjects capable of managing their life, building their capacities of self-confidence and trust in others (Dubet 2004: 74).

Of course, the 'fundamental social achievements' approach rejects *meritocracy*, which is important to refuse in order to make possible the protection of self-respect and self-esteem. As argued by Rawls, this approach entails that we reject as citizens the criterion of perfection, that is, the reference to an absolute level of fulfilment as a political principle and that we avoid any estimation of the relative worth of others' ways of life in the name of justice (Rawls 1987: § 50). Finally, the approach based on 'social outcomes' doesn't end in weaving a safety net in fundamental individual fulfilments, but it gives priority to individuals who have the lowest outcome in the dimensions considered, as high as these outcomes may be. At the end of the day, such an approach centred on 'social outcomes' is more likely to respond to instances of solidarity and autonomy than an approach based on opportunities, capabilities, or primary goods.[31]

4 Conclusion

This analysis has shown that concerns over solidarity and related duties require self-respect to be socially considered in order to guarantee its foundations. Painful feelings and unhappiness resulting from the lack of self-esteem can therefore represent a legitimate matter for social concern. In some cases, it is clear that the fact of feeling unhappy legitimately arouses social concern, regardless of its origins (which explains the existence, in France for example, of the *Centres de Clinique Psychothérapique*). At the very least, it has seemed to me crucial to identify the measures and social dispositions contributing – in redistributive terms – to a minimum of individual and social fulfilments capable of positively feeding the self-respect owed to everyone. Concerns for fundamental social achievements outlined here require institutions and social policies to take directly into account the social fulfilments of agents and, indirectly, the fulfilment within private spheres of life.

These compensatory measures focus on fulfilments or individual outcomes considered in their social dimension, being recognized that individuals take responsibility for their private fulfilments (see Guibet Lafaye 2006: 143–153). Unlike that avenue exclusively addressed to opportunities or capabilities, the approach based on fundamental social achievements takes into account the distribution of shares once everyone's fulfilments have been undertaken, in other words, at the end of distribution. This way, it rejects as an insufficient justification the notion of responsibility for the existing social inequalities or the situation of the deemed 'undeserving poor' as well as the least fortunate.[32] It finally provides the means to reconcile the concern for redistribution with the concern for recognition.

Notes

1 See Rawls (1987: 93, 122) or Rawls (1982).
2 See the article 22 of the Universal Declaration of Human Rights of December 10, 1948: 'Everyone, as a member of society, has the right to social security and is entitled to realization, through national effort and international co-operation and in accordance with the organization and resources of each State, of the economic, social and cultural rights indispensable for his dignity and the free development of his personality'. See also the "Human Development Report 2003" and "Millennium Goals" of the UN or the OMS' "International Classification of Functioning, Disability and Health".
3 Likewise, Nancy Fraser suggests a definition of recognition based on the lack of it, namely through humiliation, discrimination, contempt, disqualification, and the constitution of a distorted self, which prevent the individual from acquiring the capacity to live and act autonomously (see Fraser 2005: 159).
4 Honneth is largely inspired here by elements of Rawls' theory of justice.
5 However, I would point out that what Rawls describes as 'self-respect' would fit more adequately with what Honneth calls 'self-confidence'.
6 'The Aristotelian Principle states that, other things equal, human beings enjoy the exercise of their realized capacities (their innate or trained abilities), and that this enjoyment increases the more the capacity is realized, or the greater its complexity' (Rawls 1987: 566). Rawls reminds us that, according to Aristotle, the exercise of natural capacities is an essential good for human beings; that the most enjoyable activities and pleasures are linked to the exercise of their greatest talents, involving the most complex judgements (see Aristotle, *Ethics to Nicomaque*, VII, chap. ii-xiv, et livre X, chap. i-v). Thus a plan that an individual might pursue will lack interest for him/her if s/he is not able to express his/her natural gifts in an interesting way.
7 Stressing that a condition of self-respect is 'finding our person and deeds appreciated and confirmed by others who are likewise esteemed and their association enjoyed', Rawls considers recognition to be a necessary condition for self-esteem (Rawls 1987: 480).
8 See Honneth (2000: 197). Honneth points out that, to the extent that recognition is the fact of the one who gives recognition, in this act there is an exercise of power, even if the one who recognizes simply recognizes the claim to uniqueness which is addressed to him/her.
9 According to this principle of parity of participation, a measure or a society is fair to the extent that it makes participation possible for all members, that it ensures a parity of participation in the construction of institutionalized value patterns, in processes of deliberation about the rules of redistribution, and, more generally, in all forms of social interaction.
10 My perspective is more congruent with that of Axel Honneth (2000) who considers social esteem to be an intersubjective condition for undistorted identity-formation, that morality is meant to protect. Indeed, in this case, everyone has a legitimate right to social esteem.
11 A. Sen has well shown that the advantage that is taken from a good isn't mainly a matter of pleasure but rather the chance of realizing one's potentialities (Sen 1985: chap. III).
12 A. Sen defines the functionings as follows: 'what the person succeeds in *doing* with the commodities and characteristics at his or her command. . . . A functioning is an achievement of a person: what he or she manages to do or to be. It reflects, as it were, a part of the 'state' of that person. It has to be distinguished from the commodities which are used to achieve those functionings' (Sen 1985: 6–7).

13 Thus recognizing that economic inequality is mainly inevitable, Nancy Fraser emphasizes that a threshold is needed, beyond which the distance that separates the most disadvantaged from the wealthy is such that all practical ends are impossible – the problem being of course that of determining this threshold (Fraser 2005: 54).

14 As suggested by the question of envy in Rawls' *Theory of justice*.

15 In other words, the principle of equal freedom for all and the difference principle.

16 However, Rawls mentions the possibility that the feeling of one's self-worth may depend to some extent on one's place within the institutions and relative income. Faced with this difficulty, he suggests as a theoretical solution to include self-respect on the list of primary goods, the index of which defines expectations (Rawls 1987: 588). This concern would result in the index' consideration of the effects of agents' excusable envy in the application of the difference principle (see Rawls 1987: § 80), and in this sense, that the expectations of the most disadvantaged 'are lower the more severe these effects'. Thus we should introduce at the legislative level some adjustment for self-respect of the most disadvantaged.

17 Rawls would answer to this objection by showing that the basic principles of justice as fairness tend less to inspire excusable envy than other principles of justice and that, in a just society, economic differences are set for the benefit of the least favoured. Rawls himself emphasizes the interest and the 'several advantages' of considering political status as fitting the social need of self-esteem (see Rawls 1987: 588). Nonetheless, I don't believe that the theoretical efficiency of the solution suggested by Rawls justifies its moral validity. From providing everyone with the same political status, through the institution of basic equal liberties for all, one cannot so easily conclude (or deduct) that the distribution of material means deserves a lower place, when questions of self-respect are involved (Rawls 1987: 588).

18 For example, I will deal neither with cultural nor with gender problems.

19 This condition seems to me controversial in itself.

20 See Van Parijs (1995). This position is that of the real-libertarian theory and, more generally, that of liberalism.

21 François Ost, for example, points out the expectations of dignity generated by a system of guaranteed basic income that relies on such controls. He stresses that only anchoring social provision in the unconditional affirmation of human dignity will allow to preserve their value (see Ost 1988: 246; see also 259 and 269).

22 In social terms, the fact of participating to association fits the principle of political participation.

23 Rawls highlights the connection between shame and self-respect (Rawls 1987: 483). Regardless of its natural or moral nature, shame comes from a feeling of a diminishment of the self. In moral shame, one is harmed by the loss of self-esteem and capacity to pursue one's goals.

24 See Rawls (1971, 1982), Dworkin (2000), Van Parijs (1995).

25 See Sen (1985a, 1985b, 1987, 1992), Arneson (1989, 1991), Cohen (1989, 1990), Roemer (1996), Vallentyne (2000).

26 Among the fundamental achievements to be taken into account, one might consider the possibility of developing a conception of the good and engaging oneself in a critical reflection on the planning of one's own life; the possibility of living for and towards other human beings, expressing one's capacity for recognition and attention, devoting oneself to different forms of social and familial interaction; the possibility of living one's life within an environment and a context that one has chosen (see Nussbaum 1990). As Nussbaum notes, in the short list of capabilities she proposes, a life that lacks some of these dimensions would see its human content seriously diminished, that's why a public authority

is expected to guarantee the minimal resources that will allow the citizens to satisfy their capabilities, as well as a concern for minimal achievements within these dimensions.

27 That is to say, individual qualities and talents that is rational for everyone (including ourselves) to want us to have (Rawls 1987: 483). See footnote 59.

28 Thus natural shame comes from an injury to our self-esteem, due to the fact that we don't have some excellencies and that we have failed to exercise them.

29 Capabilities express the dimension of freedom while present *functionings* witness the fulfilments reached by agents.

30 However, it requires to limit the sphere of responsibility of people, so that agents are not necessarily able to use their autonomy the way that they might wish.

31 Indeed, the mistake of an approach centred on chances or capabilities is that of giving too much weight to past chances in spite of present chances and fulfilments. Likewise, the approach centred on resources neglects final endowments and their equal distribution.

32 Highlighting the importance of responsibility in individual well-being, social institutions neglect losers.

References

Arneson, R. J., 'Equality and Equal Opportunity for Welfare', *Philosophical Studies*, vol. 56, 1989, pp. 77–93.

Arneson, R. J., 'A Defense of Equal Opportunity for Welfare', *Philosophical Studies*, vol. 62, 1991, pp. 187–195.

Cohen, G. A., 'On the Currency of Equalitarian Justice', *Ethics*, vol. 99, 1989, pp. 906–944.

Cohen, G. A., 'Equality of What? On Welfare, Resources and Capabilities, in *Alternative to Welfarism* (M. De Vroey éd.)', *Numéro spécial de Recherches économiques de Louvain*, vol. 56, 1990, pp. 357–382.

Dubet, F., *L'école des chances. Qu'est-ce qu'une école juste?* 2004. Paris: Seuil.

Fleurbaey, M., 'Equality of Functionings', March 2004. www.univ-pau.fr/~fleurbae/publi.htm.

Fleurbaey, M., 'Equal Opportunity or Equal Social Outcome?', *Economics & Philosophy*, vol. 11, 1995.

Fraser, N., *Qu'est-ce que la justice sociale ? Reconnaissance et redistribution.* 2005. Paris: La Découverte.

Gorz, A. *Leur écologie et la nôtre.* 1964. Paris: Éditions Galilée.

Guibet Lafaye, C., *Justice sociale et éthique individuelle.* 2006. Saint Nicolas (Canada): PUL.

Honneth, A., *La Lutte pour la reconnaissance.* 2000. Paris: Le Cerf.

James, W., *The Principles of Psychology* (1890), vol. I. 1950. New York: Dover.

Nussbaum, M. C., 'Aristotelian Social Democracy', in R. B. Douglass, G. M. Mara and H. S. Richardson (eds.), *Liberalism and the Good.* 1990. London: Routledge.

Ost, F., 'La théorie de la justice et le droit à l'aide sociale', in C. Audard, J.-P. Dupuy and R. Sève (éds.), *Individualisme et justice sociale. A propos de John Rawls*, Paris: Seuil, 1988.

Rawls, J., *Justice as Fairness, A Restatement.* 2001. Cambridge, MA: Belknap Press of Harvard University Press; tr. fr., *Théorie de la justice. Une reformulation.* 2003. Paris: La Découverte.

Rawls, J., *Political Liberalism*. 1993. New York: Columbia University Press 1ère éd.; trad. franç., *Libéralisme politique*. 2001. Paris: PUF.
Rawls, J., 'Social Unity and Primary Goods', in A. Sen and B. Williams (eds.), *Utilitarianism and Beyond*, Cambridge: Cambridge University Press, 1982.
Rawls, J., *Theory of Justice*, Cambridge, MA: Belknap Press of Harvard University Press, 1971; trad. franç., *Théorie de la justice*. 1987. Paris: Seuil.
Ricœur, P., *Parcours de reconnaissance*. 2005. Paris: Gallimard.
Roemer, J. E., *Theories of Distributive Justice*. 1996. Cambridge, MA: Harvard University Press.
Sen A., *Inequality Reexamined*, Cambridge, MA: Harvard University Press, 1992; trad. franç., *Repenser l'inégalité*. 2000. Paris: Seuil.
Sen, A., 'Well-Being, Agency and Freedom, *Dewey Lectures*, 1984, *Journal of Philosophy*, 82, pp. 334–347', in L. Daboni A. Montesano and M. Lines (eds.), *Recent Developments in the Foundations of Utility and Risk Theory*. 1985a. Dordrecht: Reidel.
Sen, A., *Commodities and Capabilities*. 1985b. Amsterdam: North-Holland.
Vallentyne, P., *Left Libertarianism and Its Critics: The Contemporary Debate*. 2000. London: Palgrave.
Van Parijs, P., *Qu'est-ce qu'une société juste?* 1991. Paris: Seuil.
Van Parijs, P., *Real Freedom for All. What (if anything) Can Justify Capitalism?* 1995. Oxford: Oxford University Press.

INDEX

For Product Safety Concerns and Information please contact our EU representative GPSR@taylorandfrancis.com
Taylor & Francis Verlag GmbH, Kaufingerstraße 24, 80331 München, Germany

www.ingramcontent.com/pod-product-compliance
Ingram Content Group UK Ltd.
Pitfield, Milton Keynes, MK11 3LW, UK
UKHW020151200926
475702UK00016B/2658

* 9 7 8 0 3 6 7 5 6 9 2 1 1 *